RESONANCE

the art of the Choral Music Educator

Pedagogy, Methods, and Materials for Tomorrow's Outstanding Music Teachers

Christopher W. Peterson

RESONANCE
is available as an online book at Perusall.com

Perusall®

Perusall provides an online portal for the
full color,
interactive
version of RESONANCE.

To visit RESONANCE at Perusall go to:
https://app.perusall.com/catalog/book/bZQSNg74wMQLCYaA6

Pavane Publishing Catalog No. P5029
Hal Leonard Catalog No. 00365359
ISBN 978-1-950736-01-0

Table of Contents

I. Prelude

II. Exposition and Development

III. Coda

Register Your Copy of RESONANCE to Receive Updates

Links can change or be removed, plus new features and items can be added. The only way we can let you know about them is if you register your copy of Resonance.

You will find a link for registration that looks just like this on P5029 RESONANCE ONLINE interactive booklet you download through MyLibrary.

RESONANCE Registration Page.

CREDITS
Cover Art: Sara Littlefield
Graphic Artwork: Alicia Steinhaus
Music Engravers: Lesley Sirianni and Lyndell Leatherman
Icons: Joshua Petker and Elsa Castañeda
Editors: Elyce Berrigan
Proofer: Rich Messenger
Layout and Design: Allan Robert Petker
Poster Collaborator: Stanford Scriven

A Foreword

by Clifford K. Madsen

I do not remember having ever gone through a music education methods book that is as well grounded in scientifically demonstrable techniques, solid evidenced-based suggestions and explicit exercises as found in this work. Previously, I have stated there are pedagogical exercises that are based on imagery or seemingly odd or even ridiculous things intended just "to get the particular sound or phrase development, or whatever the teacher desires validated by seemingly good results of the activity." For example, in developing good posture one might find "Head lightly suspended by an imaginary 'string' through the spine." And "Feel grounded, free, and lifted at the same time." However, suggestions become more meaningful if nested within a solid empirical approach. This point of view finds expression in the empirically based content throughout. Yet, all of this is aiming toward developing the art of making beautiful music. The content of this book is not just well organized. More importantly, it contains a great deal of new material not usually found in such an endeavor. I highly recommend it knowing it will provide a meaningful contribution to the development of singers of all ages.

Clifford K. Madsen

CLIFFORD MADSEN, the Robert O. Lawton Distinguished Professor of Music, is Coordinator of Music Education/Music Therapy/Contemporary Media and teaches in the areas of music education, music therapy, research, and psychology of music. He serves on various international and national editorial and research boards and is widely published throughout scholarly journals in music education and therapy.

In addition, he has authored and co-authored many books and is perhaps best known for Teaching/Discipline: A Positive Approach for Educational Development, Experimental Research in Music, Competency Based Music Education, Applications of Research in Music Behavior, and Vision 2020: The Housewright Symposium on the Future of Music Education.

Dr. Madsen received the bachelor's and master's degrees from Brigham Young University and the Ph.D. from The Florida State University. He was appointed to the FSU faculty in 1961.

Introduction and Acknowledgments

by Christopher W. Peterson

The "art" of teaching is different from the "act" of teaching in that an "art" is creative, unbound, and spontaneous. The "act" of teaching can be methodical, planned, well sequenced, and clearly logical. Obviously, teachers must be well planned and methodical in order to deliver information that makes sense to their students; yet, information that only informs, without relevance to the questions that the students hold, is likely to be perceived as one dimensional, boring, and sterile. One major foundation of the Art of Teaching is the concept that "everything relates to everything." There is nothing that can be discussed, examined, or explored that is not related to everything else in the known world.

resonance[1]

noun

res·o·nance | \ ˈre-zə-nən(t)s, ˈrez-nən(t)s\

Definition of *resonance*

1a: the quality or state of being resonant

b (1): a vibration of large amplitude in a mechanical or electrical system caused by a relatively small periodic stimulus of the same or nearly the same period as the natural vibration period of the system

2a: the intensification and enriching of a musical tone by supplementary vibration

b: a quality imparted to voiced sounds by vibration in anatomical resonating chambers or cavities (such as the mouth or the nasal cavity)

c: a quality of richness or variety

7: a synchronous gravitational relationship of two celestial bodies (such as moons) that orbit a third (such as a planet), which can be expressed as a simple ratio of their orbital periods

Resonance. This one amazing word can relate to so many of the things that we, as choral music educators, do. We work to create beautiful music that is rich and resonant, and we strive to connect with our audiences so that they will resonate with our ensemble sounds and the expression of our art. We work to relate to our students so that they will be inspired to be their best, hoping that the structure and opportunities that we create for them multiply and resonate positively in their own teaching. As one resonating body can initiate sound in another potentially resonating body in close proximity, our work to train future educators ripples out to affect change in subtle and very significant ways. When things are in a state of "resonance," there is a common vibration, a sense of wellness, and a feeling of satisfaction that comes from a general sense that everything we do is affected by, and connected to, everything else. It is hoped that this textbook will inspire you whether you are an experienced teacher,

---

1 Excerpted from:
https://www.merriam-webster.com/dictionary/resonance

a new teacher, or an emerging teacher, and that you will be changed in positive ways through your interaction with and exploration of the material. I hope that you resonate with the concepts you will read and that you will be inspired to apply and "steal" everything that you think will make you a better teacher.

The title of this book "Resonance: The Art of the Choral Music Educator" is intended to relate to a philosophical foundation in my approach to teaching: instead of teaching teachers how to teach as if it were a black-and-white quantifiable science-like endeavor, I believe that we need to teach our preservice teachers how to think, how to learn, and how to solve problems creatively. The arrival of the COVID-19 global pandemic in spring of 2020 emphasized the efficacy of this approach more than ever before. In what felt like a split second, the entire world changed. Singing was determined to be a "super-spreader activity," and choral music…indeed most ensemble music making nationwide… ceased to exist except as online, pre-recorded virtual events. We were all suddenly physically alone, in quarantine, and wondering when we would be able to return to our "normal" lives in artistic resonance together. Student teachers, and all teachers for that matter, were thrust into a teaching world that few knew anything about. The environment of online music teaching and Zoom technology was foreign to all but a few of us, and the skills of being able to think, learn, and solve problems creatively became absolutely essential to our survival as teachers in a virtual classroom.

Yet, for all the challenges of virtual instruction and the constraints of making music through technology, most of the concepts, techniques, and philosophies of effective teaching remain unchanged. Good teaching is still good teaching, regardless of the teaching environment. Teachers have, by pure necessity, found new ways to mentor their students in engaging and creative ways, and we have emerged into a new world of teaching that we could not have imagined possible before COVID-19. And while many people have embraced the need for change and raced ahead to adapt and learn new strategies for instruction, others have felt left behind and sad that so much has suddenly changed in our musical and educational world. Indeed, we must all endeavor to remember how we once felt as emerging teachers, and we must strive to come to terms with the feeling of struggle that accompanies unfamiliar experiences that force us to grow. It gets easier. Great teachers are always striving to learn, even when the learning feels particularly uncomfortable. Like many, I have had to dig deep into my creativity, problem-solving abilities, and my pedagogy to try to be as effective as possible, and it would be a lie to say this has been easy for me to do in a moment's notice when the pandemic materialized. But together we can move ahead, in resonance, to create a teaching world that embraces the effective techniques we have used for decades while also capitalizing on what we have learned during COVID-19 to make our instruction even more effective than it was before.

I have had the wonderful opportunity to teach music as an elementary general classroom music educator, as a middle school and high school choral director, as a church choir director, as a community chorus director, as a guest conductor and workshop clinician, and for over twenty years, as a college professor in higher education, directing choirs and training choral music educators. With all the years of experience that I have accumulated and the many amazing teachers whom I have been honored to study with, I still don't think that you can train music educators as if what we do is more science than art.

I truly believe that preservice teachers need to grapple with ideas and concepts that will teach them how to develop creative solutions to the problems that they will likely encounter. They can't memorize enough facts and handbooks, or rules and procedures, to know exactly what to do when they are in front of real students in authentic settings, so they need to cultivate their ability to assess each new situation and to draw from conceptual understandings in order to find the most functional and constructive approaches. In other words, I don't believe that we can adequately teach preservice teachers what to do, but I do believe that we can teach them how to figure out what to do. In that light, you will see that this text offers fewer concrete directives for methods of teaching, and instead introduces broader concepts concerning pedagogy for emerging teachers to explore. Within each chapter there are multiple sections entitled "Recapitulation" where open-ended questions are presented to initiate creative thinking and possible discussion in a personal or class setting. I have not provided specific answers to these questions on purpose so that each student and each classroom can reach for new ideas that apply directly to their own experience and environment.

It is my hope that the values presented here are clearly communicated to the reader, but that no specific endorsement of a single technique is conveyed. Teaching is an Art, and each person will bring something new and creative to their classroom if they have the freedom to grow and explore as an educator. Any technique outlined in this text can be changed and adapted (or ignored) if there is a better technique that is found to implement a particular value.

You will notice that this textbook is relatively sparse in terms of footnotes and academic references. This is intentional. For my first seven years teaching choral methods in higher education, I focused my curricular approach upon much of the information I had learned from my mentors and I also drew from my varied experiences as a teacher and conductor as well as my understandings as a lifelong, curious student. I do want to acknowledge my use during these years of the excellent methods text by Barbara Brinson. I enjoyed her straightforward tone and her approach to presenting clear and practical information; we do, incidently, share some mentors as well from Florida State University. When I moved to California to teach at California State University, Fullerton, in 2007, I stopped using the Brinson text and instead taught from a patchwork of different sources, but primarily from my own perspective and experiences. I have never been a professor who photocopies a chapter from several different texts to make my own classroom materials, and I will confess that I have not read very much, if any, of the most recent choral methods textbooks that are available today that have been authored by my wonderful colleagues around the United States. In fact, it was a conscious choice not to read other people's choral methods texts once I started writing this one as a sabbatical project in February of 2015. Subsequently, any material that I have presented here without credit to the original author is an unintentional oversight or a coincidental re-statement of a concept that I have coined or learned from someone too long ago to recall. I am happy to credit anyone I have may have missed in future editions, and I apologize in advance if there is the appearance of anyone else's work going uncredited within the body of this text. My broad intention is to speak directly to the reader as if they were sitting in my methods class, drawing from my personal perspective and experiences to teach as well as I can.

As was just stated, this book was started as a sabbatical project in the spring of 2015 and was on a "slow simmer" for a number of years. I pilot tested many of the chapters with my own students at Cal State Fullerton during those years, and I believe that it is a more solid text because of the years of revisions. I am grateful for the work of my amazing colleague Joshua Palkki, Ph.D. [Pronouns: he/him], Assistant Professor of Vocal/Choral Music Education at California State University, Long Beach for his copy editing and professional feedback. He is a true scholar, a fabulous teacher and musician, and a wonderful person. I am also so grateful for the contribution of another wonderful colleague, William Sauerland, Ed.D. [Pronouns: he/him/his/they/them/their], Director of Choral Activities at Purdue University – Fort Wayne, for authoring and contributing the chapter entitled "Gender Identity in Choral Music Education." He is a leader and an authority on these issues in the world, and I am overjoyed to have his perspective included in this book.

This textbook is divided into three sections: Prelude (setting the groundwork for concepts related to the profession, including classroom management), Exposition and Development (addressing specific teaching pedagogy and approaches in the classroom), Coda (addressing issues of music education philosophy, gender identity, as well as several topics of interest), and Cadenza (addressing resources and website information as well as other information that is useful for the reader). University programs across the United States vary widely in their required classes, time set aside for student teaching, and time allotted to cover a vast array of practical and philosophical topics. Whereas a math textbook might start with addition and subtraction and then progress sequentially to more complicated concepts of mathematics, a choral music education textbook must embrace a very diverse body of knowledge and concepts that may or may not have an obvious or sequential order for study. Furthermore, some institutions offer an entire choral music methods sequence in two hours a week over a single semester, while others devote three to six hours a week over the course of several semesters to teach and reinforce the same skills and materials. While some schools require a semester of student teaching just before graduation, other schools require an entire year of student teaching after graduation. Because of the variations of requirements from school to school, no single textbook could be a one-size-fits-all resource for every choral methods class and institution. Feel free to use this book with any method or order that suits your needs and leave out any material that does not serve your curricular purposes or time constraints.

The endeavor of authoring this textbook would not be possible without the love and support of a large number of people. Much of what is contained within is the result of many years of teaching choral methods to many outstanding and talented students at California State University, Fullerton, and also previously at the University of Wisconsin-Milwaukee. I have learned so much from these amazing students, and I dedicate this book to those who have come before, and also those I am yet to meet, teach, and learn from in the coming years. I also am grateful to the faculty of the School of Music at California State University, Fullerton, for their collegial support, and I'd like to give special thanks to Dr. Robert Istad, Dr. Dennis Siebenaler, and Dr. John Koegel for their individual support on this project, as well as Dr. Jeffrey Benson at San Jose State University, and Dr. Michael Murphy at Stephen F. Austin State University for their contributions. I am also grateful to all my teachers over the years at the University of Southern Maine, the University of Maine, and at The Florida State University. I know that much of what is contained in this text has been greatly influenced, if not directly taken from, classes and interactions with many of my mentors, including Clifford K. Madsen, André J. Thomas, Rodney Eichenberger, Judy Bowers, Peter Martin, Bob Russell, and Dennis Cox. For all my outstanding teachers and my worldwide colleagues, I am forever grateful. I would also like to acknowledge and appreciate my publisher, Allan Petker with Pavane Publishing, for believing in this project enough to invest time and money into it so that the world might be changed in some way through its broader dissemination. Finally, I am grateful and appreciative for my incredible wife, Tina Glander Peterson. She is one of the finest choral music educators I will ever know, and I am constantly energized by her love and support for me and also for my busy career. Among all my wonderful teachers, Tina is truly the greatest of them all.

The world continues to change so quickly, and it is my hope that the concepts in this text will continue to be relevant to the training of outstanding music teachers in this country, and perhaps around the world, for many years to come. As I write this, I have no idea what we will all be doing a year from now, post COVID-19, two years from now, or ten years from now. But everything relates to everything, so regardless of the teaching environment, I intend that the ideas and approaches within this book can be adapted to whatever you may encounter in the future. For all of the ideas you will encounter within these pages, take and try anything that you think works, and pay it forward in your teaching until you adapt it and integrate it as your own approach. In this way, I believe that you can continue to be the best educator you can be, integrating teaching as an Art rather than a science, regardless of how the world changes around you.

I. Prelude

Chapter One

Becoming a Professional Music Educator

1. **Becoming a Professional Music Educator**

"Choose a job you love, and you will never have to work a day in your life."
~Confucius

Music Educator by Choice

Welcome to the professional world of the choral music educator! You are reading these words because you have, on some level, decided to explore the idea of becoming a choral conductor and teacher of choral music students. It is a big decision to become a professional educator, and it is not a decision that should be made without a lot of thoughtful consideration. Are you right for this profession, and is this profession right for you? There are no easy answers to these questions.

When it comes to choosing a job, there are really only two kinds to choose from: jobs that require you to shower *before* work and jobs that require you to shower *after* work. If you have never considered the "shower before or after work" concept, think about the kinds of jobs you have had in your lifetime. Did you need to wear a uniform for your job, and did you have to stand and interact with customers and smile at people? If so, then you probably had a "shower before work" kind of job. If you had a job that allowed you to wear casual, non-uniform clothes, and that required you to get dirty and smelly for the job, you certainly had a "shower after work" kind of job. There are some jobs, of course, that are both, such as working at a fast-food restaurant where you take a shower before work, wear a uniform, interact with customers, and still get dirty and smell like French fries when you're done...requiring *another shower after work*. Being a professional music educator is primarily a "shower before work" kind of job, so knowing who you are and what you like to do are important considerations as you embark into the world of the conductor/educator.

If you are a "shower after work" kind of person, choral music education might not be the right profession for you. To be happy, you will probably need to be outdoors working with hands-on materials and getting yourself dirty making, growing, or fixing things. Likewise, if you prefer to work alone on a computer and are annoyed when people interact with you, you are probably not well suited for teaching either. If you love music, but don't enjoy helping other people gain musicianship and grow to love music the way you do, you might not be a good fit for teaching. If you are using music education as a backup plan if something else doesn't work out for you, you will probably not become a passionate and effective professional music educator. If you are going to become an effective and professional teacher, you have to be someone who likes people, is a superb musician, and who enjoys the process as well as the product. Do not fall back on teaching as a plan B, but instead make a decision to embrace teaching music as your profession. Make an informed decision to become a music educator...by choice.

One thing to ask yourself is, "What could I bring to teaching, and what would teaching bring to me?" Choosing a profession that you enjoy and can thrive in is a very important decision; you could possibly remain in your chosen profession for your whole life. You need to choose a job that will help you feel fulfilled while also allowing you the chance to grow, change, and learn.

Those Who Can, Teach!

A truly effective and inspiring teacher brings a large mix of skills, knowledge, and experiences to the classroom. You may already possess some of these skills because of your own experiences and background or perhaps because of your natural dispositions or inclinations. Some people are "natural teachers" who have been enjoying interacting with, and helping, others their whole life. These natural teachers relish opportunities to explain and demonstrate things to others, and they get excited when people improve and acquire the skills that they are teaching. Not everyone, however, feels the calling to teach at an early age, and some people come to teaching after a great deal of life experience and soul searching. Still others "awake" to teaching as something they never considered, but that they are quite well suited for in terms of their personality and work ethic. And then there are some people who seem to default to teaching as a back-up plan, who aren't curious about being a great teacher, but who consider teaching as something that anyone can do if need be.

The truth is that talent for teaching is like talent in music; natural teachers can be effective with less practice because they possess the inherent skills that effective teachers develop, and they start practicing their teaching skills very early in their lives. But talent for teaching is not a prerequisite for becoming a great teacher any more than talent for music is a prerequisite for becoming a great musician. Some people work and practice to become fine musicians despite having an average aptitude for music, and some people work hard and become great teachers even if their disposition is not that of a natural teacher.

It is important that you, as an aspiring teacher, become acquainted with the knowledge, skills, and behaviors of great teachers so that you can work on the areas that you have not developed already through hard work or natural talent.

Everyone is unique, so what you need to work on and develop in yourself may differ greatly from the next person. By defining what great teachers do, and by honestly looking inside yourself and taking note of where you are, you can begin your development and transition into this wonderful and fulfilling profession.

Characteristics of Great Teachers

By the time you graduated from high school you had the exposure to, and the influence of, many good and not-so-good teachers. Each one of these teachers helped mold you and your views of what teaching is or could be. Because we tend to teach the way we were taught, you will carry with you all the good, as well as all the bad, educational experiences that you were exposed to throughout your lifetime.[1] It is so very important that you focus on the great teachers you have had and that you strive to learn and practice the best pedagogy available so that you can maximize the most positive and effective parts of your educational past with your students. Your task, then, is to be the best voice of all your greatest teachers wrapped up into one person, and to reject all the less effective techniques that you experienced along the way. However, sorting through which techniques and traits you should maximize is not an easy process because the art of teaching is not a "right and wrong" body of understanding; a technique that works well and functions in one situation can be ineffective in another class, rehearsal, or setting. But there are some traits and characteristics of highly effective teachers that are identifiable, and during your preservice studies, you should strive to grow and enhance these effective behaviors in your teaching as much as possible.

RECAPITULATION

1. In your opinion and experience, what are some of the traits of great teachers you have known? If you reference music teachers, be sure to include musical as well as non-musical traits and behaviors. What do they do, how do they behave, how might they think, and what makes them effective at their job? List at least eight traits with a sentence describing or explaining each trait.

1 https://sslc.wikispaces.com/Teaching+and+Learning

2. Do you think you are a "natural teacher?" Why or why not? What are some of the things you are already good at in terms of becoming a great teacher, and what things do you hope to work on and grow in your skill set?

3. Have you worked at a "shower before work" as well as a "shower after work" job? Describe the differences that you experienced, including how much satisfaction you had working in each one. If you have only ever experienced one or the other, describe your likes and dislikes of two similar jobs you have held. Which one did you like best and why?

Developing Your Own Musicianship and Performance Skills

If you asked an experienced choral director for advice on how you should prepare for a career in choral music education and conducting, you would probably expect an answer such as "study to become a clear and expressive conductor." And while this is good advice, you might also hear these three important bits of wisdom:

1. Study to become a competent musician.
2. Practice to become a beautiful singer.
3. Learn to play the piano with confidence.

While there are surely more ideas that could guide your focus as you are starting out, these three areas are important if you want to become a competent choral music educator. For example, students may depend on their teacher to help them learn their music, but teachers must be independent, well-trained musicians who can study and choose literature, prepare rehearsal plans, model and sequence proper singing technique, and use the piano as a teaching tool in rehearsal. It can be quite difficult to teach students to do things that you can't do yourself, and you will need to be able to help them learn regardless of their skill level and experience. Emerging music teachers are often excited to learn how to conduct from the podium and rehearse a choir, but all of this must be preceded by solid focus and achievement in the areas of personal performance and musicianship skills. Let's explore a few ideas relating to these areas to help you focus on your own progress.

The training of your voice as an undergraduate student will form the foundation of your success as a choral teacher and conductor. Most colleges and universities in the United States that have programs to train choral music educators have a fixed curriculum to develop both the teacher and the performer. Music majors are usually trained in music theory, music history, ear training, and sight singing, and a major performance focus is developed such as voice, piano, or another instrument. It is common for the music major to study on their major instrument privately with a teacher to achieve a level of mastery that may or may not be evaluated in a public recital before graduation. It is also not uncommon for there to be different academic expectations for performance majors than there are for education majors, such as longer lesson blocks, more comprehensive recital requirements, or different levels of achievement in semester-end vocal juries. Nonetheless, the choral music education major must still work to be the best *singer* possible, not just to pass the requirements of a curriculum, but to be able to break down singing technique into small, teachable steps for their own students. If you approach singing technique as one of the most important aspects of your music education, then you will spend many hours in the practice room learning to improve your singing skills. If you are not a voice major, then you can still be curious about developing your singing voice by singing in a choir, or perhaps by choosing to study voice privately. As you practice to become a beautiful singer, you will understand your own voice, your own abilities, and your own strengths and weaknesses when it comes to singing, and you will be able to teach what you have learned to your choirs.

Before you can lead a choir from the podium, it is essential that you develop your independent musicianship skills. You will need to be able to look at a musical score that you have never heard or performed and study and interpret it yourself. You will need to develop the ability to read music literature from a musician's standpoint; this means that you must be able to analyze a score comprehensively to determine the form, harmonic structure, rhythmic complexities, texture and transpositions, counterpoint, tempo variations, articulations, dynamics, expressive markings, and all other aspects of musical information in the printed music. You must be able to sing each line in the conductor's score and create rehearsal plans and strategies to teach the music to the students in your choir. Independent musicianship is developed over time when a person decides to challenge themselves in as many areas as possible, including learning to play new instruments, taking sight-singing lessons, working with software programs to develop aural skills, listening to lots of different kinds of music, and going above and beyond whatever formative training they had when they were younger. As you work to be a better musician, you will see evidence of your progress, but you may never feel fully satisfied with your present abilities, and that's normal and common. You can always grow to be a better musician, and as long as you are studying to be the most competent musician that you can be, you will be headed in the right direction.

Emulating Our Mentors

To be successful as a professional choral music educator you will have to be prepared to manage all aspects of the choir program, including budgeting, recruiting, programming, and many other tasks. Arguably the most important task that affects all others is your ability to rehearse the choir in an engaging, positive, musical, and educationally sound manner. It is the quality and effectiveness of your rehearsal process that will largely determine how your singers grow as musicians together and to what extent that your choirs will be able to create and experience well-prepared, confident, and artistically compelling performances. The art of rehearsing the choir effectively is closely tied to the art of teaching effectively, and the choral conductor that integrates sound teaching strategies into their rehearsals will be more likely to realize broad educational and performance outcomes with their choirs.

Because we tend to teach the way we ourselves were taught, we are most likely to use the techniques and pacing, and even the words and phrases, that our own conductors used when we were students in their choirs. If you have had several choir teachers in your lifetime, then you are likely to possess a unique mixture of all of them in your own teaching approach. It would be great if our brains knew how to screen out less effective techniques while memorizing only the most effective ones, but that is not how we are wired as human beings; we take in everything within our environment and we consciously and subconsciously encode this information into our brains neurologically. These brain connections become the "default" that we regurgitate when we are in front of choirs teaching for the first time, and it is a common experience for most beginning educators to emulate their mentors closely. It is really important, therefore, that you become a reflective practitioner who can sort out the effective techniques from the less effective ones, and that you can consciously enhance the best ones while minimizing the ones that function least effectively.

For example, if you had a teacher who used sarcasm as a primary tool for delivering instructions and feedback to the choir, you may find yourself doing the same thing automatically. Sarcasm can be defined as "a sharp and often satirical or ironic utterance designed to cut or give pain."[2] In certain situations, sarcasm can be perceived as humorous, but in other contexts, it can function

2 https://www.merriam-webster.com/dictionary/sarcasm

to make fun of someone or to disapprove of a group of people. It is a more effective teaching technique to communicate to the class using specific words that have clear and unambiguous meanings, especially if the class is culturally diverse or when exceptional learners are present.[3] But if a sarcastic tone is a technique that you inherited from a mentor, you will have to work — through careful self-examination and practice — to communicate clearly and directly with the choir. This kind of change will take effort and awareness on your part, but it will help you to become the best teacher you can possibly be. A good approach for you as an emerging music educator is to emulate and nurture the best parts of what your mentors did while identifying and minimizing any techniques in your practice that are less effective. If you "take the best and leave the rest," you will come to be as effective and inspiring as your former teachers while striving to be an even better teacher for your own students.

The Struggle Is Real

It is important to recognize that few beginning teachers fully emulate their mentors effectively at first. This is primarily because our mentors learned to be master teachers over thousands of hours of practice and through many years of rehearsal in front of real classes; what they make look easy is much more complex than one would expect. An experienced teacher is simultaneously and keenly aware of many things such as student engagement, social and academic student behavior, materials in the room, and the various levels of inappropriate and appropriate talking, all while gauging student achievement within the lesson, listening to the music-making, choosing what to prioritize and sequence, and conducting from the podium with intention and clarity. It is not unusual for a beginning teacher to struggle just to deliver a lesson plan as written while being completely oblivious to the classroom environment, the sound of the music-making, the clarity of the conducting, or the level of student engagement.

When you find yourself struggling to do something, always remember that your struggle can be your best teacher in the long run. That uncomfortable feeling you get can be a good thing as you strive to learn to do something better. This is because the struggle forces you to work hard while breaking down the task into smaller skills that you can improve upon sequentially. In doing so, you will be able to teach others what *you* learned in each step. For example, if you are someone who always sang beautifully in tune since you were young,

3 Saying What You Don't Mean: Social Influences on Sarcastic Language Processing, Albert N. Katz, Dawn G. Blasko and Victoria A. Kazmerski, Current Directions in Psychological Science, Vol. 13, No. 5 (Oct., 2004), pp. 186-189

then you probably never had to learn how to tune your own voice. Your natural tendency in this case would be to simply tell your students to "sing in tune" or to model for them with your own voice. But if you struggled to sing in tune (and if you worked to do it better), you may have learned that breath energy, physical alignment, listening ability, vowel color, and other elements affected your own accurate intonation. The steps you learned during your struggle to improve will inform you as a teacher, and you will naturally draw upon your experiences to help your students learn as well. You will be especially prepared to teach all students what they need to know to sing with precise intonation and to meet them where they are in their development.

You may be wondering then, is struggle necessary to become a great teacher? The answer is, not necessarily. A person who barely struggles, however, must be curious about how all students learn. It is possible to teach others even when you didn't struggle, but only if you can break skills down into smaller steps that add up to the larger task. A teacher who learns from their personal struggles, and who also develops a curiosity about how other people learn, has a tremendous pedagogical advantage over teachers without curiosity who do things without personal insight as to how they do them. When you find yourself needing to work hard to do things that others already do well, just affirm to yourself that you are developing as a teacher, and that you are going to be a stronger teacher in the long run because of your personal struggles to improve.

RECAPITULATION

1. Who would you consider to be your primary mentors in music? What musical skills, techniques, and personal traits do you think you share with them? Describe several things that they did well that you hope to include in your own teaching and rehearsing methods as well as at least one thing (if you can) that you recognize as a less effective technique that they demonstrated.

2. When you hear the phrase "sarcasm is not a great teaching tool," what comes to mind for you? What is your experience as a student with the use of sarcasm in the classroom? Have you been aware of it, and do you feel you understand it all the time? What could be some potential benefits of using sarcasm in a classroom in your opinion, and what do you think might be the dangers of using it frequently?

3. Everyone struggles in some areas of their life. What comes easily to one person may be a real challenge for another person. Describe something, musical or otherwise, that you have personally worked hard to learn over time. Does the word "struggle" describe your experience, or are there better words to explain how you progressed? What are some things that you are working on now that you hope to be better at someday, and what are you doing to make progress?

4. Make a list of activities, musical or otherwise in your experience, that came easy to you. In other words, what skills or tasks have you learned without having to work very hard at them? For example, perhaps you tried a sport like windsurfing and found that you could ride and stay on the board on your first try, and without lessons. Comment on your ability, in your opinion, to teach that particular skill or task to other people who are beginners.

The Learning Cycle

It is important to understand that not every student in your class is ready to learn what you are teaching. Some students in your class will not care at all that you have written a wonderful rehearsal or lesson plan or that you have excellent information or music to share with them. Some beginning teachers lose some enthusiasm for teaching when they realize that, especially in the first few years of their first job, student's academic interest can range from energetic and engaged to half-hearted and apathetic.

In an ideal world, all students would come to class curious and excited to learn, and teachers would impart the answers to their questions expertly and in perfect sequence and timing. Experienced teachers know that few instances of this "ideal world" actually exist, though there are certainly experienced teachers who make teaching and learning look easy, organic, and fun for everyone. This appearance of ease stems from years of expert lesson planning, masterful administration of tasks, engaging delivery, and preparing the students to be curious about the subject matter.

If you are thinking, "Why is it my problem to get the students interested in my subject matter?" Then you should read the following sentence carefully several times:

"No one wants to hear the answer to a question that they are not asking."

No one, including you, appreciates a person who gives you advice when you aren't asking for it. Think about it. Imagine that you are walking down the street and a stranger approaches you and says, "I can help you improve the style of the clothes you wear and help you look better." Assuming that you hadn't been considering a fashion makeover, your reaction to this unsolicited proposition might be to ignore and dismiss it and to move on with whatever you were doing. You weren't asking the question, "How can I dress better?"

But suppose that you *were* curious about the question. What if you had recently been with friends and noticed that you were the only one who looked out of date with your fashion choices. Furthermore, what if this bothered you on some level so that you had an uncomfortable feeling about it? What if you suddenly felt the urge to learn how you could make simple changes in your wardrobe on a small budget? What if you decided to explore ways to look better through your choice of wardrobe? In this example, the person walking up to you and saying, "I can help you improve the style of the clothes you wear and help you look better" might get your attention in a whole new way. If this individual happened to be a sales person at a clothing store you shop at, it might really get your attention! In this case, you would probably stop, engage them, and listen to their answer…*because you were asking the question before the answer appeared.* This is a basic premise of learning theory: students must be curious about the subject matter or real learning cannot take place.

So how do you get your students to be curious about music, musicianship, choir, and singing in general? Your first step is to understand something we will refer to as "The Learning Cycle," which was adapted from the "The Learning Stages" by Mr. Noel Burch, co-author with Thomas Gordon of the *Teacher Effectiveness Trainingbook* in 1974.[4]

Step One: Unconscious Incompetence

"You don't know what you don't know"

Step Two: Conscious Incompetence

"You know what you don't know"

Step Three: Conscious Competence

"You know what you know"

Step Four: Unconscious Competence

"You don't know what you know"

---

4 New York: Three Rivers Press, 1st rev. ed. ©2003, Contributors: Noel Burch ISBN : 0609809326. It is also possible that this concept first appeared in an article by Martin M. Broadwell: "Teaching for learning (XVI)," *The Gospel Guardian.* (20 February 20, 1969) http://wordsfitlyspoken.org/gospel_guardian/v20/v20n41p1-3a.html

In Step One, unconscious incompetence, you are in a blissful mindset where you are not curious. You know everything, and life is good. You feel great. You are not open to learning, and you are *not asking any questions.* You are in a condition where you "don't know what you don't know" and it doesn't bother you at all. When you are in Step One, you are like that person walking down the street getting unsolicited advice from strangers. No matter what they say to you, it goes in one ear and out the other. You dismiss people who try to help you improve because you are not asking for improvement. You are just fine as you are. You are not curious. You are completely closed to learning. Any attempt to teach you makes no lasting difference in your behavior.

Step Two, conscious incompetence, is normally entered into when a person has an experience where they fail at something, or when an uncomfortable situation creates questions in their mind. In other words, you are in Step Two when you wish you were better at something, or when you don't achieve something you expected to achieve for whatever reason. In the fashion transfer example above, the inner dialogue in Step One might range from no thought at all about your fashion to, "Man, I look great in these clothes." But everything changes as you enter Step Two. The sudden realization that you may not dress as well as you thought you did might create thoughts like, "How did I miss the memo on fashion changes?" or "Why do I have to be the one wearing this outdated stuff?" or "I wonder if I should start paying attention to what's in fashion before it passes me by?" or "How can I upgrade my look on a tight budget?"

The important thing to remember about Step Two is that it creates questions, and *once questions are asked, you are motivated to seek out, rendezvous with, and hear the answers.* There is an old saying that says, "When the student is ready, the teacher arrives." It speaks to a Step Two moment; the question allows you to rendezvous with the answer and to act on that information to change your behavior. Can you think of an instance where you entered Step Two from Step One in The Learning Cycle? Some people have described the experience as feeling like, "Once, I knew everything, and now I feel like I know nothing." Take a moment to connect how this relates to you as a teacher, but also to you as a lifelong learner.

Once you have entered Step Two, and after you have gathered some answers and have started working toward improvement, you will enter Step Three, conscious competence. There is a sense of relief in this step because you can reflect a bit on your improvement as you continue to make thoughtful progress. You will be introducing new skills and knowledge into your behaviors, and you will be in a conscious process of integrating these skills. One way this step has been described is that the student is practicing the skill "not until I get it right, but until I can't get it wrong." You can feel yourself growing toward mastery, and you have a better understanding of your achievements and limitations. In our fashion example, you are probably dressing differently but still not feeling like you have transformed your wardrobe or even your understanding of how you want to dress differently. Some people have described the feeling as, "Once, I knew everything, then I knew nothing, and now I feel like I know something again." This conscious grappling with the progress and growth is the hallmark of Step Three. You start to realize what you know and how far you have come.

At some point, when a skill has been broken down into steps over time and consciously practiced, a transition takes place in the behavior and mindset of the student. What was once a conscious effort to improve becomes an integrated skill at a higher level. The mindful work needed to activate the skill becomes second nature, and the student enters Step Four, unconscious competence. In this step you just enjoy engaging in your new behavior. You have no need to devote conscious effort toward your progress, and you are free to focus your attention elsewhere. In this sense, you don't know what you know…though you could still reflect on how you got there if you wanted to. The hallmark of Step Four is a letting go of conscious progress and a refocusing of energy away from the skill or behavior. In the fashion makeover transfer, you just dress yourself in the new way and feel good wherever you go.

You might be thinking, "What happens next? Why isn't there a Step Five or Six?" This is where the *cycle* part of The Learning Cycle comes in. When you are in Step Four, unconscious competence, you have moved into a higher level of mastery. What you once tried hard to do better, you now just do better. At the point that you believe you know all there is to know about the skill or behavior, you re-enter Step One, unconscious incompetence again, but at a higher level. You become a "know-it-all" again on that subject. You become closed to learning again. You feel great again until something comes along to push you into Step Two again. If you are not an open learner, you might never leave Step One. If you are an open, lifelong learner, The Learning Cycle will continue over and over and over again throughout your lifetime.

It is very important to note that people do not typically move through The Learning Cycle on the same step for different skills and behaviors. In other words, it is possible to be in Step One in your personal relationships, Step Two in your musicianship, Step Three in your teaching ability, and Step Four in your knowledge of current fashion *all at the same time*. Some people, however, are in Step One on most every subject. Once you understand The Learning Cycle, you can then begin to strategize how to get your students to be curious about music, musicianship, choir, and singing in general. It is your job to get them curious about the subject matter, and if you can't move them into Step Two, then everything you teach will be ignored or forgotten almost as soon as it is taught.

RECAPITULATION

1. Think about how The Learning Cycle has played a role in your education or musicianship throughout your life. Recount a time when you moved into Step Two with a skill or behavior and explain what happened and why.

2. Because of the nature of Step One, unconscious incompetence, it is difficult to reflect on your place within it. Step Two and Three, however, provide you with plenty of opportunity to build awareness of your growth as a learner. Make a list of as many things as you can where you believe that you are open to learning. In other words, what do you devote conscious time and effort toward improving in your life? Why are these things important to you?

3. Moving a choir from Step One to Step Two of The Learning Cycle will require some sort of experience that would promote curiosity and a desire for improvement. Make a list of at least three activities that a choral director could do to help students move into Step Two. For example, your list might include playing recordings of choirs that are more advanced or that have more experience than the school choir and then compare them to a recent recording of the school choir to inspire discussion. Think of and describe at least three more activities. Also, do you think that attempting to motivate students in these ways could backfire and not have the desired effect? Explain your thinking.

Intention vs. Function

Teachers should be people who care about their students. But caring, while important to building relationships, is not enough to ensure that students are making good progress in their learning. A caring teacher has the best of intentions for the students, and a committed teacher will do everything in their power to help students master the subject matter and gain the skills necessary to be successful. But when it comes to measuring educational outcomes, intentions don't matter as much as what the students are actually able to do after instruction and assessment are over. The issue of *intention vs. function* is an important concept to understand because it is the foundation of understanding your own effectiveness in the classroom and rehearsal.

Imagine going to the doctor and finding out that you need an emergency operation to remove your appendix. Because you trust the doctor and the diagnosis, you are likely to accept the course of action and go through the surgery. You know that she has the best of intentions for you, and you fully expect that the details of the procedure will be task analyzed and implemented carefully and accurately. Now imagine waking up and finding that instead of taking out your appendix, the doctor removed your tonsils. Your reaction is likely to be something between disbelief and anger, and you would probably soon be calling a malpractice lawyer with a strong claim for damages.

Now imagine that the doctor came to you after the operation and said, "I'm really sorry about all of this. I had the best of intentions to remove your appendix. It just didn't work out. I hope you understand." At this point, you probably would think that the doctor's intentions, while good, weren't enough to satisfy you based on the outcome. She intended one outcome, but the *function* of the procedure — what actually happened — was completely different than her intentions. Any conversations about her intentions will be meaningless to you, because the function of the procedure didn't align with the intentions.

The concept of intention vs. function also transfers to you as a lifelong learner and educator. If you intend to study for a test, but you don't study long enough or well enough, and then you do poorly on the test, your previous intentions do nothing to change the outcome. If you want your students to be excellent singers and musicians, but they do not make progress toward artistic singing and strong musicianship, your intentions mean nothing. Some people spend a lot of time and energy offering detailed rationales for the value of their intentions without measuring or taking responsibility for the outcomes of their efforts. If you have a tendency to think this way even a little bit, you can make a shift in your thinking to focus on how your intentions actually function and then focus your attention on changing your teaching and learning to better affect the desired outcomes.

We all have the best of intentions for ourselves and for our students. Acknowledge your good intentions (as well as other's good intentions) and then give your full focus to how those intentions function in terms of measurable outcomes. When you fall short of your intentions, and we will all fall short at times, don't waste any time explaining or worrying about it. Instead, change your thoughts and behaviors to change your outcomes. Being an effective teacher, then, is a practice that focuses not on what you hope happens for your students, but rather on what actually happens for them. By focusing on function, rather than intention, you will be able to gauge accurately how effective your teaching is, and how much of a difference you are making in the educational and music progress of your students, without wasting precious time rationalizing about your good intentions.

RECAPITULATION

1. Think about an instance when your intentions and the functions of your actions were in conflict. What did you hope would happen, and what actually happened? Why do you think your intentions didn't function properly? What do you think you could have done to change the outcome to better align with your intentions?

2. At some point in your life, someone probably disappointed you with the functions of their actions. Describe one time this happened to you. Did they try to make you feel better by explaining their good intentions? How did you feel, and what did you say to them regarding the poor functioning of their intentions, if anything? If you said nothing, what would you have liked to have said, based on how you felt at the time?

Professional and Ethical Behaviors of Successful Teachers

There are many career paths that are referred to as "professional trades." These include doctors and lawyers, plumbers and electricians, teachers and administrators, and many other professions. Each of these jobs has a body of knowledge and skills specific to the trade, and each has written and unwritten lists of professional and unprofessional behaviors associated with them. When you think of the professional behaviors of medical doctors, for example, you probably expect him or her to be clean and well dressed. You expect them to be knowledgeable and competent. You expect them to be clear minded and polite. If your doctor appeared drunk and unkept, confused and irritated, and used profanity excessively, it would make a very bad impression on you as a patient. You would probably determine that this doctor was unprofessional. You would probably not visit that particular doctor's office again in the future. Your expectations about the professional behaviors of medical doctors shape your opinion of them as professionals, and this opinion determines your willingness to be in their care.

Every profession and trade has certain rules of conduct that are generally accepted as normal, so not every profession will have the same standards of conduct as the medical profession. Behavior is, after all, dependent on the context of the situation. For example, if you have ever been on a construction site where electricians and plumbers are working, you may have observed that the use of profanity is normally accepted between workers in casual conversation, and that the standards for personal hygiene on these job sites are less stringent than for medical doctors. While a doctor would most certainly shower before reporting to the hospital to see patients or perform surgery, the plumber, knowing that the job can entail getting quite dirty, would save that shower for after work.

The online dictionary *merriam-webster.com* defines the term "code of ethics" as "a set of rules about good and bad behavior." Likewise, the website *investopedia.com* defines a code of ethics as "a guide of principles designed to help professionals conduct business honestly and with integrity. A code of ethics document may outline the mission and values of the business or organization, how professionals are supposed to approach problems, the ethical principles based on the organization's core values and the standards to which the professional is held." Many professional trades have extensive rules for the behaviors that guide the actions of its members. Other trades have larger unwritten lists of professional behaviors that are the foundations of the group norms for good behavior. Whether these behaviors are written or unwritten, certain actions in any profession could be considered either "professional and ethical" or "unprofessional and unethical." It is a very good idea for you, as a professional choral music educator, to write down and clarify your own personal list of professional behaviors and your own code of ethics.

What is the difference between unprofessional behavior and unethical behavior? Both carry negative connotations, but they are distinctly different. "Unethical" is an adjective that means "not conforming to a high moral standard, morally wrong" while "unprofessional" means "not exhibiting a courteous, conscientious, or generally businesslike manner in the workplace."[5] If you do something unprofessional, it may or may not be unethical; but if you do something unethical in the duties of your job, it will most certainly be considered unprofessional as well. For example, if you don't teach your students to read music and become independent musicians, despite your good intentions, you can justifiably be considered unprofessional in the sense that you are not fulfilling your professional duties. If you change the grade of a student,

5 https://www.merriam-webster.com

up or down, to reflect a grade that the student has not earned, that could be called both unprofessional and unethical. Likewise, if you collect money from students for trips or any other legitimate reason, and then you steal some of that money for personal use, that would be considered unprofessional, unethical, and also illegal. While discussions of morality in various cultures are beyond the scope of this book, there can be some debate as to which behaviors could qualify as unprofessional or unethical. This is especially true considering that morality is usually involved in a discussion of ethics, and what is considered moral can vary across cultures. It is clear, however, that when something is illegal, you should not engage in the behavior; always stay within the laws of your city, state, and country at all times.

The professional behaviors and expectations of music educators will obviously be somewhat different from the behaviors and expectations for medical doctors or plumbers. It is good to clarify what you think would qualify as acceptable behavior as well as what you think would qualify as unacceptable behavior in the education profession. The National Association for Music Education does have a document called "The Music Code of Ethics" on their website. Click on the Dig Deeper icon to view the full document.

But this document, adopted in 1947 and updated in the 1970s, mostly addresses the relationship between public school performing groups and the community of professional performing musicians. It focuses primarily on helping public school teachers understand when it is appropriate and inappropriate to have ensembles play in public, especially when performance opportunities would be lost to professional musicians. No other specific music code of ethics seems to exist besides this document.

The National Education Association is the professional organization for all public school teachers in every subject area in the United States, and they have a published code of ethics that can be transferred to the music education profession. It addresses specific behaviors that teachers should adhere to, and defines what kinds of values the organization believes in.[6] Here are some of the main points of their online published statement:

6 http://www.nea.org/home/30442.htm

NEA Code of Ethics

PRINCIPLE I — COMMITMENT TO THE STUDENT

The educator strives to help each student realize his or her potential as a worthy and effective member of society. The educator therefore works to stimulate the spirit of inquiry, the acquisition of knowledge and understanding, and the thoughtful formulation of worthy goals.

In fulfillment of the obligation to the student, the educator--

1. Shall not unreasonably restrain the student from independent action in the pursuit of learning.

2. Shall not unreasonably deny the student's access to varying points of view.

3. Shall not deliberately suppress or distort the subject matter relevant to the student's progress.

4. Shall make reasonable effort to protect the student from conditions harmful to learning or to health and safety.

5. Shall not intentionally expose the student to embarrassment or disparagement.

6. Shall not on the basis of race, color, creed, sex,[7] national origin, marital status, political or religious beliefs, family, social or cultural background, or sexual orientation, unfairly--

    Exclude any student from participation in any program
    Deny benefits to any student
    Grant any advantage to any student

7. Shall not use professional relationships with students for private advantage.

8. Shall not disclose information about students obtained in the course of professional service unless disclosure serves a compelling professional purpose or is required by law.

7 The terms "gender identity and gender expression" should probably be included in this list as "sex" is no longer a sufficient term to describe gender. The words "sex" and "gender" are not synonyms. For more on this see Chapter 13 "Gender Identity in Choral Music Education."

PRINCIPLE II – COMMITMENT TO THE PROFESSION

The education profession is vested by the public with a trust and responsibility requiring the highest ideals of professional service.

In the belief that the quality of the services of the education profession directly influences the nation and its citizens, the educator shall exert every effort to raise professional standards, to promote a climate that encourages the exercise of professional judgment, to achieve conditions that attract persons worthy of the trust to careers in education, and to assist in preventing the practice of the profession by unqualified persons.

In fulfillment of the obligation to the profession, the educator--

1. Shall not in an application for a professional position deliberately make a false statement or fail to disclose a material fact related to competency and qualifications.

2. Shall not misrepresent his/her professional qualifications.

3. Shall not assist any entry into the profession of a person known to be unqualified in respect to character, education, or other relevant attribute.

4. Shall not knowingly make a false statement concerning the qualifications of a candidate for a professional position.

5. Shall not assist a noneducator in the unauthorized practice of teaching.

6. Shall not disclose information about colleagues obtained in the course of professional service unless disclosure serves a compelling professional purpose or is required by law.

7. Shall not knowingly make false or malicious statements about a colleague.

8. Shall not accept any gratuity, gift, or favor that might impair or appear to influence professional decisions or action.

Adopted by the NEA 1975 Representative Assembly

RECAPITULATION

1. After reading and examining the NEA Code of Ethics statement (above), comment on if you think this document is useful or not to you as an emerging professional, and explain why you think it is or isn't useful. Also, in your opinion, what do you find to be the most important aspects of the statement and why?

2. Write your own personal "Professional Music Educator Code of Ethics" with eight specific behaviors that you would want to follow as a professional music educator. One way to organize this list is to start each of the eight sentences with "As a professional music educator, I will always..." or "Professional music educators should always...." You don't have to organize your list of professional behaviors this way if you can think of a way that better expresses your value statements.

3. Examine your personal Code of Ethics. Do you see how this list clarifies the things that you value as a professional? Compare your list to the others in your class (or colleagues that you know), and then revise your list to reflect your specific values even more precisely.

The Trouble with Gossip and The Rule of "Car"

One thing that you will find out about being a music teacher is that you are part of a small but wonderful group of artistic professionals. Each person has strengths and weaknesses that they bring to their position, and each teacher has an ability to reach students in their own unique and powerful way. The professional circles that you will be part of are relatively small, and in most situations, it will be true that "everyone knows everyone else." This will be especially true if the state music educator's association has well-attended in-service conferences or if there are statewide events where music educators gather together.

It is also true that professional music educators are human beings with opinions, biases, insecurities, and a whole host of personal preferences for music and teaching. It is a natural part of the human condition to want to voice your opinions and preferences to others, and there is nothing inappropriate or unethical about having an opinion about someone or something. But how you choose to voice these opinions will determine, in large part, how you are perceived and judged by your peers in the profession. It is very important for you to understand how public gossip functions for you professionally.

Gossip is defined as "casual or unconstrained conversation or reports about other people, typically involving details that are not confirmed as being true."[8] To gossip, then, is to create or perpetuate stories or opinions about

8 https://en.oxforddictionaries.com/definition/us/gossip

others that may or may not be true. When you engage in gossip, you become a willing participant in the potential defamation of others, and you may degrade yourself in the eyes of other professionals. In our small music education circles, if you gossip about someone, you can be fairly sure that someone will retell the gossip story to the face of the person and that they will use *your name* as the originator of the story. Once you are labeled as a mean gossiper, you will suffer professionally whether you realize it or not. If you are in any professional or public setting, such as a hotel lobby or restaurant, or an interest session at a convention, you may be able to be heard by lots of people in our small circle.

When it comes to talking or writing about other people, your best bet is to follow these guidelines:

1. If you have something nice to say about someone, use their name and feel free to go on and on about how wonderful they are or what great things they have done.

2. If you have something unkind or even disparaging to say about someone, *do not* use their name publicly, and do not provide hints to help others know the identity of the person you are talking about. Keep it completely anonymous.

3. Whenever possible, if you must listen to gossip in public settings, do not participate in it. If you listen but do not add anything, you are less likely to be linked to the gossip by others.

4. If you have nothing nice to say…*try harder*.

You may be thinking, "But if I have opinions, shouldn't I be able to express them?" The answer is yes, in the proper setting. You should limit your personal, unflattering opinions to close friends who you really trust not to gossip about what you say. One way to practice this rule of professional behavior is to adopt and practice the Rule of "Car." When something in the professional environment causes you to think of something to say that is better left unsaid in that setting, just nod to your colleagues and say "car." This means that everything will be chatted about later, usually in the car, where no one can overhear or judge the opinions of the conversation. As a professional choral music educator, you have a choice to uplift others or to diminish others…and how you do anything affects how you do everything. Remember that you can always say honest and positive things about anyone at any time in public settings, even when other people are being unpleasant or malicious.

RECAPITULATION

1. Recall and tell a story about an instance where someone said something mean about a person who was your friend. Did the person saying the mean thing know you were friends with this other person? If so, did you confront them about it? Did you want to go right to your friend and tell them what you heard, as well as who you heard say it? Did you decide to tell your friend? Why or why not? If you did tell them, what was their reaction? Would you do things differently knowing what you know now?

2. Have you ever been the victim of negative gossip? How did it make you feel, and what did you do in response to hearing about it? What have you done to change your own behavior around gossip?

3. Imagine and then describe a scenario where you hear your own students saying mean things about another student in your choir. How would you handle it? What would you do and say, if anything?

Behavioral Traits of Successful Teachers

Becoming a certified and credentialed professional music educator is an exciting journey. Many students find it fun and interesting to leave behind the behaviors they modeled as a student for the professional behaviors of the teacher. Other students struggle to embrace the habits and behaviors of competent educators. As you begin your transition from student to teacher, it is good to clarify and examine what teachers are expected to do, and what behaviors you will be required to attain and exhibit. Here are a few of the most important and universal behavioral traits of successful teachers:

- ✓ **Teachers Are Punctual**. Successful teachers are on-time professionals. When you are a student, you can arrive to class when it is starting, or you can even be a little late for class. Class starts whether you are there or not there. Teachers who arrive when class starts are rarely prepared to teach in the first minutes that class begins, so successful teachers arrive early, before the students do. For teachers "on time" means early, and arriving literally "on time" means you are late.

- ✓ **Teachers Are Well Prepared.** Great teachers invest whatever time it takes to prepare for class so that every detail of what will happen in the lesson is clarified, organized, and sequenced. Students sometimes arrive to class unprepared and hope that the teacher won't notice, but an unprepared teacher is an obvious failure in the eyes of the students. Experienced educators will, however, improvise and adjust the order and content of their lessons when student engagement or progress demands it. Inexperienced teachers sometimes mistake this improvisation as permission to make up their lessons on the spot, without careful planning and a task analysis of activities. The most artistic and effective teaching is most often meticulously planned ahead of time, but feels natural, adaptive, improvisatory, and engaging.

- ✓ **Teachers Are Lifelong Learners.** A good student is a curious student, and teachers should be curious, long-term learners too. It is your ability to ask questions, reflect on your abilities, and synthesize new ideas that will keep you growing as a teacher throughout your career. Teachers who "have it all figured out" often don't feel the need to make their teaching better, and they might even blame the students for their own teacher shortcomings. Teachers who are open to learning, and who enjoy the *process* of learning, realize that learning is never finished; they rejoice in the daily progress and unfolding of new skills and ideas. As a student, you can sometimes get good at regurgitating information on tests without actually learning or retaining anything after the test is over. As a teacher, however, you must constantly ask the questions that will spur you forward to becoming better and more effective in your classroom and rehearsals. Ask yourself this question, "Do I someday want to be a teacher who has taught for thirty years, or do I want to be a teacher who has taught one year thirty times?"

- ✓ **Teachers Are Masters of Task Analysis.** Some people think that teaching is the same thing as coaching, but there are distinct differences between a "teacher" and a "coach." A coach is a person who works on a skill or performance globally, guiding the student through imagery, modeling, and enthusiasm. A teacher is a professional who breaks down a skill or performance into smaller pieces that add up to the overall performance. The teacher creates this *task analysis* that includes a detailed list of every step needed toward mastery, and then creates an order and lesson plan for teaching those steps. The artful teacher assesses the student and determines what step the student needs. The teacher focuses on one particular step at a time, knowing that starting too low or too high on the task analysis will not create success for the student. It should be noted that some people who call themselves "coach" are really excellent teachers, and some people who call themselves "teacher" are really approaching their teaching as a coach. It is also important to understand that the difference between a coach and a teacher is discussed here primarily to clarify a global distinction in teaching approach. Every teacher "coaches" at times, and every coach "teaches." One way to discern if a person is acting more like a teacher or a coach is to determine if the teaching focus is primarily process oriented or product oriented. The teachers meets the student where they are, honing and breaking down the skills that they need to be just a little better, and building on the learning process. The coach works with the final skills, or product, even when the student is not prepared to demonstrate those skills. Some of the best teachers in the world call themselves "coaches" and some of the best coaches call themselves "teachers."

✓ **Teachers Are Morning People.** Some people love to stay up all night and others prefer to get up early in the morning. Students can (and do) pull all-night work sessions to finish academic projects by the deadline. If you are hoping to become a public school music teacher, you will need to be able to get up early, get dressed and ready for work, travel to school to get set up, and be clear minded and prepared…possibly for classes that may start at 7:00 A.M. or earlier! If you are a person who can adjust your behavior to allow you to be a morning person, you will have no problems with this teacher behavior. But if you are a person who can't get going in the morning, you may want to consider other musical career options that allow you to sleep late and stay up late.

✓ **Teachers Are "People-People."** There are two broad types of jobs: jobs where you work alone and jobs where you are required to interact with other people. Some people prefer to work alone, perhaps in an office cubicle, while others prefer an environment where they can connect and collaborate with other people. Teaching is not a solitary activity. Even though you will be teaching music to people, you will spend most of your time *teaching people* through music. Teachers must enjoy human interaction on a deep level that creates personal satisfaction on a daily basis. If you are often annoyed with people when you are required to interact with them, you might consider a job path where you have an ability to work in a cubical or private space far away from other people.

- ✓ **Teachers Understand and Form Appropriate Personal and Professional Relationships.** When you are a student, you do not need to model all of the professional behaviors that teachers must model regarding the nature of their personal and professional relationships. As a student, if you want to be friends with someone, and the other person reciprocates a willingness to be friends, you can be friends. But teachers can't really be "friends" with their students; teachers must develop and understand how relationships *function*, and their personal and professional life must be guided by codes for appropriate teacher/student behavior. As a teacher, you will need to learn how to form contingent relationships with your students, and this means creating a professional distance that is healthy, functional, appropriate, and ethical.

- ✓ **Teachers Are Organized.** When you are a student, you are only responsible for your own learning. As a teacher, you will be responsible for guiding the learning of many people. Along with this responsibility comes the need to control the environment and to manage a large quantity of details related to your teaching. This will require you to solve problems ahead of time, to plan your lessons carefully and gather the materials you will need well before class starts, and to maintain and update a personal and professional calendar. The old saying "failing to plan is planning to fail" applies here, and your ability to organize all the aspects of your teaching life is a prerequisite for your professional success.

- ✓ **Teachers Are Good Managers.** As a student, you may have worked independently, or you may have had instances where you were required to collaborate on projects with other students. But as a teacher, you will be collaborating with other people all day, every day. You will need to be able to have positive interactions with people while motivating them to work together as a team. You will need to create systems for managing fundraising events, concert events, small ensemble opportunities, trips, festivals, musicals, booster groups, and various other events. *You can't do it all on your own.* As an effective manager, you will learn to delegate certain tasks while keeping an eye on the progress and outcomes of every task. A good manager trains people to lead and trusts others to do their best work within the framework you will create for them. Good managers appreciate the people they collaborate with and give them frequent and appropriate thanks and approval.

- ✓ **Teachers Are Professionals.** A liberal arts undergraduate education teaches you a little bit about a whole lot of things. Your professional teacher training will teach you a whole lot about fewer things, and you will gain a greater depth of understanding in these areas. As a professional, you will need to be ethical, positive, competent, and well prepared, and you should most certainly be involved in your professional music and educational organizations. Professional educators treat their colleagues with respect, and they do their best to refrain from criticizing other educators in public settings. Professional educators claim the title of "teacher" as a badge of pride because they do not view teaching as a default if nothing else works out, but as a profession *by choice.*

RECAPITULATION

1. Take each of the traits of successful teachers (above) and write a few sentences describing your own abilities for each trait. Rate yourself on a scale for each one from 1–10, with 10 being the best. If you rate yourself as a "10" for "punctual," it means that you are always early or on time as a personal habit already. A "1" would mean that you are really needing to grow in the behavior.

2. List any traits of successful teachers that you think should have been included in the list above but were not.

Developing Your Piano Skills

There was a time in the past when a choral conductor was required to be an accomplished pianist. Some of these "conductor-pianists" were piano majors in college who made a choice to become choral directors somewhere along the way, and their keyboard skills were very helpful in their successful teaching. Some of these teachers were effective because of their ability to teach by rote at a very fast pace and to play parts and accompaniments accurately in rehearsal so that the students could learn the music quickly by ear. In this model of teaching, it could be said that "the better the pianist, the better the choral teacher."

Even today, some choral teachers teach notes completely by rote (or use part predominant recordings) while others use a student-centered approach to build musicianship skills, regardless of the teacher's piano skills. Singers who are trained to be independent musicians do not need to rely solely on the piano or part recordings to learn their notes, and the belief that only good pianists can train good choirs is not as prevalent today as it once was; there are many choral music educators with average piano skills who train their choirs to sing beautifully and expressively. A skilled music educator who can use the piano as a *tool* to sequence lessons and teach musicianship, with a varied approach to teaching students, can be highly effective as a choral conductor and educator, and being able to work *a cappella* is a skill that is just as important as being able to rehearse from the keyboard. When students rely too much on the piano for pitches and rhythms, they can actually have trouble tuning pure intervals and singing a sustained legato because the piano is an equally tempered percussion instrument. So, while you do not have to be a lifelong pianist and a trained accompanist to be successful, it is a good idea to work on your piano skills so that you can become capable enough on the piano to run a rehearsal from the keyboard, to play individual parts accurately, and to provide at least a basic chordal accompaniment, when needed, during the rehearsal process.

The Late-Blooming Pianist

Many students who choose to become voice majors in college, and who then choose to be choral educators, often make that decision because they fell in love with choral music in high school. Their musical experiences instilled a love of the choral arts into their consciousness and they gained a desire to inspire others by expressing that passion through teaching. Sometimes these enthusiastic students have some sort of instrumental background, but this is not always the case. If you have played the piano or have played in any band or orchestral ensemble for any length of time, you have gained some excellent experience that will aid you as a teacher of choral music. If you have gained competent musicianship skills through choir with voice as your sole instrument, you probably had excellent teachers along the way. But if you only sang in choir and never really learned musicianship skills in a sequenced and methodical fashion, you do have some ground to make up and some extra practicing to do to build your musical teaching competencies. If you did not have the good fortune to begin studying piano at an early age, you can still become a "late-blooming" pianist and train wonderful choirs just as well as lifelong pianists can. Even if you didn't start playing piano until you started attending college (or later), you can still build the functional skills you will need to teach confidently and capably from the keyboard.

It is not uncommon for college music majors without a piano background to pass their required piano classes, and even a proficiency, but still not be able to use the piano as a functional teaching tool in a classroom. This is because many undergraduate piano classes don't focus on the kinds of practical skills that are needed to lead a rehearsal. This is not to say that these classes are not valuable; beginning pianists need to have a solid introduction to the piano. But if you find yourself secretly fearing the piano when you picture yourself in front of a choir, you can focus on a few key skills that will help you to develop into a "*do-no-harm*" pianist.

A do-no-harm pianist is a person who can use the piano during rehearsal to help the choir, even if they can't play accompaniments note for note. Their ability to play parts accurately and to provide a harmonic reference for the choir when needed should not detract from (or harm) the progress of the choir. Here is a framework to help focus your progress and measure your emerging ability on the piano:

- **"Do-No-Harm" Accompanying**

A late-blooming pianist is unlikely to play every note in an accompaniment as it is notated in the score. In fact, in an attempt to play every note, there can be a total breakdown, or many missed notes and mistakes that may actually hurt the progress of the choir. If you want to help a choir with your accompaniment, then it is a good strategy to decide what you can and can't play and what you can leave out when playing. Here is a sequence to follow:

1. Choose a choral octavo with an accompaniment that you want to learn to play.

2. Study the score and write in a harmonic analysis above or below the piano score. Use a system that makes sense for you such as chord names or Roman numerals. Include inversions of the bass part, especially if these are reflected in the choral parts. When the chordal analysis is too complex for you to designate easily, refer to the choral lines for any doubled notes that the choir may need to hear. Leave out any other notes. Do not add any notes that don't appear on a given beat, so if there is no Bb on a beat, don't put one in your analysis.

3. Practice playing your chordal reduction in the tempo of the piece. Slow it down if you need to but use a metronome to keep your tempo steady. Work to teach your fingers to find the correct chords (and inversions) in time as they occur in the piece. Increase the tempo as you improve until you can maintain the performance tempo accurately. You will now be playing block chords that match the harmonic motion of the composition and in the performance tempo.

4. Work to improvise your block chords into patterns that reflect the rhythmic character of the written accompaniment. For example, if the accompaniment is primarily flowing legato 8th notes, then arpeggiate your chords in an 8th-note pattern as well as you can. Don't worry that what you are playing is not exactly what is written. If your improvisation is harmonically correct, and if your rhythmic approach is somewhat like the accompaniment, then you are providing do-no-harm support for the choir.

5. One way to help develop your ability to improvise chords and rhythms is to play from some sort of "Fake Book" during your practice. [9] You can also purchase sheet music books online that contain songs that you already are familiar with, songs that you could sing mostly from memory already. These editions will almost always have guitar chords above the staff telling you what chords to play. These can be pop or country songs, holiday songs, folk songs, or old Beatles tunes if you know those songs. Open the music and start singing and accompanying yourself. It's powerful if you know a song from a popular recording because you will begin to improvise while playing to better match the music you hear in your head, and your fingers will begin to learn new patterns that you can transfer to the choral octavos that you will be playing in rehearsal. And an added benefit to this exercise…it can be fun to sing and play songs you know and like.

- **Playing Warm Ups**

Every choral educator needs to be able to warm up the choir, and the piano can be a great tool to help build tonal and harmonic references

9 https://en.wikipedia.org/wiki/Fake_book

for the ensemble. Many experienced choral conductors who work regularly with accompanists will still play choral warm ups from the piano some of the time. Your intention should be to play warm-up patterns while remaining aware of the room, student engagement, and what the students are doing as they sing so that you can help direct their progress as choral musicians. You can work on your warm-up skills at the piano by following these simple steps:

1. Practice playing five-note major-mode patterns (do-re-mi-fa-so-la-ti-do) in every key. Use both hands if you can. Play evenly and musically as well as you can. If you can move up and down by half steps easily, practice moving up and down by whole steps. When you can do that well, move around in larger intervals.

2. Practice playing five-note minor patterns (do-re-me-fa-so-fa-me-re-do) in every key. Use both hands if you can. Play evenly and musically as well as you can. If you can move up and down by half steps easily, practice moving up and down by whole steps. When you can do that well, move around in larger intervals.

3. Learn to accompany several warm-up exercises that do not follow a simple major or minor five-note pattern. These can be anything that you think the choir will benefit from singing or warm ups that you found or learned from any source. Practice accompanying these until you can play them by memory in any key. One example of this kind of exercise is "*Sing a Little.*"

- **Playing Single-Line Parts from Choral Octavos**

When you use the piano as a teaching tool in a rehearsal, it can aid your teaching in many ways. Sometimes there is a tricky melodic line that students will struggle with, and just hearing it played on the piano will help them internalize and learn it. While your singing and modeling of vocal lines can be highly effective, the piano gives you a tool to realize one or more parts at the same time when needed. Your piano skills should be broad enough that you can play most single-line melodies from the score at sight, under pressure, and in a rehearsal. This skill is especially important when you are leading a sectional. In a sectional, the singers need to hear their part clearly, accurately, and with confident repetition. Here are a few strategies to improve your skills in this area:

1. Find, acquire, or purchase a hymnal. A hymnal is a great resource for melodic lines as it is filled with numerous examples of four-part strophic choral writing to sight read at the piano. Additionally, the voice leading is usually good enough to represent standard settings of the various voice parts. In other words, if you play a lot of alto lines from hymnals (or tenor, soprano, or bass parts), you will begin to see the common patterns of these voice parts and how they are traditionally set. Knowing these patterns will help you later as you encounter them when reading in a rehearsal.

2. Open your hymnal to a random page and choose a part to play (SATB). Set a tempo that you can keep steady and start playing. If you make a mistake and need to start over, choose a slower tempo. If you need to start over frequently, use a metronome at a very slow tempo, one that gives you plenty of time to think and be ready for the next note. If you can make it from beginning to end without stopping and with no mistakes, increase your tempo. Play all four parts using this same approach. If you finish playing all the parts, select another hymn at random and repeat the exercise.

3. Be sure to play whatever random hymn you open to, especially if it has a key that you rarely play in. Don't think, "Oh no, F#!" Instead say, "Wow, F#! Let's do this!"

4. Select some music from your single-copy choral library or find some choral music that you can take to a piano to sight read. Play each choral line and compare the general voice leading to the lines you read from the hymnal. You will see similarities and differences. Every piece of music has its own unique challenges, and ideally you will be able to study and practice any music that you may need to play in your rehearsal well ahead of time.

- **Playing Four-Part Hymns and Open-Score Octavo Parts**

There are times when playing multiple parts in rehearsal is both highly effective and efficient for the choir's progress. From a "do-no-harm" perspective, this means playing the parts accurately, in time, and confidently. When choir parts are written on a grand staff, like in most hymns with soprano and alto on one staff, and tenor and bass on a second staff, it is called "*closed score*." When choir parts are written on four separate staves, like in some choral octavos, it is called "*open score*." Playing open and closed score requires practice, and the only way to get better at it, like any skill, is to spend the time working on it.

1. Open your hymnal to a random page and scan the hymn with your eyes. Notice the key, the meter, the rhythm, and anything that looks like a technical challenge such as voicings that require three notes in the right hand or accidentals that need to be realized accurately. Set your metronome at a tempo that you think you can manage as you play all four parts together. If you make mistakes or pause as you play, *slow the tempo down by one click*. Try again. When you find a tempo that allows you to play all four parts accurately, move the tempo up by one click and try again.

2. Playing open score can be the ultimate challenge for the late-blooming pianist. Compare the two scores (below) and you will appreciate how managing four parts and three clefs is a much greater challenge than reading closed score. Sometimes open-score pieces include a closed-score piano reduction, but sometimes they do not. To practice playing these pieces, follow a similar approach to reading hymns, always using your metronome. Play all four parts unless you find it too difficult. If you do find it too difficult, try playing just the bass and soprano together in tempo. When you can do that, try to get an occasional alto or tenor note in, but keep playing bass and soprano. Eventually you will "see" the whole score and be able to get all four parts in as you play.

(Closed-Score Example)

(Open-Score Example)

- **Transposing Melodies**

There are times when you need to play a part during rehearsal in a different key than what is written. This is especially true when you are working with a soloist who is searching for a good key to pitch a song in or when you have changed the key of an a cappella song and need to transpose a part in the original key during rehearsal. Try this approach:

1. With your hymnal, play a single-line part of your choice from a random hymn. Then play it again one whole step up from the written key. Try playing it a half step down from the original key. Make note of how you keep the keys related, such as by interval, scale, or solfege syllables.

2. If you are successful transposing single-line melodies to any key, try playing two parts from the hymn in another key. Start easy by playing in a key just a step away. Add more parts as you get better. Ideally you will be able to read four parts while transposing into another key. This will take considerable practice, but it will be worth the time to challenge yourself and become a competent do-no-harm pianist.

- **Using a Rubric to Assess Piano Skills**

The best way to change a behavior is to first measure it so that you can quantify future changes and chart your progress and improvement. Measuring your piano skills can be done with the Music Assessment Rubric for Piano Skills (page 35). You can have someone fill it out as you play the various sections of the assessment or you can video yourself and do a self-evaluation. Either way, you can re-administer the assessment every few weeks to see if you have made improvements. Likewise, if you are weaker on certain sections of the rubric, you can devote more of your focused rehearsal time to those areas and skills.

Music Assessment Rubric for Piano Skills

Name ___________________

Date_________ *Total Score _____

Skills and Points	Late Bloomer (1-3)	In Progress (4-6)	Competent (7-9)	Advanced (10-12)
Supporting choral singing with "do no harm" prepared piano playing Score:	Very basic analysis of chords, possibly with some incorrect chords, possibly no inversions notated, plays tempo slower than marked tempo, stops and starts often, changes tempi, plays incorrect harmonies, insecure playing that will not inspire students to sing confidently, playing does not reflect essential rhythmic aspects of written accompaniment.	Correct analysis of chords, inversions correctly notated, plays tempo slightly slower than marked tempo, keeps tempo steady, knows what to leave out, plays correct harmonies with few mistakes, secure playing that will inspire students to sing confidently, playing somewhat reflects the essential rhythmic aspects of written music.	Correct analysis of chords including inversions, plays tempo at marked tempo, keeps tempo steady, chord choices help choir sing accurately, can monitor students while playing, secure playing that will inspire students to sing confidently, playing completely reflects the essential rhythmic aspects of written music.	Plays the accompaniment primarily as written and possibly improvises an improved piano accompaniment, can monitor and shape student behavior while playing, can bring out voice parts as needed while playing, exudes confidence that inspires students to sing confidently and musically.
Playing warm ups from the piano Score:	Not confident playing major and minor chords in all keys, weak when playing patterns with both steps and leaps, can play only a few warm ups, does not inspire confident singing, playing can possibly hinder rehearsal progress.	Somewhat confident playing major and minor chords in all keys, can play patterns with both steps and leaps with few mistakes, can play many warm ups, inspires confident singing, playing enhances rehearsal progress.	Confident playing major and minor chords in all keys, can play patterns with both steps and leaps without mistakes, can play many warm ups, inspires confident singing, playing enhances rehearsal progress, can monitor student engagement.	Very confident playing of various patterns in all keys, can improvise many warm ups, inspires confident singing, playing is musical, can monitor student engagement, use of piano integrated well into teaching.
Playing single-line parts from choral octavos Score:	Pauses significantly before playing, inaccurate pitches or rhythms played, might not keep tempi steady, might not give starting pitches, inefficient or unconfident approach to rehearsing with significant mistakes.	Plays parts without pausing often, mostly accurate pitches or rhythms played, keeps a steady tempo, gives starting pitches, can lead a sectional or rehearsal from the piano with occasional mistakes.	Plays parts without pausing, accurate pitches and rhythms played, can play at a steady indicated tempo, gives starting pitches, can strongly lead a sectional or rehearsal from the piano.	Plays parts without pausing, accurate pitches and rhythms played, can play at a steady indicated tempo, gives starting pitches, can strongly lead a sectional or rehearsal from the piano.
Playing four-part hymns and open-score octavo parts Score:	Pauses and seems not ready to start playing, inaccurate pitches and/or rhythms, stops and restarts often, awkward playing of treble and bass clef lines, unconfident.	Seems ready to start playing, mostly accurate pitches and/or rhythms, steady tempo, can play one treble and one bass clef line together, mostly confident.	Starts playing immediately, accurate pitches and rhythms, steady tempo, can play several open-score lines together, is confident leading the choir.	Plays immediately, accurate pitches and rhythms, steady tempo, musical playing, can lead singers well, reads open score well, can improvise on notes.
Transposing melodies Score:	Inaccurate playing of new key, rhythms not correct, stops and restarts, not confident.	Accurate playing of key within a second away, rhythms correct, keeps tempo, is confident.	Accurate playing within a third, rhythms correct, keeps tempo, is very confident.	Accurate playing in any key, perfect rhythm and tempo, is supremely confident.

*NOTE: The emerging pianist should practice to eventually score between 25–35 points across the entire assessment.

Playing the piano confidently and without harming the progress of the choir is a valuable skill for the emerging choral professional. You will need to be able to work in many settings, including *a cappella*, with an accompanist, and without an accompanist. With practice and experience, you will feel confident and capable in any rehearsal setting, in front of any choir, even if you are an emerging or "late-blooming" choral pianist.

RECAPITULATION

1. Everyone has a story about playing the piano. Some people took lessons from an early age and stuck with it while others started early and then quit for some reason. Still others didn't play piano at all growing up, but may have played another instrument in concert band, orchestra, or in an extra-curricular ensemble such as a folk or rock band. Discuss your experience playing piano, as well as other instruments, in your lifetime. How has your experience playing these instruments affected your skill and confidence as a future professional music educator?

2. Write a paragraph as a self-assessment of your own piano skills in relation to the various sections of the *Music Assessment Rubric for Piano Skills*. Do this *before* you take the assessment. Read the descriptions and guess where you would probably score on each section. Where do you think you would have the most success and where do you think you would have the most challenges and why?

3. Use the *Music Assessment Rubric for Piano Skills* to measure your ability to be a "do-no-harm" pianist. Find a choral octavo with an accompaniment that you can study and give yourself a few days to practice it. Have someone watch you to fill out the rubric or video yourself playing the accompaniment and fill it out yourself. Find some musical examples to test yourself on each section of the rubric. Compare these scores and results to the self-assessment you did in the previous section. Did you do the same, better, or worse than you thought you would on the actual assessment? Discuss the factors, in your opinion, that lead you to this result.

4. Create a "Practice Log" for your piano playing. Get a notebook or use an electronic device with an app that you like, and keep track of the date, location, and number of minutes that you practice the piano every day.

Do this for thirty days in a row. If a day goes by without any practice, be sure to enter a zero for that day. Be sure that you only track the minutes of focused practice; playing for ten minutes and then chatting with friends in a practice room for ten minutes is still only ten minutes of practice, even though you have been sitting at the piano for twenty minutes. Make your practice time a "no-distraction event" where you turn off electronic devices, forget about social media, and discourage friends from interrupting your practice time. After each week, create a graph to represent your time spent in focused practice. See if you can increase the total time on task for each of the four weeks. At the end of the thirty days, retake the piano assessment and score your results with the *Music Assessment Rubric for Piano Skills.* If you applied yourself over the thirty days, you should see excellent progress and improvement in all of the areas on the rubric.

Chapter Two

Career Paths in Music Education

2. Career Paths in Music Education

"Passion is what gives meaning to our lives. It's what allows us to achieve success beyond our wildest imagination. Try to find a career path that you have a passion for." ~Henry Samueli

The Importance of Learning to Teach

When it comes to studying music and becoming a trained musician, it is a true statement that virtually everyone will assume the role of a teacher in some fashion and at some point in time. Some people will become credentialed public school educators, while others will become private school music teachers. Some will become workshop and master class clinicians, and some will become college and university professors. Some people will start, build, and maintain private music studios where they will teach students one on one, while others may hold corporate jobs in the music industry where they will interact with and train others to do their jobs effectively. Professional conductors and performers (who may work with highly trained musical colleagues) will need to use the skills of a trained teacher some of the time to be most effective. Even public school administrators, who don't work with musicians most of the time, need to know how to manage and teach their staff to be valued employees in the workplace. Everyone, regardless of their professional title, will be a teacher in some form, and every person would benefit from learning how to teach others as effectively as possible.

But while everyone would benefit from learning how to teach more effectively, not everyone will study to acquire the pedagogy of highly effective teachers. This implies that there will be a good number of music teachers in the world who may be good performers, conductors, or administrators, but who are not adequately prepared to be highly effective professional music educators. Of course, if a person is born with the innate traits of a natural teacher, they will probably have a good chance of "figuring out" how to teach over time, through trial and error, without any formal education training. But for many other people, teaching is not something that comes naturally. Without any specific teacher training, most people will teach exactly the way that they were taught by their own teachers, for better or for worse.

It is presumed that you are reading these words because you are intending to be a professional music teacher someday and that you are curious about the knowledge, skills, and attitudes of highly effective music educators. But you may be a little unsure of your future role in the profession and the various opportunities that are available to you after graduation. If you are called strongly to teaching as a profession, rest assured that you will encounter ample opportunities to express your passion in the professional world. As it has been stated, everyone will be a teacher at some level. The questions to consider are, *"In what music-teaching situations could I envision myself enjoying and growing? In what situations can I see myself making a difference in the world? What kind of lifestyle do I want and what am I best suited for based on my talents, focus, and innate dispositions?"*

Keep these questions in the forefront of your thinking as you read the rest of the chapter. You will be presented with a short description of the most common career paths in music education, along with a few of the advantages of each. It is not uncommon for a person to work in several of these positions at different times throughout their career, so consider each one with an open mind, knowing that you may very well experience any of these if you choose to.

The Elementary General Music Teacher

Elementary general music teachers are normally public school educators who teach students in grades kindergarten through fifth or sixth grade (roughly ages five to twelve years old). The duties of these teachers can vary widely depending on the district they work for, the support for elementary music education in the school and district, and the facilities and resources available to them. Students usually take music together as a homeroom class, so class sizes can be small to large depending on the average class sizes of the school. The amount of time per class might range from twenty minutes or less to an hour or more. In many public school elementary music programs, one music specialist may teach hundreds of students every week, and it is not unusual for a single music teacher to be the only classroom music teacher for several schools.

In some schools, there will be a dedicated music room that students come to for music class, and sometimes the music teacher will be required to move from class to class, instruments and materials in tow, in a situation called the *itinerant* (traveling) music teacher. There are too many districts across the country, unfortunately, that do not have any classroom music instruction in the elementary curriculum, though they may offer band instrument lessons in fourth or fifth grade and choir as a school elective in fourth, fifth, or sixth grade.

Elementary music educators need to be able to teach and relate to very young students as well as adolescent students and to plan and implement musical activities that are rich, varied, and age appropriate. Effective classroom lessons require detailed and well-sequenced lesson plans that keep students engaged, interested, and experiencing music through singing, playing, listening, and moving activities. All good teachers must hold the attention of their class, but elementary music educators become masters at energetic delivery and fast-paced sequencing. Some of the very finest music educators in the profession are elementary music specialists because younger children will not behave, participate, nor thrive in anything less than a well-structured and consistent learning environment.

There are many professional and lifestyle advantages when you are an elementary music specialist. Teachers at this level normally get to know every student in the school because they teach every class in the school on a regular basis. A teacher with responsibilities of grades kindergarten through sixth grade will be able to work with a student when she is six years old until she is twelve years old and to really make a difference in the musical development of the child. Elementary teachers often have a strong sense of community within their school, and as possibly the only music specialist on campus, they often develop a strong identity as the musical leader of the faculty.

Teachers at this level will work full days with few breaks, and much planning will be required outside of class. However, there will be few concerts and evening activities to run and attend, and once school is over and students walk or ride the buses home, the elementary music specialist is normally free to enjoy the evening with family and friends and to enjoy musical pursuits and hobbies of their choosing. Like other fully certified public school teachers, elementary music specialists also are afforded a full-time salary, full benefits often including medical and dental insurance, employer-assisted retirement plans, and a generous holiday and vacation schedule, which usually includes a paid summer vacation.

Finally, recruiting students for music classes is not an expectation for the elementary music specialist because students in elementary school will be assigned to take general music classes together as a curricular requirement. If there is an elective (normally after school) choir, then there will be some recruiting that has to take place; but because every student in the school will be taking at least a weekly music class with the teacher, it is usually not difficult to get students to join the elective choirs. If the general music classes are fun, musical, and engaging, students will connect with the teacher and be interested in the after-school choir experience.

The Secondary Choral Music Teacher

Secondary choral music teachers are normally public school educators who teach students in grades seven through twelve (roughly ages thirteen to eighteen years old). These teachers are usually considered choral music specialists and their primary responsibilities are creating and implementing curricula for choir and presenting concerts and special events such as choir trips, musical productions, and collaborative arts events with the other arts teachers (instrumental music, theater, dance, and visual arts). Although the teaching load is usually two to five choir classes, it is not unusual to have other duties assigned such as advanced-placement (AP) music theory, guitar, music appreciation, or piano classes.

Class sizes can be quite large, with choirs as big as eighty to over a hundred students in some situations, depending on rehearsal space and schedule. School administrators actually depend on large class sizes to justify the teaching position of the secondary music specialist because one teacher for many students saves money in the budget. Music ensembles are one of the few classes that can be highly effective with large class sizes, and in the case of instrumental ensembles like concert band, large numbers are required simply to fill out the orchestration demands of the literature. A full-time assignment for these teachers is typically five daily classes consisting of five choirs, or fewer choirs with a combination of other music classes such as AP music theory. Occasionally, teachers with a dual certification will teach music and another subject, such as English or physical education. It is also possible, depending on state certification rules, for a choral specialist at the secondary level to be assigned instrumental duties such as concert band, orchestra, instrumental lessons, or marching band to fill out a full-time teaching assignment.

A secondary choral specialist at the middle or high school level will often have a counterpart in instrumental education heading the band and/or orchestra program in the school. In a district that supports the arts strongly, the choral educator may be part of an arts staff consisting of a choir specialist, an orchestra specialist, a wind band specialist, a dance specialist, a theater specialist, and a visual arts specialist. In very large programs, there may even be several people in one specialty area. While there are some districts that have cut elementary music in tough budget times, far fewer districts have cut music in the secondary schools, and most middle and high schools have choir and band programs, even if they are barely supported through the budget.

The secondary school choral music educator is expected to be like an entrepreneur. An entrepreneur is a word often used for independent business owners and is defined as "a person who organizes and manages any enterprise, especially a business, usually with considerable initiative and risk."[1] Most often, students are not required to sign up for choir classes, and the secondary choral educator must continually work to recruit students for the choirs. Budgets are frequently too small to run the choir program properly, so the choral educator is often responsible for managing and maintaining a parent booster organization

1 http://www.dictionary.com/browse/entrepreneur

to raise money for the activities of the choir program. The teacher at this level is also a producer of public choral events, and depending on the expectations of the school or district, there will be two to six or more major concerts to plan, produce, and conduct every school year. Many school choirs also take trips and tours, and time must be dedicated to planning these trips, collecting money, and fundraising for special travel events. As entrepreneurs, these teachers also build and brand the program so that it has a positive public image that is well supported by the greater community. Because the nature of the position requires a large skill set outside of simply teaching music, not everyone will be well suited for this kind of work. These educators must be excellent musicians, good conductors, fine recruiters, capable producers of concerts, organized business people, good public relations agents, and smart administrators.

There are professional advantages when you are a secondary music specialist. Teachers at this level often work with students for several years and get to influence their artistic education significantly at a time when students are nearing adult maturity. The schedule is not usually as impacted as the elementary music specialist, so there will usually be free periods and longer blocks of time during the school day for planning and organizing. Most secondary choral educators have their own room for rehearsing, and also a private dedicated office for running the program's many and varied activities. Like other fully certified public school teachers, secondary music specialists are afforded a full-time salary, full benefits often including medical and dental insurance, employer-assisted retirement plans, and a generous holiday and vacation schedule, which usually includes a paid summer vacation.

There is a significant lifestyle difference between the elementary and secondary music specialist. When school ends, the elementary specialist is usually free to go home and pursue hobbies and family activities. Secondary schools, however, are a buzz of activity at the end of the academic school day with clubs, sporting practices and games, and arts rehearsals. It is quite common for middle and high school choral teachers to be at school several nights a week attending events, and also rehearsing students for special concerts or musical theater productions.

The Private School Educator

Virtually everything that a public school music position can afford can be available to you in a private school setting. Normally, private schools are set up as charter schools, or schools set up and sponsored by religious organizations.[2] The main advantages to working in a private school setting are based in the values of the school; if you ascribe to these values, you might be a good fit for the position. For example, if the school is sponsored by a church denomination that you already believe in or belong to, you will take requirements like prayer in the classroom as a welcome aspect of the job. Sometimes private schools require the staff to abide by certain behaviors such as not drinking alcohol or other behavioral norms of the religion. Students who attend private schools are often from higher socioeconomic groups, which is why they can afford to pay the tuition required to attend the school. These students can be, on the whole, smart and motivated when it comes to school tasks. On the other hand, they don't always have authentic exposure to diverse populations of students and can lack some qualities of social understanding that public school students acquire naturally.

Private schools are not always required to meet the standards for curricular accreditation that the public schools are required to maintain, so sometimes music programs are less comprehensive compared to their public school counterparts. However, resources in private schools can be abundant, and when the school values and supports music and the arts, wonderful programs can thrive. Pay for private school teachers can vary widely, with some offering excellent salary and benefits, and some offering meager salaries and no benefits at all.

One other pro or con, depending on how you look at it, is that private schools that are not accredited are not required to hire certified, credentialed music teachers. When this is the case, the teachers that are sometimes hired are not always good musicians, may not have any teacher training, and may even have no experience teaching in the musical specialty area that they are assigned to.

The Independent Contractor

Some vocal music specialists prefer to express their art outside of the public and private school arena by becoming private, independent vocal educators or choir directors. Normally these teachers establish a personal business working with students one on one for an hourly rate of pay or they may teach group lessons or conduct community, church, or professional choirs. One big advantage to this arrangement is that hours of work can be

2 A charter school is defined as "a tax-supported school established by a charter between a granting body (such as a school board) and an outside group (as of teachers and parents) which operates the school without most local and state educational regulations so as to achieve set goals." http://merrian.webster.com

more flexible. Whereas the public school teacher must wake early and report to school at a time decided by the administration, the independent contractor can often decide when to start and end their teaching or rehearsing day.

One disadvantage of the private contractor is that there are no guaranteed salaries or benefits, and hours not worked equate to hours not compensated. Without benefit packages including dental and medical care, and no retirement plans set up automatically as they often are in public employment situations, the independent contractor must be really organized concerning personal finances and plans for a steady income.

The Higher Education Educator

Higher education music teachers are usually university educators who teach students pursuing a two- to four-year professional college degree (roughly ages eighteen to twenty-two years old). Many choral music education students find that they have become inspired on some level by their college professors, and it is not unusual for these students to aspire to teach and influence students in a higher education setting as well. The path to becoming a higher education teacher can be varied, and it is important to know how and when to pursue this path if it is indeed your educational goal.

Ironically, there is no teaching certification required to be a college or university professor…none at all. In most four-year colleges and universities, an earned doctorate (Ph.D. or D.M.A) in music is a minimum requirement for a position application, and in some community colleges and some smaller four-year colleges, only a masters degree will be required. Universities will hire different kinds of professors based on the primary mission of the university; if the mission is research, as it is in many of the largest schools, a proven research record and grant writing ability will be valued most. If teaching is valued over research, as it is in some colleges and universities, a track record of excellence in teaching over a number of years and levels will be required for well-qualified applicants. If musical performance on a major instrument is the primary criteria on which the school bases the hiring process, then a high-profile performance career must usually precede the college teaching career. But again, there is no certification required to be a higher education teacher, even though the researcher and performer will be required to teach college classes or private lessons.

Quite often, young, talented, and enthusiastic undergraduate music students will decide to earn a bachelors, masters, and doctorate without gaining any real-world teaching and performing experience, making them qualified on paper to apply for higher education positions, but still lacking the documented teaching experience that the job often requires. It is highly recommended that anyone seeking to teach in a university position learn how to teach by earning a teaching credential in the best program available and by teaching in a public or private school setting for a minimum of three to five years. The authentic growth and experience gained in these early teaching years is essential to shaping the pedagogy, rehearsal skills, and expertise of the young educator, and all too many people with earned doctorates and no teaching experience discover this too late and are unable to find a position in higher education that fulfills their career aspirations.

There are professional advantages when you are a higher education music professor. Teachers at this level usually work with adult students for several years and get to influence their artistic education and career paths significantly. Sometimes non-traditional students will be in the programs, so it is possible to work with students who are as old, or older, than the professor. The schedule is not usually as impacted as the secondary music specialist, and there are no requirements to be on campus when meetings, classes, or office hours are not being held.

The program will often have an adequate budget to run the choral events and classes, so fundraising and managing booster groups is rarely required. A dedicated and private office is common for meeting with students and managing class and rehearsal duties, and the teacher might be one of many music teachers on staff, as opposed to the only music teacher in the building. Much like fully certified public school teachers, higher education professionals may be afforded a full-time salary, full benefits often including medical and dental insurance, employer-assisted retirement plans, and a generous holiday and vacation schedule, which usually includes a paid summer vacation. Contrary to popular belief, however, the pay for public school teachers is often higher than university teachers, especially after ten to twenty years of experience in the profession.

There is a lifestyle difference between the elementary and secondary music specialists and the higher education educator. Even though the higher education teacher may not need to report to school every day at 7:30 A.M. and has much freedom outside of assigned teaching and meeting times, they are expected to maintain an agenda of creative activity and community service that will be used to determine if they are worthy of a positive decision toward promotion and tenure. They are required to be self-motivated and to pursue original research, write books and articles to advance the profession, and to travel, teach, and perform while building a national and international reputation in their chosen specialty area. Failure to earn tenure, usually in year six or seven for a new associate professor, results in being fired by the institution. In most public schools on the other hand, tenure is automatically awarded in year three if the teacher has proven to be competent in their teaching and has acted professionally in their official school duties.

Other Career Paths

There are many other jobs that music education majors thrive in after graduation besides the public school, private school, independent contractor, and higher education teaching scenarios. Simply graduating with a college degree sets you up for improved earning potential. Studies show that individuals with bachelor's degrees will earn $400,000 more in their lifetimes than those with just a high school diploma, and that the money earned by those graduates makes up for tuition and other costs for many by age thirty-three.[3] Click on the Dig Deeper icon to read about seventy careers in music and what you can expect to be paid in those situations.

RECAPITULATION

1. Think about the roles and advantages (and disadvantages) of the elementary public school music teacher, the secondary public school choral teacher, the private school music teacher, the independent contractor, and the higher education educator. Which ones are you drawn to as possible career paths, and which ones do you think you are less drawn to? Explain why you feel this way. Explain your thinking for all five of the situations and your desire (or lack of desire) to possibly follow each path. Remember to consider the questions, *"What music teaching situations could I envision myself enjoying and growing in, and in what situations can I see myself making a difference? What kind of lifestyle do I want, and what am I best suited for based on my talents, focus, and innate dispositions?"*
2. After reading through the seventy careers on the music webpage, make a list of the top ten careers that you think you would be happy doing and that you might be particularly good at if you applied yourself to the position. Be ready to discuss your top ten list in class or with colleagues, including why you made your choices. Is there something not on that list of seventy that you would consider doing as a profession? If so, list it below your top ten list, and you can list more than one if you want to.

3 https://www.educationdive.com

Chapter Three

Teaching for Transfer

3. Teaching for Transfer

"I cannot teach anybody anything. I can only make them think."
~Socrates

The Exponential Expansion of Knowledge and Information

There was a time, in the distant past hundreds of thousands of years ago, when a person could be aware of virtually everything that was known in the world. Early hunting and gathering civilizations didn't require vast amounts of information to ensure survival, and "education" was likely focused on the essential skills necessary for hunting and surviving in a hostile environment.

Sometime around 8000–5000 BCE humans began to stop roaming and they started putting down roots in the first recorded civilizations where, for the first time, they lived in dwellings and raised food by farming. As agricultural techniques improved, the number of people needed to produce and store enough food to feed the village decreased; this triggered the rise of new professions within the village as more and more people had the leisure time to become trained professionals, including craftsmen, bankers, poets, and musicians. As you can imagine, diversified labor created new bodies of knowledge specific to each profession, and a need was created to pass on the skills and knowledge of these professions to the next generations. There are no existing records of exactly how this early education was delivered, but we can guess that it was probably accomplished through some form of mentoring, job shadowing, and on-the-job apprenticing. Specific knowledge within the known world was beginning to expand at a fast rate, and as this expansion continued, it became more and more difficult to be an expert on everything in your immediate environment.

At some point in time the institution of the "public school" was started in order to facilitate the passing on of the ever-growing body of knowledge in the known world to succeeding generations. According to existing records, one of the oldest known public schools was founded in China in the Han Dynasty between 143-141 BC by Wén Wēng and was named Shishi Middle School. New public schools were established in Europe in the 6th, 7th, and 8th centuries AD, and these institutions were charged with deciding what to include, and what *not to include,* in the curriculum. Information was continuing to expand, and it became increasingly important to deliver education with a focus on specific disciplines and areas of study.

Today we live in the age of networked computers and digital media, and the world continues to experience a tremendous growth of data, facts,

concepts, and information. The amount of information is not only increasing, but it is increasing at an exponential rate. R. Buckminster Fuller (1895–1983), a renowned inventor and visionary, wrote about his "Knowledge Doubling Curve," noting that until 1900, human knowledge doubled approximately every hundred years, but by 1945, knowledge was doubling every twenty-five years. According to knowledge doubling theory, which measures the amount of data produced annually, the digital universe was doubling in size every two years in 2013 and was predicted to multiply by a factor of ten by the year 2020…from 4.4 trillion gigabytes to 44 trillion gigabytes. As of April 2020, the world's data was measured to be an astounding 4.4 zettabytes! It is already humanly impossible, then, for any one person to know everything there is to know about everything.

Memorizing multiple facts to pass high-stakes tests makes less and less sense in an ever-expanding data age, and today's educators are faced with the daunting challenge of not only teaching students *what to learn*, but also to teaching them *how to learn*. Because there is too much information in the world for any single person to learn and memorize, it is essential that our students learn how to make cognitive connections between their present studies and their previous knowledge and understandings. This will help them "learn how to learn" by challenging them to look beyond a single right answer and to search for shades of meaning and new insights into the topics they are studying. One way to address this need is to teach students how to think critically and to apply what they know into new situations that they have never encountered.

The ability to interrelate learned information is usually referred to as generalization or "*transfer*."[1] Unfortunately, many students you will teach in your classes and rehearsals will not have been taught how to make cognitive connections between previously learned concepts and new ones. Many of them will have spent years and years studying seemingly unrelated trivia and facts for tests in various classes without ever connecting those ideas to other subjects; what they learned in English class wasn't compared and contrasted with what they learned in math, history, chemistry, or music classes. You will need to develop and implement exercises and experiences to teach your students how to transfer knowledge within your academic subject and also across other various subjects.

When students learn to transfer information and knowledge to new situations, they are more likely to retain that knowledge; this retention seems to be enhanced when the information is presented within an activity where

1 Material from this chapter was adapted from: Peterson, C. W. & Madsen, C. K., (2010) Encouraging Cognitive Connections and Creativity in the Music Classroom. *Music Educators Journal*, 97(2), December, 2010, pp. 25–29.

creativity is encouraged. It is easy to assume that students in our choirs, for example, understand the unifying musical elements of the various pieces in their folder or the stylistic differences and similarities between the music of two different composers. But unless students are taught to make these connections, we know that they are unlikely to do it by chance. And it would be unwise to ask them to make high-level connections about anything until you teach them how to make simple connections in a safe and creative classroom environment. If you were not given opportunities to transfer knowledge in a creative setting when you were younger, it might be difficult at first for you to teach your students how to do it. But when you learn and implement some of the techniques of teaching for transfer in this chapter, you will encourage your students to be more curious, creative thinkers in your classroom and throughout their lifetime.

RECAPITULATION

1. What kinds of teaching do you remember experiencing as a student in your lifetime: more fact-based teaching where you did a lot of memorization or more concept-based teaching where you had to explore and explain ideas? One way to remember is to think about how you were tested. If you remember more "one right answer, fill in the bubble" tests, your studies were more fact based. If you remember more "essay and discussion-based" tests, you had more concept-based instruction. Which kinds of instruction and tests do you prefer and why? Did these approaches play into your strengths as a learner or would there have been better methods for you to learn and be successful in school? Explain your ideas.
2. In a normal day, how much do you rely on your smart phone, tablet, or personal computer to get your work done? What tasks do you do without technology and which ones do you always depend on technology to complete? In your opinion, is this a good thing or a bad thing? Do you think we will still be using these devices in some form in twenty years? Why or why not?

Everything Relates to Everything

The first step to nurturing transfer skills in students is to establish the concept that "everything relates to everything." Music relates to everything, including art, dance, theater, math, English, sports, popular culture, and so on. There is nothing that can be known, learned, or experienced that can't be related by similarity or contrast to anything else. For example, a chair and a car may seem to be completely unrelated at first. But with an approach that *everything relates to everything*, as well as a little creative thinking and positive encouragement, the connections begin to emerge. Most chairs, like cars, touch the ground in four places, either on wheels or on legs. Cars and chairs provide a place for people to sit. Both come in a variety of colors. Chairs or cars can be comfortable or uncomfortable depending on the materials they are made of. Cars get people from one place to another and wheelchairs do the same. Cars can have adjustable seats and chairs can be adjustable, like recliners. Both words start with the letter c, but each starts with a different sound. Chairs, like cars, can be very expensive and built for luxury, while others can be made cheaply for utility. You can take a nap in a chair and you can nap in a car. When shopping for either, you are likely to encounter a salesperson hoping to help you find (and buy) the right one.

After just a few minutes, it becomes clear that chairs and cars are much more closely related than we thought they were. For some people, this kind of thinking comes easy, and for others, it may seem more difficult. This will certainly be the case for your students. If you, as the teacher, find it difficult to brainstorm a list of connections like the one outlined above, you may need to spend some time practicing your improvised transfer skills before you model for the class. Like any skill, the more you practice, the easier it gets.

Transfer Tasks for the Music Classroom

This approach is best implemented in the upper elementary or secondary general music classroom setting, but can be adapted for any classroom and any subject matter. Starting with written prompts and class discussions employing topics and concepts students already understand is the most practical way to begin. This approach instantly accesses the real-world experiences and concepts that relate directly to the individual student's life and held understandings. As students learn to make transfer a habitual part of their daily thinking, the creative teacher will be able to embed transfer activities into more diverse musical settings with great success.

It seems obvious that students tend to view most everything as having little "practical value" unless they are capable of making transfers to their own understandings or performing situations. Yet, until each student is capable of answering the questions, "How does this information relate to me?" and "How do I use it?" it is probably fruitless to attempt to provide "solutions" to problems or to make meaningful decisions, even if the solutions happen to be firmly based. In the beginning, students need to get started by actually doing something—anything that will foster transfer. If at all possible, the goal should be to create a strong positive association with the activity and to develop a strong positive effect with the activity.

At the very beginning of class, ask all students to take out a blank piece of paper and a pen or pencil. In an online teaching environment, as was created by the COVID-19 pandemic, students can be encouraged to use their electronic devices to respond and share their ideas if they can't write and respond in person or on paper. Have them write their name and the date at the top. Remind them that "everything relates to everything" and ask each to write a common-knowledge person, place, thing, or idea on their paper. For example, they can write Barack Obama because most people know who he is, but they cannot write the name of their uncle Fred. Call on two students to reveal their word and write both words on the board. At this point, you, as the teacher, should begin to make connections between the two words aloud. Any connection is valid and even puns are acceptable. Contrasting how the two words are different is also acceptable. Do your best to model for them with creative ideas and connections.

As students catch on to the activity, you can ask them to offer their own creative connections to the words on the board. When the class runs out of ideas, ask for two more words and repeat the process. When you feel they have learned the activity, have each person copy the word of the person to their right (you will manage the people who are on the far right) so that every person has two words on his or her paper. Instruct them to "transfer between the two words" and to do it quietly and immediately. The only rule at this point is that every pen or pencil needs to be moving. Tell them to write "I'm thinking, I'm thinking, I'm thinking" if nothing else comes to mind. Most students will come up with an idea as soon as their pencil starts moving.

Next, call on students to verbally share the connections they wrote down and be sure to validate and approve of all their responses. Because there are no wrong answers, if you do not fully understand the connections that they are communicating, ask them for more clarification. Help every student feel successful, and celebrate the fun and creativity of the activity.

This first lesson should take about fifteen to twenty minutes for a class of ten to twenty students. Have the class hand in their "transfer sheets" as they exit the room at the end of period. For online classes that use digital methods for handing in class materials, students may or may not turn in these "daily transfers" based on the objectives of the particular class. Transfer tasks are best nurtured in a climate of support and encouragement rather than fear and punishment, and we are also training them to make transfers in music eventually, where there are many gray areas of thought and expression. Many musicians who once started by doing small-scale things have later moved on to produce very substantive relationships while pursuing their individual curiosity and interests.

Practicing Transfer Tasks: Sequencing Activities

Classes will normally begin in the same manner as the first one: students will take out a blank piece of paper and a pen or pencil and then will write their name and the date at the top. Each will write down a common-knowledge noun. As you assess their success at transfer, you can have them swap words, as in lesson 1, or you can have the whole class use one teacher-given, music-related concept as their second word. For example, you can have everyone compare his or her chosen word to "music." If a student wrote "vacation" as his or her first word, his or her task is to examine how music relates to vacation. Allow students to use any method they want, such as prose, bullet points, lists, outlines, or free-written associations to document the connections they discover. A transfer sheet using bullet points might look something like this:

Samuel Student
September 7, 2021

VACATION and MUSIC

- Both have duration.
- Both can be fun.
- Both can be boring.
- Both are best with planning.
- You can look forward to both.
- The prettier, the better.
- You can take a music vacation by going to music camp.
- There are professional musicians and also professional vacation planners.
- Music has form and vacations have segments too, like getting to the destination, the relaxing phase, and returning.
- A fine vacation is like a fine piece of music, with a lot of cool things to do and observe.
- People like different kinds of music, and not everyone enjoys the same kind of vacation.
- When we have school vacation, I hope to work on my composition assignment for the concert.

Students should have enough time to get momentum going toward the task, but not enough time to run out of ideas. Tell them that you do not expect them to get every idea down, but that you expect them to come up with as many connections as they can in the limited time available. It is very important that the teacher affirm all connections that the students offer. When in doubt say, something like, "I am not sure I see the connection you are making, so could you say it in a different way or explain it to me again?" Students will appreciate your desire to hear them, and most of the time, the connections they make will be obvious to most everyone in the class. The amount of time devoted to this task should be only ten to fifteen minutes, with everyone sharing verbally if time allows or with only some students sharing. As always, have them pass in their transfer sheets to you as they exit the room, or collect them digitally.

As the students build mastery in critical thinking, and when you want to challenge the class even more, you can provide them with both words to compare and contrast. You can use words that relate to concepts taught in class, such as melody and form, or Copland and Mozart, or you can use current events, such as the Super Bowl and Tuesday's election. If you ask other teachers at your school about the units they are teaching, you may be able to integrate interdisciplinary concepts, such as the Civil War or genetics, into musical concepts from your curriculum. Every class is different, so you must determine the best ways to keep students challenged and thinking while allowing them to be successful during every class meeting.

Transfer Tasks for the Rehearsal Setting

In the rehearsal setting, we are less likely to start a class with a writing prompt and discussion, and instead are more likely to begin with an engaging warm up including musicianship training. But we can still reinforce transfer concepts and the idea that "everything relates to everything" effectively in a choral rehearsal. Many of the same approaches outlined for the general music classroom can be adapted, but with less time spent on discussion, and with fewer students sharing each class. One way to do this is to have students keep a "choir notebook" in their music folder, or in a binder specifically for choir that has paper and other materials for the class. Start by dedicating only five minutes in each rehearsal to a transfer task. Have the students write a common-knowledge noun in their notebook and then verbally model how to relate the words, just as in the general music classroom approach. Let this be a kind of "game" of association for five minutes a rehearsal where you really encourage the students to think creatively.

As they get better at the game, have individual students respond and make connections between the two words. While it will take longer to develop critical thinking skills in a large performance class when only five minutes are dedicated to the activity, eventually you will be able to ask them to make connections between more challenging concepts that have a more direct connection to the literature you are studying and performing. Ideally, the "choir transfer game" should be a fun, safe, short, and creative activity that gives your choir rehearsal a nice change of pace.

Students who have acquired and practiced the skills of critical thinking through simple transfer and group discussion will have a good chance of creating higher-level connections during music-making activities. For example, players or singers in an ensemble can be asked directed questions about the music they are experiencing, such as the following:

1. What musical aspects of this work are similar to our final piece from last month's concert?
2. If this [contemporary] composer had lived and composed this piece in

the Baroque era, what musical elements do you think might have been the same or different and why?

3. What specific experience or event from your past could be underscored by this music in a movie and why?

4. If the form of this piece could be represented by a house, what kind of house could you envision and what musical elements led you to your conclusions?

5. What skills from our warm up help you most when performing this piece and what new warm ups would help us even more?

Transfer Tasks: Diverse Benefits

This approach to critical thinking, starting with writing prompts and simple transfer tasks, can have many benefits for you and your students. When classes begin with transfer tasks, students build habit strength toward focusing their thoughts right away. They will bring a pen or pencil and paper to class every day because they will need these materials for every class. The first few minutes that the class is writing provides the teacher with several precious moments to organize the classroom environment or write announcements or assignments on the board. The verbal sharing of written ideas will become a positive daily interaction where students feel heard and where there is no right or wrong answer to give.

While it is not recommended that this task be used as a graded quiz, it is beneficial to occasionally ask the students to "write down everything you can remember about the last class." The teacher receives feedback about retention while the students get a quick review of class concepts. You can also ask them to "write about something that happened to you since the last class that relates to this class." Students may even begin, over time, to think about class concepts even when they are not in class.

Students in performance classes can be challenged to share something they learned, practiced, or thought about outside of class that will help them be more informed or expressive during the rehearsal. They can be given specific assignments to learn something about the historical significance of the literature or about the various cultures where the music comes from. Other teachers in your school may appreciate that you are honing students' critical thinking skills and that you are integrating academic concepts across the curriculum. If a student asks you a question like, "Why are we singing this song?" you can ask right back, "Why *are* we singing this song? You know as well as I do that everything relates to everything." The student will answer the question in a way that makes sense to him or her and you will probably not hear the question again.

Another benefit of this exercise is the opportunity to ask for student responses to other kinds of prompts, such as, "What is your favorite activity in school and why?" or "What are the top three things you need to accomplish today?" It is not necessary to have verbal responses to every writing prompt, although the teacher should let the class know ahead of time whether what students are writing will be shared with the class. If a student does not want to share what he or she wrote during the transfer time, allow the individual to take a pass for the day, but be sure to call on that student during the next class.

Effective Transfer

The activities and sequences presented in this chapter will help to nurture the transfer skills of the students in your classes. Starting classes with sequenced writing prompts can help students make cognitive connections between music class concepts, interdisciplinary concepts, and even events in contemporary culture. As stated earlier, you may need to practice making some cognitive connections yourself before demonstrating these skills in front of your classes.

By starting with simple student-chosen nouns, the activity can be fun, engaging, and successful from the outset as students apply knowledge that they already have to new situations. When students are encouraged to retain understandings from their lessons, and to foster the transfer of these understandings to new situations, retention and understanding are greatly enhanced. You, as the teacher, will gain insight into the thinking processes of your students, and in general music classes, you can assess the writing ability of your students more frequently. If major deficits in writing come to light, you can refer the student for extra help and tutoring to improve these skills.

Starting classes with transfer activities provides immediate focus for the room and dispels the need for the teacher to stop student talking, much like a good engaging warm up provides immediate focus in a choir rehearsal; as students get out their materials and begin writing, all talking will cease.

It is not recommended that transfer sheets be corrected and returned to the class every day. The activity is intended to increase student thinking, creativity, and retention, and all answers to those ends are considered correct. After students learn how to approach the activity, the class time required will amount to about ten to fifteen minutes per period. When the teacher has confidence in the ability of the students to transfer, connections can be woven into purely musical listening, performing, and creating activities. Once you and your students experience the fun and practical benefits of this approach, you will all agree that this is on-task class time that is very well spent.

RECAPITULATION

1. Is the concept of "everything relates to everything" new for you or have you thought this way in the past? Explain. Do you think your students will be able to make lists of related things as outlined in this chapter easily or do you think they will struggle? Why or why not?
2. Starting non-performance classes with written transfer activities yields several immediate benefits, including stopping student talking by replacing discussion with writing and creating habit strength around learning to focus one's attention on a task. It may be more challenging for you to integrate these activities into performance classes, mostly because you may not have had anyone model these techniques for you in this setting. Brainstorm as many ways you can think of (that haven't been outlined here) to help students think more critically and make transfers in a choir rehearsal. Which ones are the most practical, in your opinion, and will integrate best within a normal rehearsal pace?

Chapter Four

Managing the Choral Classroom

4. Managing the Choral Classroom

"Everything we do, we do together." ~ Christopher Peterson

Understanding the Classroom Management Problem

As a professional choral music educator, you will have to develop a significant amount of knowledge and a wide array of skills to be successful. Some of these skills may seem obvious to you, such as becoming a clear and expressive conductor, working on your error-detection skills, and writing and implementing well-paced and effective lesson plans. Some other skills and areas of expertise might seem less obvious to you, such as being good at building a budget, managing the materials in your room, or relating well to your students' parents and your professional colleagues. Of all the skills you will need to develop and practice in your preservice teacher training, an ability to manage student behavior in your classroom with consistency and kindness is arguably one of most important and essential.[1] An emerging teacher who lacks the necessary skills and knowledge to create a positive and consistent learning environment will not be able to teach and motivate all of their students in an educationally sound and functional manner. You will certainly need to be good at teaching *music*, but you must also learn how to be effective at teaching *manners* to your students first. Without this first step, nothing else really matters in your classroom.

Here are several scenarios that describe some common experiences that some teachers can find themselves in with respect to classroom management:

- **Mr. Sheppard** is in his first year of teaching music at a small, private high school. He feels like he is making the choirs sound better, but he also feels frustrated when the kids won't focus in his rehearsals. As a new teacher, he feels that it is important that the students like him, so he is careful not to disagree with them if he can help it. When the students talk during rehearsal, he does his best to be patient, but sometimes he wishes that they would just listen, sing, and respect the learning process more. Deep in his heart, Mr. Sheppard hopes that someday he can teach in a school where the kids are more respectful and where they care more about being in choir.

- **Ms. Hernandez** has been teaching music for three years in a large public school. She knows that her style can be a little sarcastic

1 Much of the information in this chapter has been adapted from: *Teaching/Discipline: A Positive Approach for Educational Development,* 4th edition by Madsen, Clifford K., Madsen, Charles H., Raleigh, NC: Contemporary Publishing Company, 1998

at times, but she also feels that the kids "get her" and that they know when not to challenge her authority. Still, about once a week, someone pushes her to the edge of her patience and she has to get angry to make a point. She can't quite understand why students can't abide by the rules all the time, and after someone breaks a rule for the fourth time on a "low patience day," she lets her anger get the best of her. When she cools down, the students seem to behave better, at least for a while.

➢ **Mr. Reeff** is a choral educator with ten years of music teaching experience at a suburban middle school. He knows that if he "gives the class an inch, they will take a mile," so he keeps their behavior in check at all times. Mr. Reeff is proud that his students do not talk in rehearsal and that they have learned to stand up straight and motionless without touching their neighbor when singing; they always seem to have a strong discipline and an intense focus. His choirs sing with close to 100% of the correct notes and rhythms, and they often demonstrate clear and clean diction. They never take their eyes off him when he is conducting. He shrugs off feedback from adjudicators at festivals who tell him that the choir is accurate, but unexpressive. He knows deep down it's better to have kids be afraid of you than it is to allow them to walk all over you.

➢ **Mrs. Nguyen** is in her third year of teaching at a private religious school. She likes to involve the students in many of the decisions in the room, knowing that if they "buy in," they will abide by the rules. She values the ideal of treating everyone fairly, and she even has a poster on the wall that says, "In this room we treat everyone with honesty and fairness." She lets the students decide on the classroom rules at the beginning of every school year, and though she doesn't always agree with the rules that they choose, she agrees to honor what they come up with as a class. Occasionally she finds herself in a tough spot when one class period has established a rule, but another class chooses a different rule. For example, one class decided that being late to class would be 1 point off the final grade while another class decided not to take off any points for being late. Some students complained to her that it is not *fair* that they lose points for being tardy when the other class can be tardy without a penalty. When she agreed that it wasn't fair and changed the rule so that no points were taken off for being tardy, other students complained that changing the rules wasn't *fair*…they all agreed on the rules. Mrs. Nguyen changed her mind again several times to try to be fair, but no matter what she did, someone complained that her decision was still unfair. Deep down she wishes that they could just get along and stop complaining about the rules, and she also wishes that they could all agree on one set of rules.

These fictional scenarios shed some light on the real and varied experiences of many well-meaning choral directors struggling to manage the classroom behavior of their students. In each case, they have implemented a strategy that works to some degree for them. But each of these strategies falls short of being an elegant solution that will function well for all students and the teacher. Let's look at these scenarios a little more closely:

Mr. Sheppard is a new teacher who wants to be liked by his students. He is willing to sacrifice his *contingent relationship*[2] with the students for a more equal kind of peer relationship. He thinks that students won't like or relate to him if he disagrees with them too often, so he gives away much of his ability and authority to modify their behavior. He mistakenly thinks that kids are better in some schools and worse in other schools, hoping to teach in a school someday where the students care and show respect. In reality, Mr. Sheppard has not learned that behavior is always shaped and maintained by its consequences; his lack of clear contingencies for behavior in the classroom encourages his students to be off task and to ignore his authority. If he does not learn this important lesson in classroom management, the kids will be the same, and his frustration will follow him, wherever he goes.

Ms. Hernandez is willing to disapprove of student behavior and has established a contingent relationship with her students. She makes a broad assumption that her sarcastic approach is completely understood by all of the students, and she is unaware of the mixed messages that she may be sending to some of the students.[3] This could be one reason that the students don't always know when to follow the rules. But the main flaw in her approach is that she isn't *consistent* in her application of reinforcement. She ignores bad behavior until it makes her angry, and then she delivers significant disapproval to change student behavior. But when the behavior reappears, instead of addressing it again, she lets it go until the next time she loses her patience. A contingent relationship functions best when the following "if…then" scenarios are consistently maintained:

2 The *Contingent Relationship* is at the heart of all effective behavior modification and positive classroom management. In this relationship, the student has a clear "if you do this, then this will happen" contract with the teacher, and the teacher must be the final arbitrator and deciding authority in the relationship.

3 Sarcasm can be defined as: "a sharp and often satirical or ironic utterance designed to cut or give pain, or a mode of satirical wit depending for its effect on bitter, caustic, and often ironic language that is usually directed against an individual." https://www.merriamwebster.com/dictionary/sarcasm. Sarcasm is not recommended as an effective teaching technique because the actual spoken words do not directly correlate with the speaker's intended meaning. Some exceptional learners can be very literal with the words of the teacher and will not understand the implied meaning embedded in the sarcasm. Furthermore, sarcastic comments can be perceived as passive criticism of individuals, which may then function as disapproval or humiliation.

1. If you do nice things, then nice things happen to you.
2. If you do bad things, then bad things happen to you.

Ms. Hernandez primarily ignores good behavior, and then also ignores bad behavior until she loses her patience and delivers harsh and disproportionate disapproval. In essence, she has taught her kids the following:

1. If you do nice things, then nothing happens to you.
2. If you do bad things, then nothing happens to you…until it does!

If Ms. Hernandez could catch students being good more often, and approve of the behavior, and also catch them not following the rules and immediately disapprove of the behavior, her students would learn what to expect more of the time and would behave accordingly. She wouldn't need to "blow up" to change their behavior. Also, if she could use words that have their intended meaning more often, fewer students would be confused when she talks and teaches.

Mr. Reeff understands how to maintain a consistent contingent relationship with his students. His students have learned that if they do not follow the rules, something bad will happen to them. In fact, Mr. Reeff is so consistent in his reinforcement that his students do not dare disobey the rules. The main flaw associated with his approach is his intense focus on stopping bad behavior. He rarely approves of appropriate behavior, but instead waits for inappropriate behavior to emerge so that he can disapprove of it. He assumes that if he says nothing, his students will know that he approves of them. He has established a classroom environment where the expectations are clear, but where being a creative or expressive student could garner public humiliation.

Mrs. Nguyen understands the concept of creating a "student-centered" approach to her classroom, and she does a good job maintaining an environment where students feel empowered to create, and abide by, the rules. She believes in the ideal of "fairness" and tries to make this ideal function for all the students in her classroom. Despite her well-meaning intentions, Mrs. Nguyen will never be able to make everyone in her classroom feel that the rules are fair. She will constantly need to change her decisions on the rules to attempt to be fair to everyone, yet there is no single rule that everyone will agree upon that seems universally fair. In fact, in her attempt to be fair and honest, she instead becomes inconsistent and mutable. Her students have learned that if they complain to her about something as being "unfair," she will change her rules to accommodate a new approach that seems less unfair in the moment. Because of this, there is always a faction of students challenging the fairness of the rules. If Mrs. Nguyen could adopt a single set of rules for all the classes, and if she could embrace an ideal of "*kindness and consistency*" instead of fairness, the students in her classes would learn to accept the rules and stop challenging them. Her well-meaning intention to be fair has caused her to be inconsistent, and until she can combine a student-centered approach that is consistent, she will continue to need to change her rules over and over again.

RECAPITULATION

1. Each of the teachers in the above scenarios have strengths and weaknesses in their approach to classroom management and each one has the best of intentions for the behavior of their students. Think about classroom environments that you have experienced in the past and try to remember as much as you can about what your teachers did to address classroom management. Write a short paragraph addressing your remembered experiences by comparing and contrasting the chapter scenarios to your memories.
2. When a teacher has a consistent approach to the reinforcement of classroom behavior, the students will learn over time how to behave. Specifically, they must do their best to teach the students that good behavior will be rewarded and that bad behavior will be punished. But when good behavior is punished, and when bad behavior is rewarded, students become confused and unable to choose consistently appropriate behaviors. Think about a time where the following scenarios were true for you and then write two short paragraphs about each scenario:

   a. You did the right thing, but were punished (or disapproved of) for it.
   b. You did the wrong thing, but were praised (or approved of) for it.

   Be sure to include how you felt about each scenario, and what you think you may have learned from the experiences.

3. Fairness is an ideal. While we would all like to embrace fairness in concept, what seems fair to one person will seem unfair to the next person. Teachers would do well to dispense with attempts at being fair

by taking a stance that they will *not be fair* all of the time. Rather, if they make a commitment to being *kind and consistent,* but not necessarily fair, the students will eventually stop complaining about the teacher's lack of fairness. Think about fairness and consistency. Would you rather be treated fairly, but differently than everyone else or would you rather be treated with the same standards as everyone else, even if it feels unfair? Explain your thinking with descriptions of scenarios if you can.

Addressing the Classroom Management Problem

There is a difference between academic and social behavior. Students demonstrate appropriate academic behavior when they engage with the subject matter, do their work, and fulfill the requirements of the class. Students demonstrate appropriate social behavior when they follow classroom rules and show respect for the teacher, the other students, themselves, and the classroom environment. It is not uncommon for emerging teachers to assume that students will enter the room knowing how to demonstrate appropriate social behavior; yet many preservice teachers are unprepared to address and teach social behavior. Instead, they may attempt to teach academic behavior while ignoring inappropriate social behavior…which can be immensely frustrating. They think, "Why do I have to teach manners? Students should know how to behave." But all behavior is situational and every new environment requires a clarification of the specific rules of social behavior that apply to that situation. For example, if you asked your students if it is appropriate to stand on their chair and scream, they might say, "Of course not." But if you put that behavior into the scenario of a sporting event, standing on a chair and screaming loudly is appropriate and acceptable (though not particularly good for the singing voice). Your room is an environment that must have acceptable and unacceptable rules of behavior that are well established and it is your job to teach your students what is considered to be appropriate and inappropriate behavior in your classroom. A good rule of thumb is, "Teach manners, and then teach music."

A music teacher must be a good musician and also a good teacher and these skills are learned separately; being a good musician does not automatically make you a good teacher and becoming a skilled teacher will not suddenly make you a great musician. In the same way, learning how to teach academic and social behavior must also be learned separately and knowing how to teach music will not automatically prepare you to teach your students how to behave appropriately. It is well worth your time to investigate strategies that will help you to create a kind, consistent, and positive classroom environment. If your students can learn to focus and behave, then they have the best chance to learn your subject matter. Consider the following scenario:

- **Mr. Wilhite** has been teaching for five years at a public inner-city high school. When he started in his first year, many of the students seemed rude, uninterested, or difficult to deal with. He wrote the following rules on a poster and put it front of the room where all the students could see it:

CLASSROOM RULES

1. **Respect yourself and others.**
2. **Do your very best.**
3. **Be on Task.**
4. **Make good choices.**
5. **Be a musician.**

He decided that the rules on the poster would be his focus for the start of each class and he did his best to refer to the poster constantly. He decided to thank students for following the rules as a first step, but also to look for opportunities to correct their behavior when they violated the rules. His thinking was "catch them being good, but also help them when they stray." At first the students seemed confused when Mr. Wilhite would say things like "Thanks, Rayvon, for making a good choice. You sat in your assigned seat today." They had never been thanked for doing the right thing in any other class. They were also surprised, and a little unhappy at first, when Mr. Wilhite called them out for talking during rehearsal. Although they talked constantly in other classes, they eventually got used to the fact that when they talked in choir, Mr. Wilhite noticed and asked them to "please be on task." Some students did rebel a bit and tested Mr. Wilhite and the rules, but soon they learned that "the rules are the rules" and that following the rules also had some advantages; you could be noticed for behaving as well as misbehaving, but behaving got you smiles, kind words, nods, and possibly a "thumbs up" from the teacher, while misbehaving got you another review of the rules and a look of disappointment from Mr. Wilhite. Most students came to appreciate knowing what would happen if they did or did not follow the rules in the choir room and they started to choose to follow them. A few students did quit the class, but many stayed, and many more joined by the end of the first year. By the start of his second year, Mr. Wilhite noticed that some of the students started quoting the rules from the poster to help new choir members understand how to behave in the choir room; it was almost like they took on his role as the "teacher of the rules." He was still careful to "catch them being good" as often as possible, but it seemed like he was spending more and more time teaching musicianship and singing skills and less and less time teaching the rules and that made him feel really good about his choir members. Sometimes he even thinks, "How did I get all the 'good' students to join choir?"

- **Mrs. Wright** has been teaching for twenty-five years at a small suburban high school. She loves her job and appreciates how committed the students are to singing and performing choral music. There was a time, she remembers, when the kids tested her authority in the classroom, but now she rarely needs to give strong disapproval for inappropriate behavior in her classes. She has heard stories over the years of how students say, "Mrs. Wright is a great choir teacher…you don't want to mess up in her class. She makes you want to be your best!" Occasionally a student misbehaves in class, but Mrs. Wright addresses it immediately and moves on with a smile. Most of the students wouldn't even *think* of letting down Mrs. Wright and they would do anything for her and the choir. They love how positive she can be and they know that if they do their best and work together, they will be an amazing choir.

These fictional scenarios can help us understand the real and varied experiences of choral educators who strive to effectively manage the academic and social behavior of the students in their classrooms. Mr. Wilhite started from scratch with teaching social behavior in his classroom; there was no consistent approach with the teacher before him as to how students should behave, so all the students made their own choices about how to behave, which led to rudeness and students getting off task frequently. When he made up his rules, he was careful to choose only a few broad ones that would cover many types of student behavior without being too specific. For example, he knew that if he said, "No gum in class," the students could possibly eat other candy and say, "The rule says no gum, not no candy." But now if there is any food in class, he says, "We don't eat food in this room because we need to be *on task* and singing. It's not a *good choice* to bring food into this room." When he approved of students following the rules, he taught them that he notices when they do the right thing. When he disapproved of students breaking the rules, he taught them that the rules are real and that they must be followed.[4] Because of his consistent approach, in less than two years, the older students knew the rules so well that they began teaching them to the new students joining choir. This made it possible for Mr. Wilhite to disapprove less of the time and approve more of the time, still committing to "catching the students being good" as much as possible. The students came to enjoy being in the choir room because it was a "zap-free zone" where people were nice to each other. It was one of the few rooms in the school where they knew that the teacher would treat the class with respect, and where they felt inspired to treat the teacher with respect in return.

Mrs. Wright has been teaching for a long time and she established the rules for her room a long time ago. She does not have a poster with the rules in front of the class, but the students stay on task and do their best anyway. She has a kind and consistent approach that is embedded in every activity that happens in her room and the students want to please her and be contributing members of her choir. She has achieved what Mr. Sheppard wants, which is to be universally liked by the students. But Mrs. Wright, while being liked by the students, never relinquishes her contingent relationship with them either. She is charming with the class when they follow the rules and she has no fears about being disapproving when a situation warrants it. She has masterfully established a positive classroom environment that students feel safe and empowered within. She loves teaching at the school because the students seem to want to be there and she gets to build her "choir family" year by year. As students graduate, she always seems to get some great new ones coming into the program.

RECAPITULATION

1. Mr. Wilhite and Mrs. Wright are at different points in their career, but both are implementing effective techniques for managing their classrooms. Mr. Wilhite still finds himself "teaching manners" on most days, while Mrs. Wright rarely needs to address the classroom behavior of her students. In essence, Mr. Wilhite is *establishing* a kind and consistent

4 When someone breaks a rule there must be an immediate consequence or the rule is not really a rule. A stated rule only becomes a real rule when someone in the class breaks the rule and a consequence is administered by the teacher publicly. A real rule, then, is one that the teacher reinforces with approval or disapproval frequently and consistently.

contingent relationship with his students and Mrs. Wright is *maintaining* her kind and consistent, contingent relationship with her students. Think about a teacher that you had in your past who did a great job of managing classroom behavior. Were they more like Mr. Wilhite who follows a strict set of rules every day or more like Mrs. Wright who has no posted rules at all in the classroom? Describe what you remember about being in their classroom environment, what you liked about it, and to what extent you felt safe and empowered to learn.

2. It is a true statement that "There is no rule until someone breaks it and they are publicly punished"? One of the "rules" that people break all the time is exceeding the posted speed limit in their cars. If you drive, do you speed often or at all? Why or why not? Discuss this and also comment on what could change your present behavior around speeding. (In other words, what would encourage you to speed if you don't now and what could stop you from speeding if you already do it?) If you don't drive, is there a rule or law that you are willing to follow or break for some reason? Discuss why you are willing to follow or break this law or rule.
3. Read the following sets of classroom rules that could represent different approaches to classroom management. Copy them to a fresh piece of paper, or into a word document. Beside each rule, write or type two indications: rate the rule on a scale of 1–10 (10 being best) as to how important that rule would be in your classroom and also mark each rule as "Academic," "Social," or "Both." Discuss your ratings with a friend, colleague, or classmate.

   1. Respect yourself and others
   2. Do your very best
   3. Be on task
   4. Make good choices
   5. Be a musician

   1. Be engaged
   2. Be respectful
   3. Always show compassion
   4. Keep phones in your backpack during class

   1. Be respectful towards each other
   2. Be on time to rehearsal
   3. Refrain from speaking during rehearsal
   4. "You are kind. You are smart. You are important."

   1. Always be respectful to people and property
   2. Get rid of all distractions

3. Always bring your pencil, music, and paper
4. Always bring a cooperative and positive attitude

1. Respect everyone and everything in the class
2. Be on time and ready to begin when the bell rings
3. Bring your music and a pencil to every rehearsal
4. Food and drink other than water should be left outside

1. Be respectful
2. Be supportive
3. Work as a team
4. Be responsible

1. Be respectful and courteous
2. Give 100% of whatever % you are today
3. Everything we do, we do together
4. Support everyone around you

1. Respect
2. Kind and Courteous
3. Be a Team Player
4. Responsible

1. Be respectful
2. Be kind
3. Be engaged
4. Be willing

1. Treat others with respect
2. No "zapping"
3. Be on time and ready
4. Do everything together

1. Work hard, work well
2. How much practice? Enough.
3. Respect
4. If you don't love it, learn to love it

1. Be an informed and exquisite listener
2. Always do your best
3. Respect yourself, others, and your school
4. Come to class with materials and a positive attitude

1. Listen and follow directions
2. Raise your hand before speaking or leaving your seat
3. Respect your classmates and teachers
4. Keep hands, feet, and objects to yourself

1. Everything we do, we do together
2. Be kind and respectful to everyone and everything

3. Try your best in all that you do with a positive attitude
4. Be professional: come to class on time and prepared to learn

1. Be respectful
2. Arrive promptly on time
3. Listen and follow directions
4. Leave gum and food outside the classroom

4. Make a list of the four to five most important rules, in your opinion, from the list above, but feel free to restate or combine rules if you have a better wording that works for you. Also, create a completely new rule if you think it best fits your classroom-management style and is important to you. Create an electronic poster that you could print if you needed to with the final draft of your rules. (Like Mr. Wilhite did.)

RULES
1)
2)
3)
4)
5)

The Contingent Relationship and the Importance of Consistency

Once you understand the difference between academic and social behavior, and once you accept that it is your responsibility to teach both sets of behavior to your students, it is a good idea to work to balance your ability to teach the subject matter with your ability to create a positive, consistent, and functional learning environment. You may have noticed that the word "consistent" has been used many times in this chapter already, and that is on purpose: your success hinges on your ability to deliver consistent and appropriate reinforcement for your students' behavior. Let's explore this idea further by returning to the concept of the "contingent relationship."

If you have a contingent relationship with a student, that means that you have set up behavioral expectations that go like this: "When you, the student, behave in certain ways then I, the teacher, will reinforce you in certain ways." This "if…then" scenario is the foundation of effective classroom management and we want to teach our students these two proper associations:

1. If you do *nice* things, then *nice* things will happen to you. (Approval)

2. If you do *bad* things, then *bad* things will happen to you. (Disapproval)

But when we are inconsistent with our reinforcement, even though we have the best of intentions, sometimes we teach these two improper associations:

1. If you do *bad* things, then *nice* things will happen to you. (Approval error)

2. If you do *nice* things, then *bad* things will happen to you. (Disapproval error)

Our goal is to be consistent as the teacher, catching them being good and immediately approving of the behavior, but also catching them when they are not doing what they are supposed to, and disapproving of the behavior. Approving might take the form of kind words (well done, great, wonderful, so much better), facial expressions (smiles and affirmative nods), bodily gestures (such as a "thumbs up"), or possibly rewarding with something tangible such as a "star" on a chart for younger students or items of value for older students, like free concert tickets or gift cards. When you are being disapproving, you can also use words (not your best, that wasn't good, nope, that's incorrect), facial expressions (frowns and side-to-side head shakes), bodily gestures (such as a "thumbs down"), or possibly removing rewards like the "star" on the chart for younger students or withholding items of value for older students. It is important to know that reinforcers do not need to cost money to be effective in the classroom and many students will work for the approval of the teacher (and to avoid the disapproval of the teacher). Approval and disapproval delivered with words, facial expressions, and bodily gestures are free and unlimited for the teacher to use. Here are a few more things to consider when exploring the concept of the contingent relationship:

- **Intention vs. Function:** It probably seems to you like it would be a relatively easy thing to approve of good behavior and to disapprove of bad behavior in your classroom. But even a very aware and consistent teacher will make some mistakes in their reinforcement, such as saying "great" in rehearsal when the singing was not great (approval error) or possibly disapproving of a student publicly who is breaking a rule, but actually mistaking them for someone else in their peripheral vision (disapproval error). These kinds of errors are going to happen, but we hope to minimize them as much as we can. But while we can try to be aware and consistent, all of this is further complicated by the fact that you do not have control over how your reinforcement *functions* with the student. For example, if a student breaks enough of your rules to be sent to the office, you have no control over if the student perceives this to be a good thing or a bad thing. If the office is an entertaining environment for the student, they might actually *want* to be sent there. Your intention to disapprove has functioned differently for the student. We must try to determine if our reinforcement functions as intended for each student, and if we do not see the behavior improving, we will need to enact different behavioral contingencies until it does improve.

- **The Payoff:** Behavior is shaped and maintained by its consequences, and a consequence that helps you get something you want will encourage you to repeat the behavior in the future. Likewise, a consequence that keeps you from getting what you want might discourage you from repeating the behavior in the future. What do students "want"? This depends on the student, but in general most students want the approval of the teacher, to be popular in their peer group, to be recognized for doing something well, to earn good grades, or to please their parents or friends, as well as many other things. We can call these things that students want to have and are willing to work for the "Payoff:" when students achieve the Payoff, they feel a sense of having what they desire. But sometimes students will *want* to be sent to the office, to get bad grades, to reject their peer group, or will want to disappoint their friends and family. Students who have these negative Payoff goals will secretly hope that their bad behavior will get them what they want. This is why classroom management is more of an art than a science. To increase an appropriate behavior, you have to allow the student to receive a Payoff when they exhibit the behavior, and when you want to stop an undesired behavior, you have to find what the Payoff is for the student and then remove the chance of the student getting that specific Payoff. Behavior that is not associated with some sort of Payoff will disappear over time.

Practical Considerations for Positive Classroom Management

It will take some time and some authentic classroom practice for you to fully integrate your understanding of the contingent relationship, intention vs. function, and the Payoff. You will need to watch your students carefully as they interact in your classroom, and you will have to monitor how they seem to respond to your reinforcement decisions. If this seems like a lot of extra work, that's because it is. But remember that we need to teach social behavior *and* academic behavior, and social behavior must be taught first. Over time, if you are kind and consistent, you will spend less and less time on behavioral issues and more and more time on the subject matter.

Like many of the skills and concepts presented in this book, there is no way to tell you exactly what to do in your classroom to manage the behavior of your students effectively and positively. There are too many variables, such as intention vs. function and the classroom environment, that make every decision you will make context specific. One kind of reinforcement that works for one student might not work for a different student, but for every student there is *something* that will work. Here are some other practical considerations that will help you to create and maintain a positive classroom learning environment for your students:

✓ **You Control the Environment that, In Turn, Controls You**: As part of your lesson planning, you will need to think about all the physical aspects of your teaching environment and you will need to control these things ahead of time. Before class starts, you have an ability and a responsibility to solve as many problems as possible that will affect your teaching effectiveness and your classroom management. Once you start teaching, you have no time (unless you stop teaching) to address issues in the teaching environment. What you could have controlled before class is now controlling you. For example, if you don't control the fact that you need to order more copies of music for your choir, and then class starts, you will be teaching to students who can't see the music, can't mark their scores as instructed, or who won't understand what you are teaching. This will cause incredible classroom management problems in your rehearsal. Some of the things that you can try to control ahead of time might include:

- Having enough copies of music for each student in the choir
- Having a seating plan
- Having an accurate and quick method for taking attendance
- Having adequate lighting in the room
- Having adequate heating or cooling in the room
- Having a system for how and when students enter and leave the chairs or risers
- Having a system for restroom visits and hall passes
- Having a system for recording tardies
- Having a detailed lesson plan
- Having working technology such as projectors, the internet, and sound equipment
- Having instruments that you need such as a tuned piano, extra percussion, or other sound-producing devices
- Double-checking that your accompanist will be there on time and prepared with the right music

This is only a partial list. Your best approach will be to control *everything* in the environment that you can think of ahead of time, and then make note of what you forgot or what you didn't realize needed to be controlled. You will know immediately when something in the environment begins to impair your teaching effectiveness or classroom management, and you won't be able to do anything about it until class is over in most cases. There are some things that you can predict might happen, but that you really have no prior control over, such as fire drills or emergencies on your campus. In those scenarios, just do your best to be flexible and patient while the situation is affecting your classroom environment and your students.

✓ **Don't Try to Stop a Behavior, but Instead Replace it with a Better (and Incompatible) Behavior:** Beginning teachers eventually learn the power of redirecting student behavior away from what is not wanted and toward behavior that is wanted. For example, if students are talking and you want them to stop talking, it is less effective to ask for "no talking" than it is to ask them to hum a unison pitch. They can't talk and hum at the same time, so the behaviors are incompatible. Redirecting student behavior is an effective and elegant solution to stopping undesired behavior in most cases. Another way to think of this concept is to remember this sentence: "When students are engaged in an appropriate classroom activity, they can't do anything else." When you catch yourself trying to make students "stop," just think about what you can ask them to "start" instead. Click the icon "Lock it In," and think about how this picture from a real location relates to attempting to "stop" any behavior.

✓ **The Doomsday Contingency:** When you are reinforcing student behavior in the classroom, you will need to choose contingencies that are strong enough to change a student's behavior on the first try. For example, if being late to class reduces a student's final grade by one point, then some students will be sure to be there on time (especially if their Payoff is associated with earning perfect grades), while other students won't care if they miss a point or two on their grade (especially if their Payoff is hanging out with their other late friends or making a late entrance in front of the rest of the choir). If you make the contingency stronger and say that students will lose five points for being tardy, it may affect the behavior of more of the students depending on function and Payoff variables. So why not increase the strength of the contingency until ALL students are compelled to follow the rule? That would seem to be a logical approach and it is a good idea to some degree: if the contingency is too weak, it won't have the desired effect to modify student behavior. But it is a mistake to threaten the students with a contingency that is so strong no one would dare to ignore it. This is called the "Doomsday Contingency" and it is not recommended that you use it under any circumstances. For example, if you say something like, "The next person to be late for this class will be expelled from school forever," there is no way that you can follow through with that contingency (nor should you). Your approach should always be to try to enact contingencies with appropriate strength to change behavior on the first try, but not to create contingencies that are stronger than they need to be in order to be effective.

- ✓ **The Teacher Decides:** Your classroom is a space where your rules are always in effect, and you are the person in charge of teaching your rules, building contingent relationships with students, and creating clear expectations about appropriate social and academic student behavior. Anything that you do not decide will be decided by the students. For example, if you don't have a seating plan ready, the students will decide where they want to sit. If you don't engage them in an appropriate classroom activity, they will choose another activity, such as talking or checking their electronic devices. The teacher must be willing to maintain their authority and make the decisions that affect student learning and that keep the classroom environment safe and positive for all students.

- ✓ **Students Want Clear Structure:** Emerging teachers sometimes confuse the concepts of *strictness* and *structure*. They might think that they need to be strict with their students when what they really need to do is provide a consistent structure. Students desire to be in systems and environments where they know what to expect, and where they can feel safe to learn, take chances, and be creative. It is possible to practice strictness without adequate structure when, for example, you disapprove of students randomly for behaviors that were not clearly defined as inappropriate ahead of time. Most students will thrive in a positive learning environment where the teacher creates consistent expectations for behavior, both academic and social.

- ✓ **Behavior Is Relative to the Situation**: When you are teaching your classroom rules to a new group of students, you will need to help them understand the situational nature of all behavior. What is appropriate in one setting may not be OK in another setting. In choir, for example, we can say that *everything we do, we do together*: we sit together, we breathe together, we sing together, we focus together, and we perform together. Is it appropriate to stand on your chair by yourself and yell loudly? Yes, but not in choir. We can stand on our chairs and shout at sporting events, but in the choir room, that same behavior is not appropriate. If students attempt to argue that your rules don't hold in the rest of the school, you can agree and remind them that all behavior is situational and that in your room, your rules will always apply.

- ✓ **People Would Rather Be Praised than Punished, but They Would Rather Be Punished than Ignored:** We have explored the concepts of approval and disapproval as reinforcers for student behavior, but we haven't mentioned the technique of *ignoring*. Ignoring is a recommended first approach by the teacher for any undesirable behavior that is neither dangerous nor interfering with learning. If the behavior does interfere with learning (including the person exhibiting the behavior) or if it presents a clear danger to anyone, then it must be addressed immediately with an appropriate contingent response from the teacher. Being ignored is worse than being punished in the minds of many students, because when they are being punished, they are at least being noticed by others, which can be a powerful Payoff. If you ignore (do not reinforce in any way) undesirable behavior and then immediately reinforce appropriate behavior (catch them being good) with approval, you will train the students to work for your approval and to stay on task appropriately.

✓ **It Is Not Necessary to ZAP Your Students:** When you deliver disapproval for undesired student behavior, you have to be careful that your reinforcement does not function as a "ZAP." It is correct to have measured disapproval that can stop and redirect behavior on the first try, but a ZAP is a form of reinforcement that functions to hurt and humiliate a student in some way and is not necessary or appropriate in a positive classroom environment. It is a good approach to address a student's behavior without making judgment calls on the student as a person. For example, if you say to a late student, "This is the third time you have been late to a dress rehearsal. I expect you to be more professional in the future," it probably does not function as a ZAP. But if you were to say (especially in front of the whole choir), "This is the third time you have been late to a dress rehearsal. Are you lazy or stupid? You'll never be successful as a professional singer," you have now crossed a line from addressing the behavior to ZAPPING the person. Please do not ZAP your students.

✓ **Don't Be a Choir Corrector, Be a Beauty Creator:** When you are in front of your classroom or choir during rehearsal, your words, priorities, lesson plans, levels of magnitude, and style of communication will help you keep the class on task and appropriately engaged in your subject matter.[5] But if you continually focus on what they are doing *wrong*, you will create a different learning environment than if you focus on what they *could be doing right*. For example, if your tenors are singing a flat note, you can either say, "Tenors, you're flat. Don't sing flat. Do it again," or you could say, "Tenors, let's sing that again with a better breath preparation and right on top of the pitch center this time please." The "choir corrector" sees the problem, and the "beauty creator" focuses on the solution.[6]

---

5 "Magnitude" is a measure of a teacher's: Eye Contact, Closeness, Volume and Modulation of Voice, Gestures, Facial Expressions, and Rehearsal Pace. *Effect of Magnitude of Conductor Behavior on Students in Selected Mixed Choruses*, Cornelia Yarbrough, Journal of Research in Music Education
Vol. 23, No. 2 (Summer, 1975), pp. 134-146.

6 This phrase "Don't be a choir corrector, be a beauty creator" was likely coined by renowned choral educator and conductor Rodney Eichenberger.

RECAPITULATION

1. Using your four to five rules from the earlier section of this chapter, create four consequences for when people do not follow the rules, and also four ways that you will approve of appropriate behavior when people do follow the rules:

RULES *(Mark each rule as "Academic" or "Social" or "Both")*

1)
2)
3)
4)
5)

Consequences for Bad Behavior

1)
2)
3)
4)

Consequences for Good Behavior

1)
2)
3)
4)

2. What does the word "consistency" mean to you? Write a short paragraph about the concept of consistency and how well you interact with it in your own life right now. In other words, do you consider yourself to be a fairly consistent person in the things you do? Why or why not? Provide examples.
3. After reading this chapter and thinking about classroom management, on a scale of 1–10 with 10 being the best, how prepared do you feel to teach both academic and social behavior in your future classroom? What will you take away from this chapter in terms of information, and what do you hope to keep in your mind the next time you are in front of a class or choir?

4. Write a short paragraph describing a time when you had good intentions for an event or outcome that didn't end up functioning well in the end. Why didn't it work out, in your opinion? Also describe another time when your intention and the functional outcome of an event were the same in the end. Why did the outcome and your intentions work out in this scenario, in your opinion?

The Power of Catching Students Doing the Right Thing

As you put all of these classroom management concepts together in your thinking, there is one general principle to highlight and keep in the forefront of your thinking: *never miss a chance to catch a student doing the right thing, and be willing at any moment to bring everyone's attention to it.* Students will generally work for different things, and you always have to try to find what each student holds as their primary Payoffs so that you can better structure your contingencies to help them make better choices. But almost all students are positively motivated when they are being noticed by the teacher publicly while being praised for doing the right thing. It is a common mistake to ignore appropriate behavior and to only bring attention to inappropriate behavior as you address it with contingent reinforcement. But really, the best approach is to try to approve of specific appropriate student behavior whenever you can catch them doing the right thing and to ignore behavior that isn't dangerous or that doesn't interfere with learning. Then when it seems like the right approach to disapprove of a specific behavior, you will have the student's attention in an even more powerful way; when you catch them being good and they are working for your attention and approval appropriately, your disapproval will have much more weight to affect their behavior.

A good goal to work toward is to maintain around an 80% approval to about a 20% disapproval ratio in your teaching. Again, to achieve these kinds of ratios, you will need to capitalize on a lot of opportunities to catch students doing the right thing. This one principle is the key to building a positive classroom environment that functions to encourage creativity, artistry, learning, and kind, nurturing human interactions.

As an example of how an entire school can embrace the "catch them being good" approach, here is an actual "referral slip" that a Southern California high school uses when a student does the right thing. The teacher, after noticing an appropriate student behavior, fills out the slip and detaches one third for the office to pick up and record, and the other two thirds of the slip are given directly to the student so that they know immediately that they have been recognized as doing the right thing. Notice that the whole exercise is guided by the school's stated values: "Integrity, Honor Self & Others, and Social Responsibility." Every good and appropriate behavior can be classified under one of those three school-wide values. The full description of the school's values are stated this way:

- **Integrity**: firm adherence to a code of moral values; honesty; incorruptibility.
- **Honor Yourself & Others**: a keen sense of ethical conduct toward one's self and to the whole community.
- **Social Responsibility**: acting with empathy and concern.

The office then keeps track of the tallies of good behavior and puts all the referrals in a box for a bi-monthly drawing for $5 gift cards. Up to ten names are drawn and the names of the students are announced during all-school announcements. You can adopt similar techniques in your classroom if that seems like a good idea to you. Either way, if you work to develop your own ability to recognize appropriate behavior, and then if you find ways to approve of it frequently and honestly, your students will respond positively and you will be an even more effective teacher.

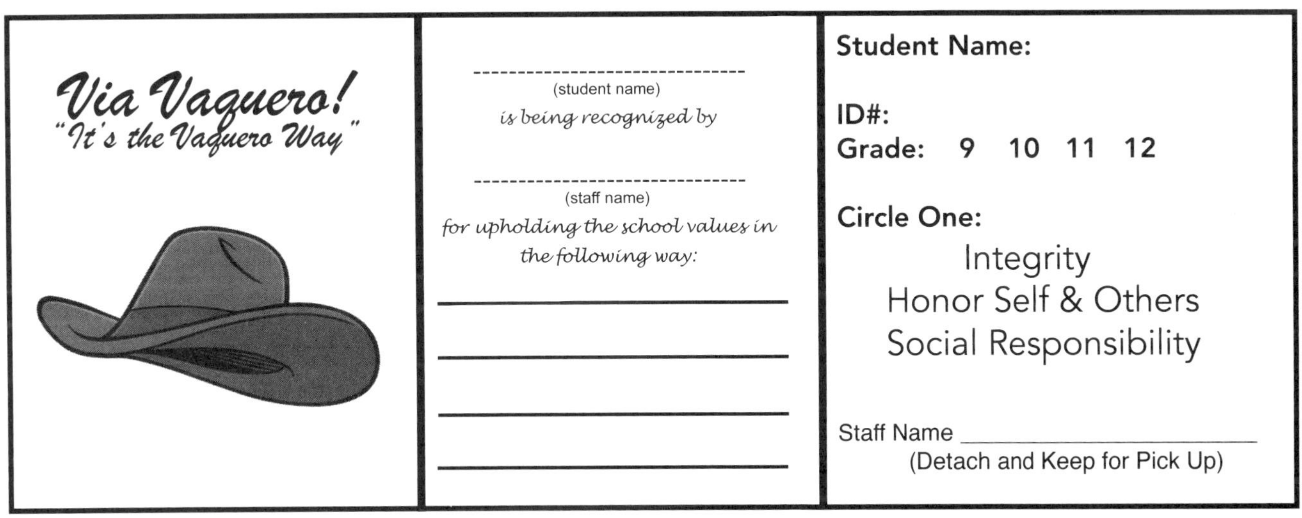
Via Vaquero!
"It's the Vaquero Way"

(student name)
is being recognized by

(staff name)
for upholding the school values in the following way:

Student Name:

ID#:
Grade: 9 10 11 12

Circle One:
Integrity
Honor Self & Others
Social Responsibility

Staff Name ______________________
(Detach and Keep for Pick Up)

Chapter Conclusion

As an emerging preservice teacher, you will have a lot on your mind when you are in front of the class. You will have a lesson plan that you are trying to remember and teach, you will have distractions that you will be managing in the learning environment, you will be monitoring and reinforcing both academic and social behavior, and you will be doing your best to listen carefully from the podium or piano as you keep your conducting gestures expressive and your teaching instructions clear. Wow! That is a lot to pull together and a lot to think about at the same time. But as you get better at running your class with all these moving parts, it will get easier and easier until you only need to think about a few things at a time. If you can, it is a great experience to get out into some real classrooms and observe exemplary veteran teachers in the field. When you see someone teaching well, and when they make it look easy, it can be a powerful example for you to integrate into your thinking. Using these experiences as a guide, you can work toward emulating their skills into your own practice.

Classroom management is the foundation upon which you will do everything else in your classroom. Be sure to make teaching social behavior a priority in your lesson planning and be ready at any time to leave academic-behavior goals to teach social-behavior goals when needed. If your students are not focused and engaged and respectful of themselves, the teacher, and the classroom environment, *nothing else matters*. You will be frustrated and start blaming the students for not caring about music and choir. Instead, take the responsibility to teach your students how to behave and how to treat each other within the walls of your classroom, and then notice how much they start caring about music and choir. When students feel safe and empowered and noticed and successful, they can achieve amazing things and you will really enjoy teaching them.

Chapter Five

Lesson Planning

5. Lesson Planning

*"Give me six hours to chop down a tree and
I will spend the first four sharpening the axe."
~Abraham Lincoln*

Preparing to Teach

A famous quote that is often attributed to Benjamin Franklin goes like this: "By failing to prepare, you are preparing to fail." This quote speaks directly to one of the most important pedagogical skills of any good teacher: the skill of constructing and implementing effective lesson plans that function well in the classroom. Teachers must learn how to organize lessons (and rehearsals) into logical and well-sequenced steps and activities so that students are engaged, on task, and learning throughout the entire class.

Beginning teachers often make the mistake of believing that they do not need to write detailed lesson plans or take the time to carefully think through all the steps that are involved for teaching. It is also common for emerging teachers to struggle as they attempt to control the classroom environment effectively, neglecting the physical aspects of the room, or underestimating the need to prepare teaching materials well ahead of time. Preparing to teach takes time and effort, and like score study and personal rehearsal on your instrument, it should not be done hastily, mindlessly, haphazardly, or at the last minute. As a beginning teacher you will have to accept that preparation is essential and that planning to teach will require you do dedicate a significant amount of your time at first.

One of the reasons that young teachers fail to recognize the need to plan thoroughly is that they may have witnessed some of their own teachers not teaching from lesson plans. While it is true that not all experienced teachers use detailed daily lesson plans, it is also important to remember that veteran teachers can make teaching look easy; because of the years of experience they have acquired implementing lessons, as well as the learning they gained from their own teaching mistakes over the years, experienced teachers can often deliver effective instruction without referring to a detailed, written lesson plan. Another way to say this is that people who have been teaching a long time know what to do because they have done it so many times. Even if what they planned to teach doesn't work, they always have a good plan B, a good plan C, and even a plan D ready for anything that they might encounter in the classroom. It is a rare teacher, however, that does not have at least a list of activities and outcomes in mind for every class or rehearsal session, even if these are not specifically written out on paper. To the observer, great teachers seem to just get up and teach really well with little obvious planning or preparation, but this appearance can be really misleading.

The Gestalt Nature of Learning

In German, the word for form or shape is "gestalt."[1] The word has been used in different contexts and applications, and it usually refers to something that is made up of many parts, but is also somehow more than the combination of its parts. Learning can be viewed in light of this concept because the ability to do something is often referred to as a single skill, such as brushing your teeth or making breakfast, for example. However, you learned these common skills through a series of smaller sequential steps in the past that you probably forgot about. In other words, things you do out of habit as a single step today were likely once learned by you in the past as many steps.

Think about a time where you learned to do something new. Perhaps you remember learning how to drive a car or learning to play a band instrument or maybe learning how to ride a bike. In all of these cases, you couldn't just drive, play, or ride in the first few minutes of your first lesson. Driver's Education classes are designed to address the multitude of steps that prepare a person to take the wheel of a car for the first time. Many band instruments need to be assembled before you can play them, and then the skills of breath support and proper embouchure need to be learned and mastered before a confident sound can be made. Riding a bike usually starts with training wheels until the person can master the skills (and courage) to pedal fast and keep moving forward with momentum. Learning a new skill, then, is really about progressing through the small steps that eventually add up to the big steps. As a teacher, you can't teach a person to do something that is complex by teaching only one step; you have to understand all the parts that make up the whole, and you have to be able to teach each small step that adds up to the larger skill.

One way to illustrate the gestalt nature of learning and teaching is to think about how one might teach a choir to demonstrate a proper singer's posture. The gestalt skill is "posture," but we can't just ask an inexperienced choir for the final skill if they haven't learned the smaller steps that add up to "posture." No matter how many times you say the word "posture," you won't get the whole choir to exhibit the behavior you want. You could, however, break the skills into teachable steps (task analysis) and then teach those steps in a logical sequence. Your teaching steps might look something like this:

---

1 A configuration, pattern, or organized field having specific properties that cannot be derived from the summation of its component parts; a unified whole. *https://www.dictionary.com/browse/gestalt?s=ts*

1. Everyone stand please
2. Feet shoulder-width apart
3. One foot slightly in front of the other
4. Slight lift of the sternum
5. Shoulders comfortably down and back without tension
6. Head lightly suspended by an imaginary "string" through the spine
7. Ankles, knees, hips, shoulders, and ears in vertical alignment
8. Muscles toned but not tense...all joints freely able to move
9. Feel grounded, free, and lifted at the same time!

But after you have taught these steps, and once the students have learned and can demonstrate them, you can collapse the steps into less specific, larger steps that simply remind the students what they already have learned:

1. Stand
2. Feet
3. Sternum
4. Shoulders
5. Head
6. Alignment
7. Freedom in the joints
8. Excellent posture

And again, these more cryptic reminders can then be collapsed into even fewer steps as the students continue to learn and build habit strength based on their practice and understanding:

1. Alignment check
2. Freedom please
3. Excellent posture

Finally, it would be possible and effective to use a single reminder for the choir that has learned the proper steps to alignment:

1. Posture, please!

Creating an Effective Lesson Plan

Now that you have a better understanding of how the steps that make up a skill can collapse into fewer and fewer steps as mastery is attained, you may be wondering how many steps should be taught to any given class during a lesson. Because teaching is an art, rather than an exact science, there is no "one-size-fits-all" answer to this question. It will be your responsibility to assess the abilities of your classes to determine just how detailed your lesson plans need to be and how many steps you will require to help your students learn effectively. In general, when you are teaching beginners, you will need to break your concepts into smaller, teachable steps that focus on basic skills. When working with intermediate students, you will probably be able to teach fewer steps than you do with beginners, but this is not always the case depending on what they have retained from previous lessons. With advanced students, you may be able to reinforce a good number of skills with only one step or a concise reminder while looking for opportunities to challenge them at a new and higher level of mastery. All of this assumes, of course, that all the students in any given class are all exactly at the same level of ability and that all students will respond to your teaching exactly the same way. This might seem like a nice idea, but it is rarely the case; within any class you will have students who get the material immediately, those who get it eventually, and those who will struggle to get it at all.

There are many aspects to consider when you are writing a lesson or rehearsal plan, and *what to teach* is only one of them. A lesson plan is a lot like a recipe for cooking or baking something. Some recipes are detailed and clear, and others are cryptic and seem to leave out a bunch of steps or details. The main reason for the difference in the level of detail in various recipes can be traced back to how much the author of the recipe assumes the cook making the meal *already knows* about cooking. If they assume that the cook already has great kitchen equipment and preparation surfaces, and that they understand what certain cooking terms mean, they can give many fewer steps in the recipe description. But if they know that the person making the dish is a complete amateur, they might break down larger steps into even smaller steps, just to be sure they get it right. Click on the icon link "Recipe Steps"to participate with your colleagues in a fun and interesting activity that relates to task analysis.

In your own situation writing music education lesson plans, you are both the author and the follower of your own plans, so it would seem logical that you would know exactly how much detail you will need to have in your lesson planning so that you can understand how to teach it. However, this idea that you are writing your plan for yourself misses the important detail that you are not actually writing the plan your yourself: you are writing the plan for the class that you will be teaching. There is a difference.

The skill level, experience, and ability of your class will determine the detail that you will need to include in your lesson plan. It is a common mistake for beginning teachers to under-plan for beginning classes, thinking that they will already understand how to perform the larger steps. When the students do not understand the larger steps, and the detail of the smaller steps is left out of the plan, the beginning teacher often will not know what to do, and the classroom management and momentum will begin to deteriorate.

As an example of what is meant by "smaller steps" and "larger steps," consider the following directive for students in the choir to perform a musical selection on solfege syllables. This is one large step:

- Students will sing *Ave Verum* on solfege syllables.

There is nothing wrong with this large step, but it will only work with a choir that knows what this means. If you ask a choir to do this step, and then they are successful, your plan was perfect for that one, larger step. But if they are not successful, then you need to break that larger step into smaller steps:

- Students will take out *Ave Verum* and identify the key and time signature.
- Students will read the notes silently as they use hand signs to demonstrate understanding of the pitches in the key.
- Students will then sing the major scale of the key together as a class.
- Students will then sing their correct starting pitch on solfege.
- Students will then attempt to sing the whole piece on solfege, *a cappella.*

The level of detail in these smaller steps should also be compared to the ability of the class to understand and perform them. If they can experience success with the detail found in these steps, you planned perfectly for them. If they seem bored and can do the steps really quickly, you may have over-planned for them. A sure way to lose any class is to give them *more* steps than they need, or *less* steps than they need. What if the class is still not successful even when you have broken down the activity into smaller steps? Then you will need to break the activity into *even smaller* steps:

- Students will take out *Ave Verum* (and a pencil) and will locate the key and time signature.
- The teacher will review how to find "do" (the last flat is "fa") as well as how to name the key ("do" names the major key, using the G and F clefs).
- Students will write in the solfege syllables for their part in pencil for the first page.
- The teacher will review the solfege hand signs and sing up and down the major scale, including any leaps that are in the music.
- Students will read their own notes silently on the first page as they use hand signs to demonstrate understanding of the pitches in the key.
- Sopranos will sing their solfege out loud as a section while the other sections demonstrate the hand signs in their part silently.

- The teacher will correct any soprano section mistakes or challenges.
- Tenors will sing their solfege out loud as a section while the other sections demonstrate the hand signs in their part silently.
- The teacher will correct any tenor section mistakes or challenges.
- Sopranos and tenors will sing their solfege out loud as a section while the other two sections continue to demonstrate the hand signs in their part silently.
- The teacher will correct any soprano and tenor section mistakes or challenges.
- Altos will sing their solfege out loud while a section as the other sections demonstrate the hand signs in their part silently.
- The teacher will correct any alto section mistakes or challenges.
- Sopranos, tenors, and altos will sing their solfege out loud as a section while the basses continue to demonstrate the hand signs in their part silently.
- The teacher will correct any soprano, tenor, or alto section mistakes or challenges.
- Basses will sing their solfege out loud as a section while the other sections demonstrate the hand signs in their part silently.
- The teacher will correct any bass section mistakes or challenges.
- All sections will then sing their correct starting pitch on solfege.
- All students will then attempt to sing through page 1 on solfege, a cappella.

As before, the level of detail in these smaller steps must be measured against the success of the choir during the lesson. If the class is engaged and on task and performing appropriately and successfully, you planned perfectly for the level and ability of this class. Would you ever need to break things into even *smaller* steps? Of course. If you have students who have never read music before, or who have never sung in a choir, you can't even break down the step "Sing *Ave Verum* on solfege syllables" into small enough steps. Your lesson for these beginners might have lots of small steps that help them understand concepts like "page-system-measure-beat" and how to know what part they are singing and how to find their voice part in the score. Don't be surprised if you need to teach very basic concepts in tiny little steps that you previously assumed everyone already knew. Students only know what they know, so you can't assume anything until you have assessed the skills and abilities of each ensemble. Until you know what they can do, you would be smart to have a more detailed plan with lots of steps to achieve your learning objectives and then also have an intention to work faster or compress steps if they don't need the level of detail that you have planned for them. Your major danger is being under-planned for a choir that needs a detailed plan, so don't be afraid to write a lot of steps in your first lesson plans.

Essential Elements of Lesson Plans

Your lesson plan is your guide for engaging the class in appropriate activities to teach your subject matter. It is much more than just a list of activities, however. You will be writing lesson plans in many different formats and for many different purposes, and there is no single format for a lesson plan. Some professors or administrators will want you to include state or national teaching standards, or adaptions for exceptional learners, or special activities to help English as a second language (ESL) students. Regardless of the format that you will be using, a comprehensive and detailed lesson plan will usually have a number of essential elements, including:

1. What to teach and what order to teach your steps, being sure that you consider the ability level of the class **(Scope and Sequence)**
2. What you want your students to be able to do at the end of the lesson **(Objectives and Outcomes)**
3. Materials you will need and room preparations **(Controlling the Environment)**
4. How you will know if they learned what you taught them **(Assessment Strategies)**
5. A gauge of how long you think your lesson steps will take **(Time Management)**
6. A list of vocabulary words and related questions that you can use to guide student learning **(Lexicon and Essential Questions)**

It is easy to believe that this list is too long and that taking the time to write all of this out in a lesson plan is not a good use of your time. But as a beginning teacher, you have to be ready for the very likely possibility that your class will need not only your academic guidance and structure, but also a consistent social structure. You will be responsible for managing the behavior of the students in the classroom at the same time that you are teaching your academic lesson plan! Without a well-thought-out lesson plan, and with the distractions of some students misbehaving or getting off task, you might get flustered easily and lose your focus; what you thought might be simple to do (teaching the class), might actually be more of a challenge for you. It is at these times that the beginning teacher should be able to rely on a solid lesson plan to stay focused, keep their pace fast, and keep the students on task.

RECAPITULATION

1. Your ability to break a skill into teachable steps will form the basis for your success as an effective teacher. Beginning students need to explore and experience more steps, and advanced students need fewer steps, but in any case, if students do not learn the material or skill, you must provide a more detailed list of steps for them. Create three task analysis lists for teaching the skill of *taking a proper singer's breath*; one list should have the heading "Steps for Teaching Breathing to Beginning Choirs," one should have the heading "Steps for Teaching Breathing to Intermediate Choirs," and one should have the heading "Steps for Teaching Breathing to Advanced Choirs." You do not need to write lesson plans for these three lists of steps. You may find it helpful to do a little research by finding and referencing several vocal pedagogy or singing method books to be sure your steps are accurate and effective.

2. Think about these two specific tasks that you do every day: brushing your teeth and making your breakfast. You learned to do these tasks a long time ago, and it is very likely that you now think of them as only a single step. Choose one of these tasks (brushing your teeth or making your breakfast) and write a task analysis that includes the steps for completing it from beginning to end. When you have completed your list of steps, read them to a friend or classmate. Let them give you feedback in terms of 1) how clear your steps are, 2) if you left out any important steps, and 3) if they think you need to revise the order of your steps in any way.

Teach the Plan or Teach the Students?

New teachers, once they have learned to write detailed lesson plans, will usually put time and energy into teaching the lesson *exactly* as it appears on the printed page. They will have lists of activities that they will initiate, and they will have specific strategies that they expect to enact during the lesson. All of this is good. A detailed lesson plan is essential to your success. But a common growing pain for emerging teachers is making the transition from teaching the *lesson plan* to teaching the *students* through the lesson plan. When you teach the lesson plan, you are solely focused on staying on track, getting through your plan, not skipping any steps, and completing all of your activities, regardless of how well the class responds to, or finds success with, the activities.

When you teach the students through the lesson plan, you are focused on the *students* to see how everything you are doing is functioning for their learning and engagement. If one of your steps doesn't work, then you will try a different step that you didn't have in your plan, or possibly you will skip to another step in the plan that you hope will work. When you are teaching the students, and not the plan, you will be more connected to the indicators of their progress and engagement, and you will be ready to move on to the next step only when you have successfully completed the step you are on. Sometimes though, you will need to abandon your plan when you sense that it is not working for your students on a given day, and that can be scary for a new teacher. Here is a transfer example to help explain this further.

If you are a fan of professional football in the United States, you will be able to relate to this example quite easily. When a quarterback on a professional team gets behind his linemen and starts calling off numbers and words, he is telling the other players on his own team when the play is going to start. When he yells just the right thing, the ball is snapped from the center into the hands of the quarterback, and the play commences all at once. But sometimes the quarterback will see something interesting in the formation of the other team, either the way they are lined up or something that indicates that a different play would work better than the one they were expecting to run. When this happens, the quarterback starts yelling different words to his team to change the offensive play, and this is done after everyone is already lined up and ready to run the play. The term for this is "calling an audible on the line of scrimmage" and it simply means that the quarterback is changing the play at the last minute without the whole team meeting up again in a circle (huddle) to talk about it first. This happens all the time in professional football, and it is the job of the quarterback to watch and evaluate the defense carefully to see if the play that was called is a good one or if they need to change it out on the line of scrimmage for a better one.

This transfer to football is applicable to your experience in the choral classroom on several levels. When you write a lesson plan with what you hope will be an appropriate number of steps and details included, it will still be based on your best guess as to how the class will receive it and how well they will be able to do what you are asking them to do. When you have been teaching for a while, and when you really are familiar with a particular class of students, your best guess will be quite accurate most of the time; your plan will succeed if you teach it well. But when you are starting out in the profession, and when you don't know the students all that well, your best guess of what they can do won't always pan out to be true. If you have underestimated their abilities and have over-planned for the lesson (too many steps), then you will be bogged down in steps and the class will be bored. If you have overestimated their abilities and have under-planned for the lesson (not enough detailed steps), you will have students who are unable to do what you ask them to do, and you will be unable to keep them engaged and on task. If you think of yourself like a quarterback in a professional football game, you can imagine yourself going in front of the class with a play that you expect to run (your lesson), but prepared to watch the defense (the class) to see if your play is going to work. If what you planned is clearly not going to function, it is perfectly alright to select another teaching strategy that will work better. Of course, when you are first starting out, you might not have another strategy to go to in your head and that can be a problem that is difficult to solve in the moment.

It is not practical to write three or four lesson plans just in case the one you expect to use needs to be changed at the last minute. With experience over the years, you will teach hundreds upon hundreds of lessons that you can draw upon in your memory when you need to, and you will be able to "change the play" as needed depending on how the class responds to your lessons and activities on any given day. There may come a day when you discover that your plan is so far removed from where the students are that you have to abandon it all together and surrender your goals for that lesson, choosing a completely different activity and direction for the rest of the period. That is OK, so long as it doesn't happen too often, and hopefully you will use the experience as a learning opportunity in your teacher training. Make it one of your professional goals to transition from teaching your plan to teaching your students through your lesson plan, and celebrate on the day that you feel you have done it successfully more than once.

Writing Your First Lesson Plans

As was stated earlier in this chapter, there is not a single universal template for creating a lesson plan. You will have to write lots of different ones to satisfy not only your own teaching needs, but also the requirements of your education classes, or perhaps the administrators of your school when you get your first job. Regardless of the format you choose for the lessons you will be writing, you should make the exercise a meaningful and useful one for you, if possible. At some point in your career you will be able to write plans that are simply peripheral organizers in your teaching environment, and you will be able to follow cryptic lists that imply many of the teaching steps that you have long memorized in your mind. Until then, you should do your best to write detailed plans that can function for a variety of students of various skills and abilities.

Your first official plans will include many of the items listed in this chapter under "Essential Elements of Lesson Plans" including your scope and sequence, objectives and outcomes, materials needed to teach your lesson and to control the environment, assessment strategies, a timeline to predict how long your steps will take, and a list of vocabulary words and essential questions that you will want to ask your students during the lesson. Additionally, you may need to reference your state or national music education standards and possibly your lesson adaptions for exceptional learners. Practice organizing this material so that you can get really good at writing these plans within the required guidelines. It will help you become an organized and efficient planner, which should translate into you becoming a well-prepared and effective teacher.

There may be times in your early career when you will realize that you haven't had enough time to write down and organize detailed lesson plans, and then you will find yourself in front of a class completely unprepared to teach. Then what? Ideally, you will never be completely unprepared to teach if you plan accordingly and consistently. But if you have only a small amount of time to plan, be sure you have these absolutely essential items organized and in place (on paper or in your mind) before you teach:

1. What you will teach and in what order **(Scope and Sequence)**
2. How long you will spend on each activity **(Timeline)**
3. Materials and equipment needed **(Environment)**
4. Goals for the lesson **(Student Outcomes)**

Over time, your authentic teaching experiences will help you appreciate the advantages of being well planned in your classroom; when you have a great lesson plan, you can do much more with your instructional time, and your students will make more progress than when you make it up as you go. Students can tell when you are prepared (as well as when you are unprepared), and they will work to be their best when they know that you are organized and that you have a clear direction for their progress. Take the time to prepare, and make it a habit to write detailed plans as much as possible.

As we stated earlier, you will be asked to write many lesson plans in many different formats as you prepare to teach, and there is no single correct template to use; it will depend on the kind of class you will be teaching as well as the authority who is asking you to write it. When you are charged to fill out any lesson plan template, learn to use it and do your best to make it practical for your teaching and planning purposes. Look at the "Choral Music Education Lesson/Rehearsal Plan" below and examine it for the kinds of information required to fill it out. This is a generic lesson plan template that has many of the most important elements that you should include in your lesson plans for any class or ensemble rehearsal. Feel free to use it to write your first lesson plans, and let it guide your thinking and pre-planning going into your first experiences in front of real classes. An unprepared teacher is rarely a good teacher, so take on this part of your pre-professional training with a diligent approach. It will really pay off when you start to feel prepared and competent in front of your classes.

Choral Music Education Lesson/Rehearsal Plan

Teacher Name: ______________________________ Number of Minutes in Lesson: __________
Class or Choir Type: ______________________________________ Date of Lesson: __________
Grade(s): ______________ Number of Students: ______ Level: Novice - Intermed. - Adv.

Goals for the Lesson (Student Outcomes): *Describe what* ***students will be able to do*** *by the end of the class.*

Materials and Equipment (The Environment): *List all the equipment, materials, and technology needed to teach, and describe* ***what you will need to do before class starts*** *to have these things ready in time.*

What You Will Teach and in What Order (Scope and Sequence): *In order, describe and/or list the* ***specific activities*** *that you will lead, and also estimate* ***how much time*** *you will need for each activity on the timeline. Use another piece of paper if you need more room. Remember that novice groups need more detailed steps than advanced groups do.*

Start Time **Activity:** *Specifically, describe what will you have the class* ***do****. (Use the back as needed)*

_________ ____
_________ ____
_________ ____
_________ ____
_________ ____
_________ ____
_________ ____
_________ ____
_________ ____
_________ ____
_________ ____
_________ ____
_________ ____
_________ ____
_________ ____
_________ ____

What You Will Teach and in What Sequence (Order of Events) *CONTINUED* **PAGE 2**

Start Time **Activity:** *Specifically, describe what will you have the class* ***do****. (continued from front)*

Evaluation of Student Outcomes: *Describe how you will* ***evaluate*** *how well the students achieved your* ***Goals for the Lesson*** *during the class.*

Vocabulary: *List EVERY* ***musical term*** *that you want your students to learn and remember from this lesson.*

Standards: *List the* ***State or National Music Standards*** *addressed in this lesson.*

OTHER: *List any other details that you, as the teacher, need to consider* ***to be successful*** *teaching this lesson today.*

Six Sample Lesson Plans

Here are some sample lesson plans with varying amounts of detail and in several different formats. Look at and read each one to see what has been included and what has been left out. Note if you understand clearly what the teacher has planned to do and also decide if you could teach the plan yourself if you had to suddenly assume the role of the teacher in the room for that lesson at the last minute. Think about what is good about each lesson plan and what could be improved in each lesson plan, in your opinion.

SAMPLE LESSON 1:

Name	CWID	Subject Area
Susie Student	*************	Music

Class Title	Lesson Title	Unit Title	Grade Levels	Total Minutes
Chamber Choir (Auditioned Mixed Choir)	The Poetry of *Silver Bells*	*Silver Bells* Arranged by Mac Huff	10-12	110 Minutes

CLASS DESCRIPTION (including specific special needs and language proficiencies)
*Not based on an actual class Will provide perspectives for teaching multiple EL proficiency levels

STANDARDS, OBJECTIVES, & ACCOMDATIONS		
CCSS Math, CCSS ELA & Literacy History/Social Studies, Science and Technical Subjects, NGSS, and Content Standards	**Content Objective(s) (cognitive, psychomotor, affective)**	**SDAIE (Integrated ELD) Strategies for developing knowledge in the content area**
Music: 2.1, 2.2, 3.3, 3.7, 4.1	Effectively analyze poetry of choral literature to enhance expression in performance.	Tapping Into Prior Knowledge: Visualization, Cooperative Learning: Pair and Share, Reduction of Teacher Talk: Only Sums Up Student Responses

Tier II (General Academic) Vocabulary	**Tier III (Domain Specific) Vocabulary**
"Glows and Grows," treasures, dressed, meeting, quartet, silver bells	Dynamics. Crescendo, decrescendo, fermata, ritardando, messa di voce

English Language Development Standards (ELD)	**Disciplinary Language Objective(s)**	**SDAIE Strategies for developing knowledge of disciplinary English**
ELD.PI.10-12.1.EM/EX/BR, ELD.PI.10-12.2.EM/EX/BR, ELD.PI.10-12.5.EM/EX/BR, ELD.PI.10-12.6.EM/EX/BR, ELD.PI.10-12.10.EM/EX/BR, ELD.PI.10-12.11.EM/EX/BR, ELD.PII.10-12.1.EM/EX/BR	Students apply their knowledge of musical articulation to their analysis of text for performance.	Cooperative Learning: Pair and Share, Reduction of Teacher Talk: Only Sums Up Student Responses, Nonlinguistic representations: Manipulative, Flow Chart

Additional Student Accommodations (Behavioral, Cognitive, & Physical)	
Specific Needs	**Specific Accommodations**
Lesson will be adjusted to suit various levels of EL proficiency.	***See Lesson Plan Rationale for accommodations/differentiations of the lesson based on EL proficiency level.**

(continued on next page)

(sample lesson 1, continued)

STUDENT ASSESSMENT				
Type	**Purpose/Focus of Assessment**	**Implementation**	**Feedback Strategy**	**How Informs Teaching**
EL	To gain cultural perspective of their views of the winter season/holidays. To see their initial interpretation of a given text. This also allows students to practice their writing and speaking skills.	Students listen to a recording of the piece and are given festive manipulative such as miniature snow globes and/or a single silver bell to hold as they listen as well as a printout of the lyrics. In their journal, students either explain the story of the piece or rewrite the story in their own words. Students then must tie the story of the piece to their experiences with their own winter celebrations in their journals. Students then pair and share with a partner. Students then share all of their answers/interpretations that they wrote with the entire class.	Students give each other feedback on their writing. Teacher gives approval for every answer. With each answer, the teacher ties the different views/interpretations into the lyrics of *Silver Bells*. Teacher essentially takes each answer and rewords/elaborates so that all students can further understand.	Teacher can modify the information so that students can apply the story to their own lives, which would enhance both reading comprehension and text expression in performance.
PM	Check for comprehension of the story, group discussion and teamwork, and a method for practicing imagery for expression.	Students are placed into quartets and must write a short story that places them into the "world" of *Silver Bells*. Students can choose any of the stanzas to write their short story. All members of the quartet then present the story. After doing so, the quartet must perform the section of music that their story is based on.	Students give each other feedback on another group's presentation and performance. Students evaluate if the group's expression matched the emotion of their short story.	This assesses if the students are able to place themselves into the story of the piece to aid with expression. This also assesses a student's ability to evaluate a performance. The activity then segues to the next activity about interpreting text.
S	To formalize the process of expressing text in a performance and to check for students' self-awareness of their performance.	Students are given a flow chart they must fill in as the class discusses the process of expressing text. After the class discussion, the entire class performs the whole piece, keeping in mind all of the activities done that connected them to the text for expression. Students then write a reflection in their journal of what they thought they did well in terms of expression, what the entire class did well, and areas of growth for both the individual and the choir. A few students will share through volunteering or selection. Journals will be turned in for teacher to look over after class.	Some students will share what they thought of the performance and what they were thinking of while singing. Teacher gives "glows and grows" feedback to the class. The "glows" are what was done well in terms of expression. The "grows" are areas for further improvement/expression.	This proves if their level of understanding of the text can be translated into an expressive performance. If the students are successful in expressing with musical accuracy, then they can be challenged with an informal public performance of the piece.

(sample lesson 1, continued)

INSTRUCTION		
Lesson Introduction/Anticipatory Set		
Time	**Teacher Does**	**Student Does**
25 Minutes	• Hands out manipulative and lyrics for students to examine as they listen to a recording of *Silver Bells.* • Plays the arrangement of *Silver Bells* on a PA system. • Instructs class to journal what they think the song is about or rewrite the meaning of the lyrics. • Instructs class to tie the story to their own winter celebrations in their journal, then pair and share with a partner. • Teacher monitors student work and clarifies any part of the tasks with individual attention as needed. • Ties student responses to themes in *Silver Bells.*	• Listens attentively to a recording of the piece while reading the lyrics and holding or examining the manipulative. • Writes in journal what they think the story is about or rewrites the lyrics. • In writing in their journals, students compare their own winter celebrations to the story. • Students pair and share their comparisons. • Publicly shares what they wrote.
Lesson Body		
Time	**Teacher Does**	**Student Does**
25 Minutes	• Places students into SATB quartets for assignment. • Provides students with starting pitches for performance portion of the assigned task.	• In a quartet, students must take a stanza of the piece and create a short story on paper, placing themselves in the setting of *Silver Bells.* • Each group presents their story; every member must speak in the presentation. • Each quartet must perform the excerpt of the music that their short story was based on. The performance must match the emotion of their story. • Students give verbal feedback to evaluate each group's attempt at expressing their story and performance.
Lesson Closure		
Time	**Teacher Does**	**Student Does**
20 Minutes	• Gives students the text expression flow chart for discussion. • Gives keywords for students to input into their chart. • Conducts the piece *Silver Bells.* • Listens and watches for expressivity in the performance. • Selects students to share their journal reflection. • Gives "glows and grows" feedback to the students about their expressiveness. • Collects journals for further student assessment.	• Listens to text expression lecture. • Fills in text expression flow chart with teacher's keywords. • Sings the piece *Silver Bells* with expressivity and greater understanding of the text. • Writes what they did well as an individual and choir in regards to expression. • Writes areas for growth as an individual and choir for text expression. • Is prepared to share their answer aloud.

Instructional Materials, Equipment, and Multimedia			
Individual copies of *Silver Bells* arranged by Mac Huff, pencils, printout of the lyrics, journal, PA system, computer with internet access, and a piano or tuning fork			
Co-Teaching Strategies			
☐**One teach, one observe** ☐**Supplemental teaching**	☐**One teach, one assist** ☐**Differentiated teaching**	☐**Station teaching** ☐**Team teaching**	☐**Parallel teaching** ☐**Not applicable**
NOTES			
This lesson plan serves as guideline and quick reference guide for the instructor. The purposes of the activities, grouping of students, and use of materials are explained in detail in the included lesson plan rationale.			

SAMPLE LESSON 2:

Warm ups

1. Mirroring
   a. Claps
   b. Nose touches, pats, etc
2. Sighs, sirens
3. [a] Sol Fa Mi Re Do
4. [i] (Do) [a] (Sol Do)
5. Altos and Basses on [do]; Sopranos and Tenors on [sol]
   a. [mi me ma mo mu] on same note; go up or down half steps and tune
6. All on same note
   a. *Piano* to *Forte* to *Piano* on open [o] vowel
7. Do, Do Re Do, etc.
   a. do it in individual rounds

A Million Dreams

1. Run through piece
2. Mm. 150 to end → Review
   a. Sopranos & Basses
   b. Altos & Basses
   c. All together
      i. Maybe add hand gestures while singing
3. Mm. 142 to end → tie it in
4. *Piano* sections, make them more full and expressive
   a. Meditation voice vs "whisper" voice
5. Give *Forte* lines good phrases/lines
   a. Loud Meditation voice vs "shout" voice
   b. Loud siren, up down up down
      i. (can you move freely in the voice while singing loudly?)
6. Fix anything that might have gone wrong during first run through
7. Run through whole piece again

SAMPLE LESSON 3:

MUSIC EDUCATION WEEKLY LESSON PLAN FORMAT					
Name	**Samuel Student**	**Grade(s)** 9 - 12	**Class**	**Beginning Choir – Period 2** **South-North High School**	
Unit	**Rehearsing music for Spring Concert**		**Week of**	**04/29/2021**	**to** 05/03/2021
Element	**M**	**T**	**W**	**T**	**F**
Lesson Topic/Repertoire	1. Kuimba 2. Ad Astra	1. A Million Dreams 2. Kuimba	1. Ad Astra 2. Kuimba	1. Kuimba 2. A Million Dreams	1. Ad Astra 2. Kuimba 3. A Million Dreams Rehearse with accompanist
Behavior Objectives	• Students will be able to sight sing musical examples in the key of C major (including first 5 syllables) with correct solfege syllable, pitches, and rhythms. • Students will be able to clap rhythm examples correctly including whole note, dotted, half note/rest, and quarter note/rest. • Students will sing each song with correct posture and focused tone. • Students will sing with accurate pitches, rhythms, attacks, and releases. • Students will sing with clear vowels. • Students will sing correctly with accents. • Students will sing correct dynamics & tempos.	• Students will be able to sight sing musical examples in the key of C major (including first 5 syllables) with correct solfege syllable, pitches, and rhythms. • Students will be able to clap rhythm examples correctly including whole note, dotted, half note/rest, and quarter note/rest. • Students will sing each song with correct posture and focused tone. • Students will sing with accurate pitches, rhythms, attacks, and releases. • Students will sing with clear vowels. • Students will sing correctly with accents. • Students will sing correct dynamics & tempos.	• Students will be able to sight sing musical examples in the key of C major (including first 5 syllables) with correct solfege syllable, pitches, and rhythms. • Students will be able to clap rhythm examples correctly including whole note, dotted, half note/rest, and quarter note/rest. • Students will sing each song with correct posture and focused tone. • Students will sing with accurate pitches, rhythms, attacks, and releases. • Students will sing with clear vowels. • Students will sing correctly with accents. • Students will sing correct dynamics & tempos.	• Students will be able to sight sing musical examples in the key of C major (including first 5 syllables) with correct solfege syllable, pitches, and rhythms. • Students will be able to clap rhythm examples correctly including whole note, dotted, half note/rest, and quarter note/rest. • Students will sing each song with correct posture and focused tone. • Students will sing with accurate pitches, rhythms, attacks, and releases. • Students will sing with clear vowels. • Students will sing correctly with accents. • Students will sing correct dynamics & tempos.	• Students will sing each song with correct posture and focused tone. • Students will sing with accurate pitches, rhythms, attacks, and releases. • Students will sing with clear vowels. • Students will sing correctly with accents. • Students will sing correct dynamics & tempos.

(continued on next page)

(sample lesson 3, continued)

CA Content Standards (Music and ELD)	• 1.1 Read an instrumental or vocal score of up to four staves and explain how the elements of music are used. • 2.1 Sing a repertoire of vocal literature representing various genres, styles, and cultures with expression, technical accuracy, tone quality, vowel shape, and articulation written and memorized by oneself and in ensembles (level of difficulty: 4 on a scale of 1-6). • 2.2 Sing music written in three or four parts with and without accompaniment.	• 1.1 Read an instrumental or vocal score of up to four staves and explain how the elements of music are used. • 2.1 Sing a repertoire of vocal literature representing various genres, styles, and cultures with expression, technical accuracy, tone quality, vowel shape, and articulation written and memorized, by oneself and in ensembles (level of difficulty: 4 on a scale of 1-6). • 2.2 Sing music written in three or four parts with and without accompaniment.	• 1.1 Read an instrumental or vocal score of up to four staves and explain how the elements of music are used. • 2.1 Sing a repertoire of vocal literature representing various genres, styles, and cultures with expression, technical accuracy, tone quality, vowel shape, and articulation written and memorized, by oneself and in ensembles (level of difficulty: 4 on a scale of 1-6). • 2.2 Sing music written in three or four parts with and without accompaniment.	• 1.1 Read an instrumental or vocal score of up to four staves and explain how the elements of music are used. • 2.1 Sing a repertoire of vocal literature representing various genres, styles, and cultures with expression, technical accuracy, tone quality, vowel shape, and articulation written and memorized, by oneself and in ensembles (level of difficulty: 4 on a scale of 1-6). • 2.2 Sing music written in three or four parts with and without accompaniment.	• 1.1 Read an instrumental or vocal score of up to four staves and explain how the elements of music are used. • 2.1 Sing a repertoire of vocal literature representing various genres, styles, and cultures with expression, technical accuracy, tone quality, vowel shape, and articulation written and memorized, by oneself and in ensembles (level of difficulty: 4 on a scale of 1-6). • 2.2 Sing music written in three or four parts with and without accompaniment.
Materials/ Resources	Piano, music scores, pencils, white board, markers, projector screen, computer.	Piano, music scores, pencils, white board, markers, projector screen, computer.	Piano, music scores, pencils, white board, markers, projector screen, computer.	Piano, music scores, pencils, white board, markers, projector screen, computer.	Piano, music scores, pencils, white board, markers, projector screen, computer.
Lesson Intro/ Anticipatory Set	1. Physical & vocal warm ups 2. Rhythm clapping 3. Sight-singing 2 examples in the key of C major	1. Physical & vocal warm ups 2. Rhythm clapping 3. Sight-singing 2 examples in the key of C major	1. Physical & vocal warm ups & ear training (using solfege syllables) 2. Rhythm clapping 3. Sight-singing 2 examples in the key of C major	1. Physical & vocal warm ups 2. Rhythm clapping 3. Sight-singing 2 examples in the key of C major	1. Physical vocal warm ups

(continued on next page)

(sample lesson 3, continued)

Lesson Body/ Student Activities	**Kuimba (15-20’)** Run through the whole piece to check for problems. Focus on page 6 (transition) • Review page 3 – 6 Focus on page 8 (transition) • Review page 6 – 8 Focus on page 8 – 9 (a cappella section) Review page 10 – 11 • Listen to separate sections to check for accurate pitches & rhythms • Check for note durations • Check for Open Vowels • ACCENTS + Dynamics Run through the whole piece again to check for improvements. **Ad Astra (15-20’)** **Review p.11 – 14** • Page 12 (m.81) – Check for Baritone’s entrance on “Movere” **Page 13 - Baritone & Alto** • Check for **note duration of ending note & crescendo** of “behind” • Forte dynamic all 3 parts **Page 14 –** 3 parts together • Check for Diction + dynamic • <u>Crescendos</u> every time repeating the phrase. **Page 15:** • Ask each voice part to sing separately to check for pitches & rhythms. ** Re-teach each voice part if needed • Check for Open vowels & legato singing • Check for accurate entrances + cut offs + note durations together • Check for Accents & Crescendo **Focus on page 6:** (Sop & Alto only) • Check for ending note duration + Crescendo & dim • Unison melody • Legato singing + Focused & relaxed sound • Check for clear diction. **Focus on page 8:** (Baritone only)	**A Million Dreams (15-20’)** **Focus on page 8 – 13** • Ask each voice part to sing separately to check for accurate pitches & rhythms • Check for ending note duration of each phrase. • Check for open vowels + clear diction • Check for correct dynamics **Focus on page 11:** • Check each voice part on the phrase “Run away to …design” (m.91 – 94) **Focus on page 13:** • Check for each voice part on “Oh a million dream…make” (measure 110–112) Run through page 8 – 13 to check for improvements Then, run through the whole piece with recorded accompaniment. **Kuimba (15-20’)** Run through the whole piece to check for problems. Focus on page 8 – 9 (a cappella section) • Pay attention to the pitch of Bass Then, review page 10 – 11 • Listen to separate sections to check for accurate pitches & rhythms • Check for note durations • Check for Open Vowels • ACCENTS + Dynamics Focus on page 6 (transition) • Review page 3 – 6 Focus on page 8 (transition) • Review page 6 – 8 Run through the whole piece again to check for improvements.	**Ad Astra (15-20’)** **Start on page 6:** (Sop & Alto only) • Check for ending note duration + Crescendo & dim • Unison melody • Legato singing + Focused & relaxed sound • Check for clear diction. **Focus on page 8:** (Baritone only) • Check for accurate entrances & cut offs together • Check for pitches and open vowels on “alone” + “guide” + “home” **Review p.11 – 14 to check for improvements from last rehearsal** • Page 12 (m.81) – Check for Baritone’s entrance on “Movere” **Page 13 - Baritone & Alto** • Check for **note duration of ending note & crescendo** of “behind” • Forte dynamic all 3 parts **Page 14 –** 3 parts together • Check for Diction + dynamic • <u>Crescendos</u> every time repeating the phrase. **Page 15:** • Ask each voice part to sing separately to check for pitches & rhythms. Run through the whole piece with recorded accompaniment. **Kuimba (15-20’)** Run through the whole piece to check for problems. Focus on page 6 (transition) • Review page 3 – 6 Focus on page 8 (transition) • Review page 6 – 8 Focus on page 8 – 9 (a cappella section) Review page 10 – 11 • Listen to separate sections to check for accurate pitches & rhythms • Check for note durations • Check for Open Vowels • ACCENTS + Dynamics	**Kuimba (15-20’)** Run through the whole piece to check for problems. Focus on page 6 (transition) • Review page 3 – 6 Focus on page 8 (transition) • Review page 6 – 8 Focus on page 8 – 9 (a cappella section) Review page 10 – 11 • Listen to separate sections to check for accurate pitches & rhythms • Check for note durations • Check for Open Vowels • ACCENTS + Dynamics Run through the whole piece again to check for improvements. **A Million Dreams (15-20’)** **Review page 8 – 13 to check for improvements from last rehearsal.** **Focus on refining page 14 – ending** **Page 14 – 15** • Check for harmony • Crescendo on “eyes” ** Model the crescendo & diction of “eyes…to see” • Check for open vowels • Check note duration of “see” p.15-16 **Page 16:** • Piano dynamic & shape the phrases • Focus on guys’ entrance at bottom of page 16 “A million dreams..” • Check for accurate pitches & rhythms • Check for Crescendo **Page 16 – 17:** • Check for FORTE dynamics • Check for note duration of “awake”+ “take” + cut offs **Page 17 (measure 150):** • Ask each voice section to sing separately to check for accurate pitches & rhythms • Check for open vowels • Check for Blending & harmony balance on “make”	**Ad Astra (15’)** Run through the whole piece with accompanist & check for problems. • Check for accurate pitches + rhythms + open vowels + dynamics + accents + crescendos + diction. • Pay attention to baritone’s pitches & vowels. **Review page.6 – 10** ** Page 6 (Sop + Alto only) • Check for ending note duration + Crescendo & dim • Unison melody • Legato singing + Focused & relaxed sound • Check for clear diction. ** Page 8: (Baritone only) • Check for accurate entrances & cut offs together • Check for pitches and open vowels on “alone” + “guide” + “home” **Review p.11 – 14** • Page 12 (m.81) – Check for Baritone’s entrance on “Movere” Check quickly page 15 • Ask each voice part to sing separately to check for accurate pitches + rhythms + dynamics + open vowels. Run through the whole piece again to check for improvements. **Kuimba (15’)** Run through the whole piece with accompanist & check for problems. Review page 3 – 6 • Focus on page 6 (transition) Review page 6 – 8 • Focus on page 8 (transition) Review page 8 – 9 Review page 10 – 11 • Focus on bottom of p. 10 – 11 • Listen to separate voice parts • Check for pitches & rhythms • Open Vowels + Note durations • ACCENTS + Dynamics Run through the whole piece again to check for improvements.

(continued on next page)

(sample lesson 3, continued)

	• Check for accurate entrances & cut offs together • Check for pitches and open vowels on "alone" + "guide" + "home" Run through the whole piece with recorded accompaniment.		Run through the whole piece again to check for improvements.	Run through the whole piece with recorded accompaniment to check for improvements.	**A Million Dreams (15')** Run through the whole piece with accompanist & check for problems. Review page 4 – 7 Review page 8 – 13 Review page 14-15 Review page 16-18 Focus on VOWELS + TONE + PHRASING + DYNAMICS + BALANCE + BLEND + DICTION • Listen to each voice section separately to check for accurate pitches + rhythms + dynamics • Listen to the whole choir to check for harmony & balance. Run through the whole piece again to check for improvements.

(continued on next page)

(sample lesson 3, continued)

Assessments (EL, PM, S)	Entry level + Progress monitoring: • Students will clap rhythm examples correctly. • Students will sight sing with correct syllables, pitches, and rhythms. • Students will sing each song with correct posture and focused tone • Students will sing with accurate pitches, rhythms, attacks, and releases. • Students will sing with clear vowels. • Students will sing correctly with accents. • Students will sing correct dynamics, tempos, and articulations. Self-Assessment: • Ask students to self-assess their own singing and orally share their ideas at any spot during the rehearsal.	Entry level + Progress monitoring: • Students will clap rhythm examples correctly. • Students will sight sing with correct syllables, pitches, and rhythms. • Students will sing each song with correct posture and focused tone • Students will sing with accurate pitches, rhythms, attacks, and releases. • Students will sing with clear vowels. • Students will sing correctly with accents. • Students will sing correct dynamics, tempos, and articulations. Self-Assessment: • Ask students to self-assess their own singing and orally share their ideas at any spot during the rehearsal.	Entry level + Progress monitoring: • Students will clap rhythm examples correctly. • Students will sight sing with correct syllables, pitches, and rhythms. • Students will sing each song with correct posture and focused tone • Students will sing with accurate pitches, rhythms, attacks, and releases. • Students will sing with clear vowels. • Students will sing correctly with accents. • Students will sing correct dynamics, tempos, and articulations. Self-Assessment: • Ask students to self-assess their own singing and orally share their ideas at any spot during the rehearsal.	Entry level + Progress monitoring: • Students will clap rhythm examples correctly. • Students will sight sing with correct syllables, pitches, and rhythms. • Students will sing each song with correct posture and focused tone • Students will sing with accurate pitches, rhythms, attacks, and releases. • Students will sing with clear vowels. • Students will sing correctly with accents. • Students will sing correct dynamics, tempos, and articulations. Self-Assessment: • Ask students to self-assess their own singing and orally share their ideas at any spot during the rehearsal.	Entry level + Progress monitoring: • Students will sing each song with correct posture and focused tone • Students will sing with accurate pitches, rhythms, attacks, and releases. • Students will sing with clear vowels. • Students will sing correctly with accents. • Students will sing correct dynamics, tempos, and articulations. Self-Assessment: • Ask students to self-assess their own singing and orally share their ideas at any spot during the rehearsal.
Adaptations (EL, SR, SN, AD, IEP)	Visual aids: • Write the agenda on the board • Write rhythms and terms on the board. • Show sight-reading exercises on the board or projector screen • Write solfege syllables and beats under the notes in the examples. Sectional practice if needed.	Visual aids: • Write the agenda on the board • Write rhythms and terms on the board. • Show sight-reading exercises on the board or projector screen • Write solfege syllables and beats under the notes in the examples. Sectional practice if needed.	Visual aids: • Write the agenda on the board • Write rhythms and terms on the board. • Show sight-reading exercises on the board or projector screen • Write solfege syllables and beats under the notes in the examples. Sectional practice if needed.	Visual aids: • Write the agenda on the board • Write rhythms and terms on the board. • Show sight-reading exercises on the board or projector screen • Write solfege syllables and beats under the notes in the examples. Sectional practice if needed.	Visual aids: • Write the agenda on the board • Write rhythms and terms on the board.

SAMPLE LESSON 4:

North/South High School – Period 2 (Choir)
REHEARSAL PLAN

Learning Objectives:

- Students will clap syncopated rhythms including 8th note/rest and 16th note/rest correctly.
- Students will sing each song with correct posture and focused tone.
- Students will sing with accurate pitches, rhythms, attacks, and releases.
- Students will sing with clear vowels.
- Students will sing correct dynamics.
- Students will sing with accents where indicated in the scores.

State Content Standards:

- 1.1 Read an instrumental or vocal score of up to four staves and explain how the elements of music are used.
- 2.1 Sing a repertoire of vocal literature representing various genres, styles, and cultures with expression, technical accuracy, tone quality, vowel shape, and articulation written and memorized, by oneself and in ensembles (level of difficulty: 4 on a scale of 1-6).
- 2.2 Sing music written in three or four parts with and without accompaniment.

ELD standards:

- ELD. PI.1.Ex - Express a variety of personal needs, ideas, and opinions and respond to questions using short sentences.
- ELD. PI.5.Ex - Listening actively to spoken English in a range of social and academic contexts.

Warm-ups (5' - 7')
- Physical warm-ups (2')
- Vocal warm-ups (5')

1. **Ad Astra (15')** [p.9 – 12 / m.52 – 73]
   Focus on pitches/ rhythms/ Vowels/ Dynamics

- Review p.9 -10 (m.52 – 64) – Have everyone sings through the pages to check for errors.
  Separate sections:
  - Baritone only (p.9 – 10)
  - Alto only (p.9 – 11 / m.52 – 64)
  - Alto + Baritone together
  - Soprano only (p.9 – 11)
  - Soprano + Alto together
  - Everyone together (p.9 – 11 / m.52 - 64)

- Teach p.11 – 12 (m.64 – 73)
  Have everyone practice speaking "To the stars" - cut offs together.
  Write on the board the "ACCENT" sign & term + ask question if anyone recognizes it.

  - Baritone only [Focus on pitches/ dictions – cut offs of "stars" + Accents]
    [Dynamics – Crescendo each time repeating "to the stars"]

  Ask Soprano + Alto to hold their notes on "Mm…" to keep them engaged.
  (Have them to practice the notes on "Ah", then close the mouth to "Mm…")

(continued on next page)

(sample lesson 4, continued)

- Alto only

(Remind Alto that Baritone sings "to the stars" 2 times before Alto joins in).
** Focus on pitches/ dictions – cut offs of "stars"
[Dynamics – Crescendo each time repeating "to the stars"]

- Baritone + Alto together [Focus on pitches/ cut offs/ dynamics]

Soprano Humming along – Tell them to stop at m.72 (p.12)
(After Alto sings 2 times "to the stars")

- Soprano only (p.12 / m.72-73) Focus on pitches/ cut offs/ Crescendo

(Remind that Alto will sing "to the stars" 2 times before Soprano joins in)

- 3 parts together on p.12 (m.72-73) if needed

- Run through p.9 – 12 (m.52 – 73)

2. **A Million Dreams (15')** Focus on p.8 - 13

- <u>Review p.8 – 9 (m.63 – 78)</u>

Check for pitches/vowels/ breath support/ cut offs/ Crescendo at m.77 – 78 / diction

Separate Sections:

- Alto only Focus on pitches/ vowels/ NO BREATH on p.9 (m.71- 75)
  Remind them to hold the last note of "oo" = 6 beats

- Soprano only Focus on pitches/ vowels/ NO BREATH on p.9 (m.71- 75)
  Remind them to hold the last note of "oo" = 6 beats

- Soprano + Alto together

- Baritone only Focus on pitches/ rhythms/ vowels & diction
  Crescendo at m.77-78

- 3 parts together

- <u>Continue review p.10 - 13 (m.79 – 112)</u>

Focus on note durations/ vowels/ tone quality/ dynamics/ diction

[If students do well and there's time]

- Review p.14 – 18 (m.121 – ending)
- Review p.14 – 15 only if needed (m.121 - 133)
- Review p.16 only (Focus on Baritone only / the bottom system)

- Review p. 17 – 18 (m.150 – ending) to check for harmony
  Focus on vowels/ note durations/ dynamics

3. **Kuimba (10')**

- Review p.3 – 6 (m.3 – 22) Focus on pitches/rhythms/ diction/ accents
- Review p.6 – 8 (m.23 – 41) Focus on pitches/rhythms/ diction/ accents

Have each voice section to sing separately to check for pitches if needed.

[If there's time]

<u>Teach p.11 (ending part) m.63 – 64.</u>

- Speaking the words in rhythm
- Teach each section their part.
- Add 2 & more sections together.

SAMPLE LESSON 5:

Lesson Topic/Repertoire: Go Down Moses

Behavior Objectives: Students will be able to sing from m.4 – 21 with accuracy of dynamics, articulation, pitch and rhythm.

State Content Standards
(Music and ELD) 1.4, 2.1, 2.2, ELD:PIII.7.5.EM

Materials/Resources: Piano, Score, Copies of score for students.
Lesson Intro/ Anticipatory Set: Brief Warmup
1) Major Scale with hand signs
2) Major Scale in Canon
3) Minor Scale (La) with hand signs
4) Minor Scale Canon

Lesson Body/ Student Activities:
1) Teacher will model opening "Oo" sequence for students and have them repeat
2) Teacher will inform students of the lift after each half/dotted half-note during "oos"
3) Teacher will have students sing the text
   - Teacher will tell them to articulate the "D" on the beat for both "land" and "stand"
   - Model it for them
   -Have them speak in rhythm
4) Teacher will isolate parts at m. 22
   -Part 1 sings first with piano
   -Model accents for them at 26
   -Add harmony part with part one (queued notes)
   -Part 2 sings with piano
   - Have part two sing the m.25-26 (From La down to Mi) on solfege
   Add words once they can get the skip
5) Add both parts together, playing on piano
6) Students will sing from m. 4 – 28 with piano.

Assessments (EL, PM, S):
EL: Teacher will listen to how accurately students can apply the solfege exercise to the motive in the music.

PM: Teacher will listen and correct the unarticulated "Oos" if students continue to articulate before the pitch changes. Teacher will listen for accuracy between each phrase with regards the quarter note lift.

S: Teacher will listen and note areas that still need improvement during the final run through of the piece.

Adaptations (EL, SR, SN, AD, IEP):
SN: Blind Student

Teacher will sing and model text aloud for class, allowing this student to learn the text and form of the piece without a visual score.

EL: Teacher will check in frequently for understanding. Teacher will read text aloud in rhythm and have students read along. Teacher will modify and slow rate of speech.

SAMPLE LESSON 6:

Lesson Plan
Canta Bella: (10:00-11:30)
Warm up (10:00-10:15)
Words (10:15- 10:20)

What I Want (10:20-10:45)
- sight-reading practice for the day
- ask what the key is - sight read from mm. 19-26 (x2)
- sopranos sight read with accompaniment
- altos sight read with accompaniment
- sopranos and first altos sight read on solfege together
- sopranos and second altos sight read on solfege together
- all four parts sight read on solfege together with accompaniment
- all four parts on the words with accompaniment
- everyone sight reads from mm. 27-33
- both alto parts sing first, focusing on dissonance
- both soprano parts sing
- everyone together
- everyone sings from mm. 19-33

Sigh No More Ladies (10:45-11:10)
- practice feeling 6/8 vs. 7/8 in 6 then switching to 7, and alternate measures between 6 and 7
- speak the words in rhythm
- sight read from mm. 5-17
- mm. 17 SA
- mm. 15-17 SA
- mm. 5-17 SA
- practice 6/8 to 3/4 patterns by clapping alternating bars
- everyone speaks the words in rhythm 18-21
- SA sight read
- S, SII sing 18-21
- SII, A sing 18-21
- everyone sings 18-21
- full run-through from mm. 1 with accompaniment

Bring Me Little Water Sylvie (11:10-11:30)
- practice movement
- run-through
- isolate parts on solfege or words to check notes while others dance or keep a beat (seen in journal)

If extra time - Buddy Interviews

Longer-Range Planning

Writing your daily class lessons is one of the most important aspects of your preparation, and if you start off writing detailed plans early on in your preservice training, you will be able to make them less and less detailed over time as you memorize the format and get completely comfortable teaching your classes. Experienced teachers sometimes keep lists of larger activities or objectives in their conductor's folder or in a small planning notebook. They are likely to have very good intuitions about what the class needs, what music needs to be rehearsed, how much to challenge the students, and exactly when the class needs "another play called from the line of scrimmage." Experienced teachers can teach with a very small amount of information in their "plan" and still be highly effective, all while making it "look easy" to outside observers.

But while you will get better and better at daily lesson planning throughout your career, you also need to think about longer-range planning. How can you plan your teaching over a week, a month, or over a whole semester or grading quarter? The first step is to consider all the things that you want to teach during the time span, and then you need to decide when you will teach each thing. Simple, right? Yes and no.

Many beginning teachers do fairly well when deciding on the scope of the material to be taught, such as "chapters 1–5 in the AP Music Theory textbook by the end of the first quarter" or "all the music for our December 12th concert by December 11th." Then, with the best of intentions, they start teaching on day one from a starting point that has no defined ending. For example, they might spend 40% of the available classes on the first chapter of the AP Theory text, leaving 80% of the material still left to teach, but having just 60% of the available time left to do it. Choral classes are sometimes taught with each song being learned from page 1, measure 1, and progressing in that fashion until there is almost no time left before the concert. Then it is realized that the last two pages of every song have not been rehearsed yet! Beginning teachers, before they learn about long-range planning, panic when they realize that the concert is just a few rehearsals away, but that the choir's preparation is many more rehearsals behind. There can be many reasons for this to happen; for example, sometimes the literature is too difficult to be learned in the time allotted for rehearsal preparation. But sometimes there is simply not enough structure and class planning over the course of the preparation cycle to be completely effective.

To provide a clarifying example of this "longer-range" approach, we will examine how you could organize a seven-week concert preparation with a long-term view of planning. When planning over weeks instead of days, the first step is to count up how many classes or rehearsals are available, and then to count up the minutes represented by these rehearsals. In this example the rehearsals are 110 minutes twice a week, so over seven weeks there are 1,540 minutes of available rehearsal time. Next, you can list all of the literature in your concert, making sure to list accurate timings for each (how long it takes to sing a piece from beginning to end without stopping). You can also list them in concert order if you like to do that and also include how each piece functions in the concert program based on Chapter 8 of this text.

Literature	Timing	Type
Gloria in excelsis Deo	2'30"	Opener
Gloria (from Missa Kenya)	2'30"	Opener
Avinu Malkeinu	3'15"	EPS
Leron, Leron Sinta	3'10"	EPF
Even When He Is Silent	5'15"	Centerpiece
Berusa Er! (Drink Your Fill)	3'30"	LPF
Ballade to the Moon	5'00"	LPS
Rejoice	4'15"	Closer
Carmina Opening	2'30"	Finale

Next, you can think about a single rehearsal. What do you need to spend time on in every rehearsal, no matter what? This is where many people begin to get a better understanding of how much rehearsal time is taken up by activities that are not necessarily rehearsing the music. For example, most every rehearsal will start with some sort of warm up or group activity that is not directly concerned with rehearsing the literature. Of course, a great warm up will ideally build some of the skills that will allow the choir to be more successful with the literature, but for now we will think of the warm up as being an isolated event in your rehearsal. If you spend just ten minutes in warm up over the seven weeks, you will dedicate two hours and twenty minutes to that activity alone…more than a whole rehearsal's worth of time. But when you also add in the things that you can predict will be needed, such as a break, announcements, occasional part testing, and possibly sectionals, these activities quickly add up to 500 minutes in this example, a full third of the available rehearsal time! It quickly becomes clear that you have a lot less time than you thought you did to work on all the music, so now you must be deliberate and efficient in allocating the rest of the available rehearsal time.

The best approach at this point is to work *backwards* from your concert dates. You obviously want every piece to be ready before each concert, and you will have to decide just how many rehearsals before the concert you want each piece to be ready. If you want a song prepared sooner, then you will need to schedule more minutes of rehearsal time early on for that piece. Songs that can be ready closer to the concert can be rehearsed for less time at first, but with more time dedicated later on. However, you also have to balance how difficult each piece is so that you chip away at the most difficult literature over a longer period of time. This balancing of minutes in relation to time and literature difficulty is an art, and you may not know how to make it all work at first. But if you create a table or spreadsheet with all of the information that you want to keep track of, you will start to see patterns that make it all fit together. Click on the icon "Check This Out" to examine the spreadsheet example (below).

Across the top in GREEN are the dates of the rehearsals, with dates in RED representing rehearsals in the performance space, and BLACK BOXES representing concert performances. Because we are working back from the concerts, the songs that are being programmed on each concert are highlighted in YELLOW. In the first concert there are only two songs being performed, so those songs will get priority rehearsal time leading up to that concert. The GREEN boxes represent the dates when each song is due to be memorized, and there is extra rehearsal time for each of those pieces leading up to those specific dates. The PURPLE boxes represent time allotted (fifteen minutes once a week) for group part testing on assigned sections of songs. As the semester progresses, these "mini-chorus tests" are phased out because the notes should be learned by most of the chorus by then. The column marked "Amount of Rehearsal Planned" is a tally of the number of minutes allotted to each piece over the course of the seven weeks. It is easy to see if one piece has a lot more time than another one, and you can also check those numbers against your assessment of the relative difficulty of each piece as well; the tougher the song, the more minutes it will need of rehearsal time.

There are many advantages to getting skilled at this type of longer-term rehearsal planning. First, you will quickly come to appreciate that your rehearsal time is precious, and you will begin to develop a strong desire to be as efficient as possible in rehearsal, not wanting to waste even a minute of time. Second, your timeline will be completely set for the whole seven weeks, so when you are writing your daily lesson plans, you will be able to plan for the exact number of minutes for each piece and activity, and this will guide your chosen teaching steps and sequences within your plan. Third, your students will be able to plan their own personal rehearsal time better when they know what will be sung in each rehearsal, for how long, and when each song is supposed to be learned or memorized. Fourth, if you write the rehearsal order on the board each day with the number of minutes allotted for each activity, and if you follow it, your students will learn that ten minutes allocated to rehearse a song is the only ten minutes for that song on that day. They might be motivated to work harder and stay on task if they know the time is limited and that all group progress must happen in the allocated time frame.

Literature	Timing	Type	Amonut of Rehearsal Planned	2/4/2021 (M)	2/6/2021 (W)	2/11/2021 (M)	2/13/2021 (W)	2/18/2021 (M)	2/20/2021 (W)	2/25/2021 (M)	2/27/2021 (W)	3/4/2021 (M)	3/6/2021 (W) MENG	COLLAGE CONCERT 3/9/2021 (Sat)	3/11/2021 (M)	3/13/2021 (W)	3/18/2021 (M) MENG	3/20/2021 (W) MENG	Choral Fest 3/22/2021 (F)	CONCERT 3/24/2021 (SUN)		
Gloria in excelsis Deo	2'30"	Opener	84	19	4	5	5	4	6	5	0	5	0		4	7	10	10	0	3		
Gloria (from Missa Kenya)	2'30"	Opener	129	20	15	5	10	4	4	5	0	15	20	10	4	7	10	10	10	3		
Avinu Malkeinu	3'15"	EPS	87	0	15	10	5	5	0	8	0	5	0		10	4	15	10	0	4		
Leron, Leron sinta	3'10"	EPF	148	10	15	10	15	18	18	15	0	12	0		10	4	8	13	0	4		
Even When He Is Silent	5'15"	Center piece	127	8	8	7	7	0	8	11	0	8	20		15	8	12	15	0	6		
Berusa Er! (Drink Your Fill)	3'30"	LPF	185	0	15	10	20	40	25	10	0	15	20	10	5	5	8	12	10	4		
Ballade to the Moon	5'00"	LPS	124	0	10	10	10	0	8	8	0	8	20		15	8	12	15	10	6		
Rejoice	4'15"	Closer	126	15	5	15	15	6	8	10	0	9	7		9	7	10	10	10	5		
Carmina Opening	2'30"	Finale Collag	20	0	0	0	0	0	10			10										
Date to be Memorized										SOLO Auditions (1-2, 4:30-5:30)						(Run Concert) after Mini Chorus Rehearsals from Memory						
Warm Up				10	10	10	10	10	10	10	10	10	10	0	10	10	10	10	0	0	140.00	
Break				8	8	8	8	8	8	8	5	8	8	0	8	5	0	0	0	0	90.00	
Announcements				5	5	5	5	5	5	5	5	5	5	0	5	5	5	5	0	0	70.00	
Mini Chorus Testing				15	0	15	0	10	0	15	0	0	0	0	15	0	0	0	0	0	70.00	
Visiting Choir Performance											0										0.00	TOTAL
Mini Chorus Rehearsals											90					40					130.00	500.00
Regular Rhearsals: 2:30-4:20 twice weekly				**2/4/2021 (M)**	**2/6/2021 (W)**	**2/11/2021 (M)**	**2/13/2021 (W)**	**2/18/2021 (M)**	**2/20/2021 (W)**	**2/25/2021 (M)**	**2/27/2021 (W)**	**3/4/2021 (M)**	3/6/2021 (W)	**COLLAGE CONCERT 3/9/2021 (Sat)**	**3/11/2021 (M)**	**3/13/2021 (W)**	3/18/2021 (M)	3/20/2021 (W)	**Choral Fest 3/22/2021 (F)**	**CONCERT 3/24/2021 (SUN)**		
Minutes Per Rehearsal				110	110	110	110	110	110	110	110	110	110	20	110	110	110	110	0	0	1540.00	
Minutes Remaining				0	0	0	0	0	0	0	0	0	0	0	0	0	10	0				
Choral Performance Evidence DUE by Friday at 5:00 pm after a Monday Assessment											Mini Chorus Rehearsals					Mini Chorus Rehearsals						

(Spreadsheet example for long-range planning)

Finally, this approach can help you see early on when you have overplanned for a concert preparation cycle. If you notice that you are rehearsing each piece for a relatively small number of minutes, you can cut a piece or two, or possibly add a rehearsal or two if you have that option (at the beginning of the preparation cycle and NOT as a surprise at the end). Adding extra mandatory rehearsals at the last minute sends a clear message to the choir that tells them: "Sorry, everyone, I don't know how to plan very well over the long term, and I don't respect your time."

As Benjamin Franklin told us, "If you fail to prepare, you are preparing to fail." Lesson planning is indeed one of the most important aspects of your training, and it is the key to your success as a professional choral music educator. It is a mistake for any emerging choral music educator to think that they can teach effectively without a lesson plan. Even if we can emulate our mentors accurately, we must always remember that our mentors made teaching look easy because of many years of planning and experience, how they were thinking when they were rehearsing, what they selectively ignored, and how they chose to reinforce classroom behavior. Emulating what your mentors looked like on the outside will only get you part of the way to where you need to be, and your attention to your own lesson planning will get you the rest of the way over time. Your students will need to know that you have a plan, that you know what you are doing, and that you can help them with both their short-term as well as their long-term success. Take the time now, early in your career, to be curious about how teachers think and prepare. Get really good at charting a path toward the curricular goals you set for yourself and your students. With time, diligence, planning, and practice, you will soon be changing the lives of your students through your effective teaching and the power of music.

RECAPITULATION

1. As human beings we must constantly change our behavior based on the best and most current information we have available to us. For example, if you are making breakfast and you break a glass on the table, you will probably abandon your current plan of eating for a little while as you clean up the broken glass. Think about the concept of "teaching the students instead of the lesson plan." Even though we have a plan, we still have to pay attention to how the students are responding to the plan, and we have to adjust our teaching as needed. Describe a situation (working a job or playing a sport or anything

else) where you had to evaluate what was happening in the moment and then you had to change or modify your actions or behavior based on what was actually happening. Describe what you were doing and how you handled this situation. Also comment on how comfortable you are improvising your actions and going "off plan" when the situation demands it.

2. Use the template "Choral Music Education Lesson/Rehearsal Plan" from this chapter to create a five-minute lesson plan using the canon "Dona Nobis Pacem." Get some feedback on the planning from your teacher or colleagues, and then teach your lesson to the members of your class or to a small group of musicians who are willing to sing for you. Choose someone to keep track of time so that you don't use more than five to six minutes to complete your lesson sequence. Video yourself teaching, and then review the video and self-critique your teaching effectiveness.

CANON - DONA NOBIS PACEM

ANONYMOUS

3. When you evaluated the six Sample Lesson Plans in this chapter, you were asked to look at and read each one to determine what has been included and what has been left out, and if you understood clearly what the teacher had planned to do, and if you thought you could teach each plan yourself if you had to suddenly assume the role of the teacher in the room for that lesson at the last minute. Respond in writing regarding each of the six plans, and be sure to include your opinion about what is good about each lesson plan and what could be improved in each lesson plan.

II. Exposition and Development

Chapter Six

Rehearsing the Choir

6. Rehearsing the Choir

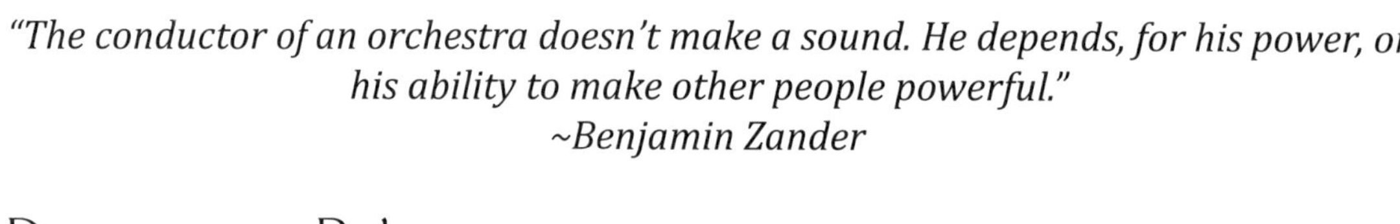

"The conductor of an orchestra doesn't make a sound. He depends, for his power, on his ability to make other people powerful."
~Benjamin Zander

Preparing to Rehearse

Rehearsing the choir is one of the most important musical activities that you will participate in as a professional choral music educator. The rehearsal is where you will do a majority of your teaching and where many of your students will connect to you, to music, and to the art of ensemble singing. Becoming good at rehearsing is essential to your success, and students will join (or drop) your choir classes based on your ability to engage the class, pick interesting and appropriate literature, and structure fun and educational rehearsal segments. How do you become *good* at rehearsing? The honest answer is that you will get better at it the more you do it, over time. But a second answer to this question is that you will do better immediately if you are prepared to rehearse, and there are some essential areas that need to be in place before you lead a choir in your first live rehearsal. Here are some of the most important preparation areas to consider:

- **Choosing music and studying your scores:** As is discussed in Chapter 8, *Materials for the Choral Music Educator*, your music is your textbook, and your overall music choices represent your curriculum. What you will teach will largely be generated and supported by the literature that the choir will be learning. You should pick a variety of music that is appropriate for the ability of the group that will be studying it. Once you have selected your music, then you must study it so that you *really know* it. Really knowing a piece of music means that you have studied all of the aspects listed in the "*Choral Literature Full-Analysis Form*" and that you have sung through (or played through) all the voice parts to know the inherent challenges of the voice leading. Next, you must know the harmonic and rhythmic language of the piece by analyzing it and writing in any chord progressions that you can't recognize at sight as well as working out and practicing any tricky rhythms. If you are also a "late-blooming pianist," you should have all the chord progressions notated in the music so that you can provide a no-harm-accompaniment if needed. (And you should also practice playing it too.) Your score study should also solve any questions of part assignments so that if the parts divide, you can know ahead of time what sections, or parts of sections, will sing them. Finally, you must know the score well enough to have created your own personal musical interpretation for the musical performance of the piece. You should have a sound in your mind that represents what the music will sound like when the choir knows and performs it well.

- **Preparing to conduct:** One main focus of this book is to help you use your conducting skills to be a great teacher, but it is not intended to be so broad in scope that it can adequately teach you conducting technique. There are excellent books dedicated exclusively to conducting, and you would do well to read as many books on the topic as you can. Hopefully, you have had the opportunity to take one or more semesters of choral conducting so that you have a basic foundation in the use of conducting patterns, cues, cut-offs, articulations, and the function of basic gestures.

  With that being said, your conducting preparation for any rehearsal should include "dry conducting" through each piece in the privacy of your own practice room while either singing the major lines or audiating them (hearing them in your head). Many conductors like to add marks in the score to designate cues for the various voice parts and accompaniment, and some also like to mark dynamics and tempo changes by highlighting them or circling them. How (and how much) you mark your score is a personal preference, but you should always have enough markings to keep you clearly focused on the mechanics of the score so that you can focus your attention on the choir and listen carefully to what they are doing musically.

- **Preparing a rehearsal plan:** Before you step on the podium, it is imperative that you create a detailed rehearsal plan that outlines the scope (what you will do) and sequence (the order you will do it) of your rehearsal. Beginning teachers sometimes overlook this important aspect of planning, figuring that they will simply "sing through the music and see how the choir does." But a detailed lesson/rehearsal plan will include much more than what literature you will sing through and in what order; it will also outline exactly what you plan to accomplish in the rehearsal segment as well as the musical concepts to be taught and reinforced and musical vocabulary that can be included. Your plan should be detailed enough that you know what to do at all times and comprehensive enough that you don't run out of things to do before rehearsal ends. A major part of the art of teaching is learning how to plan fun, educational, musical, and engaging rehearsals, and the more you do it, the better you will get at it.

- **Controlling the teaching environment:** When you have chosen your music and you know your scores, and you have practiced your conducting gestures and written your lesson plans, you still have one major thing to consider before you start to rehearse: you need to consider the physical aspects of the teaching environment. Any aspect of the teaching environment that you don't control ahead of time will control *you* once the rehearsal begins. For example, if you don't have enough copies of the music and some of the students can't see what they are supposed to be singing, you will not be able to teach your lesson plan in the way you intended. If the lighting in the room is inadequate, then you will likewise be unable to execute your plan effectively. Some other physical aspects of the teaching environment include, but are not limited to, the availability of a white board with markers that work, enough chairs (or stands) for the choir, a seating plan, a way to take attendance, sound equipment to play recordings or record the rehearsal, a plan for passing out the music (and collecting it if necessary), and being sure there is adequate heating, cooling, and ventilation. Do your best to address as many of these as you can before rehearsal begins, and don't be surprised or thrown off if a few unexpected distractions "pop up" that you hadn't thought to control ahead of time.

The Choral Conductor as Teacher

Many preservice choral educators can't wait to get in front of their first choir. You may feel the same. When you think about conductors who have inspired you in the past, you might yearn to be in the same position, inspiring others. Conducting a choir and making beautiful music is an amazing experience, and you can expect to have many transformative and artistic moments on the podium throughout your career. But when you picture yourself in front of a choir making music in the future, it is likely that you imagine a *really good* choir singing for you. And who wouldn't want a good choir to work with? But it is important to realize that while you will almost certainly have the opportunity to work with some excellent choirs in your lifetime, it is possible that few of these choirs will fully match the idealized version that you may have imagined. In fact, most conductors won't have highly skilled choirs to work with on a regular basis; almost all of us will have the challenge of teaching our choirs how to sing better, perform better, and how to be better musicians. The choir will become a reflection of you as a teacher, and your ability to *meet them where they are and then to make them better* will determine your success more than any other factor. You will be a conductor, yes, but first you must be a great teacher.

As has been stated previously in this text, a great teacher is both process and product oriented; they may work toward creating a great concert (the product), but they also enjoy creating engaging, educational, and artistic rehearsals (the process) that may be just as satisfying as the final performance. The mark of a great choral teacher is not always displayed in the final product, but rather in the progress and improvement of the ensemble over the rehearsal span. Another way to say this is, "You can't know what a teacher has accomplished when you hear their concert unless you know the improvement they made in the rehearsals leading up to the concert." A great teacher can bring a choir from *not good* to *sort of good,* and that is amazing work, which is at the heart of what we do. Don't be afraid to work with the choir in front of you on any given day, regardless of their ability, and then ask yourself after the rehearsal, "Did I teach them and help them to be a better choir today?" Hopefully, you will be able to answer, "Yes, I did." If so, you are on the right track not only as a conductor of your ensemble, but also as their teacher.

The Art of Rehearsing the Choir

There are innumerable aspects of preparation and execution that help to create an effective rehearsal environment, and no textbook can fully prepare you for everything you will need to know for the first time you are completely in charge of running a choral rehearsal. Effective rehearsing is more of an art than a science, and learning the component parts of the process will only get you part of the way there to where you feel prepared and confident in front of a choir. Skilled and experienced choral educators learn over time what to focus on, what to ignore, and how their actions will likely function during rehearsal, and much of what they do well was learned and refined by trial and error and readjustment. There are, however, some foundational principles upon which you can build your rehearsal skills, and we will outline many of these in this chapter. By learning and then following these principles, you can be as prepared as possible to start your journey toward becoming a masterful teacher and conductor.

As has been stated earlier, we tend to teach the way we were taught. Most students will emulate their mentors to some degree, and your baseline rehearsal style will be largely set and influenced by your previous experiences in ensemble rehearsals. It's important to note, however, that when we sing or play in an ensemble, we can only observe what a teacher *does*, but not what a teacher is *thinking*. The art of teaching requires decision after decision, made by the conductor in real time, that may be impossible to observe by the choir. Effective teachers manage and modify classroom behavior while simultaneously listening to the musical product, prioritizing and deciding what needs to be taught, choosing reinforcement that will function well, and executing conducting gestures that will enhance the sound of the choir while also providing musical inspiration and clarity. If we could somehow get inside the mind of the experienced teacher during rehearsal, we would probably learn a lot more about the art of teaching than we could ever observe from within the ensemble. What you do from the podium during rehearsal certainly is important, but learning to think like a teacher is probably even more important to your success. Be curious about the inner workings of rehearsing as you also compile your list of practical rehearsal techniques and activities.

Every Rehearsal Is a Coup in Progress

One of the most important lessons you will learn when you are running a rehearsal by yourself is that your leadership will need to be established and maintained constantly throughout the rehearsal segment. Because of this, it can be stated that, "Every rehearsal is a *coup* in progress." The word "*coup*" comes from the French "*coup d'état*" meaning "a sudden decisive exercise of force in politics, especially the violent overthrow or alteration of an existing government by a small group."[1] While this is intended to be somewhat humorous to compare the overthrow of a government with a choir rehearsal, any experienced teacher will likely agree that the comparison is somewhat fair. Choirs are especially good at trying to take over the rehearsal, either subtly or overtly, and you will need to recognize when this is happening so that you can thwart the *coup* before it succeeds. Here are just a few of the predictable signs that the *coup* is in progress:

- **Students are not in their assigned seats:** If you have a seating plan and students do not follow it, they are sending a message to you that they are in charge. You, as the teacher, are the person who decides what is appropriate and what is not appropriate in your classroom. Any distractions that students create in the teaching environment can potentially derail the ensemble's progress. You will have to teach and reinforce both academic and social behavior to the students in a kind and consistent manner very frequently at first, and less frequently as they learn the norms of behavior in your classroom.

- **Students ask questions that are not really questions:** When students raise their hands to ask questions during rehearsal, we always want to respect their intention to pose important questions. For example, any question that clarifies confusing splits in the voice parts or misprints in the score can save you a lot of rehearsal time; we need to know when students are confused or when they are not sure of which line to read. Any question that saves time or clarifies confusion is not part of the *coup*, so you will need to use your intuition and field these questions. However, be on the lookout for the *coup* to start when you start to hear "questions that are not really questions" such as, "Should we be singing *forte* at the top of page 6?" This sounds like an easy question to answer; but presuming that the score is actually marked *forte* at the top of page 6, it is not a real question. This question would be

1 https://www.merriam-webster.com/dictionary/coup%20d'état

more clearly stated as, "I noticed from here in the choir that the *forte* on the top of page 6 is not happening, and I was wondering if you wouldn't mind changing your teaching sequence and rehearsal priorities so that you can address what I think is most important right now." Usually this kind of nonquestion will be asked by a well-meaning student who is a smart musician. When you do hear these kinds of statements, you can simply reply with something like, "Yes, everyone, ALL the marked dynamics should be observed, as well as the articulations. You never need my permission to read the music like musicians. Now back to top of page 3, second system, third measure where we are working on getting accurate starting notes after the solo."

- One solution for soliciting student input in an appropriate forum is to create a system of "Sticky Notes" in the rehearsal. Every student receives a single Sticky Note to keep in their folder, and when they hear something or want to communicate something to the conductor, they write it on the sticky note and hand it in on their way out of the rehearsal room. That way the teacher is still encouraging students to listen and think without allowing the *coup* to knock them off their lesson sequence. The teacher must be sure to answer each question by writing on the note and passing it back at the next rehearsal. Also, have plenty of new sticky notes available to replace the used ones.

- **The accompanist does not take your tempos or follow you:** If you are fortunate enough to have an accompanist, then you get to collaborate with another musician, which is great. You should always treat your keyboard collaborators with kindness and respect. Know, however, that an accompanist can take control of many of your rehearsal decisions if you allow it to happen. This is especially true when establishing a tempo and managing changing tempos, but this potential *coup* can include other musical decisions as well. You will know that the *coup* has succeeded when the students address the accompanist directly during your teaching sequence to ask for help, and then the accompanist ignores what you are doing with the choir and helps them. Most accompanists won't try to lead the rehearsal unless they sense that the conductor is not leading or is unable to lead. Be kind, but do your best to maintain your leadership role in front of the ensemble.

- **When the singing stops, the talking starts:** Virtually every choir talks during rehearsal to some extent, and talking is a normal part of human interaction. And every teacher has a "talking quotient" that represents the highest level of chatter that they think is permissible during rehearsal, with some teachers allowing more talking and others allowing less talking. But if you don't decide how much talking you will permit during rehearsal, then the choir members will decide for you…and the *coup* is on! It is very frustrating when the choir starts conversing as soon as the singing stops, especially if the director has to waste time refocusing the ensemble before the singing can start again. Every successful teacher develops rules and procedures for when and how much the choir can talk, and you will have to find your own successful approach as well. Just know that you can train the students to focus and stay below your talking quotient, but that it may take some time and a good deal of consistent reinforcement.

- **Students stop participating in class:** This may not sound like a *coup*, but when students choose to not engage fully in class activities, they are really telling you, "I will decide if I do this, not you." This is complicated for you as a leader because engaging the class is closely connected to the energy you bring to the room, the positive environment you create that makes it safe to fully participate, your attitude toward the ensemble, and many other things that affect your relationship with the students. As a general classroom management technique, you should focus on what is going well in the rehearsal, on the students that are participating appropriately, while ignoring behavior that isn't dangerous or doesn't interfere with learning. But when nonparticipation starts spreading, and when fewer and fewer students are engaged in your lesson, it is time to adjust the focus of your leadership and to teach all of your students that, "Everything we do, we do together."

By understanding the concept of the choir *coup d'état*, you will be able to recognize it when it starts to happen. Experienced teachers can maintain control of the rehearsal and thwart the *coup* while maintaining a positive approach and while working respectfully with all participants in the rehearsal. You can learn to do this too. Do your best to provide structure and consistent leadership, and be aware when others are making decisions that you, as the teacher, should be making.

RECAPITULATION

1. Preparing to run a rehearsal requires advanced planning to build your musicianship, score-study abilities, and conducting skills. Reflect on your relative feeling of preparation up to this point in the areas listed above as you think about being in charge of running a rehearsal. Also comment on the experience you already have directing a choir, if any.
2. The phrase "meet them where they are and make them better" is a good one for a teacher who values both process and product. Do you think you are naturally inclined to be more process oriented or

product oriented when it comes to working on musical projects? What evidence can you describe to support your opinion?

3. Teachers have to think of many things when they are teaching, and they have to make many quick decisions that may or may not be obvious to someone observing the teaching. What does the phrase "think like a teacher" mean to you? Do you think you have a natural inclination to think like a teacher? Why or why not?
4. Have you ever been in a choir rehearsal and then noticed a choir *coup d'état* in progress? Describe what happened and if the *coup* succeeded. If you have never noticed this happening, describe the feeling and rehearsal atmosphere of a rehearsal you have participated in or observed. Were students on task? Was the teacher 100% in charge? Describe your experience.

Warming Up the Choir

In order to maintain a consistent classroom environment, your rehearsals should always start and end on time, and so you need to be prepared and ready to begin the moment class starts. In most rehearsal situations, your rehearsal segment will begin with a choral warm up. Warming up the choir is a very important part of the rehearsal because it sets the momentum and tone for the rest of the daily time spent singing as an ensemble. While the warm up is a very important part of the rehearsal, it is also one of the least effectively implemented parts of the typical choral rehearsal. This is because we all tend to teach the way we were taught, and many of us grew up with and experienced countless examples of autopilot warm ups in our choir rehearsals. Let's explore the concept of the "autopilot" and how it can manifest in your choir rehearsal and warm ups.

- **The Choral Autopilot**: The term "autopilot" has been defined as "a system used to control the trajectory of an aircraft without constant 'hands-on' control by a human operator being required."[2] In other words, the autopilot system in a plane can fly the plane in a single direction until one of two things happens; either it runs into something like a mountain, or it runs out of fuel. The autopilot does not look to see where it is going, and unless a human being shuts the autopilot off and takes control of the aircraft, bad things will eventually happen. Choir members can also engage their personal autopilot when they sing without paying attention

2 https://en.wikipedia.org/wiki/Autopilot

and listening carefully to what is occurring in the moment. *Choral Autopilot* is the enemy of expressive, spontaneous, and creative music making in a choral ensemble; singers on autopilot will miss cues, cut-offs, tempo changes, expressive gestures from the conductor, and will sing without the necessary awareness of the sounds around them. As a choral educator, it will be your goal to engage your classes 100% of the time, and the autopilot will work against you unless you learn to implement some strategies to help your students shut it off. Your singers will go into autopilot whenever they are asked to do routine tasks that require no immediate thinking or sensory awareness. One trigger that can turn on autopilot is when the choir is asked to do any repetitive task such as clapping a steady pulse or stepping side to side or singing an ostinato (a repeated musical pattern). Once they have the pattern established, the mind will start to wander, and it will take a change in the pattern to bring them back to the present moment. As the teacher, you have to notice when the choir is going on autopilot so that you can appropriately reengage them in the music making or classroom activity.

- **Autopilot Warm Ups**: One way to address the autopilot problem is to minimize, as much as possible, repetitive activities that allow students to disengage and daydream. One of the most common "daydream starters" is the *autopilot warm up*. This type of warm up is extremely common in both the amateur and professional choral world, and one example can be seen here:

(sample autopilot warm up)

Anyone who has sung in a choir for even a short amount of time is familiar with this kind of warm up, and most people can sing these kinds of warm ups from memory without any real thought being applied in the process. In other words, "*Choral Autopilot*...ENGAGE!" Warm ups like this one, where the choir sings unison patterns moving up and down by half steps, usually accomplish very little musically. A five- to ten-minute warm up is not sufficient to "warm up" a voice adequately, and a singer who has been awake and using the voice normally throughout the day doesn't technically need a vocal warm up. Then why do we have our choirs sing these patterns on autopilot to start most every rehearsal? The most honest answer is probably "because that's what we have always done, and that's what *everybody* does." But if autopilot is the enemy of the engaged choir, why would we deliberately choose to start every rehearsal with an activity that encourages our students to sing repeating patterns without encouraging them to pay attention or listen carefully? There is nothing magical that happens during autopilot warm ups that gets the choir ready to suddenly focus and listen once the warm ups are done. Though to be fair, great choral singers learn how to get focused at the start of rehearsal regardless of the warm up structure. We must find a way to start the rehearsal off in a way that engages the choir in voice, mind, and body so that they can create habits of focus that prepare them to sing the literature and create compelling and transformative choral experiences.

➢ **Warm Ups that Turn Off the Autopilot**: If we believe that autopilot warm ups serve very little purpose to "warm up" the voice, and if they also encourage students to go on autopilot, we have to question if they are worth the time we give them in rehearsal. One way to address the autopilot problem is to create a new paradigm surrounding warm ups, one that addresses the whole singer. Warm ups can be a good use of instructional time if they can do at least these four things:

1. Encourage the choir to focus, think, move, sing, and listen
2. Teach the choir musical skills
3. Encourage each singer to be in *A Singing Frame of Mind*[3]
4. Set the stage for challenges they will encounter in the literature

To encourage the choir to focus, think, move, sing, and listen, we will need to have warm-up activities that do not have short, easily memorized, repeating patterns that turn on autopilot. Instead, we can incorporate group movement paired with singing patterns that constantly change to bring the choir's attention to the event happening in each present moment. We can still use all of the musical patterns from the autopilot warm ups, but in a different way. For example, the sample autopilot warm up (p. 128) can be modified so that the choir members "mirror" the teacher's conducting gestures as they sing, and the teacher can vary the

3 The term "Singing Frame of Mind" was coined by the author and describes the mental state of a prepared singer. The warm up is not intended to warm up the voice as much as it is intended to warm up the mind and awareness of the singer. The theory is that most singers enter the choir room distracted by various things in their personal life and environment, and they are not always ready to focus, to listen with intent, and to make music. Warm ups that turn off autopilot require the singer to focus on sound, sight, movement, and what their own voice feels and sounds like. This helps to bring the mind of the singer "into the rehearsal" and into the present moment. Furthermore, when the singer takes some time to center the voice, to breathe with an intentional and well-prepared singer's breath, to come into tonus (see footnote page 150), and to use the foundational singing techniques they will need in the literature, they become prepared to rehearse. The five to ten minutes of "warm up" becomes a transition from a "distracted frame of mind" into a prepared and "warmed up" *Singing Frame of Mind.*

tempo, place fermatas on various notes, and vary how long each note is held or cut off. Additionally, the teacher can use gestures to get dynamic and articulation differences in the singing. Here is one example of what this might be like. Compare this to the previous example:

Note in the sample autopilot example that the teacher would probably lead the warm up from the piano and remain in one tempo. But in the example above, the teacher would need to conduct from the podium so that the students can mirror the conducting gestures together. (Each 16th note would probably need its own gesture to make the fermatas and tempos clear to the choir.) If an accompanist is present, the piano could be used to reinforce the tonal center, but the examples can be sung *a cappella*, either with the choir audiating the new key, or with the teacher singing the new tonic starting note. This approach has several immediate advantages:

1. Students must pay attention constantly because there are no predictable patterns, tempos, or articulations.
2. The students must mirror the gestures of the teacher, requiring them to be engaged visually and kinesthetically.
3. The teacher is establishing a gestural language with the choir that can be used later on in the literature.
4. The teacher can see immediately which choir members are engaged and which ones are "tuned out," and can encourage everyone to participate fully.
5. The teacher can model appropriate posture, breath, cues, and cut-offs as well as the shaping of phrases within the warm up. The choir will learn appropriate habits by mirroring the teacher.
6. When the exercises are performed *a cappella*, the singers will be encouraged to tune more carefully without reference to the equally tempered piano, building their listening and tuning skills. If a tonal reference is needed for beginning singers, the piano can always be added.

This is only one example of an autopilot warm up being adapted to function as an engaging, worthwhile use of rehearsal time. This exercise helps to prepare the choir to be in a *Singing Frame of Mind*. There are endless variations that can be adapted from this approach, and the creative teacher can experiment to find new examples that function best for their own choirs. It is important to note that the use of autopilot warm ups can be perfectly appropriate some of the time depending on the rehearsal schedule of the choir and the objectives of the rehearsal. But the concept of the autopilot warm up as the only kind of warm up, and as a default approach to begin every rehearsal, needs to be honestly evaluated for its actual function and usefulness. Click the icon "Dig Deeper" to explore an excellent book called *Choral Cantabile*.

Sample Warm-Up Sequence

The autopilot-busting warm-up adaption in the previous section is an approach that can help you to create a varied, engaging, and educational warm-up segment. In order to make your warm ups even more educationally sound and interesting, you will need to consider creating an entire "warm-up sequence" that combines different segments. These segments should change throughout the warm up and should teach and reinforce a variety of musical skills. Here is an example of a warm-up sequence that can be used as a template to create new sequences.[4] Each section is chosen for its function in the warm up, and you can skip sections or add more as time allows in your rehearsal schedule. The logic in the sequence (and any adaptions you create) is to start with physical movement to focus the choir and turn off autopilot right away and then to sing with intention in a limited range before moving to higher and lower ranges with larger leaps.

1. **Mirroring:** The teacher faces the choir and moves, stretches, and gestures while the choir "mirrors" those gestures. If the conductor raises the right hand, the choir will raise their left hand. Do this exercise until everyone in the room is anticipating and watching and moving in unison. Vary the pattern of movements continuously.

2. **Clap/Step:** The teacher steps side to side in a steady rhythm. For example: left foot steps to the left and right foot steps to the left, then right foot steps right and left foot steps right. Keep a steady pulse and have the choir mirror the movements. Begin to hold up different numbers of fingers to indicate how many claps the choir will perform on each side. For example, step left with the left foot while holding up the index finger on each hand, and then as the right foot joins the left, clap

4 Some of these warm ups were adapted from the excellent DVD "*Daily Workout for a Beautiful Voice*" by Charlotte Adams. https://sbmp.com/DVD2.php?CatalogNumber=583

once. Then as the right foot steps to the right, maybe hold up two fingers on each hand to indicate two claps as the left foot joins the right. The claps should be subdivisions of the stepping pulse. Vary the number of claps on each side between one and four and keep the choir watching, engaged, and on task. Also use two fists to indicate no claps.

3. **Hum on Vowels: u, o, a, eh, i with Movement:** Starting on a middle-range note like G, have the choir hum the pitch while you have them mirror your gestures. You should demonstrate good posture, movements that expand the space in the mouth and resonators, and any gesture that helps them sing freely and consistently on the pitch. Move up and down by half or whole steps. Move to an "u" vowel (like the word "food") as they circle the lips with the index finger. Move back to a hum. Change the pitch up or down. Move to an "o" vowel (like the word "go") as they circle the whole face with the whole hand. Work in all the vowels this way, including "a" (as in "father") using a vertical hand position in front of the mouth, the "eh" vowel (like the word "set") using the thumb and index finger near the corners of the mouth, and the "ee" vowel (like the word "see") using two extended index fingers by the sides of the mouth like "goal posts." Finally, sing all vowels using the gestures without returning to the hum.

4. **Hiss with Piano (C-D):** Instruct the choir to make a short hiss connected to the abdominal area with a short bust of air, like a wet finger on a hot stove. Have them do it on a cue consisting of holding your left palm up while the right index finger touches it from above, cuing the hiss. When the hiss is strong and unified, play the piano exercise below as they hiss. The hissing should be half in rhythmic value as it is performed, so that it is on every beat, then on every 8th note subdivision, and then to 16th notes. At the end, have each choir member sustain the hiss and cut themselves off with a "conductor's gesture" when they run out of breath.

5. **Vocal Glissandi**: Instruct the chorus to hold an imaginary tennis ball in one hand. Sing a unison (or octave) note on any vowel (G works for all voices). Pretend to "throw" the ball up as the chorus does an ascending vocal glissando, returning to the starting pitch as the ball "lands" back in the hand. Eventually, throw it higher and drop it too! Be sure the choir members keep the chin level, rather than "looking up" at the ball as it is thrown in the air. If you move one step to your left to catch the ball, the chorus should adjust the starting pitch down a half step on the

"catch." Likewise, when you move back to your starting position, the pitch should move back to your first starting pitch, and if you move to the right from the starting position, have them "catch" the ball up a half step. Be sure that the larynx remains as low as possible on the upward glissandi by having the choir members touch one finger to the front of the neck on the Adam's apple.

6. **Vocal Echoing:** The teacher sings random patterns and the chorus echoes them back as well as they can. Also include breathing hisses, bubbling, high and low notes, and articulation patterns of "S, T, K, & P." Use an easy production with lots of falsetto and support.

7. **On 1 & 1 (Clap-Mind Exercise):** Instruct the choir to clap on the number you call out, and then you should count to the number as they clap. At first, count out loud all the way to the number. For example, you will say "On 3 and 1&2&3" and the choir members should clap on three. Don't clap yourself or they will only watch your gesture for the cue. Vary the tempo of the exercise, and call out different numbers as well. If they catch on quickly, start counting out loud, but then finish the count silently. For example, you can say "On 6 and 1&2&3&......." and see if they can audiate the pulse and still clap together. For another challenge, have them clap the off beats. You would say "On the and of 5, and 1&2&3&4&5&." If they are good with rhythm, challenge them to clap the second and fourth subdivisions of the 16th note subdivisions as well.

8. **Descending 5:** Have the chorus sing unison vowels on the descending five-note pattern (5-4-3-2-1) and hold various notes according to your gestures. Have them mirror your conducting. Encourage good breathing, posture, tone, and resonance with verbal approval. Keep them off autopilot by changing your gestures constantly. Move up and down by half steps.

9. **"Sing a Little" Exercise:** Have the choir sing the exercise below. Then sing it again and ask them to be "opera conductors" as they sing, encouraging them to gesture and support the singing with sweeping movements. Move up by half steps. Try the exercise a cappella. It also works as a round, with each section coming in on beat 1.

10. **Chordal Exercise:** The graphic notation below represents two exercises that can be done in this warm up. The numbers represent the scale degrees. Have each section sing on a neutral syllable such as "ah" or "oh," with altos and basses on the root of a major chord, the tenors on the 5th, and the sopranos on the 3rd. The arrows represent movement by half steps. Play with dynamics, various vowels, vowel shapes, careful intonation, and a sustained and spinning tone quality.

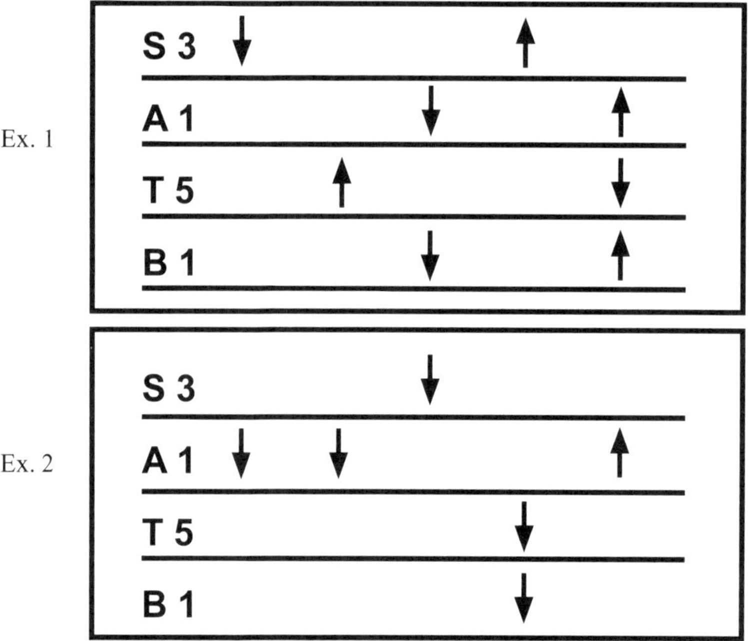

11. **"I Love to Sing" Exercise:** Use group movement to keep people engaged, and feel free to hold random words in this exercise. You can also refer back to the vowel gestures from warm up number three (above). Go high enough to help warm up the sopranos and tenors. Encourage the altos and basses to sing lightly in head voice as high as they can.

12. **Hah, Va, Va, Va, Va, Va:** For this range-extending exercise, you will not pause on any pitch. Start in A-major and play a descending five-note pattern followed by a half-step lift as the choir breathes. Singers will be forced to start in head voice because of the choice of key. Have the choir perform a gesture with both hands near the front of the face, making small circles that "wipe away tension." The movement can best be described as "fanning the face lightly." This is an autopilot exercise because we do not want the singers to think about how high they are singing. Vocalize them up to at least high C.

Used by permission of Santa Barbara Music Publishing, publisher of Daily Workout for A Beautiful Voice.

11. **Bum Biddly Bum:** This is a lower-range extender. Instruct singers to sit down when the lowest note is too low for their voice. Have them sing with a gesture that starts with one palm cupped horizontally over the other in front of the torso, and then switches positions on beat 3 and then on 1 of the next measure. On the fermata, arms hang to the sides and make small circles toward the ground. Close to the "M" on the fermata and ask the singers to chew and engage the mask and nose. Have them open to a vowel on the final note as it gets lower. Clap for the few remaining people standing at the end. Your warm-up sequence is complete and it has been fun and engaging!

RECAPITULATION

1. Think about your choir or ensemble experience in the past. Do you remember singing exclusively autopilot warm ups, or did your teacher mix in other kinds of warm ups too? How engaged, on average, do you think your "autopilot" behavior was? Describe what you remember from your past, including a few examples of specific warm ups if you can.
2. Using the "Sample Warm-Up Sequence" (above), choose three warm ups and write variations on each one. The focus and general activities can be very similar, but try to change and adapt each one slightly to be a "new" warm up.
3. Gather some willing participants and teach your "new" warm ups to them as if they were your choir. Try to keep them constantly engaged and off of autopilot. Ask for their feedback and/or record your teaching segment to make your own self-assessment.

Effective Rehearsal Sequences: Whole-Part-Whole

When you are finally at the point that you have done your best advanced preparation and you are about to rehearse the choir on a piece of literature, now what do you do? The simple answer would seem to be "we will sing the music and rehearse." And while that is technically true, that statement doesn't tell you anything about *how* to rehearse or the steps that can add up to effective rehearsing. If you have created a detailed lesson plan, then you already have a road map for what you want to do and what you want to achieve in the rehearsal. Your plan, however, can't always predict what the choir will do on a particular day and on any given piece. You may, for example, have a step in your plan to "sing page 5 and get the SA *forte* balanced with the TB *mezzo piano*." But while you might be able to predict that there will probably be balance issues on page 5, it is a mistake to assume that there will be a problem until you hear the choir sing page 5. For this reason, a good way to start rehearsing any piece of literature is with the **Whole-Part-Whole** teaching sequence. Here is how it works:

1. Following your lesson plan, have the choir take out a piece of literature that you want to rehearse.
2. Have the choir sing through the **Whole** piece from beginning to end as well as they can without stopping. (You can also sing a major section of a larger piece if that makes more sense.) Whenever possible, let

this run-through be at the performance tempo.

3. Listen to what they do musically in relation to what you predicted they would do in your pre-planning, and then decide if your plan is relevant and pinpointed to what the choir actually needs to work on *right now*. In other words, if there are balance issues on page 5, work according to your plan on page 5. But if they sing page 5 with good dynamic balance, don't execute that part of your plan. Focus on other things you hear that are also in your plan and that require attention, or focus on new things that you hear that are bigger issues.
4. Once you have let them sing the whole piece (or a significant section that you want to focus on), and once you have decided what to work on based on your plan compared to what you hear, it is time to work on smaller sections of the song. During this segment, you can stop and start the choir frequently, slow the tempo down, hear sections sing alone or in duets or trios, and experience the smaller **Parts** of the work.
5. After you have worked on the smaller sections of the piece and have made progress according to your plan objectives, you will need to save enough time in your plan for another run of the **Whole** piece (or section) at the end of the sequence.

The Whole-Part-Whole teaching sequence has important advantages to you as a teacher, and to the choir as an ensemble. For the choir, they get to experience the entire piece twice in one rehearsal, and they start building an understanding and appreciation for the musical construction of the work in real time. They will be challenged to sight read the music, especially in the early learning stages of the notes and rhythms; when a choir is expected to get "as much as they can" when sight reading, over time they become better sight readers. The choir will also be able to memorize the music much more quickly and securely when they have sung through the whole piece numerous times. Additionally, musical transitions and issues of vocal endurance that might come up in a concert performance become more obvious when the choir is asked to sing the whole piece through without stopping in rehearsals. For the teacher, this sequence allows you to evaluate where the choir is on *that day*, and to change your plan if the choir doesn't need what you thought they would need. If you don't run the "whole" and instead choose to start at a section that wasn't working in the last rehearsal (and immediately working on "the parts"), you send a message to the choir that you didn't expect them to work and improve between rehearsals. Sometimes musical problems can be solved by the choir members between rehearsals without you, so why assume that the problems will persist? You need to listen and evaluate and confirm that your plan will be an efficient use of your rehearsal time, and letting the choir sing is the best way to accomplish this. Conducting the whole work without stopping is also good practice for you as a conductor, and like the choir, you will gain insight into how to manage transitions while you also memorize your cues and cut-offs more securely. One of the biggest advantages to this teaching sequence is the fact that your rehearsal will have more uninterrupted singing than if you always worked the "parts" all the time. Choirs love to sing and perform, and you can help them love the music more when they have a chance to sing the music more.

The opposite of the Whole-Part-Whole approach, just to create a contrasting example for you, is the "front-to-back, stop when necessary" approach. In this approach, the choir starts singing at the beginning of the piece and then the conductor stops them as soon as there is a problem of *any* kind. With this approach, it is possible to work on just a few measures for the whole rehearsal segment, trying to make, say, the first eight measures "perfect." While this can certainly make those first eight bars sound very good (depending on the efficiency and effectiveness of the teaching), a choir that hasn't learned to transfer what they accomplished in the first eight bars to the rest of the piece will need to spend the next rehearsal on the next eight bars, and so on. The next time you attend a choral festival or concert with many different choirs of various abilities, see if you spot this teaching method as it can manifest in a live concert. How will you know? You will know when the first third of the piece is amazing, the second third of the piece is just OK, and the last third of the piece barely holds together.

Effective Rehearsal Sequences: Teaching Units

A rehearsal can be described as effective when 1) the goals and objectives of the rehearsal plan have been met, when 2) the choir has learned new skills or refined previously learned skills, and when 3) the choir sings the literature better because of the rehearsal experience. But some rehearsals do not meet any of these three criteria, and it is actually possible to run a rehearsal without teaching anything to the choir or making the choir sound better on the literature. How is this possible? This is possible when the conductor takes on the role of a "director of traffic," rather than the role of a teacher. In this type of rehearsal, the director just tells the choir what piece to sing, where to stop and start, and what they are doing wrong. The choir might be enjoying the singing, and there may even be a good amount of time spent singing in the rehearsal; but a "directing traffic" rehearsal is not going to be as effective as a rehearsal that implements a *sequenced* teaching approach. A sequenced approach to teaching implies that every activity the teacher initiates during the lesson is done for a specific reason, in a specific order, and for a specific outcome. A highly effective, sequenced teaching approach can engage the choir in a way that focuses their attention, guides their efforts, and gives them immediate and specific feedback about their performance results.

One very effective and sequenced teaching approach utilizes something we will call "Teaching Units."[5] Teaching Units are mini cycles of instruction that have clear goals that are communicated to the choir and clear feedback statements that let the choir know the extent to which the goals were achieved. Teaching Units are best implemented in the "Parts" of the "Whole-Part-Whole" sequence outlined earlier. Here is how to use this type of sequence in your teaching:

1. Based on your lesson plan and your listening and evaluation of what the choir did during the "Whole" segment, choose a single and *specific* aspect of the choir's performance to improve as you momentarily ignore everything else. In this case the word "specific" is important because if you are too general, or if you choose more than one thing, the choir won't know on what to focus.
2. Communicate to the choir, as quickly and clearly as possible, what they should focus on to make the desired improvement.
3. Start the choir in a place that allows them to make the improvements you have suggested.
4. As they sing, listen to determine if you hear a difference. The wording in your mind might be similar to one of the following statements:
    a. "Yes, that was improved, and we can move on to something else."
    b. "Yes, that was improved, but we can do better if we try again."
    c. "No, that wasn't better. We need to refocus and try again."
    d. "No, that wasn't better, and we need to move on to something else."
5. Let the choir sing until you decide what you will say about how well they achieved (or didn't achieve) the desired improvement.
6. Stop the choir and communicate clearly and specifically how they did. Be sure to reference the chosen goal, and include a verbal descriptor telling them the extent to which they achieved the goal.
7. Based on the choir's improvement (or lack of improvement), refocus the choir on the same goal or give them a new goal. When refocusing on the same goal, give them a slightly new way to approach the improvement, if you can; this is a good time to pair the intended improvement with an accompanying group gesture to help create a more distinct difference in the singing.[6]

---

5 The term "Teaching Units" is unique to this textbook and was coined by the author, but this concept and approach has been referred to as "closing the loop" in educational pedagogy and business management. "Metaphorically, closing the loop means that the person who issued the instruction gets a report on the outcome. The instruction goes out, things get done, and a report comes back to the person who issued the instruction." https://english.stackexchange.com/questions/301527/meaning-of-phrase-to-close-the-loop-on-this

6 Group movement is an excellent way to engage the choir, and to bring attention to the connection between gesture and expressive sound. Group movement will normally magnify the outcome of a goal, as long as the gestures are compatible with the intended goals. https://english.stackexchange.com/questions/301527/meaning-of-phrase-to-close-the-loop-on-this

8. Repeat the sequence as time allows during the "Parts" part of the rehearsal on that piece.
9. Run the piece (or section) when rehearsal time is running out for that song, possibly summarizing the improvements that were made in the rehearsal segment before you sing. Additionally, challenge the choir to keep these improvements in place during the run of the "Whole."
10. After the run of the "Whole" tell the choir how they did, and if you thought they made a noticeable and positive improvement from the first run of the "Whole" to the second run of the "Whole." Celebrate the progress in some way.

When you learn to incorporate Teaching Units into your rehearsal pedagogy, you will find that your rehearsals are focused, productive, and that the choir will retain what you taught them much of the time. This approach can also aid your ability to teach anything, not just music. The power of this approach is rooted in the simplicity of the sequence: 1. You give the students a goal for improvement. 2. They focus together to meet the goal. 3. You decide if they met it. 4. You tell them specifically how they did. And while this seems infinitely simple, doing it well is an art, and even experienced teachers don't always succeed in creating complete and productive Teaching Units. Let's clarify the Teaching Unit sequence one more way so that we can refer to it more easily, by specific "steps:"

THE TEACHING-UNIT SEQUENCE

Step One: Instruct (communicate a goal for improvement).
Step Two: Get the choir singing.
Step Three: Evaluate the choir's relative achievement of the goal (as they sing and as you conduct).
Step Four: Give immediate and specific feedback about how well they met the Step One goal.

Now that you are familiar with this teaching sequence, you may notice it working (or not working) in choir rehearsals that you observe or participate in. Here are a few of the predictable breakdowns of this approach when not administered effectively:

- **Too much time spent on Step One:** This happens when the teacher communicates the goal for improvement with too many words. In most cases a Step One can be completed in *five seconds or less.* All the choir needs to know is what the goal is and where to start singing. Extended Step Ones run the risk of losing the attention and focus of the choir and stalling the pace of the teaching. Step One is not an opportunity to tell the choir everything you know about the piece or everything they need to focus upon during the rehearsal. Instead, the teacher must learn to practice "selective ignoring" as a teaching tool. Choose *one* thing that you want to improve and momentarily ignore the rest. If you choose well, you might even solve several problems with one Teaching-Unit sequence; for example, if singing under the pitch is a problem, and the choir is also taking shallow, high breaths as they prepare to sing, addressing the breath may also solve the pitch problems.

- **Too many Step-One goals at the same time:** This happens when the teacher wants to address several different goals at the same time in the same Teaching Unit. The problem with this is that people are not normally able to concentrate on more than one thing at a time; even if you tell them to concentrate on three things, they will only focus on one...or they will try to multitask their attention, switching between each thing quickly. This "split of focus" will affect the desired achievement of all three goals, and the teacher has no way of determining who was focused on which of the three goals. Furthermore, the teacher also has to multitask in order to complete Step Four with meaning and specificity, and this is not easy to do with complete accuracy. The only exception to the "give only one Step One" rule is when the conductor gives a different Step One to different parts of the choir. For example, "sopranos and altos, let's sing higher to the tonal center in measures 44–52, and tenors and basses, let's make the low fifths louder than mezzo piano this time." In this example, the teacher must multitask, but each choir member has a single goal.

- **Step Ones that don't communicate a clear goal:** When a Step One is communicated to the choir, it must inform them exactly what to improve during the next repetition of singing. This is the main fault of the conductor who is a "director of traffic" rather than a teacher; every Step One is *where to start*, but not *what to improve*. If you don't clearly articulate what they should do to improve, you can't tell them if they did it later in Step Four.

- **Step Twos that are inefficient:** Starting the choir after a concise Step One seems easy enough, yet time is wasted in many rehearsals clarifying where the choir is supposed to start singing. Breakdowns in Step Two can be caused when the teacher uses text as a navigation tool, especially when there is a repeating text such as "*alleluia*." Sometimes a conductor will assume that everyone is looking at the same measure as they are and say something like, "Let's start right there," or, "Right after the *forte*." You can refine your Step Twos by having all singers number every measure in their music; this way you can simply say "measure 45, beat 1, everyone." But there are some times when your choir won't have the measure numbers written in, or you might not want them to write them in. The best way to work in this scenario is to give directions from big to small (page/system/measure/beat) and to tell them what they need to know to start singing, such as "I'll give you one measure...one, two, ready, sing." This seems like a lot at first, but it will become easy to say quickly, and the choir will be able to follow you as they navigate the music with their eyes. An example of a Step One/Step Two combination statement might be, "Let's start at the top of page 8, first system, second measure, beat 3, and we are going for crisper diction. I'll give you two beats." Another Step Two tip is to train your choir that you will always be starting in the same place if you don't say to start in a new place. If this functions well, then it really saves time, but if the choir is lost or unfocused, it may be more efficient to use the page/system/measure/beat approach.

- **Step Threes that don't happen in time:** In Step Three the conductor is listening to the choir perform to evaluate the extent to which they achieve the goal for improvement in Step One. Focused listening takes practice, and sometimes the choir will finish singing a segment of the music and stop before the teacher can reach a conclusion about their Step One achievement. In some cases, the teacher will be distracted by another problem with the performance and will forget about the active Step One that they should be evaluating. With practice, the teacher can develop consistent focus and listening skills to keep the Step Three evaluations on point and completed in time.

- **Step Fours that are non-existent:** To be effective, Step Four must immediately follow Step Three as soon as the choir stops singing. But of all the steps in this sequence, it is Step Four that tends to get forgotten or skipped. There are many possible reasons for this. Some teachers feel that if they say nothing, the choir "will just know" that they achieved the goal. The thinking here is, "If I didn't say it was wrong, then they know it was right." But saying *nothing* does not function as accurate and specific feedback, even if it is intended to suggest some sort of ensemble approval. Another Step Four breakdown happens when the teacher hears the goal achieved in Step Three and moves on without telling the choir, skipping to a new Step One without "closing the loop" with a Step Four.

- **Step Fours that do not adequately address Step One:** It is common, even for experienced teachers, to deliver Step Four feedback that is not specifically related to the goal in Step One. One way this can manifest is when the teacher simply uses the word "good" as a Step Four. "Good" does not give enough information to the choir regarding the extent to which they achieved the goal set forth in Step One. Furthermore, unless the choir achieved the goal at a high level, "good" really functions as approval error (saying they did a good job when they clearly did not). Any word or words that do not communicate specific feedback about Step One are similarly ineffective, such as "OK," "alright," and "great," though these are better than saying nothing at all in most cases. Another common Step Four mistake happens when specific feedback is given to the choir that is new and unrelated to the active Step One that they were working on. An example of this might be asking for *staccato* articulation in Step One and then telling the choir that the dynamics were incorrect in Step Four while failing to provide any feedback on the *staccato* articulation.

The Teaching-Unit sequence of rehearsing is simple to understand, and beginning teachers will most certainly need time to practice creating and completing meaningful Teaching Units with real classes. When this technique is delivered expertly, consistently, and effectively, the class will be engaged and focused, and the pace of the rehearsal will be fast and productive. Students will be constantly trying to achieve a single goal at a time, knowing that the teacher will let them know if they did it or not, and knowing that they will receive approval or disapproval in each Step Four. Well-structured Teaching Units help the choir retain the progress that is made by revisiting and reinforcing the concepts focused on in Step One. Another collateral benefit of this technique is that the choir members will start to listen more carefully during Step Three as they begin to predict what the teacher will say in Step Four. This awareness and increased listening can raise the artistic level of the choir in subtle but significant ways.

Each person who incorporates this technique into their teaching pedagogy will struggle with some steps and find ease in others. For some, Step One will be easy as they pick a goal for improvement, communicate it quickly and clearly, and get the choir singing immediately. Others will ramble on and on, searching for the right words to frame the goal for the choir. Still others will get completely distracted and go on and on talking about things that are not related to establishing a clear Step One. For some, starting the choir in Step Two will be a breeze; for others, they will need to work on the language and pace of getting the choir singing quickly. In Step Three, some will easily hear what the choir is doing while others will experience a common phenomenon (that most new teachers experience to some degree) where it seems like you don't hear *anything*. With practice, of course, you get better and better at listening to what is happening in real time. Finally, some people will easily and naturally find the words to create rich, specific, and meaningful Step Four Feedback while others will struggle to find words that connect to Step One or will forget what Step One was by the time Step Four arrives. There is an art to teaching, and there is an art to using Teaching Units masterfully too. Work to improve the things that are a struggle, and celebrate the things you already do well.

Experienced as well as beginning teachers, if they lack finesse on one of the Teaching-Unit Steps, will often need to work on Step Four. For this reason, we will examine in more detail some different kinds of Step Fours that can be used to communicate feedback to the choir. There are three kinds we will classify: The Unrelated Step Four, The Complete Step Four, and The Rich Step Four.

1. The Unrelated Step Four

- This Step Four was mentioned earlier, but it happens any time that there is no Step Four or when Step Four does not connect to Step One clearly and specifically. Here are a few examples of Unrelated Step Four Feedback:
  - Step One: *"On page 5, first system, second measure, instead of a high quick breath, let's all take a whole beat to take a lower, fuller breath."*
    - Step Four: (no response, just a new Step One)
    - Step Four: *"The vowel needs to be on the beat, before the consonant."*
    - Step Four: *"Good!"*
    - Step Four: *"You guys really sound great."*

2. The Complete Step Four

- This Step Four takes the language of Step One and restates it to the choir to reinforce what the goal was and to communicate specifically how well they achieved the goal. It is important to remember that Step Four should not be approving if the choir did not make progress toward the goal. Also, words like *"perfect"* run the risk of creating approval error, and phrases like *"that was better"* and *"much improved"* are more likely to be more accurate and function as pinpointed feedback. Here are a few examples of The Complete Step Four Feedback:
  - Step One: *"On page 5, first system, second measure, instead of a high quick breath, let's all take a whole beat to take a lower, fuller breath."*
    - Step Four: *"Yes, that breath could still be lower and fuller, but it was much improved."*
    - Step Four: *"I'm not sure we all remembered to prepare that breath lower and fuller."*
    - Step Four: *"Thanks for preparing that breath more fully. It was much lower and prepared."*
    - *"Nope, that was not a low full breath."*

3. The Rich Step Four

- This type of Step Four not only "completes the loop" but also adds a dimension of "why" the Step One goal is important. It helps the choir lock in not just *what* to retain, but *why* it is in their best interest to retain it. There is an Art to creating Rich Step

Fours, and as soon as you feel comfortable with your ability to deliver Complete Step Fours, you can then focus on creating Rich Step Fours. The Rich Step Four doesn't always restate Step One like a Complete Step Four does, but it nonetheless tells the choir how well they achieved the goal in Step One. Here are a few examples of Rich Step Four Feedback:

- Step One: *"On page 5, first system, second measure, instead of a high quick breath, let's all take a whole beat to take a lower, fuller breath."*
    - Step Four: *"Wow, when you prepare your breath that early, the sound is way more beautiful."*
    - Step Four: *"If you prepare every breath like that, our whole performance will rise to a new level. Well done."*
    - Step Four: *"I don't think I heard your tone improve because of the breath. Let's try again."*
    - Step Four: *"Yes, thank you! The audience will love the way we sound when we prepare every breathe like this."*

Because teaching is an Art, there is no way to determine ahead of time how what you do and what you say when you are in front of a class will function for the students. Completing Step Fours will generally function better for student learning than omitting Step Fours, but how you choose to complete them depends on the class, your established rapport, and your style of teaching. For example, you don't always need to speak during Step Four. If you teach consistently with clear Step One goals your students will become habituated to work and focus during each Teaching-Unit. It is possible that a smile or a nod or a "thumbs up" can function as a complete Step Four when the choir is looking for it and when you have been delivering rich Step Fours in your baseline teaching approach. What matters most is that the students are doing more than just singing; if they are also self-aware, thinking, listening, and growing as musicians, then your teaching is having a true and lasting impact.

RECAPITULATION

1. In your experience in musical ensembles, have you ever noticed the Whole-Part-Whole teaching sequence? If yes, then describe the ensemble, the teacher, and what you remember about your experience in those rehearsals. Did you find it to be an effective technique as a choir member? Why or why not? If you don't recall that technique being used in ensembles you were in, describe a teaching approach you experienced. What sequence was used as far as you can remember? Was it engaging and effective in your opinion? Why or why not?

2. The Teaching-Unit sequence, once you study it, is obvious and easy to observe during any choir rehearsal. But before you are aware of the sequence, you might not notice all the steps or notice when steps are missing. Comment on your own awareness of this technique prior to reading this chapter. Did you already have awareness of what complete Teaching Units are, or is this new information for you? How might this affect your teaching and how much effort do think it will take for you to be able to integrate this technique into your own approach?

3. While the Teaching-Units sequence has been introduced in relation to the choir rehearsal, do you think it could also be used in other teaching environments? Describe two teaching scenarios where this teaching sequence could also be highly effective, in your opinion: one in a music lesson or class and one in a non-music lesson or class.

4. Write a lesson plan to teach something that is NOT music related such as putting on nail polish, making a bracelet, throwing a Frisbee, making a paper airplane, or something else relatively simple. In your task analysis of steps, think about how you might give Step Four Feedback to the person you could be teaching. If you can, teach your lesson plan to someone as you record yourself. When you are done, watch the video and see if you completed many Teaching Units. To be complete, they must have clear Step Ones, Twos, Threes, and Fours.

Effective Rehearsal Sequences: Leading from the Podium

Your skill and effectiveness as a choral teacher and a rehearsal conductor will need to be developed with time and practice in front of real choirs. In fact, it is an appropriate transfer to compare conducting a choir to playing an instrument; virtually no one can pick up an instrument that they have never played before and immediately demonstrate proficiency on it. While a young child can start learning the violin at a very early age and play really well by middle school or high school, the choir as an "instrument" is not available to most people to practice with until they reach adulthood and are studying to be choral directors. With that understanding, it is alright to acknowledge that you may be starting this new "instrument" well after you have become proficient on voice or piano, with many hours of practice on those instruments; you should be patient with yourself and know that you will make some mistakes and that you will have some growing pains in the process. It can be humbling to feel like a beginner again in your musical life, but you will be surprised how much progress you can make and how much you can grow with good planning, focus, and conscious practice.

When you are beginning to assume the role of a choral conductor and educator with real students, all of your musical and pedagogical training must be drawn upon at the same time. Everything you have learned will coalesce in one place, at the same time:

- You will draw upon your musicianship, music theory, and ear-training skills.
- You will use your conducting skills.
- You will use your score-marking skills.
- You will use your literature knowledge and programming skills to select music for a concert program.
- You will use your lesson-planning skills to structure your rehearsal.
- You will use your classroom-management skills to create a positive and consistent classroom learning and teaching environment.
- You will use your piano skills.
- You will use your leadership skills to inspire your students.
- You will use your singing skills to model for your students.
- You will use your organizational skills to manage various classroom materials.
- You will use your teaching and rehearsal skills to meet students where they are and to make them better.

The conductor's podium is truly an *authentic* learning environment for the emerging choral music educator.[7] You will need everything you have learned, and anything that you still need to work on will become apparent to you. The podium is a place where *Conscious Incompetence* in yourself can be discovered. When you feel like you failed at something, just give yourself a break and say, "Well, OK then, another opportunity for me to grow and be open to learning."[8]

As has been discussed earlier, your effectiveness in a rehearsal is less about what you *do* and more about how you *think*. There is much more to think about in the rehearsal than song order and Teaching-Unit sequences; you have to be aware of every student in the room and how they are engaging with the teaching, and you have to be continuously looking for signs of the "*coup d'état*" so that you can keep control of the rehearsal pacing and teaching sequences. You must also be listening to *everything* while at the same time prioritizing only *one thing* as you selectively ignore the rest. You may also need

7 When learning and assessment are termed "authentic," this means that skills and knowledge are being applied in real-life contexts and situations. https://www.lexialearning.com/blog/creating-authentic-learning-experiences-literacy-classroom

8 See Chapter 1, "The Learning Cycle" for a better understanding of this term.

to think about your conducting patterns and gestures while you are teaching, or your attention might need to be consumed by your piano-playing technique if you are an emerging pianist. You will learn to become a master multitasker, managing these and many other aspects of the rehearsal all at the same time. Because this can seem overwhelming, and because you will need practice to get your stride, it can be helpful to boil all of this down into several of the most important aspects on which to focus. If you can keep only these five guidelines in the forefront of your teaching, you will find the most success early on.

Five Guidelines to Focus On in Your First Teaching Experiences

1) **Know your rehearsal/lesson plan:** If you have to pause and figure out what you wrote in your rehearsal plan, the class will immediately go off task and start talking. Print it out and have it at your side, but know it so well that you only need to refer to it occasionally.

2) **Engage everyone in the class all the time:** Every minute of your rehearsal, including transitions, represents your available instructional time. Find ways to have every section doing *something* all the time. The best way to stop a behavior is to replace it with another, better, behavior. When kids have time with nothing to do, they quickly find something to do…and usually it's talking.

3) **As soon as the singing stops, immediately deliver your Step Four Feedback and your next Step One:** The pause between when the choir stops singing and the teacher starts instructing is critical to the rehearsal pacing and classroom management. You have only about *two to three seconds* to pause and think, and then you need to regain the student's attention and keep instructing. Always try to know what you will say *before* you stop the choir.

4) **Teach multi-modally**: Your teaching will be most effective when you provide visual, aural, and kinesthetic teaching sequences. Model for the choir occasionally, have them sing a lot, have them stand and sit frequently, and have them move (using group gestures) as they sing, using the body to inspire the voice. Engaging their eyes, ears, and bodies will help them to learn and to stay involved in the rehearsal activities.

5) **Don't apologize for your mistakes:** You are going to make some mistakes. If you lose the inner game and start to say you are sorry to the choir over and over, they will begin to feel bad for you and your leadership may be diminished. Instead, make

light of mistakes and say something like, "Oops, that's my first mistake of the year!" When you say that line again later, it may begin to function as a benign joke, and the third time you say it, they will begin to catch on that you are making fun of your own mistakes. We all make mistakes, so see if you can have fun in the process too.

These guidelines are simple, yet powerful. If you can be prepared with a great rehearsal plan, ready to engage the choir all of the time, prepared to deliver Teaching Units with little or no down time, ready to challenge the students to sing, listen, watch, and move with intention, and determined to stay confident in your ability to lead them with purpose, you will be ready to start your journey as a choral education professional. Be brave and be willing to try, fail, and to succeed. As an open learner, you will do well to remember that the most effective teachers are willing to grow when they acknowledge that they can be more than they are. Be your best. Applaud your strengths as well as your faults...and be willing to grow.

Effective Rehearsal Sequences: Conceptual Teaching Strategies

When you create your lesson plans and rehearsal sequences, you will need to think about specific objectives for each piece of literature that your students are preparing. But there are also some sequences that can be considered more general, conceptual approaches that can be applied to many different pieces across all of your literature. These "concept rules" can be taught and reinforced at most any time, and these ideas, when applied, can address a wide array of singing techniques and performance skills.

Twenty-Five Conceptual Strategies for Building Skills While Rehearsing the Choir

1. **Listen Louder than You Sing**: The concept of "listening louder" can help any choir to be more aware of the sounds around them. When the choir sings louder than it is listening, the sound will be less unified and probably less blended than when the choir is listening with good sensitivity.

2. **Never Louder than Beautiful**: The concept of never singing louder than beautiful can help choirs who push the voice in loud dynamics without proper technique. If the voices become less beautiful at the louder dynamics, then the choir must learn to support the volume required with a more supported breath and a release of glottal tension.

3. **The Unwritten Dynamic**: Musical scores are filled with lots of information for the choral musician including dynamics, articulations, notes, rhythms, text, and the like. But if the score contained the level of detail required to create a compelling musical performance, it would be filled with markings that would almost obscure the page. The concept of the unwritten dynamic is that any long note (longer than the primary pulse) must crescendo or decrescendo, even if the dynamic is not written in the score.

4. **Permission to Be Expressive**: This concept addresses the idea that every marking in the score is important and that every opportunity to be expressive should be realized. If a choir member asks if the "accents" written in the music should be sung, the answer is clearly "yes." The choir can be given permission to observe everything in the score without asking and to be as expressive as possible *all the time*.

5. **Look Like the Music**: This concept asks the choir to move in a fashion that supports the musical phrases and in a way that encourages the voices to express the phrase more musically. A choir that stands perfectly still while trying to sing a beautiful, moving line will probably not be as successful as a choir that releases tension and sings in a state of *tonus*.[9]

6. **Breath Preparation Determines Tone**: There are many skills that are needed to create a beautiful and compelling choral sound, but breath preparation is the foundational element that affects everything else. When the choir is out of tune, unenergized, lacking synchronization, or singing with a less-than-beautiful tone, a lower and more complete preparation of the breath is often the best solution.

7. **Turn Off the Autopilot**: As was explained earlier in this chapter, anytime that a choir member sings without listening, stops paying attention, stops watching the conductor, or simply daydreams about something in the past or future, they can be said to be on autopilot. Ask the choir to "be right here, right now" and to notice everything that their eyes and ears can perceive while they are singing.

8. **Snap the Releases:** Choirs that don't end phrases together are sometimes not completely sure where the release is supposed to be. By asking the singers to "snap" their fingers on the release of sound at the end of the phrase, they will make a kinesthetic connection to the event that they can remember later. Students who have trouble snapping can also tap their lap or leg lightly to make the sound.

9. **Conduct with Me:** When the choir isn't responding to your conducting the way you hoped they would, it can be helpful to have them mirror

9 Tonus – a bodily state where the muscles are engaged, but are not unnaturally tense. For singers, this means that movement in all directions is possible while singing, and that the body is able to be used to aid the voice in artistic expression and storytelling. For more on this concept, see *Cantabile - A Manual about Beautiful Singing for Singers, Teachers of Singing and Choral Conductors* by Katharin Rundus, Pavane Publishing, (2009).

your conducting gestures. The movement will help them to sing more expressively, and it will also give you immediate feedback about what your choir perceives you to be doing as you conduct. This exercise also has the effect of switching off the autopilot and letting you see (through gesture) what the relative energy is in the choir; enthusiastic mirroring reveals an enthusiastic mind, and half-hearted mirroring reveals boredom or a lack of enthusiasm that would otherwise be hard to detect.

10. **Sound On, Sound Off:** With the technique of "Sound On, Sound Off," the choir can be asked to "turn off the sound" as they are singing, just like a remote control turns down the sound on a television or computer. When the sound is off on a computer, it does not affect the visual aspects of the screen, just the sound. The choir with "sound off" would still look like they are singing, breathe like they are singing, and move their bodies, mouths, and faces like they are singing. This is especially effective when you want to hear one section alone without everyone else immediately going off task. You can say "all voices 'sound off' except basses," and you get to hear the basses alone. A quick "sound on tenors" creates a duet, and so forth. Challenge the choir to "hear your part" when sound is off, and to imagine it sung expressively and in tune.

11. **Everyone Sing:** There are times when you need to work on a passage in one voice part while the other sections listen. But rather than having them just listen, turn sound off, or work on another task, have everyone sing the passage you are working on in unison. You can say "Page 5, second system, third measure, beat 1, everyone sing soprano in your own range. Let's focus on the staccato articulation." This is an especially efficient technique when the other voice parts have similar challenges in their own lines that can be solved and then transferred through one big sequence in unison. Also, keeping the choir sight reading and building a better understanding of what each voice part is doing will boost their musical skills in many ways.

12. **Be A Choral Actor:** Performers in Broadway musicals or in professional operatic productions are unlikely to disengage from their character when they sing. Rather, they will remain in character and use their face, body, hands, and their voice to express the persona that they are trying to portray. Yet choir singers sometimes disengage from the meaning of the text and the theme of the song when they sing. If the choir members are asked to be like characters in a musical, expressing the music by engaging in the story in some way, the performance will be more engaging, expressive, compelling, and communicative to the audience.

13. **Brand A and Brand B:** When you model something for the choir, it can be helpful to give them two contrasting examples, one way that is clearly NOT the way you want them to do it, and one way that is a good example of what you hope they will do. For example, you can say, "Listen to this passage that we will call Brand A" as you model singing with a bright and spread vocal tone quality. Then you can say, "Now

listen to this, which we will call Brand B. Raise your hand if you hear a difference as I sing." After you model Brand B in the way that you hope they will sing it, you can ask them to model both, just model Brand B, or respond by describing the difference that they hear between Brand A and Brand B before they sing. You can end the sequence with, "Let's use Brand B. It sounds so much better, and the audience will love that sound." As a general rule, regardless of teaching sequence, have the last thing you model for the choir be the example that you want them to remember and replicate.

14. **The Tonus Balloon**: Earlier in the warm-up section of this text we discussed the concept of *tonus*, a state where the body's muscles are engaged but are not tense. It can be a challenge for choirs to stay in tonus while they are busy thinking about other aspects of the music and the performance. But a tense body will create a tense mind, and a tense mind will create tension in the vocal mechanism. Have the choir imagine a rope hanging down from the ceiling of the room, one in front of each choir member. Have each of them grab on to their rope and lift themselves up and down. Then have them imagine that it is tied to a weather balloon way up in the atmosphere. Now the balloon can lift them up, down, frontward and backward, and also side to side. Tell them that, "The body is in tonus when it is free to move in any direction." Then have them imagine that the rope extends up from their spine, and have them relax their arms to their sides. As the "balloon" lifts them up, down, frontward and backward, and side to side, they are in a position to sing. Tell them that the balloon is connected, and that they do not need to worry about it as long as they don't cut the rope. When they need a reminder, you can just say, "Stay connected to the tonus balloon please."

15. **Press Save:** When the choir does something particularly well, you will want them to remember what they did. While you could say, "Please remember that," it is fun to say, "That was great. Your tuning was much improved and true to the key. Take your index finger and touch your forehead…press 'save.' Always save your work." They will smile and maybe laugh, but the act of "saving the work" will help the choir to remember to do it again the next time.

16. **Repeated Text Requires Contrast:** When a piece has repeating lyrics, it is important to add some sort of contrasting dynamics, tone colors, or articulated emphasis to keep the repeated words interesting and expressive, even if the composer does not indicate these in the score. This is especially true when there are repeated words in succession, such as "alleluia, alleluia, alleluia." A subtle but contrasting approach to singing the repeated words will increase the expressive nature of the performance.

17. **Take Control of the Note:** When a choir sings and sustains a long note, they can be instructed to "take control of the note" by adding a slight *crescendo* or *decrescendo*. Likewise, if you have the choir put their palms together in front of the torso and then move the hands away in a horizontal motion outwardly as they sing a single note, you will hear

the sound "expand" a little. This is also "taking control of the note" but without an obvious *crescendo*. They can also put one hand at belt level, palm up, with the other hand palm down covering it. As they sing a note, lift the top hand vertically while the bottom hand stays in place and notice the difference created in the sound. This "lifting" gesture will be slightly different than the "widening" gesture, but it will still be "taking control of the note." Finally, challenge the choir to crescendo, decrescendo, lift, or widen on every note longer than the pulse. If you don't hear a difference on longer notes when rehearsing, you can say, "Please remember to take control of the longer notes."

18. **Breathe for the Highest Note in the Phrase**: Sometimes choir members will forget to breathe for a long phrase, or not prepare for a high note that happens later in the phrase. Breathing for the high note will require the singer to take a consciously low and well-seated breath and to discharge any accumulated and unnecessary tension. With proper preparation of the breath and the vocal mechanism, the high notes will be as free and beautiful as possible.

19. **Walk the Pulse and/or the Rhythm:** If there is room in the rehearsal space, it can be a good activity to have the choir walk as they sing, moving around the room in all different directions. As they mix, they will hear the other parts in new ways, and they will get a better understanding of how their part fits with the other parts. If students walk the pulse, that means that they all take a step on every beat, like on every quarter note in 4/4 meter. If they walk the rhythm, that means that they will only take a step when their vocal section has a note that changes. For example, in 4/4 time a whole note on beat 1 would only require one step with a held note for four beats. A quarter note and six 8th notes would require seven steps. Challenge them to step in the character of the musical phrase, moving smoothly from step to step in a *legato* articulation and bouncing slightly on *staccato* articulations.

20. **Developing A Conscious Approach to Onset of Tone:** Every time the choir begins to sing, there should be a thoughtful choice connected to the onset of sound. The three most common onset choices are the *aspirated* or breathy onset, the *coordinated* onset, and the *glottal* onset.[10] Each of these three can be appropriate for certain kinds of choral singing, but only the coordinated onset should be used as the default for most singing because it creates a clear and beautiful initiation of sound. The choir can

10 "Coordinated onset involves closing the vocal folds simultaneously with the flow of air. To achieve coordinated onset, the abdominal and intercostal muscles must be engaged just prior to singing so that there is sufficient breath support for the onset of sound. This onset method is normally preferred because it produces a clear, resonant sound. Glottal onset, sometimes called a hard attack, involves inhaling, closing the vocal folds, and then beginning to sing. (People involuntarily close the folds when they lift a heavy object.) Glottal tension is eased just enough to cause the vocal folds to vibrate and produce sound. Many singers unconsciously use this as a default onset. Breathy onset occurs when singers inhale and then start to exhale while leaving the glottis open. Shortly thereafter, they close the glottis just enough to bring the vocal folds into vibration." http://www.vocaltechnique.info/onset.html

learn to model all three onset techniques and to use the coordinated onset unless otherwise instructed to do so.

21. **In Tune Is Loud Enough:** Every choir will sing out of tune some of the time, and bringing attention to aspects of intonation will help them to tune more accurately. The concept of "in tune is loud enough" brings the choir's attention to components of intonation that they might otherwise ignore. The idea of "sing more softly until you hear your voice tune" can help people who sing without listening, or who push their voice in certain registers. The rhetorical question "how loud should you sing?" followed by the answer "in tune" is a statement that you can make whenever the choir needs to be more sensitive to tuning as individuals and also as an ensemble.

22. **Sing Soft, Look Loud:** Choirs often sing with more resonance at louder dynamics, but then sing with less resonance at softer dynamics. This concept brings awareness to the fact that it requires *more energy* to sing softly than it does to sing loudly. When you teach the choir to "look loud" when they sing softly, they will usually bring an increased breath energy to the diction and an intention to be expressive that was lacking when they "looked soft while singing softly." In this sequence, you can ask the choir to sing as loudly and beautifully as they can, but with "sound off," and then ask them to look and feel the same with "sound on" at a very soft dynamic.

23. **The Minus One, Net Zero, and Plus One:** This concept teaches that everyone in choir has the opportunity to contribute in some way that makes the choir better. You might have an amazing and positive attitude that uplifts the other people in the room. You might have excellent musical skills that can also help people in the choir. You can be someone who serves the organization through your service and time, or someone who practices often to learn the notes more accurately. No matter what you bring and contribute, your goal is to be a *Plus One*, which is someone who makes the choir better in some way. A *Net Zero* is someone who doesn't really contribute much, but who also does not seem to detract from what others are contributing either. A *Minus One* is someone who behaves in a way that brings the ensemble down or who acts to keep others from being their best in choir. We want everyone to strive to be a *Plus One* and to contribute in the best way that they possibly can.

24. **Singlish**: When American choirs sing in English, they often incorporate speaking habits in their diction that they have practiced throughout their lifetime. This can be problematic depending on what part of the country they are from. The concept of "Singlish" is that the choir sings the *most beautiful vowel* that represents the English word, but not necessarily the vowel that is used when speaking. For example, the words "Amazing Grace" might be said "Uhh-May-Zihng-Grays" [IPA: ə-mei-zIŋ-greis] but in "Singlish" it would be sung "Ahh-Meh-Zeeng-Grehs," [IPA: a-mɛ-ziŋ-grɛs], which sounds "wrong" but is more beautiful when sung because of the pure vowels. The audience translates "English" to

"Singlish" as they listen, and what sounds "wrong" to the singer sounds more beautiful to the audience.

25. **Speaking Habits vs. Singing Habits**: Similar to the concept of using "Singlish," choirs can be taught to keep their speaking habits out of their singing. When most people speak, they do not take a full singer's breath, and they do not release unnecessary tension in the throat and resonating spaces. Furthermore, when speaking, people sometimes talk "off the breath" and at lower in pitch than they probably should. It can be an effective sequence to talk to the choir using your speaking habits (carefully *not* using your singing habits in your speech) and then to use your singing habits (low and prepared breath, clarified diction, pure vowels, open resonating spaces, and a lifted and resonant placement of the voice) to speak. Ask the choir if they hear a difference in the two approaches, and then ask them to sing using their "speaking habits," and then to sing using only their "singing habits." Later they can be reminded by saying, "Please use only your singing habits to sing."

Effective Rehearsal Sequences: Developing Your Positive Approach

As has been stated earlier, when you are running a fast-paced rehearsal, you will need to make many decisions in a short amount of time. Your ability to keep the choir engaged, motivated, and working at a fast pace will largely determine your rehearsal effectiveness. Working at such a fast pace and keeping all the elements of your lesson plan in sequence can be stressful, and it can be a challenge to manage your stress levels so that they do not negatively affect the choir. One way to address the potential for stress to negatively affect the choir in rehearsal is to learn how to create and maintain a positive rehearsal environment. But what does a positive rehearsal environment look like?

It is easy to misunderstand how a positive classroom environment might be created and maintained. You might be thinking, "A positive rehearsal environment is when the teacher approves of everything in the room." But when a teacher approves of *everything* in the room, this implies that they are using some *approval error* and that they must be giving approval for some behaviors that should garner disapproval. You should always strive to be consistent with your classroom reinforcement by approving of appropriate (social or academic) behavior, while also disapproving of inappropriate (social or academic) behavior, while also ignoring behavior that does not interfere with learning or is not dangerous. This seems simple, but it does not always happen consistently. The main reason for this inconsistency is rooted in an intention/function problem. Most teachers will disapprove of inappropriate behavior immediately, but then they will say *nothing* in the presence of appropriate behavior, believing that saying nothing functions as approval. But saying nothing usually does not function as approval.

Approval is a powerful tool for creating a positive rehearsal environment, and you will need to learn how to be approving when the choir has earned it. If you miss opportunities to approve of the choir when it is warranted, then you will run the risk of having disapproval or the act of ignoring as your primary reinforcers. Here are a few tips to help you in this area:

- **Approval as a Primary Reinforcer:** Look for opportunities to "catch the students being good" as often as possible. This can certainly be done in your Step Four Feedback when they have accomplished the goal, or it can be at any time for other behaviors like being on time, having materials ready, or giving their best in rehearsal.

- **Pivoting from Unwanted to What Is Wanted:** Pivot away from talking about what the students *don't* do to what you want them *to do*. In other words, if the pitch is low to the tonal center, don't spend too much time talking about the low pitch center. It is just as effective (and more positive) to pivot away from the concept of "low pitch" and focus on "in tune singing." Instead of saying, "You guys always seem to go flat. What's wrong with your ears today?" you can say, "Let's sing again and let's focus on lifting the pitch closer to the tonal center. I know we can do it."

- **"Feed-Forward" and the Choir as Your Mirror:** Be aware of the concept of "feed-forward." When we do something and are evaluated in some way, we usually receive some sort of "feedback" about how we did. Your choir will be a wonderful provider of feedback to you regarding your energy, your attitude, and your positive (or negative) teaching effect. The class will be like a mirror reflecting back valuable information to you about your teaching approach. If you are cranky, they will likely seem cranky. When you are happy, they may seem to be happy too. When you are stressed out, you might think that they also seem stressed out as well. Because of this feedback phenomenon, you can use the skill of "feeding forward" the attitudes and behaviors that you want your students to feed back to you.

Effective Rehearsal Sequences: Using Group Movement with Choirs

One of the fastest ways to engage a choir is to have them move as they sing. Group movement can be used with choirs of all ages to affect positive changes in breath preparation, breath support, tone and vocal color, phrasing, articulation, tempo, dynamics, and other subtle, musical elements.[11] When we involve the bodies, ears, eyes, and minds of the singers, they are more likely to be off of autopilot and to be in the present moment making music. This textbook describes some specific techniques for group movement in several sections, particularly *"Warm Ups that Turn Off the Autopilot," "Sample Warm-Up Sequence,"* and *"Twenty-Five Conceptual Strategies for Building Skills While Rehearsing the Choir."* The focus of this section will be to explore group movement as a concept, to give tips on how to use it, and to help you transition from movement used in rehearsal to movement used during a formal concert presentation.

- **The Gesture-Body-Mind-Voice Connection**: People experience bodily movement throughout their lifetime, and many of us move in similar patterns with each other. We pick up a pencil differently than we pick up a large plate of food, and we interact differently with a feather-light balloon than we do with a fifty-pound barbell. These many and varied kinesthetic experiences color our perceptions so that we have similar mental ideas of what these experiences mean to us at some level. For this reason, when you ask a choir to sing the vowel "ah" on a single pitch in unison, you will get one sound, and when you ask them to sing the same pitch and vowel while pretending to pick up a pencil, you will get a different sound, and if you ask them yet again to sing while moving as if they were picking up a big heavy object, you will get another, different sound. The mental image and the associated movement will cause the singer to unconsciously make micro-adjustments to the vocal tract, breathing apparatus, and other physical conditions, and the sound will change accordingly. It can be said that "where the body goes, the mind goes, and where the mind goes, the voice follows." Virtually *any* movement initiated while singing will affect the tone to some degree, as will a complete *lack* of movement. There are endless ways to have the choir move, and the only way to decide if you like the difference that the movement induces in the singing is to hear the choir sing while moving and then decide. The rehearsal can become a laboratory for creating beautiful singing sounds accompanied by group gestures that can later be used in performance.

- **Looking Like the Music**: Some choirs move when singing and some choirs do not. Choirs that remain motionless and rigid when singing rarely perform with a free and released vocal technique, though that is not always the case. As stated above, the body informs the mind and the mind informs the voice, so a musical body will help the mind, which will help the voice. But a choir with a musical mind can make beautiful sounds without moving or looking like the music at all. But

11 For a more complete exploration of group movement as a choral rehearsal technique, see these videos, available for purchase online: *"What They See Is What You Get (Linking the visual, the aural, and the kinetic to promote artistic choral singing)"* by Rodney Eichenberger & Andre Thomas, Hinshaw Music, Inc. (08763059) and "Enhancing Musicality through Movement" by Rodney Eichenberger, Santa Barbara Music Publishing (SBMP661).

for most amateur singers, the mind will be affected by the body, and the voice will follow every time. Choirs that stand completely still when singing are a curious oddity in the musical world; professional orchestra players move to the music when they play, and pop, rock, and folk musicians move to be expressive during performances as well. Many choirs do move when they sing, and it is a tough task to find a world-class musical performance by a performer who is standing rigidly and absolutely motionless. So why do choirs do this? There may be a few possible reasons for this including the traditions of choral singing in the Lutheran church and other religious orders, and the common need to *stop* elementary and middle school singers from *moving too much* in class or touching each other.

A useful model for movement in the choir is for each singer to be in a bodily state of *tonus* while also being free to "look like the music." But what does the music look like, you may ask. What is appropriate when it comes to the choir moving while singing? The answer is that it is up to you, the choir, and your artistic taste. Choirs that constantly sway back and forth to the pulse as they sing don't always look like the musical phrase, even if they are connected to the beat. Singers that allow their movement to reflect the movement of the musical phrase, much like a violinist would move using up and down bows with various degrees of weight and motion, will reflect the music in their gestures and voices more than a "sway to the pulse" approach might. Having the choir "conduct" as they sing is another way to connect gestures to the mind and voice, and this also allows the singers to experiment with their own expressive conducting gestures, which can be fun for them. A choir that moves musically will probably sing musically, so using group movement can be a powerful tool for your teaching, as well as a pathway to creating artistic and compelling performances for your audiences.

- **Using Group Movement in Concerts:** There are some choirs that use group movement effectively in their rehearsals, and also in their concerts.[12] Other choirs use gestures and group movements in their rehearsals, but then struggle to get the sounds created by the gestures on the concert stage without the accompanying movements. There are two tips to help with this challenge:

    1. When the choir is experimenting with group movement in rehearsals, care should be taken to try different gestures until a particular movement can be associated with a particular vocal color or tone quality that is desired. Because the gesture has informed the mind of the singer, and the mind has informed the voice, the conductor can use the associated gesture as part of the conducting pattern in the concert performance. This may take some practice by the

12 See for example any video of the St. Mary's Varsity Ensemble from Tokyo, Japan, directed by Randy Stenson.

conductor, but it can work really well to remind the choir to think and sing as musically as they did in rehearsal.

2. Gestures that are experienced in rehearsal by the choir will be transferred to the mind and then to the voice. If asking the students to remember their state of mind or the tone they created does not yield the results you want, ask the choir to imagine the gesture in their mind as they sing. Challenge them to imagine their arms and torso moving as they did in rehearsal, and allow them to move freely but without arms swinging, lifting, or conducting. Using "imaginary arms" will sometimes be enough to inform the mind and the voice during a concert. For the conductor who is concerned about the choir moving too much, this technique can be effective without being distracting.

Effective Rehearsal Sequences: Creativity and Student-Centered Teaching

Your classroom will reflect your philosophy of music education as well as the values you hold for your students as musicians and as people. For example, if you value musicianship as an important part of your student's education, you will devote time, effort, and resources to be sure that you are including music-reading sequences and skill development into your rehearsals and lessons. We should always strive to teach using the best techniques that we can, and with a limited amount of instructional time available, every choice we make to include or exclude something from our curriculum has consequences for our students and their musical education.

While the decisions to include and exclude certain skills and techniques in your curriculum are important and consequential, how you teach your students is also an important choice that you should make consciously and carefully. In this section we will explore the concepts of "Teacher-Centered Teaching" and "Student-Centered Teaching" in a creative learning environment.

- **Teacher-Centered Teaching:** Teacher-centered classrooms are learning environments where students interact with the teacher in a way that empowers the *teacher*. Students look to the teacher for the answers to problems, and the teacher imparts most of the musical decisions to the choir. Students are rarely asked to perceive, to explore, or to describe musical events in the rehearsal, but rather are instructed how to sing and perform by the teacher. In essence, a teacher-centered rehearsal focuses on communicating information to the students rather than asking students to make choices, to listen, and to respond to the music making. In a strictly focused teacher-centered environment, students are completely reliant on the teacher for the musical note learning, interpretation, decision making, and artistry.

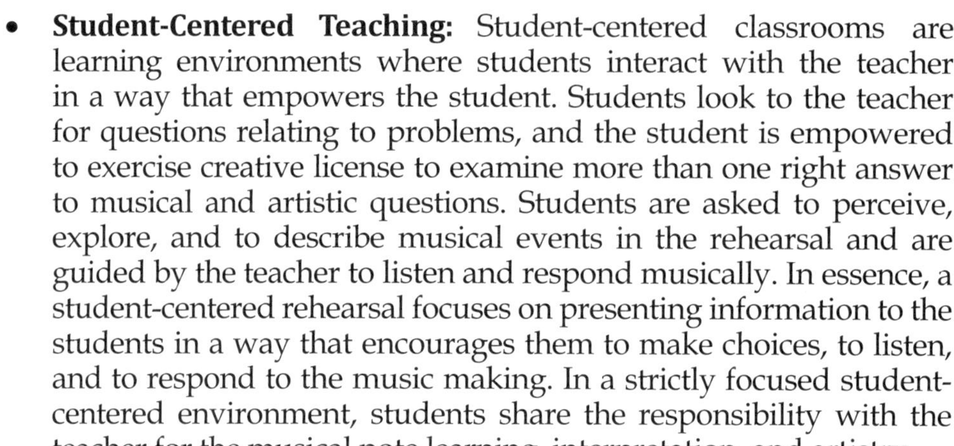

- **Student-Centered Teaching:** Student-centered classrooms are learning environments where students interact with the teacher in a way that empowers the student. Students look to the teacher for questions relating to problems, and the student is empowered to exercise creative license to examine more than one right answer to musical and artistic questions. Students are asked to perceive, explore, and to describe musical events in the rehearsal and are guided by the teacher to listen and respond musically. In essence, a student-centered rehearsal focuses on presenting information to the students in a way that encourages them to make choices, to listen, and to respond to the music making. In a strictly focused student-centered environment, students share the responsibility with the teacher for the musical note learning, interpretation, and artistry.

- **The Importance of Questioning in a Student-Centered Rehearsal:** Students in the high-stakes testing "No Child Left Behind" generation were trained to look for the one "right answer" to every question, and to rely on the teacher for solutions to problems.[13] Because creativity demands that students acquire the ability to transcend traditional ideas, rules, patterns, or relationships, students must be afforded frequent chances to explore questions that can have more than one right answer. Music is an art form that can provide a fertile learning environment for creative thinking and expression, but only when the conductor/teacher is willing to let students express and verbalize their conclusions to open-ended questions in the rehearsal. In any rehearsal the teacher will likely pose questions to the choir. Sometimes the questions will demand a response, and sometimes the questions will be rhetorical in nature, requiring the students to think but not respond. Lower-level questions have one correct answer, while higher-level questions can have several correct answers.[14] Creativity is enhanced in a student-centered classroom with the use of higher-level questions, regardless of whether they are rhetorical or not.

- **Creating A Safe Environment for Creativity to Awaken:** When students know there is only one correct answer to a question they are less likely to take risks and to attempt to guess or offer a creative answer. This is particularly true if the teacher uses "guess what I'm thinking" questioning, which often poses as a brain-storming session, but with only one right answer. If a question, can have more than one correct answer, the teacher must accept

13 "The No Child Left Behind Act (NCLB) was a 2002 U.S. Act of Congress, which set the ambitious goal of having every student in every school in America perform at state standards on tests by a certain point. NCLB came under criticism soon after proposal for its high-stakes testing, meaning that schools that failed to meet standards faced funding cuts or potential closure. Additionally, this meant that instructors were more prone to 'teaching to exam,' conducting their classes in a manner designed to enable test-passing and not ensuring that students actually knew the material."

14 See Chapter 11 "Leading a Discussion" for more on "levels of questioning."

all plausible answers as valid, and give approval for the thinking process of the student. In a student-centered rehearsal, approval for creative thinking is essential. Students who are administered disapproval for answers to questions with more than one right answer will stop offering answers over time. Students who are not used to thinking critically will need time to open up and feel safe enough to explore their own creative imaginations. The teacher is responsible for fostering this safe environment by listening and validating student responses with positive words, gestures, and follow-ups. The use of sarcasm in the classroom is not recommended because it can create ambiguity and can actually confuse some students. Using words that do not carry the intended meaning can create anxiety and a feeling of insecurity in some students (especially autistic students), resulting in a diminishment of creative thinking.

- **Musicianship as a Path to Creative Ownership and Expression:** A student-centered teacher will dedicate rehearsal time to helping students acquire the skills to become independent musicians. It doesn't matter what techniques the teacher chooses to emphasize as long as the students make progress in reading and interpreting the musical score. This text recommends the use of solfege syllables and Curwen/Glover hand signs with movable "do" and a "la-based minor" to teach pitch and numbers to teach rhythm and counting, but any system that you are comfortable with can work well if taught and reinforced consistently.[15] When students can interpret musical symbols accurately and independently, the teacher and students acquire a system, language, and framework to interact with, unlocking creativity. For example, a teacher-centered teacher will play or sing a part when asked to do so by a student. A student-centered teacher will ask the student to define the problem in musical terms and to attempt to solve the problem first on their own. By attempting to solve musical problems independently, students gain important ownership of the music-making process, and the music educator becomes a "tour guide" for exploring expressivity and musical growth in the rehearsal process.

- **Creative Listening and Responding:** When the choir has learned to sing a piece of literature well and is preparing for an upcoming concert, it can a good idea in a student-centered classroom to create mini performances in full-performance mode during rehearsal. Divide the choir into two equal halves, or have one or more members step out and listen. This teaching sequence develops what we will call the "Creative Listener," a choir member who can listen to and respond to a choral performance in a musical, creative, and thoughtful manner. Here is a sequence for using the technique. Feel free to modify it as needed so that

15 For more on this, see Chapter 7 "Developing Musicianship within the Choral Rehearsal."

it can function well with your students and your rehearsal needs and constraints:

1. Creative Listeners (CL) are listening for something that is being done well and also for ways that the performance can be improved.
2. After listening to a performance by a voice section or group of sections, the CL will raise a hand and offer a suggestion or comment.
3. On occasion, the director will randomly call on individuals to make CL comments.
4. The CL can listen for correct or incorrect notes, rhythms, expressiveness of text weight, phrase shape, tone quality, clarity of diction, facial expression, intonation, or overall affect and expressiveness of the performance.
5. The CL must describe the musical element that was good or in need of improvement. The comment of "that was good" or "I didn't like it" must be clarified to tell the singers how to perform it differently the next time.
6. There is no absolute right and wrong way to perform music. EVERY reasonable answer must be accepted, tried, and evaluated. If you disapprove of CL students in this process, you will not be successful or encourage their creative thinking.
7. Students who are singing can also offer CL observations and may be called on by the director.
8. All singers should do their best to try the suggestions of each CL. Stress the importance of hearing and performing each suggestion. Experience the way it sounds and feels in the context of the literature.
9. Every artistic performance is a choice. Let singers discuss which artistic choice they prefer, but again, there is no absolute right or wrong choice. Because the group will rarely agree 100%, the director must be clear in making his or her final choice for the performance.

The concepts in this section are only suggestions for sequences to maximize the creative potential of your students. No teacher will use these ideas 100% of the time, but using them more of the time will have positive benefits. Student-centered teaching helps foster independence in the students, and helps them become self-sufficient musicians who can pay forward the gifts you helped them acquire in music. A creative singer is an expressive singer, and an expressive singer is at the foundation of moving and artistic choral performances. In the end, if you are open to creative, student-centered teaching, you will see your students embracing it as well, with the benefits paying off through fun and interesting rehearsals, shared time in the role of "The Teacher," and stunning performances for your audiences.

RECAPITULATION

1. It is true that most people won't get to experience very much authentic practice as a choral conductor until they are older and have a real choir to lead. Comment on your experience as a choral conductor up to this point in your training. Do you think you have had more experience or less experience than the average person your age, in your opinion? Describe why you feel this way and give evidence to support your opinion. Additionally, reread the "Five Guidelines to Focus Upon in Your First Teaching Experiences" and comment on each one in terms of your ability to meet the behaviors presented in each section.

2. Comment on five of the most interesting or useful sequences in the section called "Twenty-Five Conceptual Strategies for Building Skills While Rehearsing the Choir." Why do you think these were useful or interesting to you, and have you seen any of these technique sequences used before in a real rehearsal? If so, provide some background about where you have experienced them.

3. Think of all the choral teachers you have sung for in your lifetime. In your experience, would you describe your primary choral directors as having a "positive approach" or a "negative approach" in the rehearsal based on what you read in the chapter? If some were positive and some negative, describe aspects of two contrasting mentors. If they were all similar, describe them all in one short narrative. Additionally, do you feel that you respond better as a singer in a choir to a primarily positive approach or to a primarily negative approach? Support your answer.

4. Group movement in the choir rehearsal is a very common technique that is used in many choral classrooms in America. Describe your experience with movement techniques in ensembles that you participated in throughout your lifetime. Do you think you will use some of these techniques in your teaching? Why or why not?

5. In a student-centered classroom the students are a big part of the learning and teaching, and students must take some responsibility for their own progress and mastery. In a teacher-centered classroom the teacher

has the responsibility to help the students learn the music and to sing well. Discuss the pros and cons of each approach, and describe (using percentages) how much of each approach you intend to use in your teaching. In other words, you might say "I'll use 20% of a teacher-centered and 80% of a student-centered approach." Then support your opinion and intentions with thoughtful evidence of your thinking.

Chapter Seven

Developing Musicianship Within the Choral Rehearsal

7. Developing Musicianship Within the Choral Rehearsal

"Give a man a fish and you feed him for a day.
Teach a man to fish and you feed him for a lifetime."
~Chinese proverb

Understanding The Musicianship Problem

The problem is easy to understand: virtually every choral director has the good *intention* for students to be able to read music. Many choral teachers hone that desire into some sort of instructional plan and sequence intended to help the singers develop their musicianship during the rehearsal. Unfortunately, many of these good-intended plans fall short of the goal of creating independent choral musicians. Even though instructional time and resources may be spent in the rehearsal addressing aspects of musicianship, it is often the case that the final outcome does not *function* well; despite the time and effort that is invested, it is not unusual for students to fail to acquire a functional ability to learn to read and interpret musical notation independently. This is a real problem, and it is a problem that you must examine and understand if you are to be a student-centered, comprehensive, artful, and professional choral music educator.

As the leader of your choral program you will be charged with creating choral concerts that both educate students and entertain audiences, and you will be under some pressure to maintain quality in every public performance. But some teachers stress the experience of the public concert so much that they fail to instruct the choir comprehensively in the rehearsals leading up to the performances, requiring them to rely on teaching music by ear (rote) or relying on part recordings or performance recordings to help teach the notes and rhythms. Other teachers may enact programs of sight singing that don't get the educational results and outcomes they are hoping for, causing them to question the value of the instruction and the time that it requires. Here are several scenarios that describe some common experiences that teachers can find themselves in with respect to teaching musicianship:

- **Mrs. Ledon** is a wonderful pianist who can play anything in the score accurately and musically. She picks challenging music for all the choirs, and she enjoys teaching and rehearsing with the students. The choir is always preparing for an upcoming concert, yet it seems like there is never quite enough time to perfect the subtle nuances in the music. Despite this, the concerts are solid, and the reputation of the school's choral program is good. Rehearsals are packed full of singing and part learning. Although the students are holding scores as they sing, most of them are only reading the words of the text and globally following the contour of the melodic lines as they listen to the piano. Each section takes turns hearing Mrs. Ledon play their part alone before singing along with the piano. Eventually everyone sings together while Mrs. Ledon accompanies the piece. Because they sing difficult music with a good product at the concert, Mrs. Ledon believes that she is teaching musicianship…yet she can't understand why they fail to get top ratings in sight reading tests at choral festivals.

- **Mr. Chester** is a veteran teacher of twenty years. His choirs are well respected and their concerts are always fun and interesting. He really wants to make time for sight singing and musicianship, but it usually only happens in the several days at the end of the grading quarter, after the concert is completed. It does seem like a good change of pace for the classes after the concert, and the students do their best to engage in the lessons. Mr. Chester is always frustrated, however, that students don't remember what he taught them in the musicianship lessons when regular rehearsals resume at the start of the new quarter. He often asks himself, "Why can't the students ever retain this information, especially when they hear it over and over again?" He is secretly glad that he doesn't waste too much rehearsal time with musicianship training. There is barely enough time to learn the music as it is.

- **Ms. Koppel** values teaching musicianship as part of her philosophy of music education. Every rehearsal starts with a focus on scales and vocal warm ups and then moves on to a few minutes of sight-singing examples from a sight-singing book. She enjoys when all the choirs stay synchronized on the same examples all year so that there is a "melody of the day," and she likes that the examples get harder as the year progresses. Every year starts with example one, and ends with example fifty. Her seniors can really read the examples well… practically from memory. Despite the success she feels with the sight-singing part of the lesson, she still has to rely on rote teaching for the more challenging literature. She can't understand why they can do so well at the start of rehearsal, and then struggle to read the music found in the concert literature. Deep down Ms. Koppel fears that she might be wasting valuable rehearsal time singing from the sight-singing book every day, yet she holds true to her value that students should be taught musicianship.

- **Mrs. Harrison** is interested in teaching musicianship to her choirs, and her approach is to do a lot of sight singing in every class. Her motto is, "If you want to be a better sight reader, you have to do a lot of sight singing." As students enter the room they pick up the "song of the day" and bring it over to their position in the choir. After warm ups, Mrs. Harrison conducts the choir and accompanist through the piece, at tempo, twice. She likes hearing them do their best to read the

> piece, and she knows that they will get better over time by struggling and figuring out how to make sense of the notation. She has an extensive music library, and a student helper acting as librarian, so there is always a fun and interesting song of the day. Her concerts are enthusiastic, yet a little messy, in terms of notes and rhythms, but she feels that music performance needs to have some human error to be interesting. In class when they are struggling on the concert literature, she will sometimes dismiss the choir to sectionals to learn the music on their own or assign homework on certain sections. She feels really satisfied that it is not her responsibility to spoon-feed the notes and that the students can figure it out for themselves. She is glad that they always try hard even if they don't always get it right.

These fictional scenarios shed some light on the real and varied experiences of many well-meaning choral directors struggling to teach musicianship in the rehearsal. In each case they have worked on the problem and found a solution that works to some degree for them. The issue, of course, is that none of them have really solved the problem at all. Spending time on musicianship is not necessarily the same as teaching musicianship, and if students do not become better and more independent musicians through your teaching, then you are indeed wasting both your time *and* the student's time. Let's look at these scenarios a little more closely:

Mrs. Ledon is an excellent pianist and can teach the students by rote really well. The strength of her teaching rests in the high-level development of the student's ears and their ability to parrot notes and rhythms back with accuracy. The weakness of the approach is that the teaching is completely *teacher-centered.* This means that the students are completely dependent upon the skills and rehearsal techniques of the teacher; for the most part in teacher-centered teaching, if the teacher is not present, little learning will take place. As long as Mrs. Ledon is available to play the notes and rhythms with enough time for extensive repetition, the music will be learned, and the students will be successful. But once the teacher is gone, the students will not have the same success on, or access to, the music that they learned and enjoyed through the skill and musicianship of the teacher.

Mr. Chester is doing his best to include musicianship in the curriculum, but the intense sessions for several days four times a year aren't working very well. The strength of his teaching is that there is time to cover a lot of material. The weakness of the instruction is that it takes the place of the rehearsal instead of being an integral part of the rehearsal. It's no wonder that the students don't transfer their musical knowledge to the literature, because Mr. Chester never teaches musicianship until after the concert. Musicianship is valued as something extra that is only taught when there is spare time for it and when there is no concert literature to prepare.

Ms. Koppel includes a sight-singing example into every lesson. Her weakness is that she doesn't allow the classes to progress at their own rate and that the examples have little to do with the concert literature that they are actually rehearsing. Additionally, keeping all the classes on a fixed schedule of melodies works best for the teacher, but not for the students. The strength of the teaching is that the melodies are sequenced from easiest to most difficult, but the weakness is that there is little to no transfer between the exercises and the rest of the rehearsal; the difficulty of the literature rarely matches the difficulty of the sight-singing examples. Also, because the melodies are fixed in all classes, upperclassmen come over time to remember the melodies from past years, making it seem like they are progressing in their skills when they really are not.

Mrs. Harrison has decided to make sight singing a cornerstone of her teaching, yet the students still are lacking the basic skills they will need to continue enjoying music later in life. This is because her teaching is completely *student centered,* practically to the exclusion of teacher input. A student-centered teacher will empower the students to learn the music independently, without the teacher. But Mrs. Harrison isn't really teaching musicianship from a student-centered philosophy as much as she is teaching self-reliance. The strength of her teaching is that she expects the students to learn their music and to be good problem solvers. The weakness of her approach is that she isn't teaching them much of anything. *Telling* someone to do something is completely different than *teaching* them to do it. Students require sequenced instruction and practical experiences to apply the skills and knowledge of musicianship. Her concerts are messy because the students don't really know what they are doing, and they aren't really demonstrating high-level musicianship in their concerts.

It is a fact that we tend to teach the way we were taught. If your early experiences in choral ensembles included strong musicianship training, you are more likely to provide that same kind of training to the students in your ensembles. If you were not given a strong foundation of musicianship skills in the choirs you sang in, you are less likely to make this aspect of teaching a priority with your own students. But teaching musicianship to your choir members is a *philosophical value* that you should hold as a professional choral music educator; you should strive to be curious and understand how to create strong choral musicians in your choirs as opposed to singers who depend on you to teach them the music. You should learn how to teach musicianship in the choral rehearsal every day, and to make it valuable and meaningful to your students.

RECAPITULATION

1. Each of the teachers in the above scenarios has strengths and weaknesses in their musicianship sequencing, and each one has the best of intentions for the development of their students in the ensemble. Think about the musicianship training you received in choirs that you sang in throughout your lifetime. Did any of your experiences with musicianship training mirror any of the scenarios outlined in this section? Which ones, and to what extent? Write a short paragraph addressing your choral musicianship training experiences by comparing and contrasting the chapter scenarios to your memories. If you did not sing in choirs, use memories from instrumental ensembles or private musical study as the basis for your paragraph.
2. What are some of the advantages of training strong musicians in your choirs? With excellent music readers and performers in your ensembles, what are some musical goals that you could strive for that you couldn't achieve otherwise? Describe your ideal imaginary choir, what they can do musically, and some ways that you might integrate basic musicianship into your rehearsals.
3. At the outset of this chapter this Chinese proverb is quoted: *"Give a man a fish and you feed him for a day. Teach a man to fish and you feed him for a lifetime."* Write a short transfer paragraph comparing this quote to the concept of musicianship training. Why do we do a disservice to students when we are completely teacher-centered and teach music only by rote and by ear?

Addressing the Musicianship Problem

Imagine the ridiculousness of attempting to teach young children to read and write the English language only by reading sentences from novels or poems to them as they listen, and then having them repeat the words back to you. Even if you could get them to memorize and perform Shakespeare plays, what would you have accomplished? What skills would you have taught them that they could use and apply throughout their lifetime? Yet it is all too common for choral directors to teach notes and rhythms this way, playing parts at the piano and having the students sing the notes back as they memorize the sounds, or providing part tracks for them to listen to and memorize outside of class. Some teachers may even believe that the students are learning to read the music as long as they have the music in their hands. There are certainly advantages to part tracks and rote teaching, and there are good reasons to include these approaches in your teaching at specific times; but a professional choral music educator shouldn't *rely solely* on these techniques to teach notes and rhythms because these methods do not teach all the skills that students need to become independent musicians for a lifetime.

Teaching musical literacy is very much like teaching a foreign language. But the only way to teach someone a language, and for them to become both literate and independent at reading and writing the language, is to break it down into understandable pieces that can be experienced, understood, recombined, and practiced. You have to define and explain the differences between nouns, verbs, and adjectives and give students the opportunities to experience these in both written and spoken contexts. It is easier, of course, if you are teaching someone to read and write who is already fluently conversant in the language.

Teaching musical literacy is not very different than teaching a foreign language in several important ways. It is essential that students get to make and experience music first, before attaching those experiences to the abstract concepts of musical notation. You have to teach the elements of pitch and rhythm separately, and then combine them in a musical context. And while it is easier to teach someone to read and write a language that they already speak, it is an essential first step to provide rich, multi-modal experiences with music before too much music notation is introduced. In other words, the first step to teaching musicianship is to have students experience music first-hand by singing, playing, moving to, describing, and listening to music. There is obviously a middle ground to strive for in your teaching where rote teaching and score reading are in a perfect balance and where musicianship can be an effective outcome of the curriculum. It is our job to help our students acquire the skills and abilities that will allow them to interact independently with music and musical activities for a lifetime.

There are many wonderful choral professionals across the United States who are very effective at teaching musicianship to their students every day, and who routinely help students become independent, literate musicians. They have methods that work for them, and there is no one perfect way of doing it; it has to be right for the teacher, students, and the requirements of the music program and performing schedule. There are some things that they all have in common, however. Consider the following scenario:

- **Mr. Scharf** has been teaching for six years as a middle and high school choral educator in the public schools. He enjoys the job, but also realizes that there isn't enough time to teach every student in the choir the same level of in-depth knowledge that he can teach his Advanced

Placement music theory students. He values musicianship and feels that everyone in choir should be able to read, interpret, and perform from a musical score independently by the time they graduate from his program. Because of his time constraints, he had to make some decisions about the scope and sequence of his curriculum so that he could decide what to leave out, as well as what he could include, in the musicianship training of the choir students. He decided that he would teach his students to be able to determine the key, find the first degree of the scale, be able to name all of the solfège syllables and note names, interpret a meter signature, write in and count rhythms, and be able to sing the correct pitches in rhythm on syllables, note names, count singing, on a neutral syllable, and on text. While he teaches other musical concepts during his rehearsals, he focuses on these limited goals in the sight-singing portion of every rehearsal.

He decided that musicianship was best taught and reinforced when the concepts being introduced related directly to the literature being studied, as opposed to being a separate part of the lesson. For this reason, he doesn't purchase or use special sight-singing books, but rather uses excerpts from the music in the student's folders for his daily group notation lessons. Because the music they sight sing will actually be performed in a concert later in the semester, Mr. Scharf is confident that he is not wasting class time nor sacrificing concert quality when he is teaching musicianship.

Mr. Scharf also remembered from his college methods classes that sound should precede symbol and that he should teach "rote before note." For that reason, he makes the warm ups at the start of each rehearsal more about building musical skills than about the unison singing of major scales, triads, and arpeggios in various keys. After a quick physical set of stretches, he has the choir mirror his motions as he steps and claps to a steady beat and introduces and reinforces the rhythmic skills of subdivision and syncopation through movement as well. Through a method called "sound on, sound off," he has them build *audiation* (inner hearing) skills and teaches proper alignment, body *tonus* (with muscles engaged but not tense), and breathing techniques through group movement as well. Within the first few minutes, he has every choir sing up and down scales in various keys using Curwen/Glover hand signs, which either he leads, or has students lead. As the ears of the students develop, he introduces more and more chromatically altered syllables and hand signs and more difficult keys and modes. He is especially careful to introduce the same kinds of melodic patterns and skips that the students will actually be singing later in the rehearsal as well as any unusual modes from the literature.

After "hand sign sight singing" is over, Mr. Scharf directs the choir's attention to the staff on the white board where he has notated a short musical excerpt from the literature. For the very beginning groups, it is a very brief unison line that is mostly stepwise and diatonic. For his intermediate groups, he chooses a longer excerpt in two to four parts with a few more challenges in both pitch and rhythm. For his advanced choirs, he excerpts the most difficult sections of the literature where he knows there could be problems later. With each choir, and at the proper pace for their abilities, he has the class identify the key and the meter signature. He has them name, sing, and sign the solfège syllables of the excerpt out of time, count and clap the rhythms, sing the syllables in rhythm slowly, and then sing them at a performance tempo. If there is time, he sometimes has them make up random words for every note of the excerpt, building the skills required to sing on the text rather than on the syllables or counts. In this segment of the lesson, everyone sings all the time, with basses singing soprano in their own range and sopranos singing bass up an octave. He knows that this teaches everyone what each part is doing and how the other lines relate to their own part.

Once the excerpt has been sung and experienced by the whole class on the white board, Mr. Scharf has the choir take out the piece that the sight singing was excerpted from and sing from the octavo on solfège syllables without looking back at the white board. If the pitches and rhythms are still secure, he has them sing on the actual text. If need be, he re-teaches and reinforces the musical skills needed to be successful on the excerpt. On average, from the down beat of the warm up to the end of the musicianship segment where they sing from the actual literature, he has invested fifteen to twenty minutes of rehearsal time. He invests this time in every rehearsal, all year long with few exceptions. But he knows a very important fact: he knows he hasn't *wasted* even one minute of his rehearsal time by teaching musicianship. What was taught to the group was the music that will be performed and the section that was used for musicianship training will more easily be recalled in the next rehearsal and will be solid in performance.

Mr. Scharf has been teaching long enough to realize some of the greatest benefits of his approach: students that studied for multiple years in his choral program became really competent choral musicians, so he had to start selecting harder and harder literature for his choirs to keep them challenged appropriately. He gave up worrying about learning notes and rhythms for the concert and instead picked music that he knew they would learn along with their progressing musical abilities. Even the beginning choirs seemed to learn the basics faster, and he added musicianship assessments to his auditions for the upper choirs. Because he found success through his sequencing of musicianship in the choral rehearsal, and because it didn't waste time or ruin his concerts, he sometimes wonders why anyone would want to "pound notes" with their choirs instead of helping them become literate musicians.

This fictional scenario can shed some light on the real and varied experiences of many skilled choral educators who are successfully teaching musicianship in their rehearsals. They all share a philosophical value that students should learn the musical skills to be competent, literate, and independent choral musicians. They create student-centered learning environments where information flows in all directions, from teacher to student and student to teacher, and also from student to student. They select their literature carefully so that students are challenged at, or slightly above, their present ability levels. They devote time in virtually every rehearsal for building pitch, rhythm, reading, listening, and performing skills. They are process-oriented in their approach, understanding that a lesson learned well today will pay off for years to come. They have a sense of satisfaction knowing that their students have the ability to read and interact with music independently.

RECAPITULATION

1. Mr. Scharf had to limit the number of musical concepts that he could teach to his choirs every day because of the time constraints of the rehearsal and the need to prepare quality concert performances. In your opinion, what should a "literate musician" be able to do? Make a list of at least ten musical skills, concepts, or behaviors that you would want your students to learn, acquire, and demonstrate through study in your choir program. Which ones are the most important and which are the least important? If you had to cut the list down to five, what would you cut and what would you keep? Be able to defend your opinion and choices.

2. Teaching musicianship is a very important component of a comprehensive choral music education curriculum. But it's always easier to teach something that you struggled to learn because you can often remember moving through some of the learning steps when you were acquiring the skills. It's also easier to teach something that you were taught well at some point by an effective teacher. In contrast, it is much more difficult to teach something you never learned or that you could already do without breaking it down into smaller steps. Write a descriptive paragraph assessing your present level of musicianship, and tie your assessment to the amount of time and struggle you experienced in your life working on those skills. Did you have effective teachers who taught you? What specifically do you do well, and what skills are you still working on? Feel free to include piano playing, sight singing, aural skills, score reading, notational skills, and any other musical skills you may be working on.

3. Think about the musicianship skills that you identified in the previous question relating to what you do well and also what you are still working to improve. Comment on what you already do every day to improve your musicianship skills and also what you could do, but don't presently do. Do you think you could devote more time to your personal musicianship training every day, and if so, how would you structure it? If you do not think you have the time or desire to improve your musicianship skills on a daily basis, explain your thinking in a short paragraph.

Common Systems for Teaching Pitch Concepts in the Choral Rehearsal

As a professional choral music educator, it is essential that you learn how to teach musicianship to your students. The first step is to determine a method, system, or technique that you can implement into your curriculum. But no single method will be perfect for every teacher because of the diversity of our backgrounds and experiences, and also because of the diverse populations of students that we teach. It is important to make a distinction between values and techniques: *values* are what we hold as important and *techniques* implement certain values. Teaching musicianship is a value that we should share, but we need not agree on the techniques that should be used to implement those values. For example, some people will maintain that a system of fixed "Do" (pronounced "doe") solfège is the best method, while others will say movable "Do" solfège is the best, while others still will contend that teaching pitch concepts with a number system is the best. But any of the three, when taught consistently and sequentially, could be effective for imparting and reinforcing musical pitch concepts. The most important thing is that you choose to include musicianship-training techniques in your teaching, regardless of which systems you are most comfortable with. Choose a system and use it in your teaching for a while, and if you decide to change your techniques later on, that's completely acceptable. Always hold true to your values, but be open to adapting your techniques when necessary.

There are a number of techniques for teaching pitch concepts, and each has distinct advantages and disadvantages. Here is a brief synopsis of three of the most common systems:

✓ *Movable "Do" Solfège*

In this system, syllable names are assigned to pitches of the scale as determined by the major key signature. For example, the pitch "C" is "Do" in the key of "C," but "C" is "Re" in the key of Bb. Additionally, chromatic alterations have distinct syllable names that can be sung to identify the alterations; in the key of "C," the pitch sequence of C-C#-C would be sung "Do-Di-Do," and the pitch sequence of D-Db-D would be sung "Re-Ra-Re." When the key signature in the music changes, the solfège pitches are all shifted together to reflect the new key, thus "Do" is "movable."

- **Advantage**: Students learn that key signatures create whole- and half-step relationships in the music and that these relationships create the feeling of a major tonal center. Key and mode concepts are easy to teach and are easily applied to the literature.
- **Advantage**: Students can sing specific syllables representing the diatonic and chromatic pitches in the music and can also use specific hand signs to accompany all the syllable names while sight singing.
- **Advantage**: Syllable patterns learned and memorized in one key or mode will be exactly the same in a transposed key or mode.
- **Disadvantage**: Highly chromatic music without a clear tonal center is difficult to sing in movable "Do."
- **Disadvantage**: Absolute pitch memory is not as easily acquired because the scale and note names shift with each established key. "Do" can be any note depending on the key signature.
- **Disadvantage**: Literature that changes keys frequently, especially when that key change is only reflected in chromatic alterations and not in an actual change of key signature, can be difficult to read in this system.

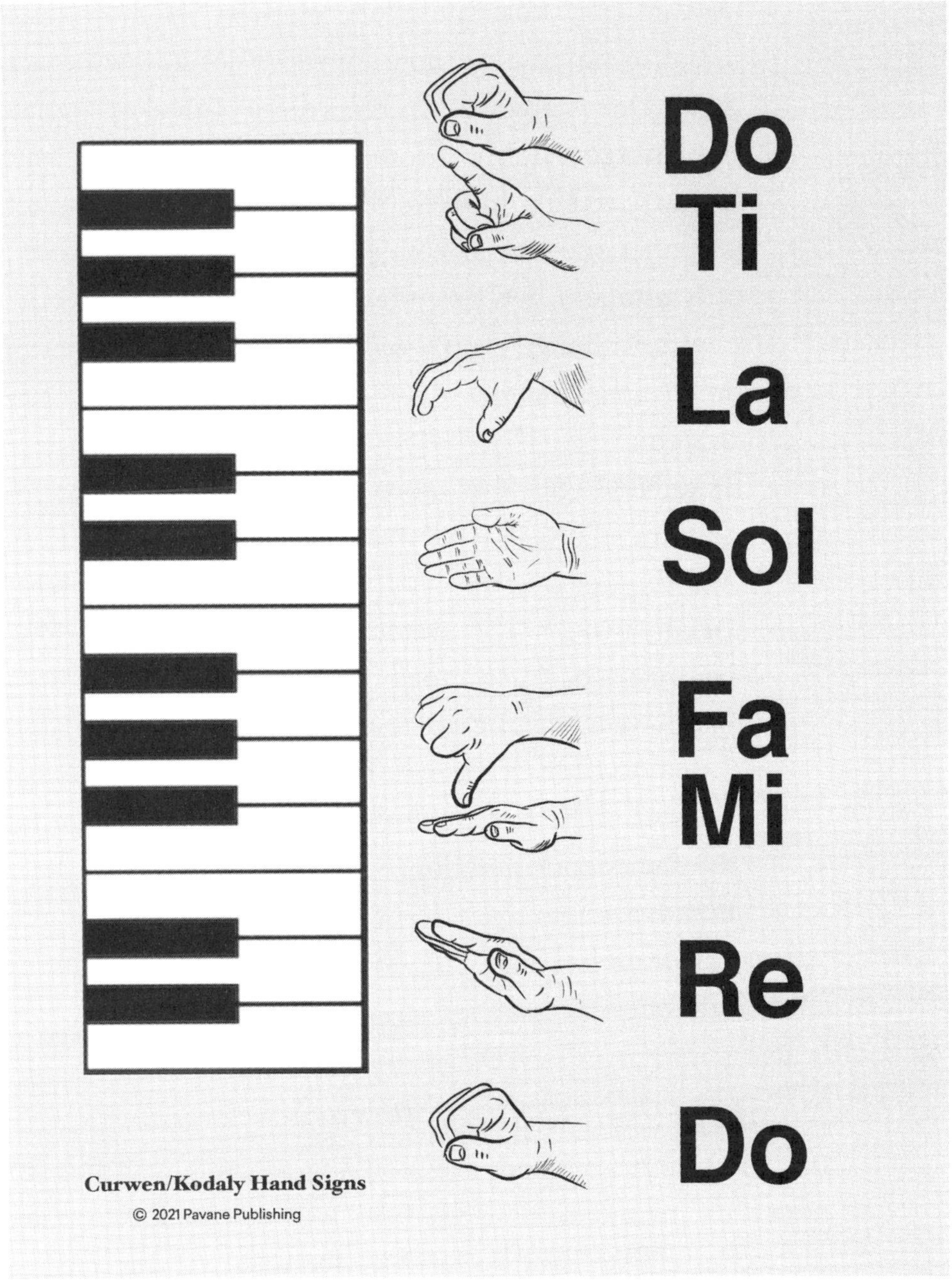

Do
Ti
La
Sol
Fa
Mi
Re
Do

Curwen/Kodaly Hand Signs

✓ *Fixed "Do" Solfège*

In this system, syllables are assigned to note names regardless of the key or tonal center. The pitch "C" is always "Do" and the pitch "D" is always "Re." For example, the pitch "C" is "Do" in the key of "C," and "C" is also "Do" in the key of Bb. Additionally, chromatic alterations do not have distinct syllable names that can be sung to identify the alterations; the pitch sequence of C-C#-C would be sung "Do-Do-Do," and the pitch sequence of D-Db-D would be sung "Re-Re-Re." When the key signature in the music changes, the solfège pitches are not shifted together to reflect the new key, thus "C" is always "Do" and is therefore "fixed."

- **Advantage**: Absolute pitch memory is more easily acquired because the scale and note names do not shift with each established key. "Do" is always "C" regardless of the key signature.
- **Advantage**: Highly chromatic music without a clear tonal center is easier to sing in fixed "Do" because absolute pitch memory is stronger once the system is acquired and practiced.
- **Advantage**: Literature that changes keys frequently, even when that key change is only reflected in chromatic alterations and not in an actual change of key signature, can be easier to read in this system.
- **Disadvantage**: It is more difficult to teach beginners that key signatures create whole- and half-step relationships in the music and that these relationships create the feeling of a tonal center.
- **Disadvantage**: The system can be really confusing to teach to beginners because a major scale can be sung with a large variety of different starting syllables and the chromatic alterations are not accounted for in the syllable system; students sing the diatonic syllable name but are required to adjust and sing the pitch to fit the chromatic alteration.
- **Disadvantage**: Syllable patterns learned and memorized in one key or mode are not the same syllable names in a transposed key or mode.

✓ *Numbers Used to Teach Pitch*

In this system, numbers are assigned to pitches of the scale as determined by the major key signature, with one as the first degree, two as the second degree, and so forth up the scale. At the octave, the number one is used again to show that the note name is the same as the octave below. For example, the pitch "C" is "one" in the key of "C," but "C" is "two" in the key of Bb. Additionally, chromatic alterations have distinct labels that can be sung to identify the alterations; in the key of "C," the pitch sequence of C-C#-C would be sung "one, sharp-one, one" and the pitch sequence of D-Db-D would be sung "two, flat-two, two." When the key signature in the music changes, the numbers all shift together to reflect the new key, so this system is very much like Movable "Do" Solfège.

- **Advantage**: Students learn that key signatures create whole- and half-step relationships in the music and that these relationships create the feeling of a tonal center. Key and mode concepts are easy to teach and are easily applied to the literature. Because students are already familiar with counting and number sequences, there is no extra step to teach and memorize solfège syllables.

- **Advantage**: Students can sing specific number labels representing the diatonic and chromatic pitches in the music and can also use specific hand signs (holding up finger combinations) to accompany all the numbers while sight singing.
- **Advantage**: Number patterns learned and memorized in one key or mode will be exactly the same in a transposed key or mode.
- **Disadvantage**: Highly chromatic music without a clear tonal center is difficult to sing in a number system. Additionally, chromatic alterations require at least two syllables (such as "flat-six") and can be difficult to execute in fast passages where a single-sung syllable would work easier.
- **Disadvantage**: Absolute pitch memory is not as easily acquired because the scale and note names shift with each established key. "One" can be any note depending on the key signature.
- **Disadvantage**: While it is easier to teach beginners pitch concepts with numbers, it can quickly become confusing when counting and meter concepts (using numbers) are also introduced and when chord function concepts are studied that require a pitch to be considered with two conflicting number labels.

Systems for Teaching Rhythm Concepts in the Choral Rehearsal

There are a number of techniques for teaching rhythm concepts and each has certain advantages. Here is a brief overview of three of the most common systems:

✓ *Counting Within the Meter*

In this system, every note is labeled in relation to its function in the measure and meter. Beats are subdivided so that numbers or rhythmic syllables can be used to count and perform the patterns, and bar lines delineate the groupings in the same way that traditional musical notation does, with each new measure starting again on the number "One."

- **Advantage**: Students learn how to dissect and label the rhythmic patterns within the context of the meter signature and measure system using the same vocabulary that instrumentalists use.

- **Advantage**: Students already have a good grasp of traditional number systems from their math classes, and the system is easily taught and learned.
- **Disadvantage:** Students may be confused if a system of numbers has also been used to teach pitch concepts.

Rhythm and Counting Concepts in Common Time (4/4)

1	2	3	4
1 1 +	2 2 +	3 3 +	4 4 +
1 e + a 1 trip let	2 e + a 2 trip let	3 e + a 3 trip let	4 e + a 4 trip let
3	3	3	3

✓ *Takadimi*

In this system, much like the counting system above, every rhythm is labeled in relation to its function in the measure and meter. In simple meter, the first part of any beat is pronounced "ta" and the second half of the beat is pronounced "di." If four subdivisions of a beat are encountered, the rhythm is performed as "ta-ka-di-mi." In compound meter, the first part of the beat is still "ta," but the first subdivision into thirds is pronounced "ta-ki-da" and a subdivision into six groupings is performed as "ta-va-ki, di-da-ma."

- **Advantage**: Students can perform and count rhythms with percussive consonants and syllables that clarify the onset of the rhythmic values.
- **Advantage**: The system can't be confused with other numbers that may be used in a pitch system.
- **Disadvantage:** Students will have to memorize a new system from scratch and it may not be as intuitive for some as it is for others.

✓ *Kodály Method*

In this system, created by Hungarian composer Zoltán Kodály, syllables are tied to specific notational values regardless of their placement within the beat. An 8th note, for example, is pronounced "ti" whether it is on the first subdivision of the beat or later in the beat, and this applies regardless of the meter. Quarter notes are labeled as "ta," and two 16th notes would be performed as "ti-ri."

- **Advantage**: Students who experienced classroom music in elementary school may have used this system, and reviewing and implementing it may be relatively easy.
- **Advantage**: The system focuses on note values rather than meter, so reading in mixed meters could possibly be easier for some students.
- **Disadvantage:** Because Kodály developed the system for elementary-aged students, it needs to be expanded when the rhythms become more complex, which can add confusion to the learning process if the adaption is not well thought out ahead of time by the teacher.

Clearly there are more than three effective methods for sequencing rhythm concepts into the choral rehearsal, so remember to be curious and open-minded to any well-sequenced methods and techniques that you learn about during your career. What matters most is that you value musicianship enough to teach it to your students and that you allow them to become independent and expressive choral musicians. Whatever musicianship techniques you decide to implement are your personal decision, and you can always change your mind and try new techniques if you decide to do so. Some new teachers find it most convenient to align with the techniques that they learned in their ear-training and musicianship classes in college or to model the techniques that their own choral director used back when they were in high school. If your college choral methods professor has a prescribed set of recommended techniques for you to explore, you should do your best to learn and implement those methods. As long as your chosen technique accomplishes the goal of creating independent and skilled choral musicians in your choirs, you have chosen well.

RECAPITULATION

1. There are other systems for teaching pitch and rhythm that are not outlined in this text. Are you familiar with any of them? If so, describe how the technique is structured and make statements of advantages and disadvantages of the techniques as you perceive them to be. Comment on one pitch system and one rhythm system if you can. If you are not familiar with any other systems of pitch and rhythm instruction, answer this question by explaining which system outlined above (one for pitch and one for rhythm) you think might work best in your classroom and why you would be inclined to adopt each in your teaching.
2. Some teachers use only part tracks to teach notes and rhythms. On these recordings, the part to be learned is either played or sung and often the other parts are also included. On most recordings, the part to be learned is louder or in a separate right-left track for the listener and the accompaniment may also be included on the recording as well. Comment on both the advantages and disadvantages of using part-predominant recorded tracks in your curriculum. Be sure to include advantages and disadvantages for the teacher as well as the students. Are you inclined to use these kinds of tracks for learning notes? Why or why not?

Implementing a Program of Sequenced Musicianship

For the purposes of ease and explanation, this book will outline a system of musicianship instruction for pitch that will use Curwen/Glover hand signs and movable "do" solfège syllables with a "la-based minor," and a system for rhythm using "Counting within the Meter." As a beginning teacher, you should strive to implement and achieve fluency in pitch and rhythm instruction that is well sequenced in the short term regardless of the techniques you may eventually adopt over the long term. There are enough advantages to these systems to warrant learning them and including them in your pedagogy, at least initially.

Sequencing Pitch Instruction: Sound Before Symbol

In the movable "do" with a "la-based minor" system, syllable names are determined based on the major key signature with the first degree of the major scale called "Do," the second degree of the major scale called "re," and so forth. When the key signature changes, the position of "do" also changes, but the relative pitch relationships (the order of the whole and half steps) from "do" to the other syllables remain the same. Once a student can hear what "do" to "mi" sounds like in one key, for example, they can more easily hear the same interval in another key. In a "la-based minor" system, the natural minor scale is named starting on the sixth degree of the major scale so that the scale is sung "la-ti-do-re-mi-fa-sol-la," rather than renaming "la" as "do" and singing the syllables as "do-re-me-fa-sol-le-te-do." This approach remains consistent for teaching all the modal scales. For example, the Dorian modal scale is first introduced as "re to re" in relation to the major key, and then it is "moved" to different keys as "do" moves with the major key signature. This system works especially well with beginners who have not studied music theory in the past because "do" is always determined by the last flat (b), which is always "fa," or the last sharp (#), which will always be named as "ti."

Because sound should always precede symbol, the first step in teaching tonal musicianship to your choirs is to teach the students how to sing and audiate (the ability to imagine musical sound) the pitch relationships of the major scale while performing Curwen/Glover hand-sign gestures. If you are working with very young students in an elementary choir situation, a common interval that is often used in the elementary classroom is the minor third between "sol and mi." From there you can add "la" and then "re" and then "do," which all correspond to the pentatonic scale relationships represented by the black keys on the piano. Once students are able to sing those pitches accurately, you can add "ti" and then "fa." For older students in high school choirs, you can usually start by singing the complete scale with an octave range starting on "do," always listening for pitch accuracy and healthy vocal production. With middle school students, you may be able to start with "do" as long as you keep the note ranges in suitable areas of the changing male voice, which means that you will often use the key of "F" rather than "C" for your initial vocalizations.

You should spend some time in your rehearsals singing the diatonic major scale with hand signs until the students can sing and audiate all the steps and leaps across all of the syllables. If you have a choir that has never used this technique before, you may need to devote five to ten minutes per rehearsal solidifying the skills needed to master these pitch relationships. You can dedicate time for these skills during the warm-up sequence or throughout the rehearsal in small segments. You should note that it is normal for students to resist these techniques and activities if they have never had experience with, or been exposed to, these techniques in the past. If you have fun and make it an engaging and fast-paced experience for them, they will probably enjoy the lesson segment with you. Always use your best judgment and intuition to determine how much time to devote to singing with hand signs and building pitch memory when you are first introducing the concepts. A little work every rehearsal will yield excellent results over time, but you will have to evaluate the progress of each choir carefully to know when they are ready for greater musicianship challenges. Be patient.

If an ensemble has had pitch training in the past, they may be able to sing the diatonic scale, and even chromatic scale degrees, on the first day you meet them. It is always your first responsibility to assess the skill level of the choir and then select and adjust your techniques to help them find the greatest success. A good motto for a process-oriented teacher is "meet them where they are and make them better." If you help make their initial experiences fun and engaging, and if you commit to providing frequent and consistent experiences with the major scale, modes, and hand signs, you will notice a steady and healthy progression of your students' abilities to hear and perform pitch relationships. These abilities are an absolute prerequisite for learning to read pitches from standard musical notation, and your teaching of tonal concepts and pitch recognition is fundamental to everything you will teach later. If you are blessed enough to have students who studied music with well-trained elementary music education specialists in the primary grades, your students may already have acquired extraordinary abilities to hear and perform pitch and rhythm relationships and you might be able to move quickly to more advanced musical experiences with them.

If you are a new teacher working with students in your first job, and if those students have never developed the skills to hear and perform pitches using the framework of Curwen/Glover hand signs, you will need to teach them how to sing and perform songs that are above their ability to sight sing for your first public concerts. Don't worry. If you continue to implement a program to teach the students the skills they need to be excellent music readers, you won't need to teach everything by rote, or use part recordings, for very long. As the students develop their skills, they will learn music faster and more independently. They will rely on you less, and on themselves more, to identify, hear, and sing pitches in the score. Work every day to reinforce pitch concepts with all your choirs, and in as little as a few weeks you will see a noticeable difference in their pitch independence, and you will feel the satisfaction of knowing that you are creating choral musicians who will be able to continue to love and perform choral music well after the teacher is gone and after they graduate from your program.

Here are some suggested sequences for five to ten minutes of pitch instruction that you can implement after your vocal and physical warm ups:

✓ Have the students stand up together and be sure you have a visual reference for the hand signs available, such as the poster from this text. Establish the key of C major and then sing the pitch G while you sign the symbol for "sol." Instruct the class to echo everything you sing and to perform the hand signs that you show to them. Add G-E as you sing and sign "sol-mi." Listen for pitch accuracy and be sure they are singing with enough breath connection and energy to be successful. If there is a critical mass of success, add "la" and "do" and "re." Sing these pitches in random patterns, including repeated pitches on the same syllable with various rhythms and dynamics as well as leaps between all the intervals. If they miss an interval leap, sing up and down the scale to fill in the pitches between the leap, and then ask them to audiate the inner pitches of the leap as you show the stepwise motion with hand signs. For more advanced choirs, you can begin to teach them the chromatic hand signs too.

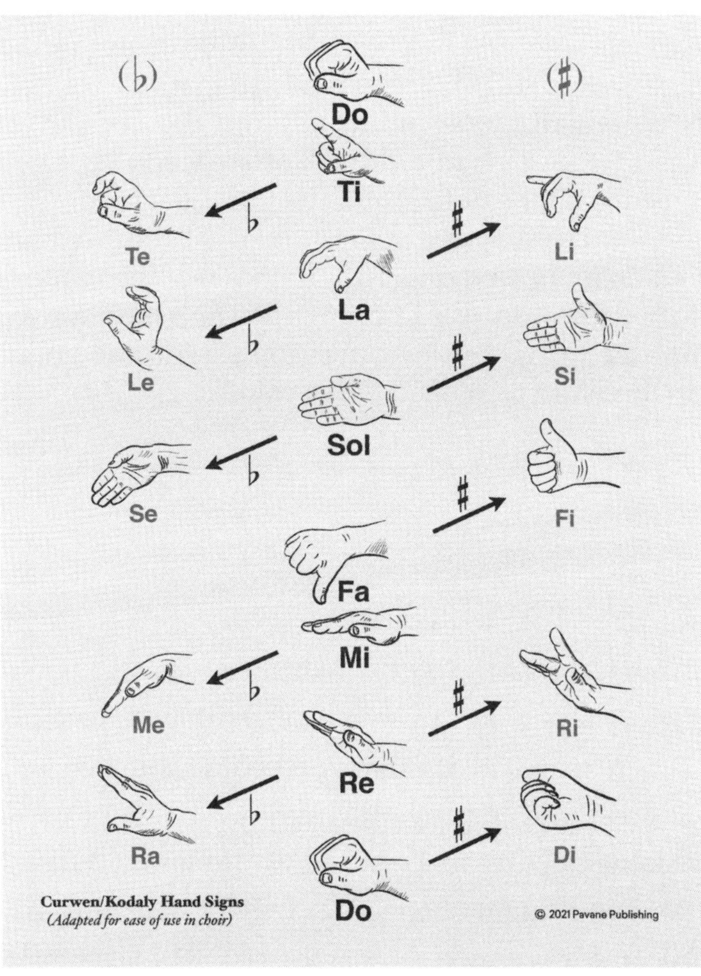

✓ Try establishing a key and repeating the exercise above and then show only the hand signs without singing them, challenging the class to perform them only from their inner hearing. Try changing the key and re-establishing "do" several times.

✓ Add "fa" and ti" to the scale and listen for pitch accuracy. Define the whole and half-step relationship of the major scale (also called the Ionian mode) using the poster (above in the section *Movable "Do" Solfège*), pointing out that "fa" and ti" create the half-step relationships down to "mi" and up to "do." Leap and step to all the syllables as you perform the hand signs with the class.

✓ When they can sing the major scale securely, break the choir into two groups and use both your hands to create a two-part texture. You can also ask individual students to lead their section when they know the hand signs well enough, creating a four-part texture.

✓ When they can sing the major scale accurately and in four parts or more, teach "fi" and "te" and challenge them to hear and perform these in parts. If their success is accelerating, add the other chromatic hand signs and intervals.

✓ Introduce the modes by singing and signing the natural minor, or Aeolian mode (la to la) and then the Dorian mode (re to re). Always relate these scales back to "do." From there, introduce the Mixolydian mode (sol to sol) and then the Lydian mode (fa to fa). Finally, introduce the Phrygian mode (mi to mi) and the Locrian mode (ti to ti). When "C" is "do," we can call the Dorian Mode "D-Dorian" because it starts and ends on the note D and the Phrygian mode "E-Phrygian" because it starts and ends on the note E. Likewise, the other modes can be named in relation to the first degree of the scale of the mode. Transfer this concept to movable "do" by teaching the class that, for example, when "D" is "do" the Dorian scale from re to re starts and ends on the note "E," and can therefore be named "E-Dorian."

RECAPITULATION

1. Audiation is an important skill for any musician, choral or instrumental.[1] Before a person can sing a pitch, they have to be able to imagine it. Describe an activity that you could sequence with a choir that would address and improve this skill over time. Describe what you would ask the class to do, how you would know if they were successful, and how you might change the activity over time as they build skill and become more successful at the task. Try teaching this sequence to your

1 "Audiation is the foundation of musicianship. It takes place when we hear and comprehend music for which the sound is no longer or may never have been present. One may audiate when listening to music, performing from notation, playing "by ear," improvising, composing, or notating music." Edwin E. Gordon, *The Gordon Institute for Music Learning (GIML)*, https://giml.org/mlt/audiation/

class, a choir, or friends who are willing to experience your sequence. Allow them to give you constructive feedback about your teaching effectiveness and planning.

2. Teaching pitch concepts to the choir during the beginning of the rehearsal is essential to setting the stage for continued learning. But it is just as important to transfer these skills and concepts to the literature being sung and studied so that meaningful connections to real music can be made and experienced. Select a piece of choral literature and create a warm up or hand-sign activity that addresses the challenges of pitch in the piece you selected. For example, if the piece has a large amount of leaps by a third in the diatonic major scale, create a short warm up or teaching sequence that focuses on leaps by thirds in the diatonic scale. Make the activity one to three minutes in length and strive to keep the class engaged in fun, fast-paced singing.

Sequencing Rhythm Instruction: Sound Before Symbol

In a system for rhythm using "Counting within the Meter," it is essential that students come to understand how meter works in printed music and how to interpret rhythmic notation so that the notes add up and make sense in the score. But before these concepts can be applied to printed music and reinforced in the rehearsal, students must be able to understand the concepts of steady beat and subdivision of the pulse. Most people who have had musical experiences in their formative years intuitively understand these concepts; yet it is not unusual for people who haven't had early musical experiences to struggle with these basic musical skills. It is essential, therefore, that you include rhythmic drills during your choral warm ups and rehearsals so that every member of the ensemble can attain and build upon the skills of rhythm.

One of the first skills that students need to master is how to move their feet and limbs to a steady beat. Students who already know this skill can easily step and dance to a pulse when music is played. But students who are still learning to move to a steady beat will be challenged to find the steady pulse in recorded music, let alone to perceive and move to a subdivision of the pulse. As basic as it sounds, you will need to provide opportunities for your choir members to experience pulse and steady beat before you can teach students to read steady beat rhythms in printed music.

A quick and effective way to get students moving to a steady beat is to have the teacher demonstrate steady-pulse movements and gestures while the choir members mirror the movements as they see them. This can be done in many various ways, both with and without recorded music. As you observe the students mirroring your movements, you will see some of them moving easily and with fluidity, while others will look awkward and jerky as they move. Of course, be sure that you, as the teacher, do your best to demonstrate clear and measured movement for the class; you may need to practice this before you model it, and consider recording a video of your preparation so that you can evaluate what the students will be seeing as you lead the class.

Here are some suggested sequences for rhythm instruction that you can integrate into your physical and vocal warm ups or as part of the pitch instruction after the warm up:

- ✓ The teacher steps side to side in a steady rhythmic pulse, for example: left foot steps to the left, and right foot steps to the left, then right foot steps right and left foot steps right. Keep a steady pulse and have the choir mirror the movements. Begin to hold up different numbers of fingers to indicate how many claps the choir will perform on each side. For example, step left with the left foot while holding up the index finger on each hand, and then as the right foot joins the left, clap once. Then as the right foot steps to the right, maybe hold up two fingers on each hand to indicate two claps as the left foot joins the right. The claps should be subdivisions of the stepping pulse. Vary the number of claps on each side between 1 and 4 and keep the choir watching, engaged, and on task. Also use two fists held up to indicate no claps.

- ✓ Instruct the choir to clap on the number you call out, and then count to the number as they clap on it. At first, count out loud all the way to the number. For example, in a steady pulse you will say "On 3 and 1&2&3" and the choir members should clap on 3. Don't clap yourself or they will only watch your gesture for the cue. Vary the tempo of the exercise, and call out different numbers as well. If they catch on quickly, start counting out loud, but then finish the count silently. For example, you can say "On 6 and 1&2&3&......." and see if they can audiate the pulse and still clap together. For more challenge, have them clap the off beats. You would say "On the and of 5, and 1&2&3&4&5&." If they are good with rhythm, challenge them to clap the second and fourth subdivisions of the 16th note subdivisions as well. Refer to the rhythm poster on page 180 to teach these subdivisions as "1e&a, 2e&a, 3e&a, 4e&a" etc.

- ✓ Clap a rhythm for the choir while they listen, and then have them clap the rhythm back to you. You can also pair this with a vocal "chant" on the counts or on a neutral syllable to help clarify the duration of longer notes. Do this within a steady pulse and implied meter. When they catch on well, add counts to your rhythms as you clap, and challenge them to clap and count just like you did. You don't have to only speak the counts that you clap on, but rather you will speak the subdivisions while you improvise over the beats. For example, if you are in a meter of 4/4 and clapping a quarter note, two 8th, two 16th and an 8th, and a quarter note, you would either count "1&2&3&4&" as you clap, or even better "1e&a, 2e&a, 3e&a, 4e&a" because of the third beat that includes the 16th notes. As the choir builds an understanding of the counting system, challenge them to improvise their own rhythms as they count, and encourage them to lead this activity in front of the class or in small groups.

✓ Instruct the choir to make a short hiss connected to the abdominal area with a short bust of air, like a wet finger removed quickly from a hot stove. Have them do it on a cue, consisting of holding your left palm up while the right index finger touches it from above, cuing the hiss. When the hiss is strong and unified, play the piano exercise below as they hiss. The hissing should then be subdivided (hissing twice as many times), so that it is on beats 1 and 3, and then on every beat, and then on every 8th note subdivision, and then on every 16th note subdivision. At the end, have each choir member sustain the hiss and cut themselves off with a "conductor's gesture" when each singer runs out of breath.

Once the choir has developed the skills to sing and audiate the pitches of the major scale and modes, and when they can repeat, count, and improvise rhythms as well as move to steady beats and subdivide rhythms, you can begin to relate what they know and hear to the little black dots in their music. The five to ten minutes spent in every class will set the stage for them to interpret the musical notation like choral musicians instead of singers, and the black dots will suddenly take on specific meanings, rather than looking like blobs on top of lines signifying relative pitch and duration.

Sequencing Pitch and Rhythm Instruction: Sound Linked to Symbol

When you get your first job, you will need to evaluate the musicianship skills of all your choirs. If you find that your choirs didn't have much musicianship training before you were their leader, don't feel bad if you have had to rely on a lot of rote teaching in the rehearsals at first. We always want to meet them where they are and make them better, and if they can't read music yet, they will need to learn the music in the best way that they are capable of learning it. Ideally, you will have already found brief mom... during rote teaching to mention things like, "That's do-mi-re, not do-fa-mi," when correcting pitches by ear, and, "That's off the beat, not on the beat, so put the release on the '&' of 3" when working with rhythms. Making the transfer from hand signs to notation takes time, but if done every day and reinforced through the literature, you will likely notice a very steady improvement in the choir's musicianship.

For many choirs, you will be able to link sound to symbol fairly soon after you introduce the hand signs and rhythmic counting concepts as outlined above. You will probably get a strong feeling when the students have begun to demonstrate enough success singing pitches accurately with hand signs and performing rhythms to a steady beat while counting, and this is your indication that it is time to introduce notation and other musicianship skills to them in a systematic way. Some choirs will be ready sooner than others, so you will have to evaluate them every day to decide when to begin your pivot from sound to symbol.

To maximize your time and teaching effectiveness, you should always attempt to teach music notation concepts while connecting those concepts to the literature chosen for performance. For example, rather than teaching sight singing by learning melodies from a sight-singing book, you should use the performance literature in the student's folders to maximize transfer and connection to the sight-singing segment of the lesson. This is a particularly effective teaching method because knowing about a musical idea, and experiencing that idea through musical inquiry and performance, are two different things. Any musical concept we teach our students should be represented in the literature they are studying so that appropriate transfers can be made and so that they can anchor and remember the concepts with repeated experiences with the music that activates both their intellectual and their *musical* intelligences.

Here is a suggested sequence for pitch and rhythm instruction that you can implement after your vocal and physical warm ups for about ten to fifteen minutes. You may still need to include your "sound before symbol" sequences to keep their musical skills progressing appropriately, but you will also learn to integrate these into the notation sequences over time. Note that you may not get very far in the first rehearsal, and that's OK. If you only get to Step Three on the first day, you will get there faster on day two. You will need to work as fast as you can while knowing that some choirs will get it faster than others. Do your best, and be ready to teach, re-teach, and reinforce, over and over again, all of these concepts. Eventually you can use two, three, and four-part excerpts to challenge the choir at their ability level, and as they get better and better, and as their musicianship skills improve, you will have to choose more challenging excerpts from the literature. Isn't that exciting?

1) Before class begins, select a short unison excerpt from the current choir literature. Write it clearly and accurately on the board, or project a hand-written version with a document camera. Make it look as neat and accurate as possible, or use a music notation program to make a fresh printed version. Do NOT use the actual score for this step. You will not include words or dynamics.

2) Establish the key by playing an "E" on the piano or by using a tuning fork. Lead the students as they sing the E major scale using hand signs. Emphasize the key, range, and leaps and steps that appear in the sight-singing excerpt. (1 min.)
3) Teach (or re-teach and reinforce) the rules for finding "do" in any music. Use the wording, "The last flat is 'fa' and the last sharp is 'ti.' If no sharps or flats appear, then 'C' is 'do.'" Write in the syllables for the scale on the staff.
4) Teach or (or re-teach and reinforce) the clefs of the grand staff. Use

the wording "Each clef has two names, the treble or G-clef and the bass or F-clef. The treble clef marks the note 'G' and the bass clef shows us how to find the note 'F.'" Write the note names on the staff. Teach or re-teach that the letter name for "do" names the major key (E major), or "la" names the key if the music is in a minor key (C# minor).

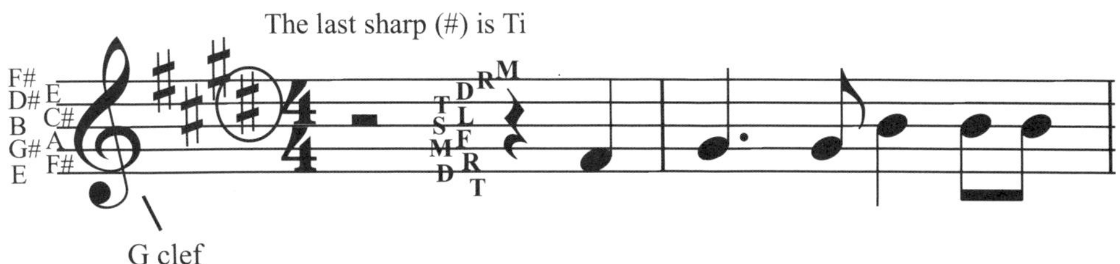

5) Identify and label the syllable names in the excerpt. Use capital letters and place these under the staff. Have students involved by showing the hand signs and/or naming the syllables out loud.

6) Re-establish the key and have the students **sing the syllables out of**

time. Help them find leaps and tricky parts. Point to the note you want them to sing, and feel free to go back a note or forward to the next note as you reinforce the correct pitches.

7) Teach (or re-teach and reinforce) the meter (time) signature. Use the wording, "The meter or time signature tells you two things. The top number tells you *how many beats there are in each measure,* and the bottom number tells you *what kind of note equals one beat.* So in 4/4, we would expect to have four quarter notes in every measure or the equivalent of four quarter notes." Write the counts in above the staff. Have the students count and clap the rhythm. Create drills for rhythm and subdivision of the pulse out of context if necessary. The students should speak the smallest subdivision as they clap, so in this excerpt they would say "1&2&3&4&" as they clap. (Note that a "+" is easier to write by hand than a "&" but both are pronounced "and.")

Have the students **speak the syllables in rhythm** while they also show the hand signs.

9) Have the students **sing the excerpt on syllables, in rhythm, at a slow tempo.** If successful, have them sing it at a faster tempo. Fix any major errors as you hear them.

10) Have the students **sing the excerpt in rhythm on a neutral syllable**, possibly showing the hand signs while singing if they are able.

11) Have the students **count-sing** the excerpt on the correct pitches, possibly showing the syllable hand signs while singing.

12) Have students **open their music folder** to the literature that contains the excerpt. In this example you might say, "Please take out 'The Road Not Taken' and turn to page 2. Find measure 4 and look at the soprano line. You probably recognize these notes and rhythms as the ones we just sang. Sing the soprano line in your own range." Establish the key again and have them **sing the excerpt on syllables** while looking only at the literature. (Don't let them write the syllable names in the music.) Then use the words from the literature in the context of the piece, using accompaniment or any other reinforcement (playing the other parts).

Commissioned by the Minnesota Valley Men's Chorale in honor of their 10th concert season
Steven Boehlke, Director

The Road Not Taken

(S.A.T.B.*, accompanied)

for Alex Mikhail Robinson

* *Also available in TTBB, P1460*

P1459

It is normal to think that there is way too much in this sequence to include in a typical choral rehearsal of sixty minutes. We would never want musicianship training to completely take the place of ensemble singing, and you will have to use your intuition to know how to balance both musicianship and ensemble performance. After you build the musicianship skills of the students to the point that they can get through this sequence in about five to ten minutes, you can continue to challenge them by not filling anything in on the excerpt before they sing it. Eventually you may be able to use the actual literature to reinforce and increase musicianship without needing to write on the board or project a printed version. Once the students develop an independent ability to name the syllables, note names, and sing on syllables, counts, and words, you will have created a student-centered learning environment of choral musicians rather than a teacher-centered class for singers.

You can fix the "musicianship problem," and you can make that fix work to everyone's advantage. Students can do anything you teach them to do, and you will be amazed at how much they can do with daily practice and good, sequenced musicianship training. You will find that your need to teach by rote will diminish greatly over time, though you should still use rote teaching occasionally when it makes sense to do so. Additionally, you will eventually need to pick more challenging literature for the ch... you discover that they can sing everything in their folder without too much difficulty. Indeed, teaching students to be independent musicians takes more time initially, but in time you will find that it is the most efficient time-saver that you could ever have as part of your teaching pedagogy.

RECAPITULATION

1. Select a piece of choral music and create a lesson plan to teach the musicianship sequence outlined above. In your plan, actually write out what you will say word for word, and practice teaching the lesson by yourself before you do it in front of the class or for another person.

2. How would you rate your own musicianship on a scale of one to ten, with one being the least skilled, and ten being the most skilled? Are you better at pitch concepts, rhythm concepts, or are you about the same at both? Do you have better music reading ability when playing the piano or another instrument, or do you do your best sight reading with your voice? What could you do to improve your musicianship? Outline a plan that would help you the most. For example, describe what you could do every day, and for how long, to make the most personal progress on your musicianship.

3. Can you think of ways to alter, improve, or expand the musicianship sequence in this chapter to make it more effective? Describe what you would change and why.

Chapter Conclusions

Teaching musicianship is an essential value that all professional choral music educators should strive to implement in their programs. Even though this text recommends using movable "do" with a "la-based minor," as well as counting within the meter to teach rhythmic concepts, it is up to the individual teacher to decide which techniques and methods are best suited to the students in their choirs. The art of teaching requires every teacher to adapt these techniques to be as effective as possible with beginning, intermediate, and advanced students. We always want students to be challenged, but we also want them to be engaged and successful in every rehearsal. When you become a student-centered choral music educator, you will value the techniques that empower your students to become self-sufficient and self-reliant musicians.

It is important that you start with sound before symbol and that you transition to notation as the students are ready to connect these sounds to symbols. This implies that you will use a rote teaching method and musical techniques that do not require students to read music much of the time (at first) when teaching students with little musical background. As their skills grow, and as you begin to introduce notational concepts, your use of a rote teaching approach will decrease. Music notation is very counterintuitive for people unfamiliar with how it is structured, and you will need to remember that the understandings of notation you learned long ago were acquired over time and not in a few short lessons. You will have to be patient with your students, and you will need to be willing to teach and re-teach these skills until your students can demonstrate competence and understanding negotiating musical and notational concepts. If you use the actual literature to be sung in concert to teach musicianship, as opposed to unrelated musical examples from another source, you will provide your students with a direct and obvious transfer to authentic musical experiences. Strive to teach musicianship during every rehearsal, even if only for a few minutes, and to relate those concepts to your literature throughout the entire rehearsal whenever possible.

The advantages to solving the musicianship problem are many. While you might think at first that you don't have enough time to teach musicianship, if you implement these techniques, you will come to understand over time that you don't have enough time NOT to teach your singers how to be excellent and independent musicians. What might seem like a lot of time for little payoff at first will become the biggest time-saver for which you could ever ask. Once you train your students to be choral musicians, and not teacher-dependent singers, you will be able to program more difficult literature as they become better sight singers. You will also find that note-learning questions that were once addressed to you as the teacher will often be solved by the students without your help, allowing you to focus more on the expressive elements of the performance. When musical issues do arise in rehearsal, you will have a musical framework to identify the problem, put it into context, and solve it once and for all. Additionally, because the students can read the music independently, you may also find that you have more time to examine the text, go into detail about musical and historical aspects of the piece, and play with choices of interpretation. Finally, when you ask students to "learn the music" either in a sectional or outside of class time, you will have provided them with the musical tools they need to be successful. As a student-centered teacher, you will be giving them the gift of independent musicianship so that they can continue to love and learn music long after they graduate from your choral program.

Chapter Eight

Materials for the Choral Music Educator

8. Materials for the Choral Music Educator

"For every minute spent organizing, an hour is earned."
~Benjamin Franklin

The Importance of Managing Classroom Materials

An experienced teacher, after being in front of choirs and classes for many years, has a wealth of experience and pedagogical techniques to draw upon while instructing in the classroom. A veteran educator has practiced and developed their teaching art, year after year, through many successes and failures, to make lesson and rehearsal time a positive, engaging, and functional experience for the students. Great teachers can both teach and manage large groups as well as small groups, beginning and advanced students, as well as exceptional students; and sometimes these groups are all in the same room, in the same class, at the same time. The knowledge and expertise that an experienced teacher gains over the years is the single most important tool that they have to teach effectively, and you will also develop these skills throughout your career.

But while the art of great teaching relies in large part upon the knowledge and expertise of the educator, effective teaching is also dependent upon the management of the physical aspects of the teaching environment. These physical aspects, which we will refer to as "materials," need to be appropriate, of high quality, well organized ahead of time, and functional for the learning environment. Your materials will include your choral literature, textbooks, musical instruments, technology, and all of the physical aspects of your teaching environment. In essence, anything that can't be stored in the brain of the educator will be classified here as an aspect of the classroom environment and materials. Your ability to organize and manage your classroom materials will most certainly shape your teaching outcomes and effectiveness because "having the stuff to teach with" can be just as important as "knowing how to teach." Beginning teachers must be willing to develop their understanding and organization of the physical aspects of the classroom and curriculum so that their developing skills and knowledge are not negatively affected by any shortcomings inherent in the quality of the chosen classroom materials.

Selecting a "Textbook" for Your Class

There are many similarities between teaching math and teaching music. Imagine, for a moment, what it would be like to be a math teacher. You would be responsible for many of the same things that a music teacher is responsible

, including motivating your students, creating and implementing teaching methods for sparking their curiosity, and teaching and reinforcing both social and academic behavior. You would be responsible for creating engaging lessons that would advance your student's understanding of math concepts. You would need to be a lifelong learner of math and to keep your enthusiasm fresh for your subject matter so that your students could observe and emulate your excitement for learning mathematical concepts.

There is one significant difference between teaching music and teaching math, however, and that difference is embodied in the materials that you have at your disposal to teach your subject matter. Simply stated, math teachers use math texts to teach math, and music teachers use music to teach music. The choral literature you choose to use in your classroom is your textbook, and how you choose your textbook is at the foundation of your successful teaching and expressive music making.

As a math teacher, you would probably start your teaching year introducing Chapter 1, page 1, in your standard-issue textbook. Every year would probably start the same way, and the concepts of addition and subtraction would be taught with the same chapter over and over again. A good math teacher would be someone who is able to maintain personal enthusiasm for the academic content year after year while reusing the exact same teaching materials. A really creative math educator might try to think of ways to supplement the material in the textbook to keep the ideas fresh and current and to adapt the concepts to each individual learner. But in the end, one plus one always equals two, no matter what source the teacher is using to teach this concept.

As a choral music educator, you will have the exciting opportunity to change your textbook over and over again because your textbook is, quite literally, the choral literature that you choose to include in your curriculum. Of course you will always be teaching vocal techniques, sight singing, musicianship, breathing technique, and the concepts of melody, harmony, form, texture, tone color, rhythm, articulation, and other expressive elements, but these will all be taught through the lens of the music you will choose for your students to study and perform. Choosing appropriate literature, then, is one of the most important aspects of the art of choral music education, and understanding what "appropriate" music is depends on your ability to assess the various needs and abilities of the choirs you teach.

In most situations you will be the only person choosing the literature that your students will prepare, study, and perform, and your expertise in choral programming must be developed if your students are to become well-versed and competent choral musicians. Like the math teacher who teaches 1+1=2, you will teach that there are four beats to a measure in common time, and that the quarter note gets one beat, but you will get to teach that concept with a music from a variety of style periods and musical genres. Your opportunity to select quality literature from the vast amount of music available to you is an enormous responsibility as well as a huge benefit. It would probably be fair to say that many math teachers get a little bored teaching from the same textbook year after year, and we are all so fortunate as choral music educators that our textbook is constantly changing and that we alone get to choose the music our students will study.

Great choral literature paves the way for great learning, great rehearsals, and great concerts. Just as you should have a clear and well-articulated philosophy of music education, you should also have a sound and methodical framework for selecting literature to be included in your rehearsals and concerts. It is not uncommon for inexperienced teachers to select choral music for a variety of well-meaning, but pedagogically incorrect, reasons. For example, selecting music that you sang in college when you were a student, but that is too difficult for your choirs, is a very common mistake. Choosing a large amount of music that is mostly in a slow tempo, because you like slow music, is also a poor choice. Choosing music that you have heard other choirs sing, but that is too easy or difficult for your choirs, is also a less-than-appropriate choice. Likewise, throwing a bunch of pieces in the folders of your choir, and singing through the pieces with the students to help you choose your program is not an appropriate way for a professional choral music educator to select music. Additionally, letting the students choose the literature for study and performance is a particularly bad idea in most instances, not to mention that it's your job, not the student's job, to choose quality educational materials for your curriculum. There are many other mistakes that can be made when it comes to selecting and programming choral music, and this chapter will provide you with some guidance to help you navigate your way through choosing the quality literature and other materials that will function well for you, your audiences, and your choirs.

RECAPITULATION

1. Many students, as they embark on becoming choral music educators, begin to understand that effective choral programming requires a large amount of expertise, experience, and artistic judgment by the teacher. In most cases, students do not pause to think about the work that conductors employ when it comes to selecting interesting high-quality literature for the choir. Reflect on your lifetime of experience as a choral singer. What varied kinds of choral music have you sung in your choral ensemble experiences? Discuss what you remember about the literature that your teacher selected for you to study and perform, and comment on what you remember about the variety of historical periods, genres, and contrasting styles you sang. If you didn't sing in many choral ensembles, comment on the variety of musical literature you have experienced in your lifetime or in any vocal or instrumental experiences that you may have had outside of choir.
2. What are some of your favorite choral works that you have studied or performed? Provide specific examples of literature when you can. Which aspects of the literature do you think contributed to your positive experience? Were there other aspects, such as the performance venue or the other people in the choir, that helped you enjoy the literature? Likewise, think of an example of a piece of music that you didn't particularly enjoy singing. Explain why you think it fell short of becoming one of your favorite pieces?

Organizing a Common Vocabulary for Examining Choral Literature

Choral music students who are just starting to learn the pedagogy of their teaching craft sometimes regard the choir director as a teacher of songs. They view the choral conductor as a person who facilitates rehearsals and creates concerts for the public. While this might seem to be an accurate assessment on the surface, and while some choir directors do fit this definition, a professional choral music educator shouldn't merely be a teacher of songs; they should be a *teacher of musical concepts.* They shouldn't just be someone who teaches the Mozart *Ave Verum* or the Schubert *Kyrie*, but rather they should be artistic facilitators who provide opportunities for students to explore musical literature through the concepts of tempo, tone color, form, harmony, melody, texture, key signature, mode, meter, rhythm, articulation, phrasing, expressive performing, text painting, and other artistic elements. An educator of musical concepts makes it a priority to select quality literature that is rich in opportunities for teaching musical understanding to every person in the choir, even if the choir is a beginning, intermediate, or advanced ensemble.

When you are a professional choral music educator, there are musical terms that are considered common knowledge that form the basis of your ability to discuss aspects of your musical art form. Many of these you have already learned in private lessons, music theory classes, or ensemble classes. Yet many undergraduate music students, even after they have studied these terms in music classes, have a difficult time defining and explaining these concepts aloud when requested to do so. This is not unusual, because being able to teach and explain a concept in a straightforward and simple way is quite different than understanding a concept in your own mind. An important step in your development as a music educator is to develop a variety of methods, and a rich vocabulary, to teach the concepts of music to your students.

Because your literature choices are your textbook, and because your textbook forms the basis of your educational curriculum, you should start by outlining the musical skills and concepts that you hope to teach to your choral musicians. What do you want them to know? What should they be able to do after a year (or more) of study in your choir? What musical knowledge and terminology should they be integrating into their awareness, and what musical genres should they explore, perform, and experience? Each student's concert folder should reflect your answers to these (and other) questions, as well as your goals and values for their learning and achievement. Just like a well-balanced diet can provide all the nutrients your brain and body need to be healthy, a well-balanced concert program should provide many opportunities to explore and perform a rich variety of musical concepts and understandings. By clarifying and defining the words that musicians use to describe music and musical concepts, and by understanding how to explain the conceptual aspects of the terms to someone who is NOT a musician, you will be able to identify music that can be used to teach these concepts more effectively.

RECAPITULATION

1. Imagine yourself teaching music to high school students at some point in the future. Outline some thoughts in writing to clarify the following questions: What do you want them to know and what should they be able to do after a year (or more) of study in your choir? What are some of the most important musical concepts and terms that you want them to be aware of, and what musical styles and genres would you want them to explore, perform, and experience in your choir program?
2. A *lexicon* is a wordlist or glossary of terms that defines and describes something. Choral music educators need to develop their professional lexicon so that they can employ musical vocabulary while teaching musical concepts through the literature. Without consulting a music dictionary or going online, define the following terms in your own words as well as you can. If you don't know the definition, guess, but don't look up the term. Try to use words that could be understood by someone who has very little musical experience so that what you say is concise and clear for the novice musician. Strive to be clear, simple, and concise for each term.
    a. Tempo
    b. Key Signature
    c. Form
    d. Meter
    e. Melody
    f. Time Signature
    g. Legato
    h. Staccato
    i. Accent
    j. Texture
    k. Genre
    l. Rubato
    m. Harmony
    n. Homophony
    o. Counterpoint
    p. Inversion
    q. Modes
    r. Coda
    s. Range
    t. Tessitura
    u. Copyright
    v. Round

w. Partner Song
x. Through-Composed Form
y. Phrase
z. Cadence
aa. Secondary Dominant Harmony
ab. Syncopation
ac. Dissonance
ad. Consonance
ee. Sonata Form

3. A textbook should explore a significant amount of the information that students need to master the essential concepts of a class. Your literature choices are your textbook. Create a sub-list of musical concepts for each of the following headings that you could teach to your students through the choral literature that you might choose. For example, because you should be able to teach time signatures through your literature, you could write the following as your first sub-list:

   1. METER: 4/4, 2/4, 3/4, 6/8, 5/4, 7/4, 12/8, simple vs. compound meter, mixed meter, shifting meter, metric modulation.

   If you can think of more to add to number 1, you can add more to it. Once you have a list of concepts related to meter, move on to the headings below. If you get stuck, just think about all the musical concepts that you could possibly teach with quality choral music and add them to your list. For this question, feel free to look up the words and search online for ideas to complete your lists.

   2. MELODY:
   3. HARMONY:
   4. RHYTHM:
   5. TEMPO:
   6. TONE COLOR or TIMBRE:
   7. ARTICULATION:
   8. DYNAMICS:
   9. FORM:
   10. TEXTURE:
   11. TONALITY:
   12. MUSICAL STYLE or GENRE:
   13. HISTORICAL TIME PERIOD:

Finding Quality Choral Literature

There is a lot of choral music available in the world, but you will need to know where to look for it. We are fortunate that the age of electronic information has made finding music a much easier task than it used to be only a couple decades ago. Before *Google* searches and the ubiquitous presence of online information on your phone, tablet, or personal computer, finding and discovering choral music was a much more daunting challenge. It is no wonder that years ago, many new teachers of choral music felt limited to music they sang in high school or college or that they experienced at choral conferences and reading sessions.

But today we can browse online literature lists, view and download public domain and purchased music from websites, and we can listen to live and recorded performances of choral music online through services like YouTube. We can communicate directly with living composers and preview their new music from the privacy of our schools and homes. We can browse our professional organization's websites for programming ideas and literature lists, and we can contribute ideas to blogs and other online sites so that others can benefit from our knowledge, recommendations, and experiences. And while it has never been easier to find, exchange, and experience new and classic choral music, it still requires valuable time and effort to seek out the highest quality literature available and to create systems for organizing the titles so that you can review and study them when you need to plan and program your concerts.

It is important that you start collecting information about choral music that you would actually use with your future ensembles and that you create an electronic database of these titles for easy reference. It is even more important, however, that you start your own single-copy library of choral music so that you have instant access to the original notation when you need it. Programming music without seeing the written notation is not a recommended practice because there is too much information in a score that can inform your choice as an educator to teach or not to teach the piece. Publishers will often let you see the first few pages of a piece, but few sources will allow you to preview an entire octavo for fear that some people will steal and duplicate the music illegally. Your single-copy library should only include legal copies of music and should contain music that you would actually use someday with a real choir. In this sense, you should limit your library to only *good quality* choral pieces.

So how do you determine if a piece of choral music is of good quality? It has been said that there are only two kinds of music in the world: *good* music and *bad* music. As a listener, music is good if you personally enjoy listening to it, or if it moves you in an emotional or intellectual way. Your personal musical tastes will determine for you what music you choose to have on your playlists and what live concerts you will attend and enjoy. Not everyone will, or should, agree on what concerts they want to attend or what recorded music they are willing to spend money on to own and experience. When you are a consumer of music, you alone get to decide what you like and dislike and what music you label as good and bad. But when you are deciding what music to include in your curriculum (your textbook), you have to let your choices be guided by more than just your personal tastes in music; you have to consider what a given piece of music can *teach* your students, and you must have a solid pedagogical justification for including or not including certain music in your repertoire choices.

You will soon be exploring and discovering new resources for finding choral music, and you will share some of these resources with your classmates and colleagues. But there is one resource that you may want to explore right away, and that is the *Choral Public Domain Library*. The CPDL was founded in December 1998 and is a website where people can post and download free choral/vocal scores, texts, translations, and other useful information. We will learn more about this online resource later in the chapter when we talk about copyright laws and fair use. But in your search for quality choral music, you will certainly want to click around this website to see what it can offer you as a choral educator.

RECAPITULATION

1. What are your favorite sources for finding choral music? Make a list to share with the class and explain the advantages and disadvantages of these sources in your opinion. If these sources are online, share the web addresses with the class as well.
2. Think of a piece of music that you feel is really good. It can be of any style or genre. What musical or expressive elements contribute to its designation of "good" in your mind? Likewise, think of a piece of music that you don't feel is particularly good. It can be of any style or genre. What musical or expressive elements contribute to it being "not good" in your mind?
3. Imagine being stranded alone on a deserted island with the recorded music of only one composer, pop band, or vocal artist. Assume that you have plenty of food, water, and shelter, and some way to have this music played through a good sound system or headphones. What composer, pop band, or vocal artist would you choose and why?

Developing Criteria for Selecting Quality Music

Choosing quality choral music takes time, experience, and skill, and there is no single equation that can determine for you if you should include a piece in your curriculum or not. As a conductor and educator, you will collect music over the years, either in your mind or in reality, that could be described as: *"Music I will do before I die, and music I will die before I do."* A common mistake new teachers make is thinking that difficult music is quality music and that beginning-level music is not quality music. But they soon discover, after a careful search for quality literature from a wide variety of sources, that there is good music and bad music available for every choir, beginning through advanced. It is essential that you, as a beginning educator, develop an ability to differentiate quality music from music of lesser quality and to develop specific criteria for making these decisions. There are many factors to consider, including the richness of the text, the variety of specific musical concepts that you can teach through the music, the genre, style, or historical time period of the music, expressive qualities of the musical writing, the historical significance of the piece, the historic relevance of the composer, the way the piece fits in a specific concert program or unit of study, and many other possible attributes that make a piece of good quality.

While it takes expertise and effort to find music, it takes time and *study* to determine if a piece of music has enough quality to justify being included in the library of music you intend to teach someday. Simply glancing through a piece of choral music to determine its educational and artistic significance is like shopping for a good frozen pizza by looking only at the boxes in the freezer area of the grocery store. The pizza might look really appetizing on the surface, but in the end it might not taste very good or be worth the money. More information is likely needed to make a firm determination of quality. The beginning choral music educator must develop a system for looking more closely at music to assess the quality musical aspects and to ultimately make a choice to include or not include a piece of music in the curriculum.

In music theory classes you learn to approach chord structure and how to analyze rhythms and motives, and in conducting class you learn how to communicate musical ideas through gesture; these skills will help you as you study your choral scores before your first rehearsal. But how does one approach a piece of choral music that has never been sung or seen to determine if it is worthy of inclusion in your curriculum? On what should you base your investigation, and what criteria should you set in your initial analysis of a piece of music?

One way to approach a new piece is to complete the following form as an initial study guide. This form will require you to look carefully and study the aspects of the piece such as range and tessitura, difficulty of the writing and accompaniment, tempo, form, text, tonality, voicing, educational aspects, state music standards addressed, program placement, and ways that you can use the piece in a concert set. If you have difficulty completing the form or coming up with at least three musical concepts that you can teach with the piece, it probably shouldn't be included in your curriculum. This form can also serve as the starting place to collect data for an electronic database that you can create as a personal reference tool of your single-copy library of choral music.

Choral Literature Full-Analysis Form

Your Name ________________

Title & Translation: ________________________________ Composer: ______________

Composer's Dates: ______________ Arranger/Editor (if applicable) ______________

Voicing: ______________ Octavo Number: ___________ Publisher: ______________

Text/Poetry Source: ________________________________ Secular or Sacred: __________

Language(s): ______________ List the accompaniment, instrumentation, or a cappella: ________

Accompaniment difficulty level: Easy/Beginner ____ Moderate/Intermediate ____ Difficult/Advanced ____

Tempo & Changes: ______________ Form ____________________ Length of Piece: ______

Tonality/Modality: ____________________ Period & Style/Genre: ______________________

Range & Tessitura:

Soprano Alto Tenor Bass

Difficulty of the piece (rubric score): __________ Designation of Difficulty: __________

Justification of difficulty score:

____

Assign this piece to all the uses that apply:

_____ Beginning Unison Songs (any voicing)

_____ Rounds and Canons (any voicing)

_____ Partner Songs (SA, SAB, 3-part mixed)

_____ Middle Level Mixed (3-part mixed, SAB)

_____ Beginning Mixed HS Choir: SATB

_____ Intermediate Mixed HS Choir: SATB

_____ Advanced Mixed HS Choir: SATB

_____ Beginning Treble Choir: SSA (including SA, SSAA)

_____ Intermediate Treble Choir: SSA (including SA, SSAA)

_____ Men's Choir: TB (including TTB, TTBB)

Why is this a piece of music worth including in your single-copy choral music library? List at least three specific musical or educational concepts that you can teach by programming this music.

1.

2.

3.

1

Assign this piece to a "menu" program (check all that apply):

_____ Opener

_____ Early Program Slow

_____ Early Program Fast

_____ Centerpiece (or "Different")

_____ Late Program Slow

_____ Late Program Fast

_____ Closer

_____ Other (Specify):

Brainstorm two possible SET PROGRAM TITLES or CONCERT THEME TITLES that you could use this piece for in a concert.

1.

2.

This piece can be listed in my single-copy library as ____ for the best use considering overall difficulty, level, and voicing (for example, *Beginning Mixed HS Choir: SATB*).

Other Notes:

Assessing Repertoire Difficulty Levels

When you are a new teacher who is learning how to choose appropriate repertoire, you will need to develop an ability to assess the difficulty of a piece of music. You will need to be sure that your groups have the appropriate musical challenges to interest them and to keep them learning and engaged, but it is also important that you choose music that will not frustrate them and be too challenging to perform well in the rehearsal time available. It is not uncommon for beginning teachers to misjudge the difficulty of music they select, mostly because they don't consider all the aspects that make a piece of music difficult or easy to learn. For example, a piece with an unfamiliar foreign text might be considered difficult to learn at a first glance, but if the piece has a repeating binary form, then the notes might take less time to learn, balancing the time needed to learn the foreign text. It is important, then, to look at all the various aspects of a piece of music to determine how challenging it might be to learn and how much time will likely be needed in rehearsal to bring the selection to an expressive public performance.

Some music publishers will include information about the difficulty levels of the literature that they sell, but many others won't. Likewise, some state music education associations will offer lists of recommended or compulsory literature for state festivals, and these will sometimes be accompanied by ratings of difficulty for each piece. Experienced choral music educators, often through years of trial and error (and success), develop a solid ability to look at an unfamiliar piece and assess the relative challenges of learning it. In one read-through (or less) many veteran teachers will be able to make a comment like, "This would be a great piece for my beginning mixed choir to find success at the start the school year," or in contrast say, "This is a wonderfully challenging piece, but it would take away from everything else we do just to learn it in time for the concert." So how can you, as a developing teacher, learn to examine new music with an eye for relative difficulty? The first step is to know what makes a piece of music difficult to learn and what aspects of a piece make it easier to learn. Here are some of the main elements to consider.

- MUSICAL FORM: The form of a piece represents how it is organized, how often there are repeating elements, and how much new material is introduced from the beginning to the end of the piece. If a piece has many sections of the form that repeat, then a lot of time is saved once the initial section is learned. In contrast, if a piece of music has few repeated sections, there will need to be rehearsal time dedicated to learning each unique section.

- HARMONY: The harmonic language of a piece plays a large role in its relative difficulty. A piece that is diatonic and stays within the primary key, without chromatic alterations, can be easier to learn than a piece that employs the use of chromatic alterations. When a song has a shifting tonal center, or uses more than one key at a time, it will require extra rehearsal time to learn.

- RHYTHM: The use of rhythmic elements in a piece of music can make the selection much easier or more difficult to learn, depending upon how those elements are presented and how much they repeat. Sometimes a rhythmic line that looks difficult can be taught quickly by rote or notation, and if that rhythm repeats frequently, it can save rehearsal time. Occasionally pieces will appear to be more difficult rhythmically because of the metric groupings and notational style, even when different choices would make the music easier to read and perform by sight.

- VOICE LEADING/RANGE/TESSITURA: It is common for new teachers to overlook how important the vocal writing is to each voice part. When a part is mostly stepwise, without angular leaps, it is easier to read by sight. Vocal lines that sit in the passage between the middle and high vocal registers for extended periods of time will require, for most choirs, extra time to develop proper technique and stamina. In contrast, when the writing stays primarily in the middle parts of the voices, the choir will be able to produce a more beautiful tone with less rehearsal time.

- TEXT: It's wonderful that we get to sing texts; it's one of the things that makes a choir expressly different than a band or an orchestra. But learning to communicate text meaning and to pronounce unfamiliar languages accurately can take up a significant amount of rehearsal time. Even English texts can range from simple to complex, with easy rhymes, repeats, and meanings to rich texts that require extra time and a dictionary to understand.

- TEXTURE/ACCOMPANIMENT: Thin textures, such as a single-line unison melodies, are easier to learn and perform than thicker textures, such as lines that divide into eight parts. Homophonic writing, where everyone sings the same words at the same time, is easier to learn than contrapuntal writing within a polyphonic texture. The instrumental accompaniment can also aid or detract from the ease of learning for the choir. If the accompaniment supports the musical aspects of the piece, it can help the choral musicians hear and learn their part. But if the accompaniment is very independent of the vocal writing, it can make it much more difficult for the choir members to learn their parts.

One tool that you can use to develop your ability to assess choral literature difficulty is the "*Music Literature Difficulty Assessment Rubric*." To use it, you would take a piece of choral music and examine it first for musical form alone. As you mark the places where the sections repeat, you should decide if these are exact repeats or if each repeat is a variation of the former section. When you are confident that you have studied the form of the piece accurately, you should be able to assign it to one of the three boxes marked "Beginning," "Intermediate," or "Advanced" based on the descriptors in each box. Next, within the assigned box you will make a subjective decision as to the relative difficulty of the piece based on its form. For example, if you have "theme and variation" as the form, is it a simple theme and variation or a more complex and changing theme and variation? If it's simple, you might assign it a score of 6 or 7, but if it's more complex, you might choose to give it a score or 9 or 10. To the far right of that column, under "Level Score," you would write the assigned numeric score and briefly note your justification. When you are done with "Form," you would then move to "Harmony" and so forth. When you have completed all six level scores, you then total them up and assign an overall rating based on the difficulty range at the bottom of the rubric. You might be surprised to see a score for a piece that you thought was easy falling into a range of intermediate or advanced, or a piece that you thought of as advanced scoring as intermediate or beginning, based on all the factors in your analysis. In time, you will learn to consider the elements from this rubric intuitively when you look at scores, but for now, it is wise to use and apply it to a good number of pieces that you study as a beginning teacher and conductor.

RESONANCE: The Art of the Choral Music Educator
Music Literature Difficulty Assessment Rubric

Name of Choral Selection ______________________ **Voicing** ____________

	Beginning	Intermediate	Advanced	Level Score
Form	A (Simple Melody) AB (Binary) ABA (Ternary) Rounds Partner Songs other ________ (1–5)	Theme and Variation Strophic with Variation ABACA (Rondo) ABCBA (Arch) other ________ (6–10)	Through-Composed Fugue other ________ (11–15)	**1–15** ________ **Notes:**
Harmony	Diatonic Simple Chromatics Major or Minor Mode Clear Tonal Center Simple Key Changes Few Dissonances other ________ (1–5)	Chromatic Possibly Modal Borrowed Chords Unusual Key Changes Tonal Center Shifts Use of Dissonances other ________ (6–10)	Very Chromatic More Dissonance Possibly Atonal Unusual Chords Possibly Bitonal Part Splits other ________ (11–15)	**1–15** ________ **Notes:**
Rhythm	Simple Rhythms Few Syncopations Same in All Parts Repeated Patterns Simple Meters other ________ (1–5)	More Complex Rhythm More Syncopation Only Some Repetition Varied in Parts Odd Meters other ________ (6–10)	Complex Rhythms Unusual Patterns Little Repetition All Parts Different Shifting Meters Unusual Notation other ________ (11–15)	**1–15** ________ **Notes:**
Voice-Leading/ Range/ Tessitura	Mostly Step-wise Moderate Ranges for All Parts Mid-Range Tessituras in All Parts other ________ (1–5)	Some Wider Leaps Extended Ranges for Some Parts Extended Tessituras in Some Parts other ________ (6–10)	Angular Leaps Extended Ranges for Most Parts Extended Tessituras in Most Parts Part Crossing other ________ (11–15)	**1–15** ________ **Notes:**
Text	Less Complex Familiar English Easier Foreign Texts Rhyming other ________ (1–5)	More Complex Old English Harder European Texts Less Rhyming other ________ (6–10)	Very Complex Non-European Texts Rich English Little or No Rhyming Large Amounts of Text/No Repeats other ________ (11–15)	**1–15** ________ **Notes:**
Texture/ Accomp.	Homophonic Texture Accomp. Supports Harmony Easy A Cappella Simple Percussion One solo Instrument other ________ (1–5)	Polyphonic and Homophonic Textures Acc. Contrast Harmony Harder A Cappella Complex Percussion Several Solo Instr. other ________ (6–10)	Polyphonic Texture Acc. Differs Harmony Difficult A Cappella Unusual Percussion Unusual Ensembles Excessive Splits other ________ (11–15)	**1–15** ________ **Notes:** **(TOTAL)** ______ **Assigned:** ________

Difficulty ranges for Literature Analysis Levels (Rubric scores)
5-35 points (Beginning Range), 36-65 points (Intermediate Range), 66-90 points (Advanced Range)

When you are striving to ascertain what constitutes music that is challenging for a choir, in the end it depends on the specific skills of the choir. A piece that is easy for one choir may be quite challenging for another choir, and the most difficult music might be easy for professional choral singers. What matters most is that you come to understand the musical abilities of your choirs and that you continue to teach them to be independent and smart choral musicians. As you become a more skilled and experienced teacher, your students will grow faster and will become more skilled as choral musicians. The music you used for your beginning choirs might become too easy for the same choir five years later, primarily because of your growth and expanded effectiveness as a teacher.

Finally, there are a couple of rules of thumb to consider when it comes to choosing literature and factoring in difficulty levels. The first rule is that you should strive to find music that fits the ability levels of your ensembles, rather than choose music that you already know and that you hope they can grow into. It's typical for new teachers to program music they did in college, thinking that it is easier than it is; music you know tends to seem easier than music you don't know. A new piece that is appropriate for an ensemble is always preferable to a familiar piece that is out of their range to learn and perform. The second rule comes from American conductor and educator Josh Haberman. He maintains that a choir folder should follow a 20–60–20 rule: 20% of the music should be *easy enough* for the ensemble to read easily and sound good on almost immediately, 60% of the music should be exactly *within the ability* of the ensemble, and 20% of the music should *challenge* the ensemble in some way. In other words, 80% of the music in the choir folder should be within their musical ability or even a little easier than their ability level. Therefore, if you are programming for an intermediate choir, you would need to include some beginning and some advanced literature while maintaining about 60% of your selections at the choir's target ability level.

RECAPITULATION

1. Think about a piece of music that you have experienced, either as a choral musician or as an audience member, and that you really enjoyed. What musical elements or performance aspects of the piece made it a favorite for you? Write a paragraph describing your experience. Why do you think you remember the experience with a positive perspective? Likewise, recall a choral piece that you didn't enjoy for some reason. Describe the musical or performance aspects of the piece that may have caused you to dislike it.

2. Have you even been in a choir or musical ensemble that wasn't able to learn their music in time for the concert? If so, how did it make you feel to be under prepared for the concert? What could the director have done differently to make the concert a more successful experience for the ensemble? Likewise, have you ever been in a group that didn't have enough challenging music to learn? How did that make you feel, and what would you have done differently if you were the director of the ensemble?

The Art of Programming Choral Music

As has been stated, your literature is your textbook, and your textbook is the foundation on which to build your curriculum. It is exciting that we get to use a new "textbook" for every concert, and it can be fun and challenging to spend your time and focus creating new and exciting programs for your students to prepare and perform in public concerts. There is, however, an art to programming music for choral concerts, and it is worth outlining some of the elements that make up an effective program. When you choose your choral literature effectively, your choices will help to serve many of the following functions:

- ✓ The music will be diverse, with contrasting tempi, tonalities, textures, accompaniments, represented cultures, texts, and languages.
- ✓ The music will be rich in musically expressive elements that can be studied during class, advancing the musicianship and musical insights of the ensemble members.
- ✓ The music will be performed in a logical, well-paced, and interesting sequence during the live concert so that the audience will be moved in some way and so that they will appreciate the concert experience.
- ✓ The music will provide enough challenge to keep the students interested and working throughout the preparation of the concert, but not so overly challenged that they can't learn the music in time. Likewise, the music will not be so easy that the students are bored well before the concert.
- ✓ The music will help the *teacher* grow as a musician through the study, teaching, and performance of the literature.
- ✓ The music will provide enough variety to allow the teacher to keep the rehearsals well paced and interesting for the duration of the concert preparation.

At first glance, this might seem like quite a large list of criteria that your music selections will need to adequately address, and it is. But these aspects of programming choral music can be learned by the beginning teacher in the same way that beginning music theory students learn to analyze and understand Bach chorales: by analyzing and understanding how the pieces function together. Once you learn to organize your own personal single-copy choral library in terms of what each piece can teach, how each title can function in a larger concert program, and how to combine works to maximize the choir and audience experience, you will be well on your way to becoming an effective and artistic concert programmer.

Engaging Both the Choir and the Audience

When you start thinking about how to create a program, it can be helpful to remember that music must be experienced in real time, note by note, during a performance. This is true for any performance art, and there are important and predictable elements that contribute to an engaging and interesting performance. Many Broadway musicals, for example, follow a predictable form that grabs the attention of the audience at the outset, introduces the characters early on, and creates ease and conflict within the story plot. Additionally, more often than not, the "good guys" prevail in the end, leaving the audience with a satisfied feeling at the completion of the musical. These predictable elements create a framework for the telling of the story, and audiences love to engage with the characters in real time as they experience a variety of highs and lows during the show. Musicals that stray too far from this form can be interesting for being different, but they rarely carry the impact and satisfaction for the audience that the more common forms do.

Because your concert program selections will embody the musical concepts that you want your students to learn, your literature selections must be rich in contrasting styles, tempi, languages, modes, and textures. Well-crafted literature choices will engage your choir in rehearsals more effectively because the pace and challenges will be constantly changing from piece to piece. Likewise, your audience, who will only get to hear the music one time in concert order, should be compelled by your literature selections to focus and engage during the concert; we want them not just to *hear* the music, but to *experience* it as fully as possible as an art form. A well-selected concert program will hold an audience's attention and interest, and the whole concert and rehearsal experience will function well for the choir and the audience alike.

Ideally, any concert program that you create will be engaging, interesting to sing and study, and perfectly suited for the choral musicians studying it. There are many creative ideas to pursue those ideals, and there is no right or wrong way to program choral music. There are different kinds of choral programs, just as there are different styles of music, and through your career you will most certainly explore a good variety of programming styles. It can be helpful to examine a few of these programming style templates so that you can understand how certain kinds of programs function for both the choir and audience alike.

These examples are to the choral director like recipes are for a cook; the recipe provides guidelines, but the cook adjusts the ingredients until the meal tastes best. You will need to experiment with different combinations of choral works to make a great and engaging program, and following and understanding programming templates is a good place to start. Let's explore a few common forms of choral programming that will help you plan for similar kinds of success in your concerts.

The Menu Program

The most common form for choral programming is what we will call the "Menu" approach. When you sit down to a nice and expensive dinner at a restaurant, you expect to be treated to a variety of tastes, textures, and experiences throughout the meal. You expect that the food will be presented in appealing ways and that the order in which the food is brought to your table will make sense to both your palate as well as your sensibilities. Your experience eating the meal is dependent upon the quality of the food, its careful preparation, the timing of the service as well as the presentation of the food on the plate. Great chefs understand that certain culinary flavors are best served before other flavors and that certain foods go well together, while other foods do not complement each other very well in the same sitting. Likewise, a great meal usually has set stages, such as starters, salads, main courses, palate cleansers, and desserts. We expect to eat our meal from front to back, in real time, with dessert last.

When you choose music in the Menu Program format to create a public concert performance, you are like a chef creating a meal for a patron of a restaurant. You are entrusted to choose music that is interesting and that flows in a logical and appealing way. The Menu approach to programming categorizes music based on its *function* in the program rather than its aesthetic appeal as a stand-alone piece of literature. Just as you wouldn't want to eat seven salad courses back to back at a fine restaurant, you wouldn't want to sequence too many pieces in your concert that fulfill the same function in the program. As you start to think of music in terms of what it can teach as well as how it will function in a live concert, you will begin to see the literature you choose in a different light.

Here are the basic building blocks of the Menu Program, and a brief description of how each kind of piece functions in this approach:

OPENER
EARLY PROGRAM SLOW
EARLY PROGRAM FAST
CENTERPIECE (Change of Pace)
LATE PROGRAM FAST
LATE PROGRAM SLOW
CLOSER

The OPENER is a piece of music that grabs the attention of the audience and engages them in some way. It can be argued that just singing the first song, in any style or tempo, will get the attention of an audience that was sitting and waiting for the concert to start. While this is certainly true, the opener should have something special about it that serves as an attention getter and momentum starter. An Opener does not have to be fast and loud, but music in a faster tempo and at a louder dynamic will announce the start of the program strongly. If an Opener is in a slower tempo and softer dynamic, surrounding the audience or processing to the stage works well to get the audience engaged in the music. Fanfare-type pieces, works that employ added instrumentalists, and antiphonal works can serve to open a program effectively as well. Generally, the Opener in a menu-type program is usually not a particularly lengthy composition, and it is rarely the longest piece compared to the rest of the program. The Opener is to the Menu Program what the appetizer is to the meal: a first taste that awakens the senses and prepares the listener for the next selection. A creative conductor can use the physical space of the performance hall and other added elements to create effective openers. Walking onto the risers quietly and singing a soft, long, and quiet piece is a sure way to have the first piece *not* function as an Opener in a Menu program.

The EARLY PROGRAM SLOW is a piece of music that flows well after the piece that preceded it and that creates interest for the listener by introducing new and contrasting musical elements. Because the audience is focused and fresh, this piece can challenge the listener with more dissonant harmonies, thicker textures, and a longer duration than the Opener. Unfamiliar texts and languages, mixed modes, and polyphonic textures are some possible elements of an Early Program Slow piece. Music from any time and style period can be used as long as the work has a certain amount of interest and complexity compared to the other pieces in the program. The Early Program Slow is to the Menu Program what the salad course is to the meal. A great salad is made up of many ingredients, including rich greens and lettuces, cheeses, nuts, fruits, and meats, all with a salad dressing that brings the tastes together as a complete experience. If you think of this piece as a rich salad, as opposed to a piece of iceberg lettuce without any salad dressing, you will be able to identify Early Program Slow pieces more easily. This piece can be, but need not be, long in duration. Finally, if the chosen Opener of the program were to be a slow-tempo piece, you would not follow it, as a general rule, with an Early Program Slow piece; rather, you would choose an Early Program Fast piece to create the desired contrast between the two selections.

The EARLY PROGRAM FAST is a piece of music that flows well after the piece that preceded it and that creates interest for the listener by introducing new and contrasting musical elements. Because the audience is still focused and fresh, this piece can also challenge the listener with complex musical elements, harmonies, rhythms, and texts. It shares many of the same functions that the Early Program Slow has, but with a faster tempo that creates momentum in the flow of the program. Music from any time and style period can be used, as long as the work has a certain amount of interest and complexity compared to the other pieces in the program. The Early Program Fast is to the Menu Program what the soup course is to the meal. A great soup is made up of many ingredients that are combined together, often over high heat and with time to simmer, to create a unique and interesting taste experience. If you think of this piece as a hearty soup, as opposed to a simple bowl of hot chicken broth, you will be able to identify Early Program Fast pieces more easily. This piece can be, but need not be, long in duration.

The CENTERPIECE is a piece of music that creates a midpoint in the arch of the Menu Program that stands out as a feature in some way. Usually this is the longest piece in terms of duration, though it doesn't have to be. A Centerpiece can be musically complex or it can be particularly interesting for other reasons. Sometimes these kinds of works will change tempi several times within the piece, may have shifting or mixed modes, or may offer aleatoric or chance elements. Music from any time and style period can be used, as long as there are musical elements present that serve to feature the piece in some way as compared to the rest of the program. Everything that the audience has heard thus far should set up the Centerpiece in some way, so finding a work that contrasts with the chosen Opener, Early Program Slow, and the Early Program Fast pieces is essential. Multi-movement works, performed as a set without applause between movements, work well as Centerpieces. The Centerpiece is an arrival point in the early part of the program and functions as a kind of pivot point to the last half of the program. The Centerpiece is to the Menu Program what the main course is to the meal. A main course is considered the "meat" of the meal, is often served in a larger portion, and usually embodies interesting combinations of flavors and textures with side dishes included. Creative conductors can make a piece function as a Centerpiece by adding instrumental accompaniments, multi-media elements such as slide shows, or by featuring dramatic elements such as staging, lighting, narration, or soloists. None of these elements are absolutely necessary for a piece to function as a Centerpiece, as long as there is a "main course" feeling to the work within the program.

The LATE PROGRAM FAST is a piece of music that flows well after the Centerpiece that preceded it and that recreates momentum in the program if the Centerpiece ended slowly. If the Centerpiece does not end slowly, the Late Program Fast should add musical elements not heard in the Centerpiece or program thus far, with rhythms and harmonies that are somewhat easier for the audience to listen to. Multicultural pieces and faster-tempo contemporary pieces make good choices for this point in the program. The Late Program Fast is to the Menu Program what a palate cleanser is to the meal. A good palate cleanser, such as fresh ginger or a small cup of fruit sorbet, serves to clear the taste buds after the main course, and it is meant to offer simple, less complex tastes that transition well to the final courses of the meal. What makes an Early Program Fast different from a Late Program Fast is the relative lack of complexity and ease of listening for the audience. If the early selections required a good amount of conscious focus and energy from the listener, then the late selections should require *less* focus and energy in comparison. Ideally, this piece will not be longer in duration than the Centerpiece.

The LATE PROGRAM SLOW is a piece of music that flows well after the piece that preceded it and that allows the audience to take in the music without a lot of intent focus. At this point in the program the audience is less fresh and has experienced a good number of contrasting musical elements throughout the concert. The Late Program Slow piece is designed to provide something familiar, either in title or genre, in a way that the audience can experience the musical sonorities without much aural effort; they are ready to just listen and enjoy the sound of the music. The Late Program Slow is to the Menu Program what a tea or coffee course is to the meal. It is a light, enjoyable, easy-to-digest part of the dinner. Late Program Slow pieces are often in English, but they don't have to be, and arrangements of folk songs and familiar tunes, as well as popular songs, work well in this part of the program. Besides being in a relatively slow tempo, these pieces are characterized by some sort of familiarity, ease of listening, or particular beauty in the compositional writing. If you think of this piece as a warm cup of coffee or tea, as opposed to another helping of steak and potatoes, you will be able to identify Late Program Slow pieces more easily.

The CLOSER is a piece of music that brings the program to a logical conclusion by providing musical elements that create energy and finality in the audience's experience of the concert. For a piece to function as a closer, it has to *end well*, in contrast with the Opener that has to *start well*. It is common for a closer to be in English, but multicultural and mixed-language pieces can work well as closers too. The Closer is to the Menu Program what the dessert course is to the meal. A good dessert is appealing and alluring to the senses, and it is the last taste the diner will get for the evening. Likewise, a good Closer will not challenge the ears or instincts of the audience more than what preceded it, and it will usually have some familiar elements in terms of genre or style. Many people think of spirituals as good (if somewhat overused) closers, which they can be; but a creative conductor can find many other kinds of pieces that can function well as Closers, including pop song arrangements, jazz, folk, and multicultural song arrangements. Combining these pieces with group movement, added instruments, or multi-media elements can enhance the effect of the Closer, bringing the concert experience to a unified and satisfying conclusion.

As you begin to classify music in terms of Menu Program function, you will notice that there are some kinds of pieces that do not fall easily into any of the categories above. Specifically, there are two types of pieces that you will encounter somewhat frequently that don't fit the menu: 1. A piece that has both fast and slow sections and 2. A piece that has a moderate tempo that stays constant but is neither fast nor slow. For 1, we will use the designation of MT (meaning that it has a "mix of tempi") and for 2, we will use the designation of CP (meaning "change of pace"). Both of these designations can be added to the traditional menu designations so that, for example, a changing-tempo centerpiece could be labeled Cen/MT, and a Late Program Fast piece could be labeled LPF/CP.

The parts of the Menu Program described here function together as the building blocks of literature choices that will interest and engage the choir while they learn and study the music. Likewise, programming this way will engage an audience who will be experiencing the music in sequence, in real time, during the concert. As a beginning choral music educator, you can benefit from learning to use this approach in your first concerts, and then you can experiment with other ways of programming to test what works best for your tastes, your students' learning, and your audience's response to your concerts. This format ensures that your literature will be varied in tempo and complexity and that you will have an interesting program that flows well from start to finish.

Not every concert situation will require a full menu-type program, and more often than not you will be building smaller Menu Programs for your choir's concerts. The framework and function of the pieces will always work the same, and shorter concert segments should strive to have the same flow and impact as longer concerts. Here are the basic building blocks of a five-song Menu Program:

OPENER
EARLY PROGRAM SLOW
EARLY or LATE PROGRAM FAST
LATE PROGRAM SLOW
CLOSER

And here are the basic building blocks of a three-song Menu Program:

OPENER
EARLY or LATE PROGRAM SLOW
CLOSER

It should be noted that effective programming in the Menu Format is not as simple a task as it sounds. The preceding language was precise in declaring that a piece of music should "flow well after the piece that preceded it and create interest for the listener by introducing new and contrasting musical elements." You will have to look at key relationships, modes, textures, and all the musical elements that characterize a particular piece of music to decide if it fits appropriately and artistically in the flow of your program. Imagine having seven stacks of music in front of you, all sorted into piles by Menu function:

1) OPENERS
2) EARLY PROGRAM SLOWS
3) EARLY PROGRAM FASTS
4) CENTERPIECES
5) LATE PROGRAM FASTS
6) LATE PROGRAM SLOWS
7) CLOSERS

Although it seems like you could, you wouldn't necessarily be able to randomly select one piece from each pile and still be sure that your program would work effectively. The *art* of programming is based on studying a piece, getting a feeling for what it brings musically and aesthetically, and creating combinations of literature sequences that make musical and artistic sense. There is no perfect way to teach a beginning choral educator exactly what makes choral pieces fit well together, so you will have to create lots of programs, experience them, and decide for yourself what works for your tastes and sensibilities. Selecting a well-crafted choral Menu Program is like preparing a great meal and requires careful attention, knowledge, taste, experience, and skill to select, combine, and present all the elements in the most aesthetically powerful and satisfying way.

RECAPITULATION

1. When you start exploring choral music with an eye for programming in the Menu format, you will need to either see the musical score or hear a performance of the music in order to determine the function that the music can serve in a concert. Sometimes one single piece can serve all the functions of a good Opener, Early or Late Program Fast, or Closer, so you will have to think about the *best* use of the piece in your selected program. Most of the time, a piece with several possible functions will work best in different places in the concert sequence based on the other literature surrounding it. For the pieces below, find scores or performance recordings online and make two Menu Programs, using each piece only once. There isn't one right answer for this task, so be ready to explain your thinking and choices to the class or your colleagues. However, these fourteen pieces can combine well into two separate Menu Programs, so if you are left with a choice or two toward the end that don't make sense in the format, you will have to go back and move something around until it does makes sense to you.

Program 1:
OPENER:
EARLY PROGRAM SLOW:
EARLY PROGRAM FAST:
CENTERPIECE:
LATE PROGRAM FAST:
LATE PROGRAM SLOW:
CLOSER:

Program 2:
OPENER:
EARLY PROGRAM SLOW:
EARLY PROGRAM FAST:
CENTERPIECE:
LATE PROGRAM FAST:
LATE PROGRAM SLOW:
CLOSER:

Select your two programs from these choices *(do not use any pieces more than once).*

My Soul's Been Anchored in the Lord **Moses Hogan** (1957–2003)
Hal Leonard Music Pub. (HL 08703235) SATB, a cappella (3′00″)

O Magnum Mysterium **Tomas Luis de Victoria** (1548–1611)
Mark Foster Pub. (MF 2130) SATB, a cappella (3′30″)

My Spirit Sang All Day **Gerald Finzi** (1901–1956)
Boosey & Hawkes Music Pub. (Hal Leonard) SATB, a cappella (2′00″)

Innisfree **Gerald Custer** (b. 1953)
Santa Barbara Music (SBMP 04) SSA/TB, piano (2′00″)

Betelehemu **Arr. Barrington Brooks**
Lawson Gould (52744) SATB choir, a cappella, percussion (5′00″)

Hallelujah **Ludwig v. Beethoven** (1770–1827)
Hal Leonard Music Pub. (HL 50293600) SATB, piano (4′00″)

Leonardo Dreams of His Flying Machine **Eric Whitacre** (b. 1970)
Hal Leonard Music Pub. (HL W08501444) SATB, a cappella (8′30″)

Sanctus **Randall Johnson** (b. 1959)
Santa Barbara Music Pub. (SBMP 1052) SATB, piano, timpani (4′15″)

Halleluya **Bill Derksen**
Hal Leonard Music Pub. (HL 08501356) SSATB, marimba and percussion (2′30″)

Serenity (O Magnum Mysterium) **Ola Gjeilo** (b. 1978)
Walton (WW1480) SATB div., a cappella, violin, or cello (5′45″)

i carry your heart with me **David Dickau** (b. 1953)
Walton (WJMS1104) SATB, piano (4′00″)

Rytmus **Ivan Hrusovsky** (b. 1927)
Santa Barbara Music Pub. (SBMP 319) SATB, a cappella (2′00″)

Come Mighty Father **George F. Handel** (1685–1759)
Alliance Music Pub. (AMP 0185) SATB, piano (2′20″)

Oh, My Love's Like A Red, Red Rose **R. Scott Coulter** (1925–1979)
Santa Barbara Music (SBMP 04) SSA/TB, piano (2′00″)

2. Using music you already own, or with music you find online, find a good example of each part of the Menu Program. These pieces do not have to represent a program, but rather each should represent a good example of each kind of piece. In other words, don't select them because they combine well together, but rather because they are, in your opinion, good examples of pieces that function in each spot in the Menu format. So that you can share your choices with the class or your colleagues, find a recording online for each of the examples you choose. If you can't find a recording, choose another good example to replace it.

   Examples you found (one of each):
   OPENER:
   EARLY PROGRAM SLOW:
   EARLY PROGRAM FAST:
   CENTERPIECE:
   LATE PROGRAM FAST:
   LATE PROGRAM SLOW:
   CLOSER:

Set, Themed, and Multi-Choir Programs

Once you have studied the Menu Program format and have a better understanding of how it functions to create interest for the choir, the audience, and the conductor, you can apply these insights into other approaches to programming. The most common variation of the Menu approach is what we will call the "Set" approach. While the Set program maintains most all of the aspects of the Menu Program, including varied tempi, textures, accompaniments, and other musical elements, it groups the choral selections based on some sort of organizing characteristic or theme. This organizing element can be a title, such as "Songs of Spring" or perhaps a historical grouping such as "Music of the Renaissance." The pieces within the Set should function in a similar fashion to the Menu Program, with contrasting pieces that create flow and momentum. One way to think of the Set approach is to imagine each Set as a "mini Menu" with an organizing theme of some sort.

One aspect that makes a Set program different than a Menu Program is that the "sets" within the Set program will be performed from beginning to end *without applause*. This lack of applause makes the experience of the Set different than the "Sing, pause for applause, repeat" nature of the Menu Program. The audience experiences a longer period of uninterrupted music that is linked together, without the discharge of energy that happens during clapping. It is common to hear choral programs that are made up entirely of several sets with several pieces in each Set, or for there to be a mixture of Menu and Set elements represented with, for example, an Opener (with applause), an Early Program Slow (with applause), and then a Set of several pieces performed without a break for applause, followed by a Late Program Slow and a Closer, each with applause. In this particular example, the Set portion functions as a kind of Centerpiece in the Menu Program.

Here is an example of a two-set program for TTBB Chorus using an "all-Sets" programming approach. Notice that, for this example, each Set has an organizing theme and that all the composers and arrangers are different within each set:

Sacred Latin Texts

I. Medieval Gloria — Vijay Singh (b. 1966)
Belwin Pub. (OCT9614) SA/TB, a cappella (2′30″)

II. Adoramus te Christe — Giovanni da Palestrina (1525?–1594)
Choral Public Domain Library (TTBB (1′45″)

III. Gloria — Eugene Butler (b. 1935)
Alliance Music (AMP0471) TTBB, piano (2′30″)

Singing Is for Girls (Songs about Women)

I. Viva Tutti — Anonymous, ed. Ralph Hunter
Lawson Gould (LG00778) TBB, a cappella (1′20″)

II. Gentle Annie — Steven Foster, Arr. Parker/Shaw
Lawson-Gould (LG 859) TTBB, piano, (2′45″)

III. There is Nothin' Like A Dame — Oscar Hammerstein & Richard Rodgers, Arr. William Stickles
Hal Leonard (HL 00346949) TTBB, piano (3′00″)

The above examples have three songs for each Set, but this is not a prerequisite; you can have two songs or many songs in any given Set. It is also possible to have a Set organized by the music of a single composer, even if the pieces were not composed within the same opus:

Praise and Glory
Anton Bruckner
(1824–1896)

I. Ave Maria
Choral Public Domain Library, SATB, a cappella (3′05″)

II. Locus Iste
C. F. Peters, SATB, a cappella, (3′00″)

III. Christus factus est
Choral Public Domain Library, SATB, a cappella (3′15″)

The example above represents a good offering of music by a wonderful composer, but it also creates a possible programming risk because all three selections are Early Program Slow a cappella pieces. This can be particularly problematic if you create a set called "Ave Maria" and select pieces that all feel and sound similar to one and other. Bruckner never intended that these three pieces be sung back to back in the same setting, so the organizing theme of "Praise and Glory" had to be created by the concert programmer. The audience will get an extended experience of the compositional style of Bruckner, but without much contrast of timbre, accompaniment, or tempo. However, Sets like this one can be interesting despite the lack of variety. If you were to program a Set like this one, it would be recommended that you have other contrasting elements in the rest of the program. In other words, if you have ten minutes of Early Program Slow music in a row, don't repeat that choice again in the same program.

Sometimes composers themselves write music in pre-programmed sets, and in most cases the function of a Menu Program is built in for you. Here is one such example:

Three Madrigals
Emma Lou Diemer
(b. 1927)
Boosey & Hawkes (1254432) SATB, piano (4′40″)

I. O Mistress Mine, Where Are You Roaming?
II. Take, O Take, Those Lips Away
III. Sigh No More Ladies

In the above example, Diemer creates a fast-slow-fast tempo scheme with related but contrasting musical material in each movement and sets texts selected from the same source. These kinds of composer-created Sets can be quite interesting and compelling for your choir and the audience alike, and there are many of these types of Sets available if you look for them. When you discover Sets like these, you should make a note if you think the Set works as written, or if you would prefer to combine some, but not all, of the movements. You are never under any obligation to perform every movement of a composer-created Set, and you should always consider the flow and variety of your chosen program to keep it interesting, artistic, and educational. Occasionally, you will see a composer-created Set performed, but with one or two selections substituted from another work by the composer, or even with a selection or two from a completely different composer. In the end, you get to choose the music that makes your literature serve your overall programming goals.

Another common variation of the Menu approach is what we will call the "Theme" approach. The Themed program can use Menu or Set elements, or a combination of both, but with one over-arching idea to tie together the entire concert. Every selection in the concert will relate to the theme in some way, so a very broad theme works best. Here are but a few examples of possible titles for a Theme program:

- ✓ Love Songs Through the Ages
- ✓ Freedom, Protest, and Human Expression
- ✓ Bach, Beethoven, and the Beatles: Centuries of Great Music
- ✓ Salute to Broadway!
- ✓ Selections from the American Songbook
- ✓ Seasons of Music (Summer, Fall, Winter, and Spring)

Theme programs can be fun and are especially easy to promote to audiences if they have a catchy title. If they are organized like Menu Programs, then there will be applause after each selection, and every selection will relate back to the theme. If there are Sets within the Theme program, then each Set should have a clear relation to the Theme as a sub-heading. For example, if the Theme of the entire program was "Salute to Broadway," then you might create Sets with the following headings "Sondheim," "Bernstein," and "Rogers and Hammerstein."

Finally, just because you list your literature in Sets in your program, you are under no obligation to keep the audience from applauding after each song. If your intention, however, is to *not allow applause* during a given Set, you should probably tell the audience (either verbally or in the written program) not to applaud after each piece, especially if the audience does not have a lot of formal choral concert listening experience; additionally, when conducting a Set you should learn to keep your hands high after each final cut-off and then to start the next piece without bringing the arms down too far or too fast, which will help cue the audience to hold their applause.

In your collegiate choral ensembles, you may have experienced the Menu, Theme, and Set approaches in combination during semester concerts lasting twenty-five to thirty minutes per ensemble. But when you become a middle and high school choral music educator, you will need to learn to use an approach called the "Multi-Choir" method. In this approach, you may have three to six choirs on the same concert and not enough time to learn and perform an entire twenty-five-minute concert segment for each group. Using a Menu approach, each choir would perform two to four pieces of literature, for a total of ten to twenty selections on the entire concert. The choirs would, in essence, split a larger Menu by contributing pieces that function in the overall scheme of the Menu, while no one choir would sing the whole Menu cycle. Here is another way to visualize this approach in a high school setting with five choirs:

- Beginning SSAA Choir
  - Opener
  - Early Program Slow
- Advanced SSAA Choir
  - Early Program Fast
  - Early Program Slow
  - Late Program Fast
- Beginning Mixed Choir
  - Early Program Fast
  - Late Program Slow
- TTBB Choir
  - Centerpiece
  - Early Program Fast
- Advanced Mixed Choir
  - Early Program Fast
  - Late Program Fast
  - Late Program Slow
- Combined Choirs
  - Closer

You can see that all the choirs combine to create a varied and flowing Menu Program, with each choir only responsible for learning three or four pieces, including the combined piece. This is a much more practical and realistic approach for choirs that are developing their skills and for concert preparations that may be only four to six weeks in duration. It is a common mistake to program for each choir first, without considering how everything will combine for the audience at the actual concert. When this happens, you may find that you have too many selections that serve the same function within the Menu Program, making your concert flow stall or making the literature feel too uniform.

It should also be noted that there is no one correct way to sequence the order of choirs in the program, so any choir can start or finish the program, and any choir can serve the various Menu functions across different concerts. There is nothing keeping you from including Sets in a Multi-Choir program or using Themes for the entire Multi-Choir concert. You can be as creative as you choose to be, and you can combine all of these elements of programming in the most fun and interesting ways that you can. Your literature is your textbook, so strive to create the best one you can in every concert cycle.

"Break-the-Mold" Programs

There are programming approaches that "break the rules" and follow few, if any, of the above template choices. It can be fun to experiment with these programming choices as you go through your career, but they will carry certain risks that can derail the success of your concerts if you are not careful. The functions of the Menu approach can still apply to these unusual programs, but more often they will stray away from the *usual* to the *unusual*. There are as many of these creative approaches as there are creative conductors, and it is good to keep an open mind when experiencing them as an audience member. Often these kinds of programs combine a chosen element or elements for the entire concert to create an artistic experience. Here are just a few examples:

- The music of a single composer
- The setting of the same text by different composers
- Choir selections that feature soloists on every piece
- Music of a single style or historical period
- Music in a single language other than English
- Music all with a specific accompaniment, such as string quartet or percussion ensemble
- Music that is experimental, new, or unusual
- Performances underscoring a narrative story
- Concerts that are staged, with the choral musicians moving around the stage in choreographed positions (not show choir)

Assessing Program Balance

Any program that you create will have to include elements of balance and diversity in terms of tempo, key, texture, genre, and many other elements. It is not unheard of for a conductor to select a program, feel that it is perfect, and then realize later that everything is a cappella (presuming that that was not the intention), or realize that every piece is in the same key. One way to double-check your literature choices for these issues is to fill out the "Concert Program Analysis Form." In this form, you will list all the specific musical aspects of each piece, in program order, so that you can determine if you have a good balance of these elements, or if you need to replace some of the pieces for different selections. At the bottom, once you have evaluated the data in your form, you will write a sentence or two making note of the musical elements that are well represented, including the things that create good variety, as well as anything that you feel is represented too much or too little. There is no score for this form as there was in the "Music Literature Difficulty Assessment Rubric." It is intended to bring clarity, new information, and perspective to your program choices so that you can become aware of any big errors of intention that you may have made as you focused on each piece separately. In the end, it is always your personal taste and creativity that will determine your final literature choices. As you grow throughout your career, you will consider the information from this form almost automatically in your mind when you are selecting your choral literature.

Concert Program Analysis Form

	Title	Key	Voicing	Accomp.	Tempo	Length	Sec/Sacred	Text
1.								
2.								
3.								
4.								
5.								
6.								
7.								
8.								
9.								

Number of Keys: Major ______ Minor ______ Modal ______ Mixed _____ Other _____

Voicings: SATB _______ TTBB ________ SSAA __________ Unison ______ Other __________

Accompaniment: Piano/Keyboard _______ Unaccompanied _______ Other accompaniment(s) ________

Tempo: Fast ______ Slow ________ Medium ________ Changing ________

Total Length: Under 1:00 ____ Under 2:00 ____ Under 3:00 ____ Under 4:00 ____ Under 5:00 ____ Over 5:00 ____

Sacred _________ Secular ________

Languages: English _____ French ______ Italian _______ German ______ Latin ______ Spanish _____ Other ______

Good representation and variety in these areas:

Possibly too much of the following:

To aid in your understanding of how to use this form, below is a nine-piece menu sample program, followed by a completed Concert Program Analysis Form.

Tshotsholoza (O/CL) **Trad. So. African, Arr. Jeffery Ames** (b. 1969)
Walton Music (WLG114) TTBB, percussion (2′10″)

Jerusalem (EPS) **Michael McGlynn** (b. 1964)
(https://store.michaelmcglynn.com/Sheet-Music/Detail/Jerusalem), Unison Treble, a cappella (4′55″)

Exsultate Justi (EPF) **Ludovico Viadana/Ed. Klien** (1564–1645)
GIA Music Publishers (G-2140), SATB, brass (2′01″)

Cantique de Jean Racine (EPS/CP) **Gabriel Faure/Arr. Rutter** (1845–1924)
Oxford University Press (6540107636) SATB, piano (4′55″)

A Jubilant Song (Cen/MT) **Norman Dello Joio** (1913–2008)
Hal Leonard (HL 50302650) SATB, piano (6′30″)

Arroz con Leche (CP) **Carlos Guastavino** (1912–2000)
Kjos Music Publishers (8910) SATB, a cappella (3′05″)

Black is the Color of My True Love's Hair (LPS) **Arr. Rene Clausen** (b. 1953)
Hal Leonard (HL 08501551) SATB divisi, clarinet (4′40″)

Ching-A-Ring Chaw (LPF) **Aaron Copland** (1900–1990)
Hal Leonard (HL 48003285) SATB, piano (2′05″)

Desh (CL) **Ethan Sperry** (b. 1971)
Earthsongs (S-252), SATB, a cappella, percussion (4′50″)

Concert Program Analysis Form (example)

Title	Key	Voicing	Accomp.	Tempo	Length	Sec/Sacred	Text
1. Tshotsholoza	Ab maj	TTBB solo	a cappella	Fast	2:10	Secular	African
2. Jerusalem	F Maj	Unis. (round)	a cappella	Slow	4:55	Sacred	English
3. Exsultate	A maj.	SATB	a cappella	Fast	2:01	Sacred	Latin
4. Cantique	Db Maj	SATB	piano	Slow	4:55	Sacred	French
5. Jubilant	Various (E)	SATB div.	piano	Fast/Slow	6:30	Secular	English
6. Arroz	Bb Maj	SATB	a cappella	Mod	3:05	Secular	Spanish
7. Black	F minor	SATB	a cappella (Clarinet)	Slow	4:40	Secular	English
8. Ching	D maj	SATB	piano	Fast	2:05	Secular	English
9. Desh	Modal (D maj b6)	SATB	a cappella	Fast	4:50	Secular	sounds

Number of Keys: Major 6 Minor 1 Modal 1 Mixed 1 Other 0

Voicings: SATB 7 TTBB 1 SSAA ____ Unison 1 Other ____

Accompaniment: Piano/Keyboard 3 Unaccompanied 5 Other accompaniment(s) 1

Tempo: Fast 4 Slow 3 Medium 1 Changing 1

Total Length: Under 1:00 0 Under 2:00 0 Under 3:00 3 Under 4:00 1 Under 5:00 4 Over 5:00 1

Sacred 3 Secular 6

Languages: English 4 French 1 Italian 0 German 0 Latin 1 Spanish 1 Other 1

Good representation and variety in these areas:
Five languages. Three voicings in a mixed concert. Variety of tempi. Enough fast tempi. Good to have the clarinet. Sacred to secular balance OK. Generally good balance of elements.

Possibly too much of the following:
Too much major mode? 5 of 9 songs are on the longer side, but not too long. Maybe another accompanied piece and one less a cappella?

Now that you have been thinking about how Menu Programs can be organized in combinations of Sets, Themes, Multi-Choir, and Break-the-Mold concert programs, you will begin to notice these literature combinations more often when you look at printed choral concert programs. If you are familiar with the literature of a concert, you can enjoy exploring the possible logic behind the choices and sequences of the selections. With a little experience, you will begin to make more informed decisions concerning whether the literature flows well or if there are too many pieces that serve the same function within the same concert. If you are not familiar with the concert literature, but if you are attending a live choral concert, you will be able to decide for yourself if the program works for your artistic taste as an audience member as you experience the concert in real time. As has been stated, there is no specific right or wrong way to program choral music, but there are more effective and less effective artistic and educational choices that you can make. Choral programming is more of an art than it is a science, and the more you do it, the more effective you will become.

RECAPITULATION

1. Look online for websites that list choral concert programs. (Hint: try key words such as *"All State Choir Concert"* or *"Honor Choir Music"* or *"Choral Concert Literature."*) Look for an example of a Set program as well as a Theme program, and try to find recordings of the literature for the pieces with which you are not familiar. This may take a little time and investigation because most programs are "Menu" Programs without organization into Themes or Sets. Copy the program to a word document and decide on designations for each piece in both programs in terms of possible functions (Opener, Closer, Early Program Slow, etc.). Label each piece to the best of your ability with your determined function. Next, write a short paragraph about each program on how well it flows in terms of interest, balance, and variety for the audience (in your opinion) and how you would recommend changing it by adding or subtracting pieces or rearranging the order in some way. If you would leave the literature and order as it is, comment about why it works well "as is" and why you wouldn't change it.

2. Go to the website of J.W. Pepper, the largest sheet music retailer in the world with over 750,000 titles in its catalog. On the website you will find choral music that is published by many of the music publishing companies in the United States, with a searchable database by title, composer, voicing, genre, and keyword. Brainstorm two creative Theme program titles, write them down, and then search the website for titles of published choral music that would fit your theme, regardless of voicing or difficulty. List at least five titles that could fit your theme for each of your two program themes, along with publisher and voicing information. For this assignment, you do not have to know or study the music, nor find recordings.

Creating Your Single-Copy Choral Library

If you haven't already started collecting choral octavos that you can use with your choirs when you start teaching someday, now is a great time to begin. We have already discussed earlier in this chapter how important it is that you only keep and catalogue choral music that you would actually use with your future ensembles; unless a piece is of good quality and can be used to teach a variety of musical concepts, it is not worth having in your permanent single-copy library. You will also need to organize your library in a way that you can find music easily, and you will need to think about the practical considerations of storing the music in a convenient location. Remember too that your single-copy library should only include legal copies (and not photocopies) of music.

If you have used and become familiar with the "Choral Literature Full-Analysis Form," (pg 211) then you have had practice looking at music and collecting all the information you need to determine if a piece is good enough to use in your classroom. The purpose of this full-length form was to help you learn what to look for when studying a piece of music and to collect the kind of information required to create a detailed database of your music. But while this information is important to have, you are unlikely to take the time to fill out this long form for every piece of music you consider. Instead, you can use the "Choral Literature Simple-Analysis Form" to collect the most important information needed to create your single-copy library. This information includes title, composer, publisher, voicing, style, language, accompaniment, relative difficulty, ensemble programming uses, and the possible uses for the piece in a Menu Program.

Choral Literature Simple-Analysis Form

Title & Translation: ______________________________ Composer: ________________

Arranger/Editor (*if applicable*) ____________________ Voicing: ________

Octavo Number: __________ Publisher: ______________ Genre or Style: ________

Language(s): ______________ List the accompaniment, instrumentation, or *a cappella*: ______

Designation of difficulty of the piece (your estimation): ______________________________

Justification of difficulty score (your opinion): ______________________________

Assign this piece to all the programming uses that apply:

_____ Beginning to Advanced Unison Songs (any voicing)

_____ Rounds and Canons (any voicing)

_____ Partner Songs (SA, SAB, 3-part mixed)

_____ Middle Level Mixed (3-part mixed, SAB, SATB)

_____ Beginning Mixed HS Choir: SATB

_____ Intermediate Mixed HS Choir: SATB

_____ Advanced Mixed HS Choir: SATB

_____ Beginning Treble Choir: SSA (including SA, SSAA)

_____ Intermediate Treble Choir: SSA (including SA, SSAA)

_____ Advanced Treble Choir: SSA (including SA, SSAA)

_____ Men's Choir: TB (including TTB, TTBB)

_____ Other (a voicing not listed above) *specify*: ____________________________

Assign this piece to a Menu Program (check all that apply):

_____ Opener

_____ Early Program Slow

_____ Early Program Fast

_____ Centerpiece (or "Different")

_____ Late Program Slow

_____ Late Program Fast

_____ Closer

_____ Other (Specify):

Other Notes (*use back of form as needed*):

Collecting good information through the analysis forms will aid you greatly when organizing your library and being able to access that information is crucial to your ability to *use* that information in a practical and efficient manner. One way to organize this information is to set up a software database using a program such as Microsoft *Excel*, Apple *Filemaker*, or Google *Sheets*. The cross-platform benefits of Excel make it a good choice, and the web-based access of *Sheets* makes the Google option also a good choice. While these databases are relatively easy for you to set up and learn to manipulate, a template can be helpful.

The headers on the sample *Excel* spreadsheet are as follows:

Title / Title Translation /Composer (last, first) / Arranger/Editor / Voicing / Publisher / Catalog # / Language(s) / Accompaniment / Length / Genre/Style / Difficulty / Opener / Early Slow / Early Fast / Centerpiece / Late Slow / Late Fast / Closer / Other / Contributor / Analysis

There are many benefits to creating your personal database. One benefit is being able to check to see if you have a good variety of music (voicings, difficulty, Menu Program functions) in your collection. If you have a lot of Early and Late Program Slow pieces, for example, you can make an extra effort to search for music with faster tempi, or specifically for Openers or Closers. When you know what you have, you know what you need. Another benefit is being able to share your database with colleagues and friends. If you are asked to recommend music to a colleague for a specific choir or occasion, you will be able to search your database and find options, including all the publisher information required to order the piece. Another benefit of creating and using your database is your ability to update it, adding titles throughout your career, and possibly adding fields that you find useful, such as "date and venue performed" or "worth programming again?" Finally, it can be really frustrating to know you have a copy of music, but then waste valuable time looking for it in your files. If you have multiple filing cabinets or notebooks housing your single-copy library, you can use your database to specify exactly where to find that single copy in your physical environment.

It is not uncommon for choral music educators to collect piles and piles of single-copy choral music from convention reading sessions, mailings, or through some other means. It is in your best interest to decide early on to create some sort of system to organize that music before it becomes a cluttered and overwhelming mess. Step One, based on what you are learning about selecting good choral music, is to recycle every piece of music that you believe does not meet the standards of quality for your choral classroom. Unless you would choose that piece of music to teach musical concepts through choral performance with your ensembles, get rid of it. This one step will reduce your piles by at least half. Step Two is to organize the remaining pieces in a practical physical system. Here are some possible approaches:

- Enter the data from your analysis forms into your database, and then put the single copies (in any order) into file folders or choral library boxes marked numerically. In your database you would add a field called "file number" or "box number" that connects the title with the physical location. In this system you do not have to worry about sorting the individual files or boxes because each one will have a limited number of pieces in it. When you need to find "Ave Verum" by Mozart, for example, you would check your database and see that it is in box 14, and in a minute or so you could sort through the box and have the piece in your hands. As you find new music, you just fill up more boxes without the need to sort and organize them by title or composer.
- Enter the data from your analysis forms into your database, and then put the single copies into notebooks or files by Menu function. In this system you would have a file or notebook called "Openers" and one called "Early Program Slow," and so on. As you get more and more music, you will need to add additional files or notebooks, which is easy to do. In your database you would have a primary function for each piece to tell you where to look for it. For added organization, you could alphabetize each notebook or file, but you wouldn't need to. This approach can be particularly useful when you are looking for, say, a good Closer for a program that is otherwise complete. You can browse your database for Closers or you can physically take out the Closers notebook and look right at each piece of music.
- Enter the data from your analysis forms into your database, but then create a physical filing system by title in alphabetic order. In this system you would look to see if the piece is in your library database, and then you would go to the "A" file for a piece starting with "A." For larger libraries, it can be useful to have a separate, alphabetized section for "Mixed" and one for "TTBB" and one for "SSAA" and even one for "3-Part Mixed." This system is especially practical when you don't have access to your database or you don't have the time to look something up. If you need the Bruckner "Locus Iste," you just go to the "Mixed" files and find the "L" section, and it should be in your hands quickly.

There are certainly other ways to organize your single-copy library, and you will need to decide on the system that works best for you. Additionally, you will need to keep track of the physical multi-copy choral library that your school owns. You may choose to inventory and merge both of these libraries into your database, with designations that mark which pieces are single copies and which titles are multi-copies. A well-organized choral library is a joy to use when you program, and a disorganized library can be frustrating and time consuming. As a new teacher, you should get a jump on this task and choose a system that you can use and maintain throughout your career.

RECAPITULATION

1. Do you have a single-copy choral library started yet? If so, describe it in a short paragraph (when did you start it, how many titles do you think you have, where did you get most of the music, and what kinds of music and voicings does it contain)? If you haven't started one yet, write a paragraph addressing at least three things you can do to start collecting music, and also what kinds of music you want it to contain.
2. Download the database template or create one of your own. Find at least ten pieces that you would actually use in a classroom, any voicing or difficulty, and fill out either the full-analysis form or the simple analysis form, and then enter these data into your database. Save it and back it up. Let this be the start of your personal database to use throughout your career.
3. Discuss the recommendations given in this chapter for organizing your physical single-copy library in terms of which ones you think you might prefer. Think of at least one other possible organizational approach that is not outlined in the chapter. Is your idea better than the ones that were recommended? Why or why not, in your opinion.

Musical Copyright and Fair Use

Have you ever walked into a choral classroom and seen piles and piles of photocopied music on the piano, in choral folders, or on tables around the room? You probably have experienced this because it is a relatively common practice for teachers to make photocopies of choral music. But until you understand why this is unprofessional, unethical, and even illegal, you won't know to avoid doing it yourself someday. It is important that every professional choral music educator gain a solid understanding of the broad issues surrounding musical copyright and something called "fair use."

When you look at published printed materials, you will notice, quite often, that the symbol "©" appears at the bottom of a page or somewhere else in the document. This is certainly the case with professionally published music – it will always appear at the bottom of the first page of music. The symbol © informs the user that the material is protected by United States copyright law, and that the user *does not* have permission to make unauthorized copies. Copyright laws are intended to protect the people or businesses that spend their own money creating the materials so that they can sell them to make a profit and continue to produce similar items in the future. Publishers and authors lose money every time someone steals (through unauthorized use or copying) materials that are protected by copyright law.

Common materials that are protected under copyright law include, but are not limited to, printed choral and instrumental music (including lyrics), books, plays, dances and choreography, films, photographs, paintings, graphics, audiovisual works, video games, computer software, and sound recordings. Copyright law does not apply to some things, such as ideas, names, procedures, numbers, methods, systems, processes, or concepts. Likewise, when a work is made up of commonly available information that is not original, such as written tables and public documents, it generally won't be protected by copyright. If you make up a song or a story, but don't write it down, it is also not protected; the original work must exist in some sort of fixed and tangible form of expression.

Copyright protection does not last forever. Traditional copyright lasts for ninety-five (95) years from publication if an item is owned by a corporation. Materials owned by individuals are protected until their death plus seventy years.[1] Eventually most materials will fall under something called the "public domain." If something has a public domain designation, it can be used and

1 All works published in the United States before 1924 are in the public domain. Works published after 1923, but before 1978 are protected for 95 years from the date of publication. If the work was created, but not published, before 1978, the copyright lasts for the life of the author plus 70 years.

copied freely, even for commercial purposes. A material that was created before 1923 is usually in the public domain, and you can also determine this designation if the owner actually specifies the item as "public domain."

There is also something called "fair use" that allows certain materials to be used by particular individuals, even when those materials are protected by a valid copyright. Fair use is a bit confusing, and you will need to understand all that you can to be sure that you are aligning with fair use laws and not violating copyright laws by mistake. According to the *Copyright Act of 1976*, there are four factors used to determine if a work can fall under fair use:

1. the purpose and character of the use, including whether such use is of a commercial nature or is for nonprofit educational purposes.
2. the nature of the copyrighted work.
3. the amount and substantiality of the portion used in relation to the copyrighted work as a whole.
4. the effect of the use upon the potential market for or value of the copyrighted work.

Various guidelines exist for different types of media (books, music, audio, etc.), so it is important to look at the fair use law descriptions for each, depending upon what you intend to do. The Copyright Act (1976) and subsequent amendments, including the Digital Millennium Copyright Act, serve as guidelines for what you can do legally. Feel free to "Dig Deeper" to see what the various guidelines suggest for legal compliance.

Here are some basic guidelines for you to consider:

Fair Use allows you, as a music teacher, to do the following:

- ✓ Multiple copies of sheet music may be copied in an emergency (for an imminent performance) to replace purchased copies that are not available, provided purchased replacement copies are substituted as soon as possible.
- ✓ For academic purposes other than performance, multiple copies of excerpts of works may be made, provided the excerpts don't include more than 10% of the whole work or make up a part of the whole that would constitute a performable unit, such as a section, a movement, or an aria. The number of copies may not exceed one copy per student.
- ✓ For academic purposes other than performance, a single copy of

an entire performable unit (section, movement, aria, etc.) may be made if the unit is out of print or available only in a larger work.

- ✓ Sheet music that has been purchased may be edited or simplified if the fundamental character of the work is not distorted and that lyrics are not altered or added.
- ✓ A single copy of a sound recording of a student performance may be made for evaluation or rehearsal purposes and may be retained by the educational institution or individual teacher.
- ✓ A single copy of a sound recording of copyrighted music may be made from sound recordings owned by an educational institution or an individual teacher for the purpose of constructing aural exercises or examinations and may be retained by the educational institution or individual teacher.

Fair Use does not allow you to do the following:

- ✓ Copying to create, replace, or substitute for anthologies, compilations, or collective works; copying works intended to be consumable, such as workbooks, exercises, or standardized tests; copying for the purpose of performance (except in an emergency); copying as a substitute for purchase; and copying without the inclusion of the copyright notice are not permitted.

Earlier in the chapter you were encouraged to visit the *Choral Public Domain Library*. If you are on a limited budget, you can always use music that is in the public domain. At this website, you will find approximately 30,000 choral and vocal works by over 3,000 composers that can be freely and legally copied, distributed, and performed. The site includes large numbers of scores from the Renaissance and Baroque eras, including excellent editions of works by William Byrd, Tomás Luis de Victoria, and many other early composers. In addition to sheet music, the site also offers access to original texts, sources and translations, composer data, and other important information. Users can download music in a number of different formats, including score images in TIFF, PS and PDF format, sound files in MIDI and MP3 formats, and in notation formats such as Finale, Sibelius, Encore, and others. Because anyone can create editions of old music or compose new music, there is a wide range of editions and compositions of greater and lesser quality available. For some more well-known pieces, you will often find multiple editions available, so you will need to look each one over to decide which edition will work best for your purposes. Errors and misprints are common, and what money you save not buying the pieces may be offset a bit by the time you will invest checking the editions and choosing suitable scores. One added benefit to searching CPDL is the fact that contributors can provide links to their own outside websites that also offer free scores for download, as well as resources that can help you with your programming efforts. It is more and more common for living composers, who want their music to be known and enjoyed, to upload their music to CPDL and to grant limited permission for choral directors to copy and perform their works for free.

At this point you might be thinking, "If there are laws against stealing materials that are protected by copyright, then there must be penalties for breaking those laws." The official term for this is "Copyright Infringement." Copyright infringement is the act of violating any of a copyright owner's exclusive rights granted by the federal Copyright Act of 1976. Some possible legal penalties that you (and possibly your school) could be responsible for if you are caught and found guilty in a copyright infringement lawsuit are:

- The infringer pays the actual dollar amount of damages and profits.
- The law provides a range from $200 to $150,000 for each work infringed. This could possibly mean a charge for each copy, not just each piece.
- The infringer pays for all attorney fees and court costs incurred during the infringement trial.
- The infringer can be sent to serve a term in jail.

Even if you do not personally know of anyone who has ever been charged and convicted in a copyright infringement case, there are people and institutions who do get caught and convicted of this crime. If you do violate copyright laws chronically and publicly, you may be putting yourself at great risk of becoming a criminal, owing a lot of money, and ending your teaching career forever. The best advice is to know the laws and to do your best to uphold them.

Every choral music teacher will make occasional copies of music for their classroom, hopefully in accordance with fair use laws, yet no one is perfect. You should strive to be an ethical and professional person who knows, follows, and understands these laws. When you first try to digest all the clear and gray areas surrounding copyright and fair use laws, don't be surprised if you get tired and confused digesting all the information. Not understanding the information is not a valid excuse for breaking the law. What really matters is that you learn and follow as many of the guidelines as often as you can and that you don't steal music from the people who make a living creating it. At the very least, you should try to adhere to these few simple guidelines that are sometimes ignored by some people in our profession:

- **Don't photocopy music to avoid buying it.** Even if your budget has no money for music, you can reuse music from your multi-copy library, you can borrow music from colleagues, and you can find music that is in the public domain. Additionally, stealing music for your choirs by photocopying discourages your school from ever funding your program adequately.
- **Don't scan music and encourage students to download it for choir.** Scanning music for download in class is the same as photocopying it. The copies were not paid for, and it's still stealing from the publishers and composers.
- **Don't purchase some, but not enough, copies for your choir and then photocopy the rest.** Publishers that require minimum orders of music (often five copies) do not grant permission to photocopy beyond the five purchased copies. It is acceptable to have students share music in class (if necessary) and to have different classes use the same legal copies. But as soon as you need to make photocopies, what you really should do is buy more legal copies.
- **Don't buy one copy of music and then project it in the classroom for students to sing and memorize.** In the spirit of the law, you still have not compensated the publisher and composer for their work, and you are making it harder for them to stay in business.
- **Don't attend an adjudicated choral festival and provide the judges with illegal copies of your literature.** Nothing says "I'm unethical, unprofessional, and clueless" more strongly than using photocopies at a public choral festival. The saying "how you do *anything* affects how you do *everything*" applies here, and the message you send to everyone is that you steal *all* your music. Additionally, the message you give your students whenever you infringe on a copyright is damaging to our profession in every way for years to come.

If you are curious and want to know even more about this topic, the internet is full of information that you can find easily. J.W. Pepper has a good presentation on copyright issues, and it is targeted to professional music educators who use their music services. Feel free to "Lock it In" if you are curious. Additionally, an informational video on YouTube can be found at "You May Like It." There are also several good books in print that detail the specifics surrounding copyright law as they affect you as a music teacher:

- *Music Copyright Basics* (Joel Leach - Alfred Music Publishing)
- *Copyright Handbook for Music Educators and Directors* (Pam Phillips & Andrew Surmani - Alfred Music Publishing)
- *Copyright: The Complete Guide for Music Educators* (Jay Althouse - Alfred Music Publishing)

RECAPITULATION

1. Have you ever stolen something, even something small, perhaps long ago when you were very young? What did you take and why? What justification do you have for your past behavior? Would you do it again? Why or why not?
2. In your opinion, is it ever alright to steal something? Try to think of and describe a couple scenarios where you can somewhat justify taking something that you didn't technically pay for.
3. Having read this section of the chapter, what did you learn about copyright and fair use that you didn't already know? Do you think this will affect your professional behavior throughout your career? Why or why not?
4. Imagine walking into the choral classroom of a colleague and seeing only photocopies of music on tables, on the piano, and in choir folders. Is it your job to say anything, in your opinion? Why or why not?

Sacred vs. Secular Choral Music

When you become a practicing professional choral music educator, you will need to learn the norms and standards of the school and district that employs you. You will familiarize yourself with the policies, rules, and procedures that all employees follow, as well as the expectations of professional behavior. These rules and expectations can vary from school to school and district to district, and it is best not to assume that any one school is exactly like any other school. For example, some private religious schools require their teachers to maintain certain behaviors outside of school such as believing in specific church doctrine or even completely abstaining from behaviors such as drinking alcohol. Public school districts are unlikely to have prescribed behaviors for teachers when they are not teaching, but you should attempt to learn what specific behaviors are expected of you when you are teaching.

Sacred music is music that references or promotes themes or texts from a religious tradition. *Secular* music is music that is not associated with a religious text or tradition. Among all the expectations that will be present in your school district, there may be an expectation that you will balance your programming choices in terms of sacred and secular music. There are public school districts in the United States that require music teachers to submit, to the school board or some other special committee, literature choices ahead of time to determine if there is a balance of sacred, secular, and other cultural offerings present. Many other school districts do not have these requirements, though the parents of the school may voice an opinion informally regarding the balance of the literature choices. In contrast, if you work in a private religious institution, you may be required to program exclusively sacred music in your choral concerts and services. Again, it is best to find out what the expectations are in your community and to be sure you are sensitive to these norms and expectations.

Some music is clearly sacred and some is clearly secular, but some music exists in a gray area in between. Look at the following songs and decide if you consider each one to be either sacred or secular, even if you are unfamiliar with some of the music. Be ready to defend your opinions as well as you can:

- Mozart: *Ave Verum*
- Copland: *Simple Gifts*
- Schubert: *Mass in G*
- Any arrangement of *Rudolf the Red-Nosed Reindeer*
- Whitacre: *i thank You God for most this amazing day*
- Barnum: *Afternoon On a Hill*
- Any arrangement of *Silent Night*
- Levine: *Hiney Ma Tov*
- Arr. Jason Robert Brown: *Chanukah Suite*

The first piece, Mozart's *Ave Verum*, is a setting of a sacred text from the Christian Bible. It is clearly sacred based on the origin of the text. Copland's *Simple Gifts* is an arrangement of a Shaker song, and the text does not come from a religious text and could probably be considered secular. However, because the Shakers were a group of people known as the *United Society of Believers in Christ's Second Appearing*, a Christian sect founded in the 18th century in England, should their song be considered sacred to their tradition? The *Mass in G* by Schubert is a traditional setting of the Christian Mass, and it is clearly sacred. *Rudolf the Red-Nosed Reindeer* is a familiar song that is sung during the Christmas season. If not for Christmas, a sacred Christian holiday, would we even sing this song? Should it be considered sacred? Eric Whitacre's beautiful setting of ee cumming's text *i thank You God for most this amazing day* includes the word "God" in the title, but it is not taken from a specific sacred text. In this case, can a song referencing the word "God" be considered secular? Eric Barnum's *Afternoon On a Hill* is a beautiful setting of a text describing an afternoon in the natural beauty of the outdoors, without reference to anything else, and is clearly secular. *Silent Night,* like *Rudolf,* is traditionally sung at Christmas. But *Silent Night* is probably sacred because the text describes the circumstances surrounding the night of the birth of Jesus Christ. The text of *Hiney Ma Tov* by Iris Levine is taken from the first verse of Psalm 133 in the Hebrew Bible, which reads, "Behold, how good and how pleasant it is for brethren to dwell together in unity!" The text seems unrelated to a specific religious holiday, and possibly could be considered secular; yet because it does come from the Old Testament Bible, should it be considered sacred? Finally, Jason Robert Brown's *Chanukah Suite* is a celebration of Chanukah, a lesser sacred Jewish festival and should probably be considered sacred.

As you can see, some pieces are easy to classify while others are less obvious. Of the nine titles, only one, *Afternoon On a Hill,* has nothing to suggest a sacred designation. Four of the nine (*Simple Gifts, Rudolf the Red-Nosed Reindeer, i thank You God for most this amazing day, and Hiney Ma Tov*) fall into a gray area that could allow someone to argue for a designation of either sacred or secular. And four titles (*Ave Verum, Mass in G, Silent Night, and Chanukah Suite*) would probably best be classified as sacred. If somehow you were to program all of these pieces on a single program, would you have a balance of four sacred to five secular, or would you have eight sacred and only one secular? Does it make a difference? It quite possibly could, depending on the expectations of your community and how much the school district is allowed to oversee and approve your literature choices.

Sacred music represents a large segment of the canon of the Western choral tradition. This is primarily because the Christian church sponsored and protected music for worship over the centuries. Composers were paid to write music for the church, and the church often helped to preserve the music during dangerous times of war and struggle. Some of the most beautiful and musically expressive choral music was commissioned by the church, and we should study and perform some of this music in our public school choirs. To ignore the sacred music of Wolfgang Amadeus Mozart or Franz Schubert in the choral curriculum would be like an English teacher excluding the works of William Shakespeare or Charles Dickens; the works are arguably *historically significant* to each discipline. As choral music educators, we will need to build a case for including sacred music in the curriculum, and our reasons will need to be logical, educational, and backed up with a sound justification that can be communicated to parents, students, colleagues, and administrators.

We are very fortunate in the United States to have a well-organized professional organization, the National Association for Music Education (NAfME), that addresses all aspects of music education. It is among the world's largest arts education organizations, and it advocates at the local, state, and national levels for K-12 choral, instrumental, and general music education. As a professional choral music educator, you should belong to your primary national professional organization NAfME, as well as your main national choral professional organization, the American Choral Directors Association (ACDA). Membership in these national organizations automatically includes membership in the state professional organizations as well. Your dues to these organizations will help to continue the important work they do advocating for the profession, providing resources for teachers, parents, and administrators, supporting and encouraging academic research, publishing professional journals, hosting professional development events, and offering a variety of opportunities for students and teachers. The websites of these professional organizations are filled with tips and information that can help you do your job better, and every professional music teacher should maintain membership in these organizations throughout their career and benefit from the resources and opportunities that they provide.

At the website for NAfME, you will find a page that includes a number of position statements. A position statement explains where an organization stands on a topic or debate question. Position statements adopted by your national professional organizations are powerful tools for you to advocate locally on important topics. NAfME has developed a number of well-articulated position statements on many issues, including Alternative Certification, Inclusivity and Diversity, Assessment, Homeschooled Students' Participation in Public School Music Education, and many others. Among these statements is one addressing the use of sacred music in schools. Your justification for the use of sacred music in your school's curriculum should be informed by the national position statement because it represents the general consensus of the entire music education profession in the United States. Excerpted here, it reads:

> "It is the position of the National Association for Music Education that the study and performance of religious music within an educational context is a vital and appropriate part of a comprehensive music education. The omission of sacred music from the school curriculum would result in an incomplete educational experience.

The First Amendment...

The First Amendment does not forbid all mention of religion in the public schools; it prohibits the advancement or inhibition of religion by the state. A second clause in the First Amendment prohibits the infringement of religious beliefs. The public schools are not required to delete from the curriculum all materials that may offend any religious sensitivity. For instance, the study of art history would be incomplete without reference to the Sistine Chapel, and the study of architecture requires an examination of Renaissance cathedrals. Likewise, a comprehensive study of music includes an obligation to become familiar with choral music set to religious texts.

The chorales of J. S. Bach, the "Hallelujah Chorus" from George Frideric Handel's "Messiah," spirituals, and Ernest Bloch's "Sacred Service" all have an important place in the development of a student's musical understanding and knowledge.

In order to ensure that any music class or program is conforming to the constitutional standards of religious neutrality necessary in public schools, the following questions raised in 1971 by Chief Justice Warren E. Burger in *Lemon v. Kurtzman* should be asked of each school-sanctioned observance, program, or institutional activity involving religious content, ceremony, or celebration:

1. What is the purpose of the activity? Is the purpose secular in nature, that is, studying music of a particular composer's style or historical period?

2. What is the primary effect of the activity? Is it the celebration of religion? Does the activity either enhance or inhibit religion? Does it invite confusion of thought or family objections?

3. Does the activity involve excessive entanglement with a religion or religious group, or between the schools and religious organizations? Financial support can, in certain cases, be considered an entanglement.

If the music educator's use of sacred music can withstand the test of these questions, it is probably not in violation of the First Amendment.

Since music with a sacred text or of a religious origin (particularly choral music) constitutes such a substantial portion of music literature and has such an important place in the history of music, it should and does have an important place in music education."

The statement goes on to include issues of legal history, a discussion of religiously neutral programs, and includes footnotes, as well as a suggested bibliography for more information. It is recommended that you read all of the NAfME position statements at some point in time to familiarize yourself with these topics.

With this clear and persuasive position statement on sacred music from

NAfME, you will be able to advocate for the inclusion of sacred music in your choral curriculum, especially if your sacred music choices can be considered historically significant and conforming to the "constitutional standards of religious neutrality necessary in public schools." But what does this mean in practical terms? Here are some guidelines that can help you clarify these issues as you are selecting music for your classroom:

- ❖ Only choose music (sacred or secular) that is rich in musical concepts and expressive qualities. As we explored earlier in the chapter, only choose "good" music for your choirs.
- ❖ If a piece of music is clearly sacred, look it over carefully to be extra sure that it passes the "good music" test. There is a lot of sacred music that is composed specifically for small church choirs with less developed musical skills and very little rehearsal time. These church anthems rarely pass the "historically significant" and "good music" tests and have no place in the public school curriculum.
- ❖ Examine every choral performance program that you choose to be sure that there is a balance of sacred and secular selections, as well as an approach to diversity in terms of genre, style, tempo, and social and multicultural elements.
- ❖ Be prepared to defend your music selections in terms of what you can teach your students through them, why these selections belong in your curriculum, and the kinds of expressive effects that the literature will create for the audience and the choir.
- ❖ When you teach music that is sacred, be sensitive to your own biases regarding your personal religious beliefs. Examining, for example, that a text is drawn from a Biblical prayer is quite different than saying "Let's pray." The fact that the piece is drawn from a sacred religious tradition should never be the main justification for teaching the piece, so focus always on the musical and historically significant elements of the music.

RECAPITULATION

1. Sacred music in the schools can be a controversial topic, especially in religiously diverse communities. Your own experience was certainly affected by the religious and cultural environment that you experienced in your formative years. Write a paragraph describing your own experience growing up in your community or communities. Describe the cultural

and religious diversity that you experienced and if you feel it affected the music in your environment. Include, if you can, information about the music you sang, played, or listened to growing up.

2. Randomly select (you choose how) six pieces of choral music from your single-copy library, or from the library of a friend or an institution. Examine each piece and make a list of the six titles on paper. Under each title, assign a designation of "clearly sacred" or "clearly secular" or "possibly sacred or secular." Under each designation, write a short justification supporting your opinion.
3. Using either online sources or physical choral octavos, find two pieces that are clearly sacred in designation. One should represent a piece that you think passes the "good music" test. The second one should be one that you feel was composed specifically for a small church choir with less developed musical skills and very little rehearsal time. Describe the various elements of each piece that led you to form your opinions.
4. In a public school teaching position, the use of sacred music should be carefully balanced and justified based on the expressive and historically significant aspects of the music. In a private religious school you can use sacred music specifically to teach and reinforce religious doctrine and beliefs. In light of this, do you think you would prefer to teach in a religious, private school or in a public school? What might the advantages and disadvantages be to you personally, in your opinion?

Middle-Level Choirs and the Changing Voice

The secondary choral music educator has to be adept at working with students in grades six through twelve, including unchanged, changing, and changed voices. All too often well-meaning middle-level choir teachers do not choose literature that will address the male changing-voice ranges appropriately, causing these singers to feel unsuccessful and to quit singing in choir. Both males and females will undergo voice changes as they transition through puberty, but the female changing process is less disruptive for the individuals than the extreme voice changes that males experience. For this reason, it is very important to have a general understanding of the male changing voice in particular so that male singers can be encouraged and retained throughout the middle school years. With a little information and some targeted strategies, you will be able to help all the singers in your middle school choir program to be successful through the uncertainty of the voice change.

The issues of the changing voice have been studied in many settings, and there is a large amount of information available in books, articles, dissertations, and online research. In music education, a few of the leading authors on this subject are John Cooksey, Don Collins, Fredrick Swanson, Irvin Cooper, Duncan McKenzie, Janice Killian, Patrick Freer, and Henry Leck. The beginning teacher can easily be overwhelmed by the specifics of the information provided by these and many other researchers. This text is intended to provide a general overview, based largely on the work of these scholars, in order to give you a practical framework that you can apply to your first teaching experiences. At some point, based on your curiosity, you should expand your understanding by examining some other books, articles, and videos addressing more detailed information pertaining to the changing adolescent voice.

The traditional elementary school program normally includes students in kindergarten through grades five or six. A traditional junior high school includes grades seven and eight, and sometimes grade nine. Middle school programs are typically grades six, seven, and eight, and high schools with middle school feeders are usually grades nine, ten, eleven, and twelve. Here is another way to visualize these three scenarios:

- School District 1: Elementary K–5, Middle 6–8, High 9–12
- School District 2: Elementary K–6, Jr. High 7–8, High 9–12
- School District 3: Elementary K–6, Jr. High 7–9, High 10–12

Other variations also exist, but even in most K–8 schools, there will be some sort of division, either within the building or through the schedule, grouping elementary students apart from middle-level students. Regardless of the school district scenario you may find yourself teaching in someday, you will likely encounter issues of the changing voice.

Because every person is unique, the exact onset of puberty and the accompanying changes in vocal range can be unpredictable. Generally, the male voice will begin to change in sixth grade, though it can happen much sooner or later than that. In school district 1, the middle school choral music educator will have male sixth graders who, at least early in the year, will mostly be treble-range unchanged voices. In school district 2, the educator will have seventh graders who may have unchanged, changing, or changed voices and eighth graders with changing and changed voices. In school district 3, the educator will also have ninth graders who, on the whole, will have undergone their voice change. By tenth and eleventh grade, most male students will be settling into a voice part that suits their emerging adult range, yet the voice will still be young and developing well after high school graduation. As you can see, a middle school choir director needs to be ready for anything in terms of vocal range and voice change for their male singers, and literature choices with appropriate vocal ranges need to be chosen carefully and consciously.

Prepubescent children sing in approximately the same range, with comfortable notes from about middle C up to about F at the top of the treble clef. All of this begins to change with the onset of puberty and a significant amount of growth and change in the physical body. You may have noticed that middle school females, especially sixth and seventh graders, tend to be considerably taller than their male counterparts. This is because females go through their maturity growth spurt about two years before males do. For both genders, the voice change is accompanied by an enlarging of the larynx, an increase in the size of the vocal folds, and a downward shift of vocal range. For males, the amount of physical growth in the vocal mechanism can be about twice that of females, lowering the speaking and singing ranges much more dramatically.

For females, the voice change can be characterized by a difficulty singing in certain registers and a breathiness in the sound that can also be accompanied by a tendency to sing slightly sharp of the intended pitch. For males, the voice change can be characterized by a greater lowering of the singing range and a deepening of the vocal timbre, as well as an unsteadiness of phonation. This can be quite unnerving for young males, especially if they sang in their treble voice with beauty and agility before the voice change. Care must be taken to assure them that the changes are completely natural and temporary, and that you will help them be successful as they grow into their "new" adult voice.

Your most important tasks when working with changing voices are determining what ranges the students can sing, picking appropriate literature, and assigning the best possible voice parts that fit the ranges. Female voices will not change so much that they need to be assigned a voice part outside of the typical treble range, but there will be predictable limitations that they will encounter. Here are some general guidelines to help you:

- ✓ **Encourage and teach the female voices to sing without too much heaviness in the lower ranges.** At the beginning of their change (probably before middle school), they may have trouble singing certain notes, and especially lower notes. But by the time they are in middle school, they will probably have developed more strength and weight in their lower notes. Because these lower notes may feel strong and can be sung fully, there will be a tendency for some singers to push and over-sing these notes. Teach them the rule that *"we never sing louder than beautiful."*

- ✓ **Encourage them to sing different parts on different pieces rather than assigning them permanently to a soprano or alto part.** Young, changing female voices are unsettled and will not have the timbre or agility of adult voices, so it is unwise to limit them to a voice range too early in their development. It is not uncommon for a female who sang an alto part too early to have trouble singing in the higher vocal registers in adulthood or for a female who sang soprano too early to have trouble harmonizing below a melody. Every choir member should be taught to read music, to harmonize accurately, and to develop a consistent and connected vocal registration throughout the entire range. You can also look for music written for this age group that assigns parts such as Part I, and Part II, as opposed to soprano and alto, and have the singers switch parts on different songs to avoid identifying too strongly with one traditional voice part.

- ✓ **Encourage them to sing with an age-appropriate tone that is well supported and free of tension.** If you try to make your female singers sound "older" by asking for unnecessary tension or an excessively dark vocal color, you may be teaching them bad habits or harming their natural vocal growth. Females at this stage of development can sound beautifully expressive even if they have some natural breathiness or sharpness evident in the singing. Focus on a well-supported breath and tension-free vocal production.

- ✓ **Allow the voices to mature at their own natural rate.** There will be some female voices that gain a more mature sound earlier than others, but you cannot control this. At the age of about fourteen or fifteen, the voice will still be a bit unstable but will also begin to possess more clarity of tone. Additionally, the timbre will become fuller and richer, even developing a natural vibrato. Teaching good vocal technique will encourage all of this to happen at the perfect time for each person.

While the female changing voice will stay generally in the treble range throughout the entire transition, the changing male voice will move from a treble range to variations of an alto/tenor, an "in between" voice with very little range, and finally to a kind of baritone.[2] You will need to be able to test your singers to know what part they should be singing, and you have to remember that their voice change will be ongoing…with some male voices potentially changing to a new part right before a concert! Ideally, you should test every male singing in your middle-level choir every month or so to identify and track the progress of their voice change to be sure that they have a part to sing that best fits their present range. Realistically, you probably will not have the

2 Simplified and adapted from "Working with the Adolescent Voice" by John M. Cooksey (St. Louis: Concordia, 1992)

time to do this for each individual as often as you would like to. What you can do, instead, is test the whole group of males by singing a song in various keys, listening carefully to which key fits their voice best, and in which octave they choose to sing.[3] You will be testing to see which of the following broad categories of voice parts they seem to align with:

1. **Unchanged treble** can sing part 1 or 2 (soprano or alto)
2. **Alto/tenor** can sing limited-range tenor and alto parts in SATB
3. **Limited-range baritone** can sing part 3 in 3-part mixed music
4. **New baritone** can sing bass in SATB if the lowest note is around Bb

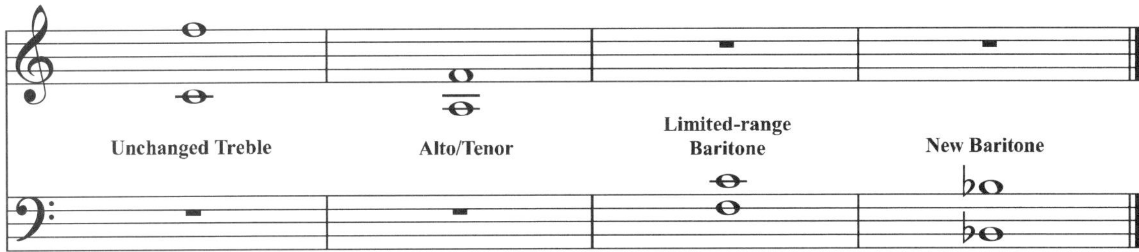

You will need to teach them a song with primarily stepwise motion and a range of about a 5th or 6th. Two possible songs are "America" (also known as, "*My Country, 'Tis of Thee"*) and the first two lines of "Sarasponda," both of which they may have sung when they were younger. The octave leap in measures four or five of Sarasponda shouldn't be used for this particular range test. You can choose any song that you think will work and that they will like singing, as long as it is primarily stepwise and within a limited range.

3 Also adapted from the methods of John M. Cooksey

Start by having the male singers stand in a group together or possibly in a circle with you in the middle, if space is available. Tell them that you are going to check to see what voice part will fit them best today, and that they should just do their best to sing as well as they can. Remind them that the voice change is natural as they grow into their adult voice, and that every adult male singer, even the most famous ones, went through this very same voice change at some point. Be light and even try to make it a fun experience for them. Use this sequence:

1. Have them sing the song in the key of C (approximate range C up to G). Listen for which students are choosing to sing the whole song in the higher octave and which ones are singing in the lower octave. Some will be struggling in this key to match all the notes but will still be trying in a lower or higher octave.

2. Move them into two groups: higher octave and lower octave, making a mental note of those having trouble singing in the key of C. Check the higher and lower octave groups to be sure you didn't miss someone that you thought was singing in a different octave.

3. Have the lower-octave group sing the song in the key of F (approximate range F up to middle C). Listen to see if any of the "strugglers" in the key of C can find more success in the key of F. Divide them into two groups: those who can sing it in C (low octave) and those who have more success in F. Your low C group is your "New baritone" section and your F group is your "limited-range baritone" section. You may decide to just call them "Group 3 and Group 4" to avoid using the term "limited range."

4. Have the higher-octave group sing the song in the key of A (approximate range A below middle C up to E). All voices should still be singing in the higher octave. Listen for those who can phonate the lower notes and for those who struggle because it is too low. Divide them into two groups: those who can sing it in A and those who had more success in C. Your low A group is your "alto/tenor" section, and your C group is your "unchanged treble" section. You may decide to just call them "Group 1 and Group 2" to be consistent with the lower voices.

5. It is possible that you will have some non-pitch-matching singers in the choir. This is not unusual, and you will need to help them find their voice over time. For the purpose of this test and voice placement, try to get a rough idea of the speaking voice in terms of if it sounds thicker and husky or lighter and unchanged. You probably can get a sense of this based on the relative range of the non-pitch-matched notes too. If unchanged (to your ear), then assign part 1 or 2 depending on the literature, and if changed or changing, assign part 3 or 4. Always have strong pitch-solid singers close to these voices and behind them, as opposed to putting the developing singers in the back row.

Once you become practiced at this voice-placement test, it will not take you long to check the progress of the male singers in your choir. Celebrate their changing voices and be positive and enthusiastic when you tell a singer "Justin, let's move you to part 3. Your voice sounds really great in that range now." You will even begin to hear when students need to be tested again based on their speaking voices and singing accuracy in choir rehearsals. When you can, test individuals using this group method and consider charting their progress in some way. They will take their lead from you and your attitude toward their vocal transition, and if you are supportive and excited for them, it is likely that they will feel the same way.

RECAPITULATION

1. What do you remember about your music classes in elementary school and middle school? Perhaps you didn't have any music classes. Either way, comment on some of the things you remember about your school situation during these years. Did you have a favorite teacher or teachers and which classes did you enjoy the most and why?
2. Have you had any experience working with students between the ages of twelve and fifteen? If not, perhaps you have relatives or friends with young people in this age group. Describe your impressions of how many young people this age interact and behave with others in three different situations: 1. With peers their own age, 2. With adults they don't know, and 3. With their parents and family. You will probably notice that your impressions are slightly different for the three situations, so also make a few observations about why you think they behave differently in each situation.
3. Based on your experience so far in the choral music education profession, do you think you might be well suited to teach middle-level students in choir? Why or why not? Comment on what you think might be easy for you, as well as on what you think could be a challenge for you.

Selecting Literature for Middle-Level Choirs

As has been stated, it's important to know what part your middle-level students should be singing by testing their voices frequently. But it's just as important to know what kinds of literature will best fit those voice ranges. If you are working with an elementary-aged choir with all unchanged voices, it is wise to choose unison music, rounds, and partner songs to start with that have a range of approximately middle C up to high F on the treble clef. When working with high school choirs, a majority of the students will have changed voices and voice ranges that are beginning to settle, and much of the standard SATB-range music will be appropriate in most instances. But when you are working with middle-level students, it is almost impossible to select unison music that will fit the ranges of every voice. This is counterintuitive because you might think that singing in unison would be easier than singing in parts, which would be true if everyone could sing all the notes in the melody. But let's revisit the general range chart:

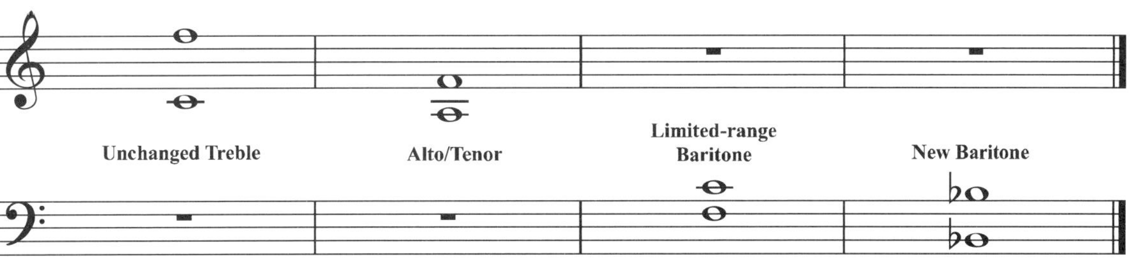

As you look for overlap of the ranges in this chart, you will see that there are no notes that are shared by all four parts. The closest and most usable notes are these:

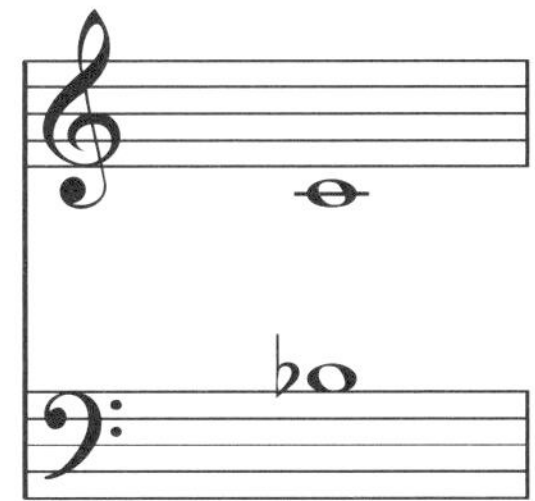

Imagine a melody using only these two notes; it certainly would be boring and repetitive and would also keep the voices at the high or low ends of their usable ranges. Middle school singers, then, must sing in parts and must have options for each voice part to sing notes in the middle of their best usable range. A middle-level choral teacher that thinks, "How can I teach them to sing in parts when they can't even sing a unison in tune?" does not understand this important concept of appropriate ranges for this age. If you give them a part that they can sing in their most-usable vocal range, they will have the best chance to sing it accurately and in tune.

Here are some general guidelines for selecting music for this age group:

- ❖ For a choir of exclusively sixth graders, you will encounter mostly unchanged male singers and changing female singers. You can choose 2-part music that has a tessitura primarily on the treble clef, and then let the male singers who are entering a change sing down the octave when necessary. Pieces in the keys of E, F, and G can work well, as long as the range is limited to notes on the treble staff. If a piece has a melody that has a wide range and stays off the treble clef for a while, you may need to write a new part for the voices that can't match the notes.

- ❖ For a choir of sixth, seventh, and eighth graders, you will encounter some unchanged, some changing, as well as some changed male singers. You can choose *3-part mixed* music that has a part that will fit the Limited-range Baritones, with two treble parts above, and then allow your New Baritones to sing the soprano or alto part down an octave as needed.

❖ For a choir of seventh and eighth graders, you will encounter many changing, as well as some changed, male singers. You can choose 3-part mixed music (as above), or you can sing SATB music with the following approximate ranges:

You will see that these range suggestions are a little wider than the ones presented earlier, but the intention would always be to keep the singers in the middle of the ranges as much as possible. The alto/tenor (singing written alto) may have the hardest time singing the top of the alto range, so a lower tessitura for the alto would be best. The limited-range baritone (singing tenor) will always have the most constricted range, so finding a tenor part that stays in the middle of this range might be a challenge. If this part is the only one that does not conform to the range suggestions, and if you really think the piece is of good quality, you can always re-write a part for the tenors (limited-range baritones), or if the part jumps occasionally higher, encourage the use and development of a light falsetto. The new baritone won't have much, if any, sound below Bb, but your eighth-grade males might drop to basses before graduation, allowing you to program some lower bass parts as long as they are not too low for too long. If your choir includes ninth graders, you will be able to sing music with a higher tenor part and a lower bass part compared to the range chart, but you will still need to consider the limited-range baritones by possibly writing an adapted part for them. This chart is only a guideline, and you will always need to listen to your singers and test their ranges to determine what they can and can't do.

Consider the following SATB piece from CPDL:

The range considerations for each part work well, with the bass only hitting an A below Bb, and the tenors dipping down to D. If you try it with your students, you may find that it works, as written, with those students. If you needed to, you could adapt this piece to fit the outlined considerations in the range chart by having the basses always take the low A up an octave, leaping up a fourth instead of leaping down a fifth, and also doubling the tenors in measures 18–19. The tenors could likewise double the altos in measures 18–19 and 29–30. When working with changing voices, you are always free to change the key of the piece, rewrite parts, double at the octave, or double on a unison. Range is everything, so you must provide each singer with a part that they can sing regardless of how you achieve it.

One excellent resource for literature that is tailored to fit the range considerations of changing-voice singers is Cambiata Press. This website is dedicated to providing arrangements and compositions that are specifically tailored to the changing voice and are rooted in the best research and scholarship in this area. Besides providing music for purchase, this site also will help educate you more specifically on this subject than will the broad guidelines presented in this text.

RECAPITULATION

1. As we have explored, vocal range considerations are crucial to the success of the middle-level choral ensemble. But when selecting choral literature for this age, there are other factors that you should also consider. What are some of these factors, in your opinion? Make a list of these things, along with a sentence or two about why you think each factor is important.
2. Using music from your single-copy library, a choral music store, or online, find some music that you would consider to be of good quality for the following choirs: sixth-grade chorus (2-part treble); sixth, seventh, and eighth-grade chorus (3-part mixed); seventh, and eighth-grade chorus (SATB). Find at least one piece of literature for each choir. Fill out either the Full-Analysis Form (page 211) or the Simple-Analysis form (page 240) for each piece.
3. Find a piece of SATB literature that you believe would be suitable for a middle school choir in terms of theme, text, difficulty, and voice leading, but that is not quite right in terms of range considerations. Using a pencil, cross out and rewrite sections of the piece that don't work well in terms of range for this age. Consider voice leading and chord completion as much as you can so that the lines are stepwise whenever possible and so that original chord tones are not completely missing. Consider range first, then voice leading, and then chord-tone completion, getting all three whenever possible.

Voice Testing and Placing High School Singers

The middle-level choir can be considered a constantly changing ensemble, with students maturing physically, mentally, and vocally. In contrast, the high school choir is much more stable; students will still be growing, changing, and maturing into young adults, but without the seemingly dramatic variability of middle school students. This is especially evident when it comes to vocal ranges. By the time that male and female students are in eleventh grade (about age 16) their voices will have settled in large part, and they will begin to develop ranges and timbres that will suggest either a higher voice or a lower voice. But as in middle school, it is important that all students develop their whole voice including high, middle, and low registers to become the most expressive musicians possible. Because of this, it is still advisable that you listen to each voice in your choirs to determine *possible* voice placements as well as *best* voice placements.

When voice testing your high school choir students, you should consider both range and quality of the voice. Just because a student can phonate a pitch doesn't mean that the note is a good one for them. When possible, test one person at a time. Consider using this simplified sequence:

1. Engage the singer in a short conversation by asking them a few questions such as, "What is your experience as a singer?" or "Do you have any favorite hobbies outside of music?" or "Tell me a little about yourself." Listen carefully as they speak to determine if the voice is naturally resonant or breathy, if it sounds like a lower or a higher voice, and if it sounds clear and healthy or unclear and possibly damaged.
2. Individually have the student sing a stepwise vocalise of your choice with the range of a fifth, starting and ending on middle C (or the octave below for basses and tenors). Have them hold the last note and listen to the quality of vocal color, tuning, and support. Does it sound like a thin note that is at the bottom of the range or a completely full note in the middle of the range? Make note. Move up by half steps, repeating the assessment. Here is a possible example:

3. At first all the notes will be sung in the same register, but as you move up by half steps listen carefully to the top note and the way it is produced. At some point you will hear the singer "lift" or "flip" into a different register on the top note, which may be subtle or pronounced. Make a note of which key this seems to

happen in and keep going up by half steps. Vocalize them, if they can, up to a key that starts in the higher head register and listen for color and tuning in this range. Does it sound more in tune or less in tune in the higher ranges? Does it gain color or lose color? Does it sound more freely produced or more strained? It is possible that a new singer will have very little experience singing in the higher registers, and they may not be comfortable or able to phonate in those registers. Again, make a note of this.

4. Next, have the student sing a stepwise descending vocalise of your choice with the range of a fifth, starting on G and ending on middle C (or the octave below for basses and tenors). Have them hold the last note and listen to the quality of vocal color, tuning, and support. Does it still sound like a thin note that is at the bottom of the range or a completely full note in the middle of the range? Compare your initial impression in Step One for this note. Move down by half steps, repeating the assessment. Here is a possible example:

As you move down by half steps, you will hear the notes on the bottom getting stronger and fuller, remaining the same, or diminishing in color and strength. Make a note of what you hear. If the bottom note in the first key, ending on C, is already barely phonating, then there is no need to go any lower. If it is a usable note with a clear pitch, move down by another half step. Continue down until you hear the lowest clear note, which will be a half step above the first fuzzy, barely phonating note. Make a note of this pitch. Be prepared for an inexperienced singer (with a higher voice) to have few usable low notes and also an undeveloped head register. Remember, all singers will need to develop the higher registers, regardless of voice type.

At this point you will have heard the voice in the highest and lowest ranges, and you will have heard the voice gain or lose color and strength in several registers. You will have heard the first note that the singer seemed to "shift" or "flip" into a head or mixed register, and you will have noted if certain registers are more in tune than others. Here is one possible way to apply this information:

- ✓ In Step One, if the singer flipped into a head register on the top note on C or D (in the key of F or G), then that is evidence that the voice type could be a baritone (bass) or mezzo soprano (alto). However, if the singer flipped into a head register on the top note on F or G (in the key of Bb or C), then that is evidence that the voice type could be a tenor or a soprano.

- ✓ When the singer sang higher and completely in the upper registers, was the sound production freely produced, colorful, and in tune, or did it feel less free, less colorful, and perhaps a little less in tune? Freedom, tuning, and color in the higher ranges would suggest a soprano or tenor voice, especially when the voice lift was around the F-G range. When you have a beautiful, colorful, and in-tune high range, but a voice lift at C-D, make a note of this.

- ✓ In Step Three, if the lowest notes gained clarity and color, and if the lowest clear note was around a low G, then that is evidence that the voice type could be a baritone or a mezzo soprano. Additionally, a bass voice would be able to phonate even lower, perhaps as low as E, D, or C. However, if the singer lost color and clarity as they moved down from middle C, then that is evidence that the voice type could be a tenor or a soprano.

- ✓ If the singing and speaking quality of the voice is higher, it would suggest a soprano or tenor voice designation, and if the speaking and singing quality is lower and richer, it would suggest a bass/baritone/mezzo soprano/alto designation.

With all the data collected from the vocal audition, and using the considerations outlined above, you should be able to assign an appropriate voice part in the SATB choir for each singer. As has been stated earlier, every voice will need to develop as consistent a registration as possible with the lowest and highest notes sounding clear, in tune, and expressive. If a singer *can* sing both high and low, then you might encourage them to experience different voice parts on different songs. A voice that can't sing below middle C (or the octave below for tenors) should not be asked to sing alto or bass. Remember that high school voices are still developing, so you will need to allow them to sound warm and beautiful without asking them to sound like fully mature voices by creating artificial tension or color. Your literature selections can be made with your specific singers in mind, so do your best to pick music that best fits the ranges of your singers.

To help you in the practical implementation of this audition process, consider using the "Choral Voice Testing and Placement Form." Remember that your goal is to asses usable vocal ranges, high- and low-register quality, and to gather enough information to assign the most usable as well as the best voice parts that are appropriate for each individual. It is possible that you will have an occasional student who seems to have no best part to sing, and others who can sing several parts with equally good quality. It is alright for you to assign several (or no) "best parts" or just one or several "usable parts." When

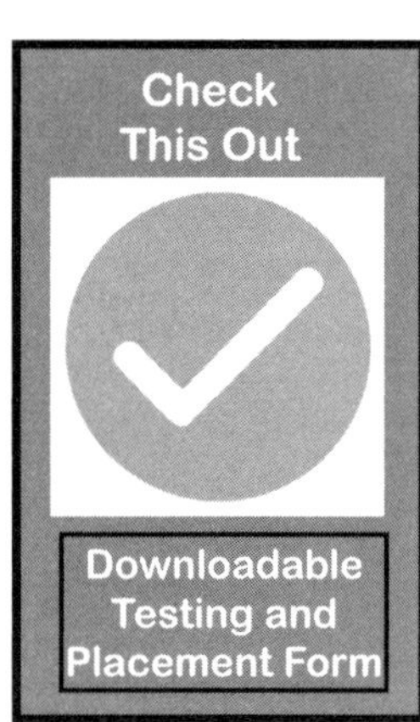

balancing the various vocal sections of the choir, you will need as much accurate information as possible to keep everyone feeling successful and singing with a healthy technique. Students who have trouble matching pitch will need special consideration and help both inside and outside of class, so be sure to note when pitch matching is a challenge for the student during the voice placement. Even a non-pitch-matching student can be guided to an appropriate voice part based on the quality and timbre of the speaking voice, as well as the relative ranges of the pitches they do sing while struggling to find their intonation.

Choral Voice Testing and Placement Form

Singer Name ______________________ Singer Grade: 9 10 11 12 Other ___

1. Engage in a short conversation. Listen carefully to determine if the voice is naturally resonant or breathy, if it sounds like a lower or a higher voice, and if it sounds clear and healthy or unclear and possibly damaged.

RESONANT _________ BREATHY _________ OTHER _______

HIGH SOUNDING ______ LOW SOUNDING _____ OTHER _______

CLEAR and HEALTHY _______ LESS CLEAR _______

2. Sing a stepwise vocalise with the range of a fifth, starting and ending on middle C (or the octave below for basses and tenors). Hold the last note and listen to the quality of vocal color, tuning, and support.

Middle C VOCAL COLOR:	1 (thin)	2	3	4	5 (full)
Middle C TUNING:	1 (out of tune)	2	3	4	5 (in tune)
Middle C SUPPORT:	1 (less supported)	2 (well supported)	3	4	5 (full)

3. Move up by half steps and listen for the singer to "lift" on the top note. Make a note of the pitch lift. Have the student sing completely in the higher head register. Is it: more in tune or less in tune/more colorful or less/more free or more strained? How usable is the head register?

Head Register "Lift" note(s)

Head Register Quality

VOCAL COLOR:	1 (thin)	2	3	4	5 (full)
TUNING:	1 (out of tune)	2	3	4	5 (in tune)
PRODUCTION:	1 (strained)	2	3	4	5 (free)

Other Observations of Register: ______________________

4. Sing a stepwise descending vocalise with the range of a fifth, starting on G and ending on middle C. Move down by half steps. Are the lower notes getting stronger and fuller, remaining the same, or diminishing in color and strength? Continue down until you hear the lowest clear note, which will be a half step above the first fuzzy, barely phonating note. Make a note of this pitch.

Lowest Usable Note(s)

Lower Note Quality (while descending)

GETTING STRONGER	☐ Yes	☐ No
REMAINING THE SAME	☐ Yes	☐ No
DIMINISHING	☐ Yes	☐ No

Other Observations of Lower Register: ______________________

5. Circle ratings for each usable vocal range that apply to this voice. A Plus (⊕) means the person is *able* to sing that part, an X (⊗) means that they *shouldn't* sing the part, and a Star (✪) indicates a possible *best part* to be assigned.

Soprano 1	⊕	⊗	✪	**Soprano 2**	⊕	⊗	✪
Alto 1	⊕	⊗	✪	**Alto 2**	⊕	⊗	✪
Tenor 1	⊕	⊗	✪	**Tenor 2**	⊕	⊗	✪
Bass 1	⊕	⊗	✪	**Bass 2**	⊕	⊗	✪

Selecting Literature for High School Choral Ensembles

The high school choral music educator may have five or more different choirs to choose literature for, and each group will likely have different needs in terms of music selection. Most programs will have a roster of choirs from this list:

- The Beginning Treble Choir
- The Bass Chorus
- The Advanced Treble Choir
- The Beginning Mixed Choir
- The Intermediate Mixed Choir
- The Advanced Mixed Choir
- The Show Choir
- The Jazz Choir

You worked with the *Music Literature Difficulty Assessment Rubric* earlier in this chapter, so you already have a tool for determining the relative difficulty of a piece of choral music (5-35 points for beginning choirs, 36-65 points for intermediate choirs, and 66-90 points for advanced choirs). But a beginning piece of music won't always be right for every beginning ensemble, and you will need to think about the needs of each choir to make the best selections that you can. Let's examine each of these choirs to provide some guidance and insights for your literature choices.

It's helpful to acknowledge that the same choir levels at different schools can vary widely in ability depending upon how strong and comprehensive the feeder-school music programs are in middle grades, so a beginning choir in one school may be much more advanced than a beginning choir at another school. Other factors affecting this are how much the school schedule supports students rescheduling choir from year to year, and how well the students are taught musicianship training and singing techniques at each level. In the end, as you give concerts with each choir, you will figure out if you did a good job assessing their abilities and ranges before you selected the music, or if you misjudged what they were capable of doing. Over time, and through trial and error, you will get very good at knowing what your choirs can and can't do. But when you are starting out as a new teacher, here are a few general things to consider:

- **The Beginning Treble Choir:**
  This choir will normally be for younger treble voices (ninth and tenth grades) and for inexperienced older voices (eleventh and twelfth grades) who need an introduction to choral singing and musicianship. The average singer

in this ensemble will need time to work on basic singing techniques, and the literature should have moderate ranges and tessitura, as well as a predominance of forms that have repeating sections. Repeating forms allow you to break down a section of music while implementing basic choral techniques and then apply the learned notes and rhythms to repeated sections, saving rehearsal time. Homophonic textures and primarily diatonic harmonies will also provide this choir with enough time to learn the notes and rhythms while developing other skills. Unison, 2-part, 3-part, and 4-part voicings are possible, depending on the complexity of the writing. Accompaniments that support the harmony and choral writing will work best, and some *a cappella* music can be introduced as well. As with every choir, you will need to have some very accessible music that they can sing on the first day as well as some music that will challenge them to grow musically and artistically over time. Beginning choirs will usually need more rote teaching than advanced choirs, so you should consider their developing tonal memory skills and choose the music accordingly; most of the writing shouldn't be so complex that they can't digest and perform it by ear if necessary. Text themes and poetry can be simple or intricate, even if the musical writing is more accessible. Foreign-language texts can work with this choir as long as they are not too complex and especially if they repeat within the piece. For a list of sample repertoire for beginning treble voices, click "Check This Out."

The Bass Chorus:

This choir will normally be for younger tenor and baritone voices (ninth and tenth grades) who need an introduction to choral singing and musicianship. In some schools, all of the ninth grade bass-clef voices will sing in this choir and then move up to a mixed choir the following year, while other schools may not offer this choir at all depending on the number of students enrolled in this voice type. Like the beginning treble chorus singer, the average singer in this ensemble will probably need time to work on basic singing techniques, and most male singers will need to develop a usable high register that is clear, freely produced, and in tune. There is a good amount of published literature in two parts for tenor/bass that will work well with this choir. Appropriate arrangements for this choir will keep the bass and baritone singers above a low G at the bottom of the bass clef and up only to about middle C and D, and tenor-clef singers will not be required to sing much lower than C below middle C and up to E and F above middle C. Repeating forms, homophonic textures, and primarily diatonic harmonies are also well suited for this choir. Students in a bass choir can be motivated by group challenges and accomplishments, so singing in more than two parts can be a good goal for this ensemble. Like the treble chorus, accompaniments that support the harmony and choral writing will work best, and some *a cappella* music, including simple barbershop-style harmony, can be introduced as well. Music for this choir need not be too complex because the best way to build and sustain membership in this choir is to make the ensemble members look good in public performances by choosing music that they can perform really well. For a list of sample repertoire for beginning bass chorus, click "Check This Out."

- ## The Advanced Treble Choir:

  This choir will normally be for older treble voices (eleventh and twelfth grades) who have some experience singing in choir and who have intermediate to advanced musicianship skills. The average singer in this ensemble will already have developed an in-tune and pleasant singing technique, and the literature can have more extreme ranges and tessitura as well as more complex contrapuntal and through-composed forms. This ensemble will be expected to sing on solfege syllables and to read and count rhythms at sight. Fewer notes will need to be taught by rote during rehearsals, and students will be able to make faster progress on more challenging music than the beginning choirs. Singers in this choir can be challenged to sing 4-part music (SSAA) with divisi. Accompaniments that contrast with the harmony and choral writing are possible, and *a cappella* music will work well. Complex texts and themes will be appropriate for this choir, as will a wide variety of foreign texts. For a list of sample repertoire for advanced treble voices, click "Check This Out."

- ## The Beginning Mixed Choir:

  This choir will normally be for younger voices (ninth and tenth grades) and for inexperienced older voices (eleventh and twelfth grades) who need an introduction to choral singing and musicianship. This choir is usually offered in a school that does not have beginning treble and bass choirs and may serve as the initial training ensemble in the choral program sequence. Like the other beginning choirs described above, the average singer in this ensemble will need time to work on basic singing techniques, and the literature, ranges, tessitura, and forms will need to be moderate and accessible. Four-part (SATB) voicings with limited divisi will work best, but other voicings can also work as long as each part has notes within their usable ranges. Because you may have bass-clef voices that are still changing in this choir, you will need to choose music that will fit their ranges, much like the middle school mixed choir. Harmonically supportive accompaniments will help the singers develop their ears, and some *a cappella* music can be introduced. Keep in mind that you will need to teach some of the music by rote as they develop their musicianship skills and that you will have four distinct parts to manage most of the time. Simple foreign-language texts can work with this choir if they are not too lengthy and if they repeat within the piece. Text themes and poetry can be simple or intricate, even if the musical writing is more accessible. For a list of sample repertoire for beginning mixed voices, click "Check This Out."

- The Intermediate Mixed Choir:

This choir will normally be for all older voices (tenth through twelfth grades) who have some experience singing in choir and who have basic musicianship and vocal skills. The average singer in this ensemble may still be developing an in-tune and pleasant singing technique, but the basics of choral performance and sight singing will be familiar to them. The literature can be more complex than the beginning choirs, but ranges and tessitura should still be moderate and not too vocally taxing. This ensemble will be advancing their ability to sing on solfege syllables, and to read and count rhythms at sight, yet some notes will still need to be taught by rote during rehearsals. Singers in this choir can be challenged to sing standard 4-part music (SATB) with occasional divisi sections. Accompaniments that support and contrast with the harmonic and choral writing are possible, and *a cappella* music will work well. Simple as well as complex texts and themes will be appropriate for this choir, as will moderately simple foreign texts. For a list of sample repertoire for intermediate mixed voices, click "Check This Out."

- The Advanced Mixed Choir:

This choir will normally be for older mixed voices (eleventh and twelfth grades) who have experience singing in choir and who have intermediate to advanced musicianship skills. Most everything that was stated about the advanced treble choir will also apply to the advanced mixed choir. The average singer in this ensemble will already have developed an ability to sing well and in tune and will have musicianship skills that allow them to learn music independently in sectionals or after school. Depending on the prior training that students receive in the choral program, this choir may be able to sing college-level literature. Few notes will need to be taught by rote during rehearsals, and students will be able to make faster progress on more challenging music than the intermediate choirs. Singers in this choir can be challenged to sing 4-part music (SATB) with extensive divisi. Accompaniments that contrast with the harmony and choral writing are possible, and *a cappella* music will work well. Complex texts and themes will be appropriate for this choir, as will a wide variety of foreign texts. For a list of sample repertoire for advanced mixed voices, click "Check This Out."

- ## The Show Choir:

This choir is considered a "pop" ensemble and in some choral programs it may be offered as an extra elective, and in other programs it may receive most to all of the curricular focus. Show choirs can be any ability level from beginning to advanced, and students of all ages are often members of the ensemble. The main difference between a traditional classical choir and a show choir is that a show choir performs a wide variety of choreography while singing and they often wear colorful costumes to enhance the impact of the performance, much like a Broadway cast in a musical. All music is memorized to allow the choir to move and dance while singing, and the accompaniment can include keyboard, bass, drums, electric guitar, and even wind instruments. The literature is usually arranged to be easily sung and memorized, and the songs tend to be popular hits that are well known to the singers and audience. There is a large amount of commercially arranged music for show choir that is available for purchase, and accompaniment tracks are frequently available for choirs that do not have the resources to use live bands in performance. In programs where the show choir is the main curricular focus, there may be beginning, intermediate, and advanced show choirs, as well as bass and treble show choirs offered. In these big programs, there will normally be a focus on choir competitions, with each show choir competing in several or more competitive festivals per year. At the highest competitive levels, these choirs will often contract musical arrangers to create unique choral medleys for each choir to showcase in their performance sets. It is not unusual for these choirs to learn all their music by rote and to focus less on musicianship skills, though that is not always the case. Apart from memorizing the music, significant time will need to be spent learning and perfecting the choreography and practicing the show set with costumes and props. While most show choir competition sets will feature fully accompanied songs with a live band, it is often a requirement for one of the songs to be an *a cappella* slow ballad-type piece. For a list of sample repertoire for show choir, click "Check This Out."

- The Jazz Choir:
  In some schools the main "pop" ensemble will be a jazz choir. Like the show choir, this ensemble may be offered as an extra elective, but it is rarely the sole curricular focus of a program. While a jazz choir can be of any ability level from beginning to advanced, the complexity of jazz music requires the singers to have good ears and a certain amount of musical ability and independence to be successful. The main difference between a show choir and a jazz choir is that the jazz choir won't perform choreography while singing, though they will often memorize music for performance. The jazz choral musician will also have opportunities to improvise solos much like instrumental musicians, and accompaniment ensembles usually include piano, bass, drums, and electric guitar. The literature is more chromatic and rhythmically complex than show choir music on the whole, so extra time will be needed to learn and perfect the syncopated rhythms and sometimes-dissonant harmonies. There is a large amount of commercially arranged music for jazz choir that is available for purchase, and accompaniment tracks are also available. Jazz choirs are less likely to compete in a large number of choral competitions, though some programs do include competition in their curricular focus. Like the show choir, the jazz choir will sing both accompanied and *a cappella* music. For a list of sample repertoire for jazz choir, click "Check This Out."

Performing Major Works of Choral Music

Many collegiate choral programs, depending on size and resources, will include the study and live performance of major choral works such as the Brahms *Requiem* or the Beethoven *Ninth Symphony*. Major works are called "major" because they are usually composed for adult choirs and are often multi-movement, extended (longer in duration) pieces. It is also common for these works to be accompanied by an instrumental ensemble or full orchestra, and they can be as short as about fifteen minutes or as long as sixty minutes or more. Because these works are often conceived with adult voices in mind, the ranges and tessitura of the vocal writing can be extreme. Additionally, the choir may be required to sing at very loud or very soft dynamics for extended periods of time and sometimes with a very large orchestra.

If you had the wonderful opportunity to perform major choral works during your collegiate experience, you may have developed a very enthusiastic desire to perform some of these works with your own students. Indeed, major works can provide students with extended challenges that will inspire them, and these challenges can align well with your curricular goals. But while you may want your students to explore the challenges and musical experiences of these amazing choral works, is it possible and realistic to program these works with your high school choral students? The answer is yes…and no… and it depends. Like the preceding discussion of appropriate choral works for various-level choirs, major works can be appropriate for some choirs if the singers are prepared musically and vocally, but they can be completely inappropriate for other choirs if the singers do not have the musicianship and vocal maturity to be successful.

Let's examine this question in light of all three of the answers above:

- *Yes, major works can be studied and performed by high school choral ensembles.* There are a number of major choral works that are perfectly appropriate for many high school choirs and that do not require completely mature voices and professional-level musicianship. It may be possible to collaborate with your school's orchestra if you have one that is able to play at a high-enough level or you can use a piano reduction in many cases. You will need to consider how difficult the vocal writing is and the range and tessitura of each part to decide if your choir can perform the work effectively. Some appropriate major works for a good high school program include Vivaldi *Gloria*, Faure *Requiem*, Schubert *Mass in G*, Thompson *Frostiana*, Rutter *Gloria*, J.S. Bach *Wachet auf*, J.S. Bach *Ich lasse dich nicht*, Britten *A Ceremony of Carols*, Durufle *Requiem*, and G. F. Handel *Zadok the Priest*.

- *No, major works can't be studied and performed by high school choral ensembles.* There are a number of major choral works that are not appropriate for many high school choirs and that do require completely mature voices and professional-level musicianship. While it is technically possible for high school voices to perform these works, the rehearsal hours and vocal stamina needed to prepare these works, as well as the musicianship needed to learn them accurately, make them a daunting challenge for the average high school choir. Some major works that probably won't be appropriate for a good high school program include Bach *B Minor Mass*, Verdi *Requiem*, Mahler *Symphony No 8*, Orff *Carmina Burana*, Bach *St. Matthew Passion*, Brahms *Requiem*, and Beethoven *Ninth Symphony*.

- *Can major works be studied and performed by high school choral ensembles? It depends.* There are many high school choral programs in the United States that create opportunities for their students to sing and perform many easier and more challenging major choral works. In some scenarios, the program supports young singers with vocal and musicianship training that prepares them to learn and perform these works, and in some choral programs there is a healthy collaboration with other musicians (often adults) in the surrounding community. These directors may hire local instrumental musicians to accompany the choir in the dress rehearsal and concert or they may invite a university or community choir or orchestra in their area to collaborate with them in concert. Another option is to combine several high school choirs from different high schools and pool resources to hire instrumental musicians and an appropriate concert venue if needed. If you do an online search for recommendations for major works for high school choir and orchestra, you will see a large number of recommendations ranging from easy to extremely challenging. What you can do depends on your particular program, the training your choral musicians have received, and the resources you have available to you.

Sometimes it can be a great idea to excerpt a single movement from a major work to give the choir time to learn and digest the piece more deeply. A shorter major work that is appropriate for an ensemble can also make a very nice Centerpiece in a Menu Program or can stand alone as a featured piece. Like any literature choice, you will need to be sure that the music is appropriate for your choirs in terms of range, tessitura, demands of tone color and vocal stamina, and musical difficulty. Before you program any major work, be sure to study the score carefully and to do some research on performance practice to be sure that you have a good handle on what will be required of you, your students, and your available resources.

RECAPITULATION

1. Voice testing choral singers is an important part of your training and skill set, and it will take some practice for you to get completely comfortable doing it. To begin your practice in this area, find at least three people (any age from middle school through adult) who will agree to let you voice test them and then audio record your assessment at a piano. These can be family members, friends, or acquaintances. Use the "Choral Voice Testing and Placement Form" during your assessments. Ask a choral music professor or choral music colleague to listen to the recorded sessions and evaluate your process while they reference your completed Placement Forms. Ask them to provide some feedback about your approach and effectiveness. Be ready to provide

this feedback to your colleagues as well.

2. You are now more familiar with what makes a piece of music appropriate for several of the most common choral ensembles. It is also important to keep in mind that for every ensemble there will be a variety of music from various time periods and styles that can work well. To help illustrate this, do your best to find the following pieces, supported by a completed "Choral Literature Simple-Analysis Form" for each:
    a. Beginning Mixed Choir (from the Renaissance period)
    b. Beginning Mixed Choir (from the Baroque period)
    c. Beginning Mixed Choir (from the Classical period)
    d. Beginning Mixed Choir (from the Romantic period)
    e. Beginning Mixed Choir (from the 20th Century)
    f. Beginning Mixed Choir (composed in the last 10 years)
    g. Beginning Mixed Choir (from a Broadway musical)
3. The words "multicultural choral music" have been used in the recent past to describe music that is from outside of the traditional Western-European choral tradition. However, "multicultural" is simply an adjective that means "relating to or constituting several cultural or ethnic groups within a society," and the word does not necessarily denote certain cultures.[4] Discuss your own musical and cultural background in terms of the musical styles and genres that you would consider to be central to your own culture, and also describe which kinds of music you would consider to be less common to your particular culture and background.
4. Did you perform any major choral works in your high school or collegiate choir experiences? If so, what are some of your favorite memories of the experiences? If you did not experience singing a major work, discuss an extended work (choral or instrumental) that you are familiar with and that you would like to program someday if you have the chance. What musical aspects of this work make it appealing to you?
5. Use the internet to research and make a list of recommended major works for choir and instrumental ensemble. Find at least twenty works. Group the titles and composers in *one or more* of the following ways: 1. By composer, 2. By performance duration, 3. By difficulty, 4. By instrumentation, 5. By the frequency of positive recommendations on different websites.

---

4 Apple Dictionary Version 2.2.2 (203)

Materials in the Teaching Environment

Any teacher who is leading a class will need to maintain behavioral control of that class in some obvious and subtle ways. Effective classroom management is a skill that can be practiced and improved throughout your career, and beginning teachers often struggle to maintain a positive, contingent, and consistent teaching approach. The teacher must make continuous decisions to reinforce certain behaviors while ignoring others, and the students will need to know that the teacher is constantly aware of all the aspects of the room. Any behavioral decision that is not made by the teacher will be made by the students, and while the teacher will make a single decision at a time, a class will make many (often contradicting) decisions together that will usually lead to a disruption in learning. For example, if the teacher does not decide how and where the class will be seated, every student will decide for themselves where they prefer to sit, how they will sit, and how they will get to that seat.

Some of the most important decisions that you can make as an educator involve investing time and forethought into the practical, physical aspects of your teaching environment. Experienced teachers understand that they must control the teaching environment as much as possible before the class begins and that they will be completely controlled by the physical environment during the entire lesson. Inexperienced teachers, through trial and error, will learn the importance of controlling the teaching environment and will learn to plan more and more effectively regarding the physical elements that enhance or interfere with student learning. Here are just a few of the most important aspects of the teaching environment that you must think about and plan for before you start teaching your first classes.

- ✓ **<u>Taking Class Attendance:</u>** You will need to create or adapt a system for taking attendance that is accurate, quick to administer, and that doesn't encourage your students to be off task. Your administration can help you with ideas for this, as can colleagues who teach choir and other performance ensembles. For very large classes, if you call off each name and wait for a verbal response from each student, you will waste a great amount of rehearsal and teaching time. Additionally, attendance that takes more than a minute or so can stall any momentum that you are trying to create at the beginning of the class. Some schools require attendance to be submitted to the office within the first few minutes of each period, and creating an efficient and accurate attendance system will need to be among your top priorities.

- ✓ **<u>Seating Students in the Classroom:</u>** As noted above, if you don't decide how and where students will be seated, they will decide for you. An accurate and well-thought-out seating plan can help the class get settled and start on time, and it can also aid you in taking quick and accurate attendance. In a choir rehearsal, the seating plan is essential for helping the choir sing in tune and listen across sections and voices. Students struggling to match pitch can be placed beside or in front of strong pitch matchers, and different seating arrangements can be tried to experiment with aspects of choral sound and blend. There are many approaches to seating a choir, and there is no one right way to do it. Generally, there are two ways to seat the choir: in sections or mixed. Here are several examples of just a few ways to do this:

Three options for SATB in Sections:

Soprano	Alto	Tenor	Bass

Soprano	Bass	Tenor	Alto

Bass	Tenor
Soprano	Alto

Two options for SATB Mixed:

T	T	S	S	B	B	A	A
A	A	B	B	S	S	T	T
B	B	T	T	A	A	S	S
S	S	A	A	T	T	B	B

A	T	B	S	A	T	B	S
T	B	S	A	T	B	S	A
B	S	A	T	B	S	A	T
S	A	T	B	S	A	T	B

✓ **Visual and Aural Aids in the Classroom:** As you teach musical and social skills to your students, you will need to be sure that you have adequate visual and aural materials for them. All students learn best when there is a multi-modal approach to any concept. If you can explain a concept (aural), demonstrate it (visual), and have them experience it (kinesthetic), the class will have the best chance of understanding and remembering it. Ideally your classroom will have concept posters, a piano, a white board with a musical staff and fresh markers, a document camera, a way to show video clips, and a sound system that is of good quality. If you visit effective and experienced choral music educators and notice how the room is set up in terms of visual and auditory teaching aids, you will see some of the ways that these materials can be most effective.

Here are a few samples of musical concept posters that you can buy or create for your classroom:

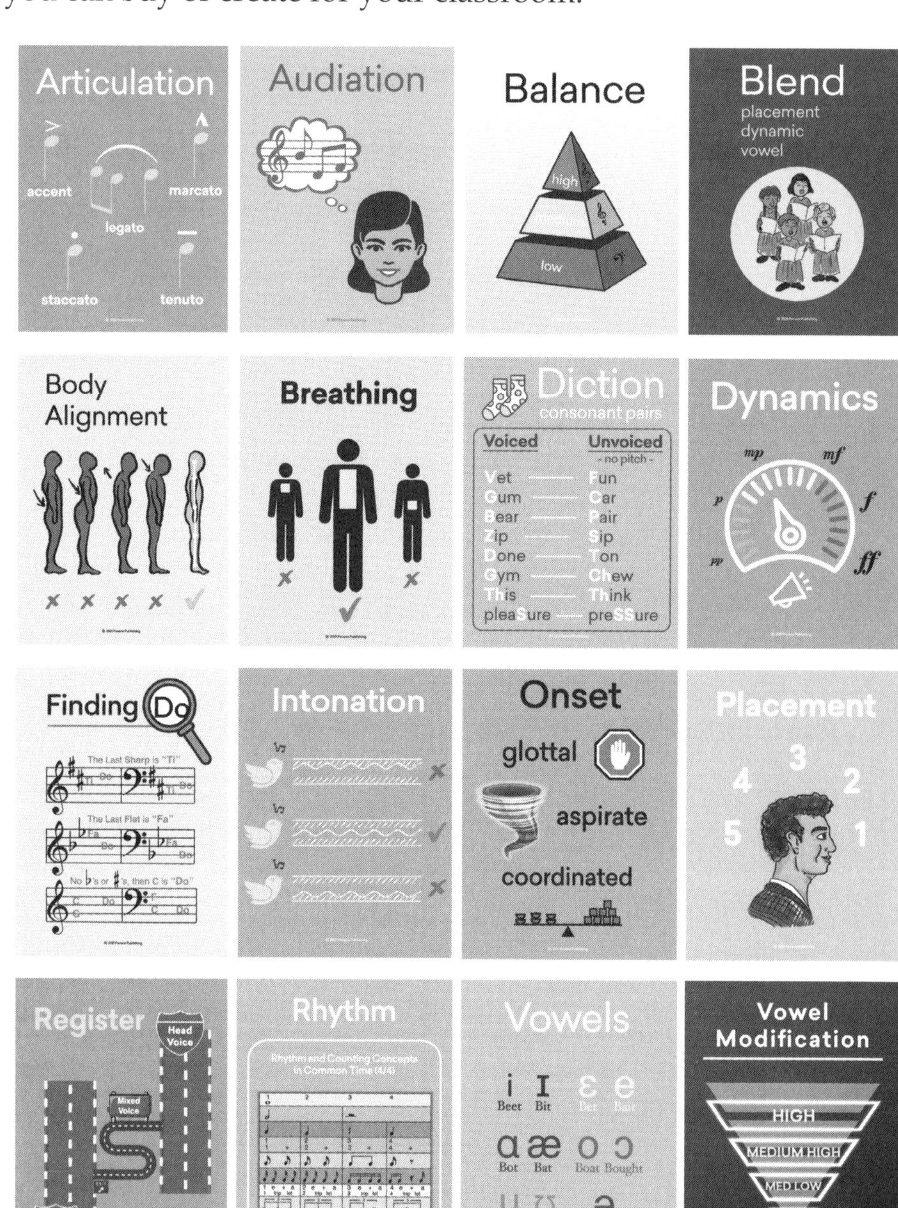

Distributing and Collecting Choral Music: One often overlooked aspect of the teaching environment is the need to pass out and collect choral music during the rehearsal. If you have stacks of music on the piano or on a table, you will need to pass out the music and collect it every rehearsal, which can take a lot of valuable rehearsal time. Some programs require a music folder for each student with all the music inside, which can solve this problem. But then you have to decide if students will be required and encouraged to take the folder home to practice. If so, you will need to have some extra music available for students who forget their folder at home, or at least a plan so that they can see a copy of the music during rehearsal. If you require students to leave the folder in the classroom as they leave, then you will need to have a storage system that allows students to find their folder quickly on the way back into the rehearsal space. If you have the technology and budget to have your literature legally scanned and on student's iPads or tablets, you will be able to bypass most of the problems associated with physically passing out music every rehearsal. If the system you choose is working well, every student will have the materials they need for each rehearsal, and you will not waste rehearsal time sorting out who needs a copy of the music.

- ✓ **Controlling Distractions in the Classroom:** Every room will have certain built-in distractions that will affect the ability of the students to remain on task during the lesson. You will have to be perceptive to notice some of these, and some you will be able to control while others you may not be able to control. One potential distraction is the direction that the choir faces during rehearsal, especially in relation to what happens *behind the teacher*. If the main door to the room is behind the teacher then people leaving and entering the room may draw the attention of the choir away from making music. Sometimes it is possible to realign the direction of the choir to control this, and sometimes it is not possible. Another potential distraction can be a clock in direct sight of the choir; some experienced teachers have even removed the clock or relocated it behind the choir. The general acoustical environment of the room can also create a distraction, especially if the room is very big and very live. In this instance, you may need to talk more loudly and slowly, or you may be able to work with your administration to treat and deaden the acoustic of the teaching space. There are many other elements to consider such as the temperature of the room, the lighting, air flow, the placement of the piano and podium, how loud school-wide announcements sound, and the like. Do your best to know about these distractions, and work to control as many of them as you can so that your students can focus their attention, stay on task, and become the best musicians and performers that they can be.

- ✓ **Controlling Electronic Media During Rehearsal**: Students who have not been given a policy for cell phone use during rehearsal will often decide to use them when they should be participating in class. Some will be very stealthy and it may be hard for you to even notice, while others will not even try to conceal their phone to text or check email or social media. You will need to have a policy for cell phones and electronic media, and it will need to be consistent and effective and approved by your administration. Some experienced teachers make students turn off their devices while others require them to leave them on a table or shelf as they enter the room. If you have a policy that allows students to have electronic devices turned on and in pockets and purses during the rehearsal, you will need to develop a contingent rule for anyone who breaks the rule, and you will need to enforce this so that everyone knows it's a real rule. Even when you don't notice students using electronic devices in rehearsal, the other students *will notice*, which can distract and lower morale within the choir.

✓ **Controlling How and When Students Enter and Leave the Room:** Most every teacher in a school setting must develop a system for allowing students to leave during class to use the bathroom or visit another location for some reason. Most schools require some sort of hall pass or permission for any student to be out of the classroom during a scheduled class period, and you may find that departing and arriving students can cause significant distractions in the learning environment. In some classrooms, students fill out a written hall pass that the teacher must sign each time, and in other schools, there will be an official "hall pass" that can be reused, such as a big block of wood with the room number on it. If you have to stop teaching to sign a hall pass, it will obviously affect the pacing and flow of your teaching in a negative way, especially if student after student needs your attention and signature. When the hall pass is a reusable object that students can pass on to the next person, it will minimize the times that you are taken away from your teaching to sign the hall pass, but it can also create a distraction if someone is always leaving or departing from the rehearsal. If you limit student departures to "critical issues," you will significantly cut down the number of students requesting to leave the classroom while still allowing them to use the facilities when they really have a need to do so.

✓ **Controlling the "Uncontrollable:"** Professional choral music educators can plan ahead for many things that could distract students in the learning environment. Everything noted above is predictable and likely to occur in any position you hold. But there will also be things that may happen in your school situation that you will need to be aware of and prepared for as much in advance as you can be. Consult your administration and ask about school policies for the following scenarios:

- <u>Weather-related emergencies and fire drills</u>: Depending on where you live, there will be safety drills to address possible weather emergencies such as earthquakes, tornadoes, hurricanes, and other possible natural disasters. Every school will be required to have fire drills. When these are scheduled in advance (and the administration tells you when to expect them), you will be able to adjust your lesson plans to accommodate the time disruption. Sometimes these drills will not be announced ahead of time and you will just have to adjust your lessons and rehearsals in real time. Always take these drills seriously and participate fully with your students. If a real emergency does happen, you will be prepared to keep everyone as safe as possible by following practiced procedures that the school has adopted. By not learning, practicing, and following the school procedures, you may open yourself up to personal legal liability that can cost you a lot of money, and that could even end your teaching career.

- School-wide testing: Most states require students to be tested at certain intervals such as the seventh, ninth, and eleventh grades. The schedules for these tests will usually be announced to allow teachers to plan around the disruptions. If you are not planning ahead for this type of disruption, you may find yourself missing half your choir the week of a performance or scheduling a trip or retreat when students are not available. The testing in most states is mandatory, and the test scores can often be used to evaluate the school as a whole and may even be tied to funding sources based on the performance benchmarks and student test averages. Your administrators will probably give considerable and serious focus to these tests, and you should not try to negotiate with them for anything that will disrupt the testing. Plan ahead as well as you can or live with the fact that you could have planned better, but always do everything you can to support your administration when school-wide testing is happening.

- Students in personal distress: There will be times that students will come to you, in or out of class, with some sort of personal problem or distress that they want you to know about. You have a legal responsibility to report your knowledge of certain issues as soon as you are aware of them, so it is a good idea to check with your administration to know exactly what you can and cannot keep in confidence with a student. Two examples of reported information that you can't keep to yourself and that you must report to school authorities include reports related to sexual or physical abuse and a communicated intention that a student is considering suicide. Know your school and state policies regarding mandatory reporting and know what the procedures are for students in distress in your classroom. For medical emergencies, your school should have a written policy available, and maybe even an "emergency button" in each classroom to alert the office of a dire circumstance unfolding in a classroom. Be well informed and as prepared as possible.

- Fights, weapons, and active shooter scenarios: It is an unfortunate but real possibility that you may encounter a student fight, students with weapons, or a person with a gun on your campus at some point in your career. As in the scenarios above, your best approach to any of these scenarios is to know your school policy ahead of time and to follow it exactly. For example, your school may want you to intervene to stop a student fight or they may require that you call for help if you are the only faculty member in the area. If you have knowledge of a student hiding a weapon, you will need to know how to report it and how to handle the student in the most effective way. Most schools have developed an "active shooter" protocol that can vary greatly from school to school, so take these guidelines and drills very seriously and prepare for these possibilities. No concert, rehearsal, or music trip is more important than the safety of your students, so be sure to keep this balance in your mind always.

RECAPITULATION

1. Class attendance is going to be a task that you will need to complete quickly and accurately. Think back on your own experience as a student and the various ways that your teachers took class attendance. Comment on the different ways that you remember this being done, and also comment on which methods you think were the quickest and most accurate. Look online or interview some veteran teachers to determine how they take attendance in their classes. Do they use different methods for different classes? As choral directors we sometimes have very large choirs and classes. Discuss what ways you might take attendance in a rehearsal or class of 1. 10 students, 2. 40 students, 3. 80 students, 4. 150 students.
2. Refer back to the "Three options for SATB in Sections" diagrams page 281. There are some benefits for seating the choir in each of these options. Study these diagrams and then discuss what you think some of the benefits might be for each option. Do you see any drawbacks or possible problems with each one as well? Discuss these too. Are you familiar with any other seating options besides these three or can you create another option? Create a new diagram and list some of the reasons you selected that arrangement.
3. Some choral educators like to use both mixed and sectional options for seating plans in choir. In your opinion, what are some of the pros

and cons of mixed vs. sectional seating for a choir? When would you use one over the other? If you sang in choir, which ones did you prefer and why?

4. Revisit the "musical concept posters" page 282. Do you fully understand what you would teach with each one? Are you unsure what some of them mean? Discuss with your colleagues or your teacher what they might teach with each poster and some of the steps and methods they would use to help students understand each one. What big concepts could you teach and reinforce with a new poster? Brainstorm several poster ideas that you could create that are not included in this chapter. If you can, sketch out your ideas graphically in basic form.
5. The concept of controlling the materials in your teaching environment is critical to your success in the classroom. Summarize several things that you think you learned or that surprised you in the section "Materials in the Teaching Environment" and comment on how and why these ideas might help you to be a more effective teacher. What is your biggest "take away" from this section?

Chapter Nine

Recruiting for the Successful Choral Program

9. Recruiting for the Successful Choral Program

"Pretend that every single person you meet has a sign around his or her neck that says, 'make me feel important.' Not only will you succeed in sales, you will suceed in life."
~Mary Kay Ash

Why Do You Have To Recruit?

Being a secondary choral music educator is different than being a math or an English teacher in several important ways. One significant difference is that you, as a music teacher, are responsible for attracting and retaining students into your program. Classes like English and math have attendance requirements built into the curricular offerings of the school and a significant number of students will always be required to populate the seats of those classes, ensuring that those teachers will always have a minimum number of class sections offered in the schedule and full-time employment guaranteed as well.

But while many schools require some sort of "fine arts credit" to graduate, students can often earn that credit in visual arts, photography, drama, dance, concert band, orchestra, and even in classes like industrial arts in some instances. In that sense, it is likely that very few students will be required to be in any of your choirs. It is essential, then, that you learn how to recruit students for all your classes and that you also strive to build a comprehensive choral curriculum that will keep students engaged and interested so that they will continue to choose to be involved, year after year, in your choral program.

Successful recruiting for any organization or cause is largely based on specific skills and methods that you can learn and adopt, and many of these skills are the same ones shared by professionals outside of the education profession. People who work in the fields of product sales, psychology, design, advertising, and many other professions are constantly creating positive scenarios that will help attract people to their products, and we can learn a lot from what they know and practice in their professional duties.

It may not seem fair that you have to recruit while some other teachers are guaranteed students in their classes by the requirements of the general education curriculum, and it's true…it's not fair. And while it certainly isn't your fault, it certainly is your problem, and you will have to solve that problem if you want to be successful. But the sooner you get over that, and the sooner you start preparing to be an excellent recruiter, the sooner you will begin to enjoy how much fun it can be to encourage students to make music a central part of their personal expression and education.

Talk Less, Listen More: the Rule of 50-50

People love to hear their own voice. When we are face to face with someone, it is a natural human inclination to want to share our thoughts and views with the person, especially if we share common interests. It also seems to be a human tendency to enjoy a conversation where we get to speak more than we listen…where we talk more than 50% of the time. But have you ever noticed that when someone else dominates a conversation, and you get to talk much less than 50% of the time, you don't usually feel heard or satisfied with the interaction?

People who talk more than they listen can come across as self-absorbed, overly important, or as uncaring self-promoters. On the other hand, have you ever noticed that when you are sharing a conversation with someone, and the talking and listening ratios are approaching a 50–50% balance with each person contributing and listening equally, that you both can come away with a satisfying feeling from the interaction? We like to be heard and we also enjoy knowing that someone else is interested in what we have to say. The 50–50 rule of talking and listening is a recommended guideline for friendly relationships where you want to maintain good, healthy communication; both people feel that they are valued and that their opinion matters.

But when you are recruiting for your choral program, you can throw the 50–50 rule out the window. Your goal is not to be friends with your students, but to encourage them to try singing in your choir. Remember, people may judge how much they like interacting with you based on how much you listen to them talk and by how you engage them while they share their thoughts. When recruiting, you should invoke the 30–70% rule where you only talk 30% of the time and where you listen 70% of the time. If you are engaging an outgoing person, this will be easy because of the other person's natural inclination to talk when prompted. If you are engaging a shyer person, you will have to get really good at providing multiple questions and verbal and nonverbal prompts to keep them speaking. Just remember that they will, as a general rule, enjoy the interaction more if they get to talk about themselves most of the time. Any experienced salesperson understands that letting the customer talk, while engaging them in full eye contact, is a basic ground rule for making them feel comfortable. Many possible sales have been lost by novice salespersons who didn't have any self-awareness, and who didn't know how to listen to or engage others when others are talking.

Your first step toward self-awareness is to simply notice your own inclination to speak and listen in your normal daily conversations. Are you demonstrating a balance in your speaking interactions or are you noticing an imbalance? Do you look people in the eye when they are talking or do you look at your phone or dart your eyes around the room as they speak? Are you always thinking about the next thing you want to say or are you considering their words and changing your responses to fit their conversational momentum? Once you observe your own behavior, you will begin to get clues as to how you can expand your ability to create balanced and satisfying conversations. The beauty of this is that you will get to practice these skills every day and you will get to chart your progress with every new conversation you have.

While most people will find that they need to learn to listen more, another just-as-important skill is learning how to sustain a conversation without dominating it. One professional who uses this skill proficiently is the television talk show host. T.V. talk show hosts understand the importance of asking their guests probing questions to get them to speak during on-camera interviews. They get really good at keeping the conversation going by acknowledging what was said and then following up with new, often related, questions. Talk show hosts usually have the advantage of knowing about the guest in advance, and it's not uncommon for many of the questions to be pre-scripted before the interview, making it easier for the host to sustain the conversation. But the best hosts learn to improvise their follow-up questions when doing so has a chance to make the interview more interesting for the audience, and you can learn to do this too. You can learn how to be a good "interviewer" when you talk to students in your school, and you can even enjoy it as a kind of "game" where you happily help others talk about themselves, rather than having them listen to you talk about yourself.

The successful "game" of interviewing someone (while conversing) depends on your ability to ask rich questions and follow-up questions that allow the other person to elaborate and expand on the details of their story. One professional who uses this skill is the improvisation comic. A golden rule of improv comedy, where two or more people are making up a conversation on the spot to be funny, is never to disagree with the other person. No matter what the other person says, the response affirms the original statement, and when possible, offers new information to help expand or exaggerate the dialogue. Here is an example of a bad start to an improvisation skit:

Comic 1: "I just had a terrible ride to work."
Comic 2: "No you didn't."
Comic 1: "Yes, it was dreadful. I broke down, and there was an accident on the highway."
Comic 2: "I'm sure it wasn't dreadful."
Comic 1: "I'm going to use another way to get here next time."
Comic 2: "But driving is the best way to get here."

Because Person 2 is not agreeing with the statements in some way, there is a limited opportunity for Person 1 to expand the conversation into a humorous line. If you think of this conversation like an imaginary game of catch (with a ball), Person 2 is not doing a great job of throwing the ball back once they catch it. The improv comic knows to agree and expand the statement, allowing for a richer, more creative unfolding of the story, and allowing for a spontaneous "twist" in the conversation. Consider this dialogue in contrast to the previous example:

Comic 1: "I just had a terrible ride to work."
Comic 2: "Did you? Oh my, so did I. Did you break down like I did?"
Comic 1: "Yes, it was dreadful. I hit the brakes and there was an accident on the highway."
Comic 2: "An accident? How terrible. I saw an accident too. But the real reason that I broke down was that I had my dog in the car."
Comic 1: "Did you? You had your dog in the car? I love dogs. But what made you break down?"
Comic 2: "Actually, I broke down crying when my dog, who needed a walk, had an accident on the car seat."
Person 1: "Oh my, that is a terrible accident…but those *are* the breaks."

Because both parties are agreeing in some way and affirming the other's statements; the imaginary game of "catch" is working well, with each person "throwing" the ball back every time they catch it. Consider these two conversations between a choir teacher and a potential student recruit for choir in light of the improvised comedy dialogues:

Conversation A

Student: "You are the band teacher, right?"
Teacher: "No, I teach choir."
Student: "I heard the band at the game last night. They were good."
Teacher: "They were loud, for sure."
Student: "I played clarinet for a year in fourth grade."
Teacher: "I didn't play in band."

Conversation B

Student: "You are the band teacher, right?"
Teacher: "I'm a music teacher, yes. I teach choir. Do you like music?"
Student: "I do! I'm not a good singer, but I like to listen to music. I heard the band at the game last night. They were good."

Teacher: *"They ARE good, aren't they? A concert band on a football field can be loud, but it's also really fun. Do you have any musical experience?"*

Student: "Kind of. I played clarinet for a year in fourth grade."

Teacher: *"You did? That's great. Why did you stop?"*

Student: "I liked the playing in the band part, but I didn't like to practice very much."

Teacher: *If you liked hearing the band, you should consider hearing our choir in a concert too. It's also fun and we also sound really good. Our concert is in two weeks. Have you ever been to a choir concert here at school?"*

Student: "No, but no one ever invited me either. Thanks, maybe I will."

Teacher: "Great! I hope to see you there."

In Conversation A, the teacher is not doing a good job agreeing and extending the conversation by asking another question. In essence, the teacher is "keeping the ball" in the imaginary game of catch. In the second example, the teacher affirms what the student says and then prompts the student to talk more, like tossing the ball back to the student in the imaginary game of catch.

Like an improvisational comic, you will have to be creative and pose new questions to students to keep them talking, especially if the students aren't very good conversationalists…as many middle school students are not. Many students in middle school (about ages twelve to fourteen) will walk up to an adult and just stand there, wanting to engage in a conversation, but having absolutely no idea how to do it. This may also be true with students who may have exceptionalities, such as autism. If you start asking them questions that they can answer, such as their name, their favorite movie, or if they are having a good day, these young students will launch into a dialogue with you. You just have to be good at starting the "first throw" in imaginary "catch" and to keep the game going.

If there is a perfect ratio of talking to listening, no one knows exactly what it is. It is all about how the interaction *functions*, of course. Making someone talk when they would rather listen to you can certainly have negative consequences if you are not careful. There is a point where just listening, and not talking *enough*, can negate the positive effect of an interaction. One other thing to think about is that ESL (English as a second language) students may feel uncomfortable conversing with you in English, so pressing them to speak could backfire on your efforts to get to know them.

The ability to manage a functional listening-to-talking ratio in your professional duties is a skill that the experienced psychologist understands and uses expertly; when it functions well they listen carefully, and when it functions best they speak. To become a skilled and effective recruiter, you will have to learn to be present with people while you notice how every conversation weaves and runs. Every face-to-face situation is an opportunity to evaluate the interaction and work to make it positive and affirming for the student. A smile, a nod, engaging eye contact, and a few kind words can go a long way in every human interaction, even when you are not officially recruiting for your classes.

On the other hand, there are some individuals who can charm people in a positive way even when they themselves are the one talking more than they are listening. It is fairly rare to see someone ignore the 50–50 rule and be successful when recruiting, so be careful if you think you can be an exception to the rule. When in doubt, ask a professor or close friend who can be honest with you about how your natural conversational flow functions. In general, there are fewer choral educators who can persuade and recruit students while dominating the conversations they have, and these people have a rare and charming personality that seems to overcome the 50–50 rule. Also, many more people *think* they have this ability to captivate others with their words than actually do. When you first start teaching, you would be wise to assume you don't have it, choosing instead to observe the 30–70 % ratio when recruiting for your classes. Remember that you want the potential recruit to feel good about interacting with you, and the safest way to do this is to listen more and talk less while sustaining the conversation with rich and related follow-up questions.

RECAPITULATION

1. What do you think your natural tendency is in terms of talking and listening? Give yourself a rating of talking to listening as percentages, with talking first and listening second (example 40% talking, 60% listening). Do you think the ratio changes with interactions with different people? Ask someone who knows you well to rate you, but don't bias them or tell them what you think it is. Let them reflect honestly back to you. Did they rate you the same as you did? If so, you may have an accurate perception of how much you talk vs. how much you listen. If they gave a different ratio, why do you think this happened? Do you want to change the ratios? Why or why not? What would you have to do to make these changes?
2. Have you ever had an interaction with a friend where the 50–50 rule was way out of balance in one direction or the other? Tell a story about this event. How did you feel after the conversation was over? If you wanted to, what could you have done to change what happened? How does this balance affect how you feel about this friend, if at all?

3. Television talk show hosts understand how to sustain conversations during interviews, but they often will know something about the guests before the show goes to air. You, however, won't necessarily know about a student and their likes and dislikes before you engage them in a first-time conversation. What are some of the outward clues (things that you can observe with your eyes and ears) that can help you start a conversation with a stranger? Brainstorm a short list. Additionally, based on your brainstormed list, write at least five initial or follow-up questions that you could ask someone to get them to keep talking to you.

Visibility

When it comes to connecting with potential students for your choirs, nothing is more important than your ability to be visible in your school's community. Students will feel much more comfortable talking with you in the hall or lunchroom if they already have an idea of who you are before you approach them. Teachers who hide in their room between classes and skip school events in the evenings are less likely to be recognized and known by the greater population of students in the school. This means that you will have to invest some of your time and energy chaperoning school dances, attending sporting events, supervising the hallways, volunteering for teacher duties, and advising non-musical clubs. You may be thinking, "When will I, as a beginning teacher, have time to do all of that?" The answer is that you won't have much extra time, but your success (and employment) hinges upon your ability to connect with students in the greater school population.

When you are in your first few years of building a program, you will have to invest more time than when you are an established teacher, so think of this extra time as part of the job at first. Just like an English teacher who will dedicate many hours after school reading and correcting written essays, stories, and other homework, you should accept as part of your "homework" a certain amount of time dedicated to service at the school after hours. Your commitment to being a part of the greater school culture, and also to being highly visible at school events, will possibly be the most important thing you do in your recruiting efforts during your first few years at a new school. Students who aren't in choir need to know who you are, that you are approachable, and that you are a teacher that they might want to have a class with someday.

You don't have to (nor should you) try to do *everything*. Rather, you should work to find a balance between your academic school life (teaching your classes), your personal life (spouse, significant other, friends, family), and your school/community life (being visible and connected in the school). Most people struggle to maintain this balance, and in reality this balance is an *ideal* rather than a perfect state of being. When you sense an imbalance, work to bring it into a better balance knowing that it will always be in a state of change and flux. Once you establish yourself as a known and visible teacher in the school, and once you get some momentum going in your recruiting efforts, you will be able to give less focus to your school/community life while maintaining a connection to all of your students.

Appropriate and Inappropriate Aspects of Visibility

It is also essential that you understand the difference between being visible at official school events and frequenting places where students hang out outside of school. As a teacher, it is absolutely inappropriate to spend unstructured social time hanging out with your students outside of school, and you must always maintain a professional and contingent relationship with them. In other words, you can interact with them in school settings as their teacher, but do not hang out with them outside of school. If you are a young, beginning teacher, you might not be much older than your oldest students, but you are an adult, and they are not adults. You might, depending on your community and circumstances, become friends with adults who happen to be the parents of your students, but this is different than you behaving as a member of a student peer group. While you may have the best of intentions, you do not want to put yourself in a situation where your behavior could be perceived as unprofessional or inappropriate.

In this age of electronic communication and interaction, you will need to clarify and maintain your own personal rules for interacting with your students through social media. If hanging out with students outside of class, outside of school, is professionally inappropriate, what about being friends on social media? Many school districts have policies to limit the contact that teachers can have with students on social media, but many do not. You must remember that your footprint on social media is often completely public, and as a professional, you will need to think about your *professional image* as it is portrayed on your social media pages. It is highly recommended that you consider electronic interactions as carefully as physical interactions, limiting your circle to adults you know well and family and friends who are not your students.

It is not unusual for emerging teachers, who have spent many years as students, to have to adjust aspects of their social media footprint to better reflect their new professional status. Because of this, you may need to "clean up" your pages and posts if you have already had a public social media presence before becoming a professional music educator. Remember that behavior is situational, and what may have seemed appropriate behavior for you as a college student might not be completely appropriate and professional for you as a teacher. If you have posts (or reposts) on your social media pages that do not align with the values and standards of a professional music educator in your city or town, your community members might act to create problems for your employment status. Examples of some of these inappropriate posts might include pictures that are sexually provocative, posts or images that promote or imply involvement with illegal drugs, or any other activity that would be considered illegal or immoral to the greater community of families that you teach. If you are not sure if something is appropriate, ask your fellow teachers or your administrators who you teach alongside for advice.

Finally, when you enter the professional world, you should examine your list of email addresses to determine if they are appropriate. Most college and university students have a school email and one or more personal email accounts, such as a Gmail account. Most students who graduate from college stop checking their college email on a regular basis and turn to their personal email accounts for everything, including applying for teaching positions. If your email is something like Ssmith261@gmail.com, there is no problem with using this email for professional business; but if your primary personal email is something like partygirl692@gmail.com, you will need to create a new account or use another personal email that sends a more appropriate message to your potential employers. When you do secure employment at a school, you will most certainly be given an email account for that school district to communicate with you, and it would be wise for you to use this email for all future professional business and to keep your personal email accounts for exclusively personal matters.

RECAPITULATION

1. You should work to find a balance between your academic school life (teaching your classes), your personal life (spouse, friends, family), and your school/community life (being visible and connected in the school). Rank these three areas in terms of your natural tendencies right now, with 1 being the one you are already prone to giving your

focus to, 2 being the one you give less focus to, and 3 being the one you give the least focus to presently. Why did you choose this order? How close are you to having a healthy balance among the three right now? What are some things you can do to improve the balance now or that you see yourself doing when you are building a choral program?

2. You will have to invest some of your time and energy chaperoning school dances, attending sporting events, supervising the hallways, volunteering for teacher duties, and advising non-musical clubs. Make a list of anything else not on this list that could be considered increasing your visibility in your school's community. Combine your list with the list above and reflect on which ones you would enjoy doing and which ones you would enjoy less. For example, if you do not care for football games, you would reflect on what you don't prefer about the activity such as "sitting in the cold," or "large crowds of screaming people." Is it important that you attend events that you might not prefer to attend? Why or why not?

3. The transition from full-time student to professional choral music educator requires that you reflect upon your social media past and consider "cleaning up" anything that might be considered less than professional. Comment on your own situation in terms of how you might interact with students, if you need to sanitize anything on your pages, or if you can continue without any changes. Do you have any email accounts that send negative or mixed messages to a potential employer? Reflect on this and anything else that relates to your appropriate visibility in your community.

Kinds of Students in the School Population

Recruiting for your classes requires you to be visible and to connect with many different kinds of students. This conversation is only possible with a certain amount of political *incorrectness*. We are going to identify and discuss some stereotypical groups of students, but in no way are we making value judgments about any of these groups. Cliques and congregations of similar students do exist at every school, and for convenience, we are going to give them name identities here:

Some Examples of Student Clique Names

Geeks, Jocks, Nerds, Preps, Bros, Skaters, Loners, Overachievers, AP Kids, Hipsters, Floaters (no group)…

There are many other groups intentionally left off this list. Again, we are not making value judgments about any of these groups, we are just admitting that many of these groups exist at every school depending on the culture, location, and school climate of the district. It is also important to remember that any one student can be a member of more than one group and that membership in a group is not always a conscious choice by the student, though it can be. Sometimes being included in a group comes as a reaction to the rejecting of another group, while some people are associated with a group only through the stereotypical and judgmental perception of others. It seems to be part of the human condition to want to belong to something, and most high school students gravitate to identifying with some sort of group at some point. A great aspect of music classes and choral ensembles is that they can be a place for everyone to belong, regardless of the cliques and groups in the school.

Think back to your experience in middle school and high school. What kinds of cliques existed at your schools and which groups did you find yourself associating with? Did you change groups over the years, or did you identify with more than one at a time? Chances are you did move between groups and you probably had friends in various different cliques. It is likely that the kinds of kids you hung around with when you were in high school are not too different than the adults you prefer to socialize with today, though that is not always the case.

When it comes to recruiting, know that you will relate to, and interact with, some groups of kids easier than others; the cliques that you identified with as an adolescent will probably be the same cliques that you will approach and interact with easily as a teacher. The groups of students that you didn't identify with could present a challenge for you in terms of starting conversations, making them feel comfortable, and getting them to choose your classes. You may think, "I didn't like those kids when I was in school, and I still don't like them now." Remember, however, that you are a *teacher*, not a student. Your job is to teach everyone, even if you can't easily identify with them and their interests, and even if they don't seem to connect with you immediately. You must develop the skill to talk to every student in your school and to help them to become interested in your classes, ensembles, and clubs.

It isn't difficult to look at any choir and make a quick assessment of how many diverse kinds of kids there are participating. It's a bit harder to determine when everyone is in concert dress, but it's easy when you see a choir in their rehearsal space, dressed in their daily school clothes. Teachers who can relate to diverse populations of students will be able to attract and retain many kinds of students in their choirs and classes, and those who can't relate to diverse populations of students may find that their choirs are smaller and more homogeneous. If your philosophy of music education supports teaching *everyone* who wants to express themselves through music, then you will have to learn to relate to and engage every student in your school from every group and social interest. This may require a little earnest, yet predictable, homework on your part.

Maintaining a conversation with someone who does not share your passionate interests can be awkward for both parties. But it doesn't take much homework to know a little bit about what students are interested in. Search out some things that are popular that you might not normally know or care about, and learn a few things about them. For example, if you normally skip the Super Bowl for a day at the movies, check to see who played, who won, and any stories from the game or halftime show that kids might be chatting about in the halls. If there is a popular novel that kids are reading, find out who the characters are and a little about the plot lines. You might even read the novel series over the summer. If you could care less about video games, find out what games are popular and know a little about what the themes are so you can recognize the references in a conversation. If you never read or listen to the news, find a news source and know what the top stories are. By expanding your knowledge of popular culture beyond your own specialized interests, you will broaden your appeal to the students who you interact with, and you will have the best chance to attract and retain healthy numbers of students into your choirs and classes.

RECAPITULATION

1. Remember the list from this chapter of some examples of student cliques: *Geeks, Jocks, Nerds, Preps, Bros, Skaters, Loners, Overachievers, AP Kids, Hipsters, Floaters (no group).* Based on your own experience, make your own complete list of possible student cliques in a public school setting.
2. What do you have for popular interests in your normal life? Make a list. Compare and contrast your list of interests with the list you made of student groups and cliques. How many of these groups are likely to be interested in the same things you are? Which ones probably won't relate to your specialized interests? Think of some things that

you can do to broaden your appeal to the kids who you have nothing in common with and write these down. Which interests would you actually be willing to explore and which ones are you unwilling to explore? Why and why not?

3. Do you think that there are some topics that everyone is interested in? What might some of these be? Are all of them appropriate to discuss in school? Brainstorm some questions you might ask a student that could have broad appeal and also some questions that you should probably not ask because they could be considered too personal, may elicit responses you don't want to hear, or could be viewed as inappropriate conversation between a teacher and a student.

Going For the Sale

Being a successful choir recruiter is much like being a good car salesperson. You have a product (the class) that you want to sell to the buyer, and you need their commitment (time and credits) to get them signed up. The car salesperson doesn't greet you in the parking lot with, "Hello, would you like to buy this car?" Rather, she introduces herself, makes small talk, listens to what you have to say and what your interests are, and then starts showing you cars that could meet your specific needs. The car salesman also knows that a potential buyer is more likely to say "yes" when they feel comfortable. Because of this, they start you off with easy questions like, "What color of car do you prefer?" and "What options do you want in a car?"

The car salesperson doesn't "go for the sale" until most of the smaller details are known and when the buyer is close to being able to decide whether or not to make the purchase. In the same way, walking up to a student you don't know and asking, "Would you like to join choir?" is less likely to elicit a "yes" than when you have spent some time making small talk, making them feel comfortable, and finding out what the student is interested in. Once you have established a rapport with a student, you can "go for the sale" by simply saying, "I think you should join choir!" Sell them on it based on what you know about their interests, and if they just tell you, "Maybe I'll join," consider it a success.

On the other hand, there are some teachers who have the courage and personality to walk up to students they don't know, and have never spoken to, and immediately "go for the sale" by asking them to join choir. In professional sales this is called "cold calling" and it survives on something called *The Law of Averages*. The cold call implies that you are speaking to someone who hasn't come to you to buy something, as opposed to a car salesperson that knows, at the very least, that the customer might want to buy a car.

A professional example of the cold-call approach would be the salesperson that goes door to door through a neighborhood, knocking on doors and hoping to sell a product that the customer may or may not want. The Law of Averages contends that if they ask enough people to buy something, eventually someone will say yes. Cold calling means that they will hear "no" most of the time, but that they will also get a few "yesses" every now and then. If you have a thick skin, meaning that your feelings don't get hurt easily, and an outgoing and loquacious personality, then you might be able to use cold calling in your recruiting approach, while also establishing a comfortable rapport with other students over time before "going for the sale." In the end, if your efforts are functioning properly, you can measure your success by the increase in the number of students that sign up for your classes.

RECAPITULATION

1. Have you ever had to sell anything to people you don't know? Tell a story about it including what you sold and what made it easy or challenging for you. What did you learn and what skills did you hone that relate to recruiting for the choir?
2. As a rule, it is easier to sell a quality product that you believe in. Hopefully your choir program will meet both of these criteria once you get it going. Make a list of the positive qualities of your program (or your vision of what it will be) and also why you stand behind it in terms of artistic experiences and educational outcomes. Let this list represent your "selling points" when you recruit. Put it in a form that works for you and that you will remember. Share it with your class.
3. Do you have any experience selling anything in a professional setting? If you do, comment on your experience. If you don't have this kind of experience, what are some things that you think you could sell effectively? Make a short list. Do you think you are someone who could be a "cold call" salesperson? Why or why not? Describe some of the aspects of your personality that contribute to this self-perception of your potential sales ability.

Why Students Join Choir

Students will join choir for many different reasons, just like people will buy cars for a variety of needs and reasons. Think about why you joined choirs or interest clubs when you were in middle and high school. Was it because of a deep-felt love and respect for the subject matter or topic (even if this came later), or did you do it for simpler reasons? Most students won't join choir for the first time because of a love for artistic expression, but rather for some of the following reasons:

Some Examples of Why Students Join Choir

- My friend is in choir.
- I need the fine arts credit.
- Nothing fits in my schedule.
- It's an easy A.
- It looks good on a college transcript.

There are many other possible reasons intentionally left off this list. These can include interest in the subject matter, but just be aware that not everyone will join choir for the first time because they love choir and love to sing. But if things are going well in your classes, loving to sing in the choir will become one of the main reasons students return year after year to the choir experience.

Who Can Sing? Everyone Can Sing!

For a professional choral music educator, there are only two kinds of people: those who sing and *those who haven't sung yet*. There was a time in the United States, many decades ago, when it was a common and accepted practice to divide elementary students into groups of "singers" and "non-singers." This was primarily based on the student's innate ability to match pitch without any vocal instruction, practice, or time to develop their skills. As you can imagine, the so-called "non-singing" adolescents often went on to become non-singing adults. This "teach only the talented" philosophy still exists today in some classrooms and institutions. If your philosophy of music education includes making music a part of every student's life, you will be happy to know that everyone can participate at some level and that most students can participate and enjoy music at a satisfying level. It is your job to meet them where they are and to make them better with a sequenced curriculum that develops their musical skills. Start reminding yourself that everyone can sing, and then make it your goal to see this prophecy fulfilled again and again in your classroom.

There is good evidence that suggests that most everyone can sing a recognizable melody when given proper vocal instruction, practice, and time. Most experienced choral music educators find this to be true. Some students join choir with an ability to match pitch while others arrive without pitch-matching ability. By working with these students and placing them carefully in the choir, you will find that almost every person can find their voice over time. The very few exceptions to this could be students who have major disabilities, such as Down syndrome (though sometimes these students match pitch well) or students who have some true form of inner-ear physical disability. But of the students lacking true physical disabilities, virtually all can match pitch when given positive and affirming vocal instruction and time to develop. Knowing that everyone can sing will help you recruit and stay positive while new ensemble members find their voice in choir.

Self-Perception of Singing Ability

If everyone can sing, then why are there so many people who don't *think* they can sing? This is because of a phenomenon called *self-perception of singing ability*. Research indicates that self-perception of singing ability does not correlate to singing ability reliably enough to predict someone's level of singing skill without actually hearing them sing. In other words, if you ask a person if they can sing, no matter how they answer, you can't trust their response to be accurate. You can visualize this using the following graphic:

Four Kinds of Self-Perception of Singing Ability	
1 Self-perception: Believes that he/she is a highly skilled singer Reality: He/she is actually a highly skilled singer	2 Self-perception: Believes that he/she is a highly skilled singer Reality: He/she is NOT a highly skilled singer
3 Self-perception: Believes that he/she is NOT A highly skilled singer Reality: He/she is actually a highly skilled singer	4 Self-perception: Believes that he/she is NOT a highly skilled singer Reality: He/she is actually NOT a highly skilled singer

As you can see in quadrant number one, some people believe they can sing well, and they are correct in that self-perception, while other people (quadrant two) believe they are highly skilled in singing, but really are not. Quadrant three represents people who don't believe they can sing well, but who really can sing well, and quadrant four represents those who don't think they sing well, and indeed they are yet to develop their singing skills. When you are recruiting, always remember that no matter what anyone says about their singing ability, for better or worse, *you won't know how skilled they are until you hear them sing*. If they say they are a good singer, tell them you hope they will join choir, and if they say they can't sing, tell them that they may be better than they think they are. Assure them that you can teach them to sing better regardless of their skill level. Let them know that you believe they can be a better singer with your help, no matter what they think about their singing up to that point. Tell them you hope that they will join choir.

When you ask someone about their singing ability, you will get several possible predictable responses. One is an overwhelming positive reaction and a willingness to talk about their singing experience. This person will likely welcome your interest in their participation in choir. Another possibility is a lukewarm but positive response followed by, "I like to sing, but only in the car or shower where no one can hear me." Telling this person that there are many people singing in the choir, and that they are not required to sing any solos, will often help them consider joining. If they have any other reason to join, such as many friends already in the ensemble, you have a good chance of getting them to sign up if the schedule works out.

Another possible response is, "I'm not a good singer, and I could never do choir." Tell this person that you can teach them to be a better singer. Let them know that there are lots of singing ability levels in the choirs and that they can fit in and get better. Offer to hear them sing something in a safe setting (not in front of their friends), and tell them that you will give them an honest assessment of their ability. You may be amazed to hear that they have a very nice singing voice and good ability to match pitch. If they have skills to develop, including pitch matching, help them feel good about joining a choir.

A fourth predictable response is to tell you that they can't or don't sing. You might say, "Now who told you that?" Most of the time a name comes right out of their mouth such as, "My mother says I have a bad voice" or "My boyfriend said so." Consider following up with the ridiculous question, "Who are your primary voice teachers? Who have you studied voice with?" They will say, of course, that they have never studied voice. Tell them that no one expects to play the piano without getting lessons, yet people think they should be able to sing without lessons. Let them know that you are a voice teacher and that you want to help them find their voice and that you will give them opportunities to improve their singing in choir class. These people are usually the most difficult ones to convince, so don't be surprised if you need to work on them for a while before they get the courage to join. Be sure to show your enthusiasm and belief in their potential to become a contributing member of your ensembles. Remember, there are only two kinds of people: those who sing and *those who haven't sung yet.* All they need to be able to sing a recognizable melody is proper vocal instruction, patience, positive encouragement, practice, and time.

RECAPITULATION

1. Students join choir for the first time for some of the following reasons: *My friend is in choir; I need the fine arts credit; Nothing fits in my schedule; It's an easy A; It looks good on a college transcript.* Make a complete list of all the reasons you think that students might choose to join choir.

2. Why did you join choir (or band or orchestra) for the first time? Do you remember? Do you think that your reasons for participating changed over the years? Write a paragraph explaining your memories of joining a musical ensemble for the first time, including the factors that kept you participating over the years.

3. Because self-perception of singing ability does not always correspond to actual singing ability, it is important to take anything someone says about their singing potential with skepticism until you actually hear them sing. When recruiting for choir, we need to assume that everyone can be successful at singing and that we can give them the support they need. What are some statements that you could say to someone who does not think they can sing in order to try to convince them to try singing? Create a short dialogue that could be read by two people from your class like a short scene from a play.

Other Tips and Practical Recommendations

Once you decide to commit some of your focus to becoming a successful recruiter, it is to your advantage to design a plan of implementation. This way your time is spent wisely, and you can get as many students as possible to sign up for your classes. Here are some general tips and statements that can inform you and that also can stand as reference points for discussion with your colleagues. Remember that for every rule there is an exception and that you always will need to look carefully at the situation and circumstances of your school, position, colleagues, and students to decide if these statements hold true for you.

- ✓ The guidance counselors have much of the power in many schools to guide and encourage students as they choose classes. If the counselors like you and are on your side, they will help you, and if they are not on your side, they will work against you. The time to start building a rapport with them is the day you meet them and not the day you need them.

- ✓ If you are a really successful recruiter, you will get kids who are in your colleague's classes to quit those classes to join choir. This will not go over well with these colleagues and you may make enemies on your staff. Be careful how aggressively you recruit kids who already have a class in their schedule during choir, especially if it is another arts class or foreign language class. Be relentless recruiting kids who have no class or a study hall during one of your scheduled classes.

- ✓ Be sure to build a quality curriculum and make your choirs sound good in every concert. Quality programs attract talented students, and if you do not have a quality product, no gimmick that gets kids through the door will retain them past one grading cycle. Your program will be maintained over time by offering interesting and varied music to study and perform, building musicianship so that students are proud of the skills they attain and the challenges they can overcome, and through artistic and engaging concerts that inspire both the choir and the audience alike.

- ✓ If you don't already have one, consider creating an "all-district" concert that features all the choirs from elementary through high school. Many districts have these concerts, and they are outstanding recruiting events. Emphasize that any student moving up from elementary to middle school, or middle school to high school, has a place waiting for them in the choir program. Have a combined song that everyone sings as a finale and be sure all the choirs sound great.

- ✓ Create a "step up" day where students moving up from the lower grades can visit the older choirs, observe a rehearsal, or rehearse along with the older students for a class period. Let your students meet and greet them and make them feel welcome in your room.

- ✓ Bring your students on a short one-day tour of the other schools in your district, ideally the ones feeding your program. Ask the administration to give you twenty-five to thirty minutes to give a short concert for the school or for any interested classes. Be sure to give a good "pitch" about why they should join choir when they move up to the higher grades. Consider having your own students say a few words about how much they enjoy choir and the benefits they get from participating. It is recommended that this be scripted or at least auditioned ahead of time.

- ✓ Create a social media page for your choirs, and invite your feeder school students to like the page and check back for events and concert information. Consider having free tickets to one of your concerts for anyone in a feeder school who connects with your program through the social media page.

- ✓ Make recruiting posters and put them up in your school and your feeder schools. Make them eye-catching and fun.

- ✓ Take your choirs on trips. They can sing at festivals, music educator events, in churches, or at other schools as part of exchange programs. Trips don't need to be expensive, and choirs that travel create wonderful memories that kids will hold on to for a lifetime.

- ✓ Hold a "Recruiting Contest" with your present choir members. Decide on prizes, such as iTunes gift cards, or maybe conducting a song in a concert, or maybe some other attractive prizes that might motivate your students to invite friends to choir. Celebrate everyone who brings friends to choir, and make it a fun event for the whole choir.

RECAPITULATION

1. Make a recruiting poster for your choir or choir program (you decide the name of the school and choirs). This would be a poster that you could duplicate and put up all over the school. You only need one copy for this class assignment, and it can be hand-drawn or done by computer. Make it fun, colorful, and interesting. Present it to the class and share your choices for the poster. Scan and upload your work and share it with the community.

2. What other ideas or strategies, besides the ones presented in this chapter, can you come up with for recruiting singers into your choirs? Which ones do you think would be particularly effective and why? What do you think kids want in a choir class, and why do you think they will want to join *your* choirs?

3. Comment on the following statement:

> *"Recruiting never stops! It is done one conversation, one interaction, one uplifting moment at a time."*

Does this speak to you in any way? What implications does it have for you in terms of your recruiting efforts?

Chapter Ten

Assessment Strategies for the Music Classroom

10. Assessment Strategies for the Music Classroom

"Everyone is a genius. But if you judge a fish on its ability to climb a tree, it will live its whole life believing it is stupid."
~Albert Einstein

Grading on Attendance Only

Every teacher has the responsibility to set learning goals and objectives for the students and to track their progress across time and through instructional tasks. Ideally, students will make significant and sustained progress toward the learning goals of the teacher, and the student's skills, attitudes, and behaviors will be enhanced and molded in positive ways. All good teachers have good intentions for their students to learn and progress, but not every teacher is completely effective when it comes to making their good intentions function positively for the students. This is further complicated if the teacher is not skilled at evaluating and assessing the progress and outcomes of the student's academic work and musical skills. Being able to measure student progress is one of the most important aspects of the art of teaching, and it is sometimes overlooked in college methods classes except for a few references to the fact that you will need to learn how to do it effectively.

Many student teachers do not learn methods of assessment until they reach the student-teaching phase of their development, and often they observe and adopt the methods of their master/cooperating teachers in the field. This can be good or bad depending on the training and experience of the master teacher. Because we tend to teach the way we were taught, it is not surprising that student teachers often adopt the methods they have seen being used with real students in the classroom. But there are too many practicing, veteran teachers who were never properly trained in college to create assessment tools, and these teachers often default to what their college choirs may have used for grading: attendance only.

Attendance has been used for grading in college choir classes for many years, and in a performance-based class, attendance is an important part of the experience. In some non-artistic college academic classes, students do not have to attend classes as long as they can pass the written exams. In music performance classes, like choir and band and orchestra, where artistic expression is major part of the experience and educational outcomes, attending rehearsals is essential. It's actually amusing to entertain the thought of choir members performing in a public concert without attending ANY of the rehearsals as long as they know the words and notes. Likewise, imagine a football team that only plays together during the games, but practices alone as individuals; it seems absurd. And while games are won or lost as an outcome of the final score of the game, music is not something that is completely right or wrong. Rather, music can be considered an investigation into the realm of human artistic expression, a realm that requires skillful interaction with the art form over time. Attending choir class is important, but grading only on attending class does not give an accurate gauge of what the student can do, what he/she has learned, how they have progressed, or what is required to sustain artistic growth in the future. To meet these assessment ends, other kinds of assessment instruments must be acquired and implemented.

Grading only on attendance is not a good idea, and it may even be illegal in some school districts. You will need to decide on your grading procedures so that they align with your teaching outcomes and so that you can have multiple measures of progress and achievement over time. Anything you figure into your final grade *must* be measurable, countable, and as objective as possible.

Grading on Progress vs. Achievement

One of the first concepts to explore as you learn to assess student learning is the difference between *progress* in a class and *achievement* in a class. In a progress-based grading system, student grades are higher when students work toward being better than they were when they started on day one, regardless of the skill levels attained at the end. In other words, if a student makes progress and improves, they get a better grade. In an achievement-based grading system, student grades are higher when they achieve a certain level of proficiency, regardless of where they started. In other words, if a student has a high level of proficiency on day one, and if they can achieve success on a final assessment regardless of any noticeable improvement, they get a good grade.

Let's use assessing musicianship as an example. Imagine that you have measured each choir student's ability to sight sing at the beginning of the year, and one student (let's call her Ayanna) was able to read the pitches with 95% accuracy and the rhythms with 100% accuracy and earned an "A" for the test. Another student (let's call her Mia) was only able to sing the same example with 50% of the correct pitches and 70% of the correct rhythms for a grade of "C+" on the test. One month later you measure them again, and Christina, who has been working really diligently on her musicianship, improves her pitch accuracy to 70% and her rhythmic accuracy to 90% on a musical excerpt of similar difficulty. Should Mia earn an "A" for progress or a "B" for achievement? Meanwhile, Ayanna once again achieved 95% accuracy for the pitches, but missed a rhythm and scored 95% on that measure. If we use progress as our measure, should

Ayanna get a "B" or less for not improving? She still has better musicianship than Mia, but she appears not to have worked to get better, and even scored a little lower.

What if you decided to give Ayanna, because of her well-developed musicianship skills, a more difficult musical excerpt than Mia, and what if she missed half of the challenging notes and rhythms? Mia scored higher, but her test was easier, and Ayanna scored lower, but her test was much harder. It's possible that Ayanna scored lower on the harder assessment because she didn't work to make progress, but it could be that she made progress and the test was just too difficult. I'm sure you can see that grading student work can be much more complicated than giving the same test to everyone. Indeed, deciding on progress or achievement, or a combination of the two, is something that every teacher must consider when assessing student outcomes.

RECAPITULATION

1. In your lifetime of experience, how have you been graded in your choir classes: attendance only, attendance plus other factors, or just on other factors? If you were graded on more than attendance, what were those other factors? It could be that you don't even remember how you were graded in these classes. If so, comment on how you think you may have been assessed and graded. If you did not sing in choir before college, choose another performance class, such as band or orchestra, and transfer these ideas to those classes. If you have never had a musical performance class, reflect on any class you have taken in your lifetime to explore these ideas.

2. As a student, do you prefer to be graded more on progress or more on achievement? If you could choose to have a mix of both, what percentages would you choose (such as 50%-50%) and why would this mix be an advantage for you? As a teacher, would you be more inclined to use progress or achievement in your classroom or a mix of the two? Explain the thought process that led to your conclusions.

The Objective vs. the Subjective Mode

Evaluating students in your music classes will take time and effort as well as careful observation and record keeping. Grades that are accurate, and that represent student work and progress, are your ultimate goal. Ideally, assessment will be ongoing and varied, and students will be guided in their progress often and not just awarded a final percentage at the end of a grading period. So if you are to measure more than attendance, and if your grades are intended to assess and guide student progress and achievement across time, what can you do to create and implement effective grading instruments? What amount of time and effort are you willing to devote to this important aspect of your job?

Your first step is to make a clear distinction in your mind between the *subjective mode* and the *objective mode* of judgment and belief. It is not that one is good and one is bad, because both modes are important avenues to how we live and think. In the subjective mode, beliefs about what is true and correct are based on faith, hunches, and the broad scope of personal experience. Little objective proof is required to make distinctions and decisions from the subjective mode. From the subjective mode, the following statements could all be possible, true, and correct for the individual holding these views:

- ✓ It is a fact that most people hate vegetables.
- ✓ It is a fact that cats are better than dogs.
- ✓ It is a fact that everyone likes football.
- ✓ It is a fact that politicians cause all the world's problems.
- ✓ It is a fact that dogs are better than cats.
- ✓ It is a fact that *Star Trek* fans are better than *Star Wars* fans.
- ✓ It is a fact that the weather is colder than it used to be.
- ✓ It is a fact that listening to Mozart makes you smarter.

Each of these statements has one thing in common: each stems from the personal perspective of a person who forms the basis for calling it a "fact." One can believe that politicians are the of cause all the world's problems, but someone with a different perspective may disagree. Because personal opinion comes from the subjective mode, it does not require objective evidence to validate its "truth."

If you believe that most people hate vegetables, then that observation is true for you, and it can become a compelling foundation of your perception and behavior. Do most people hate vegetables? Probably not, but that doesn't mean that most of the people *that you know personally* like them. Likewise, if you are a "cat person," you may contend that cats are better than dogs, and if you are a "dog person," you may believe the opposite to be true. From each person's perspective, they speak the "truth." Climate change has been documented to be true in thousands of scientific studies, and the data suggest that there is about 97% confidence that humans are contributing to the rise in global temperatures based on these *objective* data. [1] Still, if your town feels colder this year, it may be natural to assume that your local weather and global climate are somehow linked together. It just *feels* true from the subjective mode.

Why should you, as a professional teacher, understand and differentiate between the subjective and objective modes when it comes to assessing and grading your students? The main reason to make this distinction is to be sure that you structure your grading so that every measure and assessment that you include for your classes comes from the objective mode rather than the subjective mode. Consider the following two statements:

1. Rigo is lazy and never turns in his homework.
2. Rigo has only turned in three out of twelve assignments this quarter.

The first statement, from the subjective mode, makes a value judgment about the person; he is lazy and that is why he hasn't turned in his assignments. The second statement, from the objective mode, states a measurable fact that he has only turned in 25% of the homework assignments.

If you were conferencing with the parents of this student, it wouldn't be advisable to say that his grade of "C" for the quarter was based on his laziness. In reality, we probably don't really know why he didn't complete the assignments, and it could be that he has been working really hard in other classes. As humans, we all will have subjective thoughts and opinions, but we should base our grades on as much objective data as possible. Instead, we should explain to the parents that Rigo earned a "C" for the quarter because he turned in 25% of the homework assignments, attended two out of three of the extra scheduled rehearsals, was on time to class 75% of the time, and improved his sight-singing evaluations from a 50% level to a 90% achievement level. These statements communicate and describe measurable behaviors and skills and are objective enough to stand parental and administrative scrutiny. It is also important to remember that a student's grade point average will often be used to determine which colleges will accept them, so your grading needs to be based on objective data rather than subjective opinions to assure as much accuracy as possible.

1 J. Cook, et.al, "Consensus on Consensus: a synthesis of consensus estimates on human-caused global warming, "Environmental Research Letters Vol. II No. 4, (13 April 2016)

RECAPITULATION

1. Every person has thoughts and ideas that stem from both the subjective mode and the objective mode. Describe an idea or belief that you hold that could be considered true for you, but maybe isn't true for everyone. Consult the list (above) as a starting guide, and feel free to have fun with these ideas; if you want to say, for example, that chocolate ice cream is the best flavor of ice cream, then you will need to explain why you believe this to be true *for you*. Remember that from the subjective mode, all you need is your opinion to back it up. Likewise, list some ideas from the objective mode that you know to be backed up by some body of scientific data; if you want to list, for example, that global population is increasing, you would be able to find statistics quite easily to back up the claim. It's not just your opinion.

2. In your opinion, what are some strengths and weaknesses of both the subjective and objective modes of thinking? In other words, why do we need both modes, and what are the advantages and dangers of failing to make distinctions between each?

Evaluation vs. Assessment

These two terms are sometimes thought of as the same thing, but they are distinctly different. When you observe the behavior of your students during class, you make judgments in real time about what they are learning and how they are progressing. When you teach them and interact with them, and as you make subjective observations of their learning processes, you are evaluating them. Evaluation is an ongoing, formative exercise that teachers use to identify areas of student progress. Assessment, on the other hand, is a summative measure that is implemented to arrive at an objective score for grading. Assessment can be defined as testing for the purpose of arriving at a final score to measure academic achievement. A concise way to organize all of this is to remember that Informal Evaluation and Observation (ongoing) leads to Formal Assessment (tests and measures) that then leads to Grading (as a percentage).

Assessment and Rubrics

Teachers are trained to teach, but most teachers are also entrusted to assess student achievement and to report a grade that is expressed as a final percentage or letter grade. It is not an easy task to teach a creative art form such as music, where personal expression with more than one right answer is encouraged, while also being required to differentiate between, say, an 87.5% and an 88% final grade. How are we to assign specific grades when much of our class is based in participatory, creative, and expressive activities, rather than lecture and fill-in-the-bubble tests? The answer is that we need to find ways to evaluate behaviors that exist in the gray areas of student performance, and to quantify those behaviors into numbers somehow. One way to do this is with rubrics.

Rubrics are assessment instruments designed to pinpoint levels of student achievement by describing how each level of mastery might look to an observer. The teacher first chooses the skills they want to assess, and then they describe what the behaviors or skills would look like at various levels of mastery. One way to do this is to start with the highest level of mastery (the exemplar) and work back to establish lower levels of mastery, but this is not the only way to approach it. Most standard rubrics are organized in boxes with the skills listed in the far left vertical column and the levels of mastery described in the horizontal rows to the right. There can be as many skill boxes and achievement levels as are needed for the particular assessment. The skills can be organized around a single interdependent outcome, such as *the skills required to drive a golf ball* (proper standing position, speed of the swing, rotation of the torso, etc.) or the skills can be more independent for a larger outcome, such as *playing golf at a high level* (driving, putting, bringing proper equipment, etc.). Regardless of the skills chosen by the teacher for the rubric, there must be clear and observable descriptions of each level of mastery so that the evaluator can pinpoint a score as objectively as possible.

Rubrics can be classified by how many skills they address and how many levels of mastery are identified. A two-by-two rubric is organized around two identified skills and two levels of mastery, and a three-by-three rubric is organized around three identified skills and three levels of mastery. You can have as many skills and levels of mastery that you need for your evaluation purposes.

2 X 2 Rubric Template

	Level 1	Level 2
Skill 1		
Skill 2		

3 X 3 Rubric Template

	Level 1	Level 2	Level 3
Skill 1			
Skill 2			
Skill 3			

The wording of each skill level determines a range of achievement, and within each level box you can include a range of possible numbers to assign. Read and study the "Music Assessment Rubric for Piano Skills" (below).

Music Assessment Rubric for Piano Skills Name ________________

Date________ *Total Score _____

Skills and Points	Late Bloomer (1-3)	In Progress (4-6)	Competent (7-9)	Advanced (10-12)
Supporting choral singing with "do no harm" prepared piano playing Score:	Very basic analysis of chords, possibly with some incorrect chords, possibly no inversions notated, plays tempo slower than marked tempo, stops and starts often, changes tempi, plays incorrect harmonies, insecure playing that will not inspire students to sing confidently, playing does not reflect essential rhythmic aspects of written accompaniment.	Correct analysis of chords, inversions correctly notated, plays tempo slightly slower than marked tempo, keeps tempo steady, knows what to leave out, plays correct harmonies with few mistakes, secure playing that will inspire students to sing confidently, playing somewhat reflects the essential rhythmic aspects of written music.	Correct analysis of chords including inversions, plays tempo at marked tempo, keeps tempo steady, chord choices help choir sing accurately, can monitor students while playing, secure playing that will inspire students to sing confidently, playing completely reflects the essential rhythmic aspects of written music.	Plays the accompaniment primarily as written and possibly improvises an improved piano accompaniment, can monitor and shape student behavior while playing, can bring out voice parts as needed while playing, exudes confidence that inspires students to sing confidently and musically.
Playing warm ups from the piano Score:	Not confident playing major and minor chords in all keys, weak when playing patterns with both steps and leaps, can play only a few warm ups, does not inspire confident singing, playing can possibly hinder rehearsal progress.	Somewhat confident playing major and minor chords in all keys, can play patterns with both steps and leaps with few mistakes, can play many warm ups, inspires confident singing, playing enhances rehearsal progress.	Confident playing major and minor chords in all keys, can play patterns with both steps and leaps without mistakes, can play many warm ups, inspires confident singing, playing enhances rehearsal progress, can monitor student engagement.	Very confident playing of various patterns in all keys, can improvise many warm ups, inspires confident singing, playing is musical, can monitor student engagement, use of piano integrated well into teaching.
Playing single-line parts from choral octavos Score:	Pauses significantly before playing, inaccurate pitches or rhythms played, might not keep tempi steady, might not give starting pitches, inefficient or unconfident approach to rehearsing with significant mistakes.	Plays parts without pausing often, mostly accurate pitches or rhythms played, keeps a steady tempo, gives starting pitches, can lead a sectional or rehearsal from the piano with occasional mistakes.	Plays parts without pausing, accurate pitches and rhythms played, can play at a steady indicated tempo, gives starting pitches, can strongly lead a sectional or rehearsal from the piano.	Plays parts without pausing, accurate pitches and rhythms played, can play at a steady indicated tempo, gives starting pitches, can strongly lead a sectional or rehearsal from the piano.
Playing four-part hymns and open-score octavo parts Score:	Pauses and seems not ready to start playing, inaccurate pitches and/or rhythms, stops and restarts often, awkward playing of treble and bass clef lines, unconfident.	Seems ready to start playing, mostly accurate pitches and/or rhythms, steady tempo, can play one treble and one bass clef line together, mostly confident.	Starts playing immediately, accurate pitches and rhythms, steady tempo, can play several open-score lines together, is confident leading the choir.	Plays immediately, accurate pitches and rhythms, steady tempo, musical playing, can lead singers well, reads open score well, can improvise on notes.
Transposing melodies Score:	Inaccurate playing of new key, rhythms not correct, stops and restarts, not confident.	Accurate playing of key within a second away, rhythms correct, keeps tempo, is confident.	Accurate playing within a third, rhythms correct, keeps tempo, is very confident.	Accurate playing in any key, perfect rhythm and tempo, is supremely confident.

*NOTE: Grading for this assessment is (F=0 to 5 pts., D=6 to 15 pts., C= 16 to 25 pts., B= 26 to 40 pts., and A=41 to 55 pts., A+ = 56 to 60 pts.)

The rubric above was designed to assess the piano-playing competency of preservice music teachers. This five-by-four rubric has five specific assessments, with four levels of mastery, each with a range of possible points. The wording in each box helps the evaluator pinpoint what the student has achieved in terms of competencies and which number to assign for each skill (low, middle, or high). The skill-level descriptors were chosen by the creator of the rubric, but these could have been different; for example "Late Bloomer-In Progress-Competent-Advanced" could have been "Basic-Intermediate-Skilled-Professional" or any other descriptors that show a progression of ability. At the bottom there is a key to determine the grade, which in this case is based on achievement as opposed to progress. As you can see, there are still subjective elements that the evaluator must consider, and no assessment instrument can really achieve 100% objectivity for the evaluator. All grading will have some aspects of subjectivity, though we should do our best to be as objective as we can.

Rubrics can be customized by the teacher to assess specific skills being taught in the curriculum, and students can also be trained to assess their own work and progress and practice using rubrics.

RECAPITULATION

1. Rubrics need to have enough detail to be practical, but without having so much information that they are not useful to the observer. Likewise, if a rubric does not have enough details and observable outcomes, the evaluator can't use it effectively to assess a performance outcome. Go online and find examples of assessment rubrics that other people have already created. Find one that you think is really detailed and practical and also one that you think is not detailed enough. Explain several things that you would do to change and improve the one that is not detailed enough.
2. Using the template (below) create a three-by-four rubric for assessing something outside of music that you already know a lot about. Try to include skill descriptions that would be clear to anyone reading the rubric. Include a grading scale and point total ranges. Have fun adding skill-level descriptors.
3. How do you think you could adapt the grading criteria of the "Music Assessment Rubric for Piano Skills" to measure progress instead of achievement? Describe your ideas for modification of this rubric to achieve this.

3 X 4 Assessment Rubric Name ____________________
Skill ______________________________ Date__________ *Total Score ______

Skills and Points				
Score:				
Score:				
Score:				

**Grading Ranges:*

Assessing Student Attitude, Preparation, and Participation

As was made clear earlier in this chapter, grading solely on attendance is not recommended. And while rubrics are wonderful tools for evaluating certain performance outcomes and should be included as one of your assessment and evaluation strategies, you will need to collect other measures of data to grade your students fairly and objectively. Many beginning teachers consider grading their students on "attitude." But the concept of a "good attitude" is very subjective and may differ widely between different people and cultures.

For example, in some cultures the student with a "good attitude" would be a silent, compliant, diligent person who doesn't ask too many questions, whereas in other cultures the student with a "good attitude" might be an outgoing, kind, and curious students who asks many questions. By these standards, both students are displaying good attitudes, but they are also exhibiting completely different observable behaviors. If you value curiosity and like when students ask questions, and if you use these traits to define attitude, you will most certainly grade shy students lower than outgoing students, and at the very worst, you might grade people you like higher than people you don't like. So while we may think that attitude is a good thing to measure in the classroom, it introduces too much subjectivity into the evaluation to be consistent across diverse student populations.

It is, however, possible to break down the concept of a good attitude into multiple, observable behaviors and to teach and reinforce these behaviors in your classroom. For example, you might decide that the following behaviors begin to add up to a good attitude: the student…

- ✓ is on time to class
- ✓ has all materials in hand and organized
- ✓ practices music outside of class
- ✓ sings when it's time to sing
- ✓ listens when it's time to listen
- ✓ follows directions during rehearsal

There are additional behaviors we could list, but it is easy to see that all these behaviors could be communicated, reinforced, and counted in the classroom setting and could be used to help determine a student grade. But rather than use these behaviors to justify the grade based on attitude, consider instead using *preparation* and *participation* as your categories:

- ✓ on time to class *(participation)*
- ✓ has all materials in hand and organized *(preparation)*
- ✓ practices music outside of class *(preparation)*
- ✓ sings when it's time to sing *(participation)*
- ✓ listens when it's time to listen *(participation)*
- ✓ follows directions during rehearsal *(participation)*

Preparation and Participation are broad categories that can account for a large amount of student behaviors, and these behaviors can usually be observed and counted. Here are some ideas to use participation as a basis for grading:

Participation

- **Attending Concerts** (Attending and singing in the concert of the choir they rehearse with during school)
- **Transfer and "Sticky Note" Exercises** (Activities at the outset of class that require on-time attendance and student engagement)
- **Exit Slips** (Assignments during class that must be turned in as students leave)
- **Kinesthetic Tasks** (Moving appropriately when the class includes group movement)
- **Theory Exercises** (Written assignments during class to improve musicianship)
- **Following the Rules** (Demonstrating appropriate behavior based on posted classroom rules)
- **Being On Time to Class** (Arriving before the class begins, or if tardy, bringing a signed excuse note from another teacher)
- **Following Directions** (Doing as instructed by the teacher)
- **Concert Reflections** (Reflecting, either verbally or in writing, on the experience of performing in the concert)

This is not an exhaustive list, and based on your values and philosophy, you will find some of these to be more useful than others. Here are some ideas to use preparation as a basis for grading:

Preparation

- **Small Ensemble Singing Evaluations** (Students sing music in quartets or octets that they have prepared during class.)
- **Individual Sight-Singing Evaluations** (Students read melodies that they have not prepared.)
- **Recorded Homework Voice Assignments** (Students record assigned sections of the literature at home and send the recordings to the teacher.)
- **Having Materials Ready for Class** (Students have the music, their pencil, and anything else they were instructed to bring to class.)
- **Rehearsal Assignments** (Students demonstrate, during class, progress on music assigned as homework.)
- **Administrative Homework Assignments** (Students write in the solfege syllables, measure numbers, IPA, translations, etc.)
- **Sitting in Assigned Seats** (Students are in place within the choir and ready to start class.)

Again, this is not an exhaustive list, and based on your values and philosophy, you will find some of these to be more useful than others. When you are observing in the field and then student teaching, you should find out how different teachers determine grades for their classes and how they evaluate and assess student progress and outcomes.

RECAPITULATION

1. Brainstorm a list of "participation and preparation" tasks that were not specifically listed above, but that could be used to evaluate and assess student progress and achievement in a music classroom. Which of the tasks you listed would you consider using to grade your students and why? Which of the tasks listed in the chapter would you consider using?
2. The broad categories of "participation and preparation" work well to organize grading tasks in the classroom. Can you think of any other broad categories similar to these two? If yes, list some of the observable behaviors that would be associated with the categories.
3. Look online and find as many syllabi for choir/music classes as you can. Make a list of the grading criteria as well as how much each of these counts as a percentage toward the final grade. For example: (School 1, Participation 30%, Attendance 50%, Sight Singing 20%), etc. Look for insights into how you would like to organize your grading criteria someday and highlight these in your list with underlines, stars, or with an asterisk.

Make-Up Assignments and Extra Credit

It is true that people will do what they are supposed to do if two things are present: 1. They know what to do and 2. They want to do it. What this means is that students need to know the specific details of class assignments, concert schedules, due dates, and what is required for each task, and we need to be explicitly clear as teachers when we give assignments. It is inevitable, even when students know what to do and want to do it, that they will occasionally miss a concert for sickness or an exam for a conflict in another class or an assignment for some other reason. It is your responsibility to create a consistent mechanism that allows students to make up graded evaluations that they miss, regardless of the reason. Of course, your school may have a district-wide policy addressing these issues, and you can then just follow those guidelines. But most schools will allow the teacher to decide how student work can be made up and if and when to offer extra credit assignments to students.

If you give an exam in AP Music Theory and a student misses the test, you should offer another time for the exam to be taken that works for both you and the student. Participation in daily classroom activities is impossible to make up for obvious reasons, so there are some grades that have to either be ignored or not figured in for a missing student. One of the most challenging activities to make up is the public choral concert. Many colleges and universities have had policies that state that a student fails for the semester if they miss a concert, but this is not a policy you should enact in the public schools. Concert attendance should be part of the grade, but not all of the grade; you should have a make-up method for the concert grade.

Students who don't want to miss concerts rarely miss concerts. Students who want to miss concerts often miss concerts. How you decide to let them make up the grade will largely determine if they miss the next concert. Some teachers have had students write a historical research paper on a musical topic or composer to make up the grade, but that doesn't give the teacher a chance to evaluate the skills needed to sing in a public concert, which is what the student missed. Also, this contingency may or may not function well for the student, and it may or may not encourage them to attend the next concert. Some teachers have given students who miss public concerts a chance to sing their part as a solo or in a small group, dressed in concert dress, for other students and teachers to watch during the next school day. While this would give the teacher a chance to evaluate the student's performance more closely, it may or may not function well for the student. You will have to decide on the make-up plan that works well for you and your students and ensure it is a plan that encourages them to participate in the original concert assessment. One concept to understand is that the make-up task shouldn't be easier or more convenient than the original assignment. If it is, the same students will continue to miss concerts in the future.

Extra credit assignments have a similar problem. If students know that they can miss assignments or fail tests early in the semester or quarter, and then just make them up later, they may be encouraged to do so. You should have a clear policy for extra credit make-up assignments, and then you should be consistent implementing the policy. Watch the behavior of the students to determine if you need to make adjustments to the policy. Ideally, students will know what to do and they will want to do it the first time.

Organizing and Reporting Grading Data

Once you have decided how you will grade your students, you will need to create a system for collecting and organizing those data from your assessments and evaluations. This is much harder than it seems because most teachers will already have their hands full keeping the class engaged, answering questions, reinforcing classroom rules, etc. For example, having an accurate and fast system for attendance is essential if you don't want to waste rehearsal time or slow your teaching pace to a standstill. Class assignments that are turned in at the end of class can be graded by the teacher after class, and any written work or recordings that are submitted can be evaluated outside of class time as well. The most challenging behaviors to grade are the ones that must be observed continuously during class, such as "follows classroom rules." Should students start with 100% and lose points when they break rules, or should they start at 0% and gain points when they follow rules? For practical purposes, it is easier to deduct from a student's grade when you can document that they misbehaved than it is to document every appropriate behavior in the classroom as it happens. Regardless, you will need a system to organize your numbers, and you will probably need to defend your grading system to an administrator or parent at some point.

Once you have your system for collecting grade data, you will need a way to organize, crunch, and report those grades. If you have a school that provides this system for you online, all you have to do is learn how to use it. If you don't have this provided, you will have to fill in a grade book or create a personal database. The grade book, filled in by hand, is fast and convenient at first, but it will take a significant amount of time to complete when you need to report grades. A database that you design in Microsoft *Excel* or Apple's *Numbers*, for example, will take more time at first, but when it comes time to report grades, the database will compute everything for you once you have entered all the numbers. Your database might look something like this, depending on what you select for your grading criteria, evaluations, and assessments:

Name	Theory test 1	Theory test 2	Sight singing 1	Sight singing 2	Sight singing 3	Sight singing 4
Student 1	100	100	100	100	100	100
Student 2	100	70	100	75	80	90
Attendance	Entrance / Exit 1	Entrance / Exit 2	Entrance / Exit 3	Entrance / Exit 4	Entrance / Exit 5	Entrance / Exit 6
Student 1	100	100	100	100	100	100
Student 2	100	75	50	100	75	100
Name	FINAL AVERAGE				Theory Tests	Sight Singing Tests
Student 1	100				20	20
Student 2	74.75				17	17.25
20%	Theory Tests (2)					
20%	Sight Singing Tests (2)		95-100% =	A+		
30%	Concert Performances (2)		91-95% =	A		
5%	Concert Reflections (1)		89-91%=	A-		
5%	Concert Report (1)		85-89%=	B+		
10%	Entrance / Exit Slips		81-85%=	B		
5%	Preparation		79-81%=	B-		
5%	Participation		76-79%=	C+		
			73-76%=	C		
			69-73%=	C- *	*C- grade and below	
			67-69%=	D+	constitutes a	
			64-67%=	D	"non-passing" grade	
			60-64%=	D-	in this class.	
			0-60%+	F		

Excel sheet continued

Concert Performanes 1	Concert Performanes 2	Concert Reflection	Concert Report	Preparation	Participation
100	100	100	100	100	100
100	0	100	80	90	80
Entrance / Exit 7	Entrance / Exit 8	Entrance / Exit 9	Entrance / Exit 10		
100	100	100	100		
75	75	50	100		
Concert Performances	Concert Reflection	Concert Report	Preparation	Participation	Entrance / Exit
30	5	5	5	5	10
15	5	4	4.5	4	8

As most new teachers find out early, you will work really hard in your first few years learning about your school's policies, setting up systems for grading, organizing and managing a music booster group if you choose to have one, and planning and preparing concert programs, events, assemblies, and trips. All the time you spend in your first years will pay off once you have done it for a while, and you will be able to relax into your organizational systems and refine them as needed. Of all the things you need to learn immediately, your list of grading policies and systems should be at the top of the list. You can learn many other things as you go, but you will need to start evaluating your students on day one and assessing them soon after. Do all you can to be curious, and don't be afraid to ask as many experienced choral music educators what their system is so that you can create something that works for you as soon as possible, and certainly before you have your first job.

RECAPITULATION

1. In more and more public schools in America, it is becoming illegal, or at least not advisable through school policy, to grade only on attendance for any class. What this means in many cases is that the choral educator must devise ways for students who miss concerts to make up the grade for the concert. Can you think of two possible tasks that students could complete to make up a missed concert? Describe exactly what you might have them do, how you would grade the make-up activity, and why you think the activity is a good substitute for the original live concert task.
2. Create a grading database sample workbook using a database program such as Microsoft *Excel* or Apple's *Numbers*. Decide upon your grading criteria and class percentages and create grading fields for two students. One should have a perfect score (A+ and 100%) and the other should have a less-than-perfect average, just to test your database functionality. Explore how the formulas work and figure out how to manipulate them to make your database work properly for your grading criteria and data. Be ready to reflect upon your successes and failures working with the software with your classmates. To aid your understanding, download the grading template and examine how it works and how it is set up. Adapt yours accordingly.

3. Think back to all the classes you have taken since you were very young. Recall a time when you felt that your grade in a class was not a good measure of your work in the class. In other words, describe a class where your grade was lower than you think it should have been. Why do you think this happened? Likewise, recall a time when you got a higher grade than you probably should have. What were the circumstances that made this possible? Do you think it is important that grades accurately reflect the progress and achievement of the students in the class? Why or why not?

Chapter Eleven

Leading a Discussion

11. Leading a Discussion

"A good discussion increases the dimensions of everyone who takes part."
~Randolph Bourne

You May Like This

Body Language TED Talk

Discussion as a Teaching Tool

Leading a discussion is possibly the least understood and probably the least rehearsed technique that beginning teachers will implement in their classrooms. In fact, even some experienced teachers find that they have some difficulty moderating and planning effective discussions in their classes. Additionally, it is not unusual for teacher-training programs to ignore or minimize some of the crucial aspects of this important teaching technique, presuming that emerging teachers will "figure it out" as they go. The art of leading a discussion, like any technique or skill, can be perfected over time in front of real classes, but it is important to know some of the best practices and potential pitfalls of this teaching technique before you practice it in an authentic setting with students.

It can be easy to assume that leading a discussion is the *easiest* teaching technique to use in a classroom, especially if you believe that all one has to do is let the students talk about a topic. Discussion can also be misperceived as a logical choice for a teacher who has no lesson plan or who has run out of material to teach. It can even be regarded by some as a fallback lesson plan rather than as a primary plan. But leading a discussion is far from being the easiest teaching strategy, and it could possibly be *the most difficult* teaching approach to master and implement. Leading a discussion effectively requires the teacher to manage many various elements of the classroom environment, to read body language, to summarize and restate points made by the students, and to use proximity and extended questioning to keep the students engaged, listening, thinking, and on topic.

If you try to recall the class discussions that you have participated in during all your years in school, you will probably remember various teachers who made the discussion experience a positive and interesting one and also some who made the experience seem like a difficult exercise in random or specific recall. This is because some teachers understand how to structure a discussion effectively so that students think and respond critically to well-crafted, open-ended and high-level questions, while other teachers try to lead discussions with lower-level questions and "guess what I'm thinking" teaching. High-level questions are essential for setting the stage for interesting class discussions, and "guess what I'm thinking" teaching should not be confused with leading an effective classroom discussion.

"Guess What I'm Thinking" Teaching

Well-meaning teachers sometimes use this technique in their classrooms with the belief that they are leading a discussion, when in fact they are asking the students to respond with one correct (and possibly random) answer that is held in the mind of the teacher. Similar kinds of questioning techniques are best used to quiz the students verbally on topics and facts that they have been taught previously or that they may have learned in readings or through some other mode of discovery. This line of discourse can be effective for reinforcing facts and for reviewing specific bits of information that are presumed to be in the short-term recall abilities of the students. Here is a simple example of this type of questioning when done effectively:

> **Teacher**: Last class we learned how to find the solfege syllable "do" in any piece of music. There were three rules. Raise your hand if you can remember the rule for flats. Brandi? *(The teacher calls on a student with a raised hand.)*
>
> **Student**: The last flat tells you what line or space is "la."
>
> **Teacher**: Yes! That's correct. Good job remembering. What about sharps? Raise your hand. Ming? *(The teacher calls on another student with a raised hand.)*
>
> **Student:** The last sharp tells you where the note "C" is.
>
> **Teacher:** No, but I see why you remembered it that way. You combined two of the three rules together. Who can recall the rule for sharps from last class? Jayden? *(The teacher calls on another student with a raised hand.)*
>
> **Student**: Doesn't the last sharp mark where "ti" is?
>
> **Teacher**: Yes, that is correct! "ti" is indicated by the last sharp in the key signature. Who knows the rule for finding "do" when there is no key signature…no sharps or flats present on the staff? Raise your hand. Tzipora? *(The teacher calls on another student with a raised hand.)*
>
> **Student**: If there are no sharps and no flats then the note "C" is "do."
>
> **Teacher**: That's right. You can use the "G" and "F" clefs to count up and down to the note "C" and establish "do" when there are no sharps or flats present. Well done!

In this fictitious example of a dialogue, the teacher is reviewing material that the students have already been taught previously. There is a right and a wrong answer to each question, and the teacher guides the recall of facts and reinforces correct answers with even more information as review. And although the students and the teacher are communicating verbally to recall and reinforce facts, this is not a classroom discussion. It is just an effective review of facts, and the students do not need to think beyond the level of remembering specific rules and procedures to be successful.

"Guess what I'm thinking" teaching can also be used ineffectively, especially when it masquerades as thoughtful discussion that evokes critical thinking. In this example, the teacher has one correct answer, but the students have not learned previously what the answer is. Note the differences from our first example:

> **Teacher**: Let's have a discussion about composers from the classical era. Who can name the most significant composer from this period? Andrew. *(The teacher calls on a student in class before hands are raised.)*
>
> **Student**: J.S. Bach?
>
> **Teacher**: Nope. He was earlier than the classical period. Lily? *(The teacher calls on another student.)*
>
> **Student**: Brahms? I think he wrote classical music, didn't he?
>
> **Teacher:** No, no. Not classical music, Lily, but the classical period of music. I'm looking for a *significant* composer from the *classical* period. Jackie*. (The teacher calls on another student.)*
>
> **Student:** Is it Haydn?
>
> **Teacher:** No, I am looking for the *most significant* composer everyone. Think. Mackenzie? *(The teacher calls on another student with a raised hand.)*
>
> **Student**: Beethoven?
>
> **Teacher**: Close. He was significant, but he really was a bridge between classical and romantic styles. Think everyone. Macy? *(The teacher calls on another student with a raised hand.)*
>
> **Student**: Franz Schubert!
>
> **Teacher**: No, no. Come on, you guys. The most significant composer. You know the name. Think. *(No hands go up, but the teacher calls on a student anyway.)* Nicole?

Student: Is it Mozart?

Teacher: YES! Yes...it's Mozart. Very good thinking, Nicole. Mozart is the most significant composer of this period!

In this example, you can see that the teacher has one correct answer in mind and that the students are supposed to guess what it is, but they probably haven't been taught this particular "fact" in class. Additionally, the "correct" answer that the teacher is looking for is probably more of an opinion than a fact in this case. Even if the teacher was looking for a true "fact," it would be impractical to quiz the class in this manner unless that fact had been taught previously at some point. The only thing the teacher is actually doing is surveying the students to see what they already know, and if they share the same biases, but not what they remember about their studies in the class.

RECAPITULATION

1. Now that we have defined what "guess what I'm thinking" teaching is, it is more likely that you will recognize it in classes that you are taking right now or that you have taken in the past. Can you remember a time when you experienced this kind of teaching? If so, describe what the teacher did and also how it functioned for you personally. Did you feel comfortable participating, or did you feel reluctant to contribute answers? Why did you feel this way, in your opinion? If you can't recall a time when a teacher used this technique, describe any other teaching technique that you remember a teacher using in a class you took. Was it effective in your opinion? Why or why not?

2. Using your own words, describe the difference between a *fact* and an *opinion*. Can a fact also be an opinion? Do you think that teachers need to separate facts from opinions in their teaching? Why or why not?

Levels of Questioning

When you ask someone a question, how you ask the question, and how you choose to phrase the question, will largely determine the kind and quality of answer you get in return. Questions can be asked at various levels, and the level of the question affects the level of thinking required to respond to the question. Different levels of questions are effective for different kinds of teaching tasks, so a teacher needs to be able to ask questions at various levels depending on what kind of thinking they want the students to initiate before responding. Levels of questioning have been classified by various people over time, including Benjamin Bloom, who chaired a committee of educators that came up with something referred to as "Bloom's Taxonomy of Educational Objectives in the Cognitive Domain." These levels of questioning were classified into six areas: Knowledge, Comprehension, Application, Analysis, Synthesis, and Evaluation.[1] As you read the descriptions of each level, take note of how students might be prompted to think differently for each one, and also think about how each level of questioning could be used effectively during a lesson or rehearsal for different educational objectives.

Level 1 – Knowledge

This level requires students to remember previously learned materials by recalling facts, terms, basic concepts, and answers. Sample questions might include:

- Who was the composer of the famous choral-orchestral oratorio *Messiah*?
- How many beats per measure are there in *common time*?
- Which one of the following composers was born in the twentieth century: Mozart, Haydn, Copland, Bach, or Morley?
- What British rock band wrote the hit song *"Crazy Little Thing Called Love"?*
- What is the name of the musical form associated with a common church hymn?
- Write down the order of the seven sharps in the key signature of C#.
- Name the four major families of instruments found in an orchestra.

Level 2 – Comprehension

This level requires students to show that they understand facts and ideas by organizing, rephrasing, or comparing the material. Sample questions might include:

- What are the main similarities and differences between an oratorio and an opera?
- Explain the differences between simple and compound meter.
- Describe the length of lifespan (years lived) compared to the overall musical output (number of works composed) of two of the following composers: Mozart, Haydn, Copland, Bach, or Morley.
- How would you classify and describe the musical style of the hit song by Queen, *"Crazy Little Thing Called Love"?*

1 https://en.wikipedia.org/wiki/Bloom%27s_taxonomy#The_cognitive_domain_(knowledge-based)

- What are the main similarities and differences between strophic form and ternary form?
- What is the connection between the circle of fifths and how key signatures are constructed?
- Summarize the differences between the following families of instruments and how each family creates their characteristic sound (what vibrates, what energy is used to initiate vibration, and what is used as a resonating body?): woodwinds, brass, strings, and percussion.

NOTE: When leading a discussion, you should not use questions from levels 1 or 2. These kinds of questions don't encourage a rich discussion because they typically have a limited number of "correct" answers.

Level 3 – Application

This level requires students to solve problems to new situations by applying acquired knowledge, facts, techniques, and rules in a different way. Sample questions might include:

- What would happen if Handel's *Messiah* were staged as an opera as opposed to an oratorio? What production staff members for the oratorio would you be able to keep, and what people would you need to hire to produce this kind of staged performance?
- Using what you know about how meter works, how would you teach a student to understand and perform the rhythmic pattern of 2 against 3?
- What evidence can you find to support the statement that Mozart was one of the most gifted musicians and composers ever to live? Compare and contrast Mozart to another composer who you also think deserves to be called one of the most gifted in history.
- What evidence would you select to make a case that some of the most famous rock bands in history tended to blend more than one style of music into their records over time?
- What musical forms are used most often in popular music?
- Describe a sequence for teaching the circle of fifths to someone who does not read music. What do they need to know and what can you leave out, and in what order would you teach each concept?
- Describe the various challenges of learning to play (as a beginner) the following instruments of the orchestra: clarinet, trumpet, violin, and timpani.

Level 4 – Analysis

This level requires students to examine and break information into parts by identifying motives or causes and to make inferences and find evidence to support generalizations. Sample questions might include:

- Handel's oratorio *Messiah* has remained extremely popular over the centuries. What elements of the oratorio help contribute to its popularity and its frequent performances?

- When writing music for beginning choirs, why should a composer make careful decisions concerning the use of simple meter, mixed meter, compound meter, and polyrhythms?
- We know that Mozart was one of the most musically gifted composers in history. Do you think his talents and successes were primarily based on nature or nurture? In other words, how much talent do you think he was born with, and how much of his talent was developed? Provide evidence to support your opinions.
- Why would a rock band evolve their musical styles, especially if they had already found success with a particular sound or hit song?
- Why do you think that composers choose some musical forms over other musical forms when writing their music?
- Why do we teach the circle of fifths to music theory students?
- Why do you think orchestras are typically seated with strings in the front and the woodwinds, brass, and percussion sections toward the back of the ensemble?

Level 5 – Synthesis

This level requires students to engage in original and creative thinking or to solve problems. Synthesis questions generally have more than one right answer. Sample questions might include:

- If you were going to write a modern screenplay adaption (a movie version) of Handel's oratorio *Messiah*, what songs, characters, and sections of the work would you include, and which ones would you leave out? Explain why you would make these choices.
- Imagine that you have to compose a piece for an ensemble. What if you had to choose between using any rhythm but only a single pitch, or only one rhythm but using many pitches? Which scenario would you choose and why?
- We know that Mozart died at a relatively young age. Based on your understanding of his compositional change and development during his life, what might his music have sounded like if he had lived to be one hundred years old?
- Do you prefer rock bands that stay true to a particular style for which they have become famous, or do you prefer when they change their sound over time? Why or why not?
- Does the choice of musical form limit the creativity of a composer, or does it help them focus their musical creativity in your opinion?
- Do you prefer to listen to music with clear, common-practice chordal progressions, or do you prefer music that has a more varied modal and tonal language? Why do you feel this way?
- If you were a conductor and could reseat your orchestra to have them in different places on the concert stage, how would you choose to reseat them, and what effect do you think it would have on the sound of the ensemble?

Level 6 – Evaluation

This level requires students to make some sort of judgment about something and form a personal opinion. Evaluation questions generally have more than one right answer. Sample questions might include:

- Do you think that people will stop going to live music concerts someday and instead just listen to recordings or watch movies? Why or why not?
- If you had to choose the music of only one composer (or popular rock or folk band) to listen to for the rest of your life, which would you choose and why?
- Do you think talent in music is more important over the long run than acquired musical skills? In other words, can hard work over time overcome deficits in innate musical aptitude?
- What rock band do you think should be called the greatest (or most influential) in the history of music so far? Support your opinion.
- If you could choose one musical form to describe your life, which one would it be and why? Give concrete examples from your experience.
- Some people say that there are no new musical ideas, and that "new" compositions are just variations of ones that have already been written. Do you think music has evolved as far as it can go, or do you think there are new areas of composition that are yet to be explored?
- Do you think orchestras will still exist and will have the four common instrument families (strings, woodwinds, brass, and percussion) 100 years from now? Why or why not?

As you read and compare the questions from each level, you will notice that they move from one right answer (level one) to more complex answers requiring more knowledge of the topic and finally to opinions that require new answers stemming from informed opinions. The progression from level one to level six certainly has some gray areas, and there is room to disagree with what makes a perfect question at each level. However, if you try to use the technique of discussion using any of the level one questions from this section, you will not be successful. Level one questions should be used to test for knowledge and recall only, but not to initiate class discussions. Level six questions are open-ended and can have a large number of "correct" answers, and can be used quite effectively to start and maintain an interesting class discussion. As you start your teaching career, you can learn to become aware of how you ask questions to your classes, and you can choose your questions more carefully depending on the type of thinking you want your students to use.

The Rhetorical Question

There is one kind of question that needs to be mentioned and clarified here but that is not included in the levels of questioning above: *The Rhetorical Question*. A rhetorical question can be defined as "a figure of speech in the form of a question that is asked to make a point rather than to elicit an answer."[2] When you ask a rhetorical question, you are not asking for students to respond to the question. This may sound confusing to you; why ask a question if you do not want students to think and respond? Yet when you hear some examples of rhetorical questions, you will recognize how they are used all the time, especially by conductors in ensemble rehearsals:

- "Can you crescendo at the top of page 5?"
- "Would you like to stand up?"
- "Can you take out *Ave Verum*?"
- "Can you start at the beginning?"

None of these "questions" are really questions. If they were intended to be questions, then the proper response would be a resounding "yes" from the class or possibly a "no" from some of the students. Rhetorical questions can be thought of as harmless, and you can certainly train your class to ignore rhetorical questions as cues to think and respond. It is certainly more effective in general, as a teaching tool, to only use a questioning technique when you want to invite students to think and respond. It is just as easy to phrase these rhetorical questions as statements that direct behavior, rather than as potentially confusing interrogative cues.

- "Let's start that crescendo at the top of page 5."
- "Everyone please stand!"
- "Let's take out *Ave Verum*."
- "Let's go back to page 1, from the top."

When you make conscious choices to ask different levels of questions in your classes based on how you want students to think and respond, it will make practical sense to you to use rhetorical questioning sparingly. That way, when you do ask any question, students will learn to pause and think and respond without second-guessing your intentions. Because we tend to teach the way that we were taught, you may find it difficult to make this change in your own language and teaching, especially if your own teachers used these kinds of rhetorical questions constantly in the classroom or rehearsal setting. The words we choose while we are teaching are extremely important, and being aware

2 https://en.wikipedia.org/wiki/Rhetorical_question

of how your words function for students is essential to the art of excellent teaching. A good rule of practice when teaching is to always *"say what you mean, and mean what you say."*

Elements of Leading a Discussion

Once you have decided to use this technique in your class, and after you have chosen a topic and written some rich and high-level questions, there are some other practical aspects to consider. As was stated earlier, leading a discussion is possibly the most complex teaching technique to master, yet when it is done well, it can appear somewhat easy to administer to the observer. There are many things that the teacher must manage and be aware of in real time, and it takes practice to keep all of these elements functioning well during the live discussion. Here are some of the most important aspects to consider as you prepare:

- **Setting the stage for your question**

    - Rather than just asking your discussion question to the class, it can be helpful to expand on the topic to give some additional background information. Additionally, this allows extra time for people to think about their personal opinion before responding. As a general rule when teaching *any* class, always give a little time for people to think before asking them to respond to your questions. For example, rather than ask the question, *"Do you think that talent in music is more important over the long run than acquired musical skills?"* you could say, *"Some people think that musical talent is the most important part of success as a professional musician. Other people say that if you work hard, you can be successful, as long as you are willing to devote a lot of time to your progress and get a great teacher. Other people would say that you need a combination of both talent and hard work to be successful. What do you think? In other words, can hard work over time overcome deficits in innate musical aptitude?"* A question that is stated clearly and that is set up well will have the best chance of initiating a robust and interesting discussion. One indicator that your question has been stated clearly and set up well will be the hands you see in the air indicating that people are ready to explore your topic. If no hands go up, you should take that as a sign that people are confused about your question or that they are confused in some other way. Calling on people to speak (because no one raises their hands) is not recommended because it will disrupt the safe environment required to have high-level discussions that include critical thinking and thoughtful opinions.

○ Setting up the talking queue

- If your question has been stated clearly, and if the class has had a chance to think and form an opinion regarding the question, you will probably see several hands raised to respond to the question and contribute to the discussion. If you call on someone and ignore the rest of the people raising their hands, it is likely that some students will put their hands down, but that others will keep their hands up so that you can call on them when the other class members are done talking. This encourages two problems: people who put their hands down are not completely sure if they will be able to make their point and may begin to feel uninvolved in the discussion, and the people who constantly keep their hand up begin to look ridiculous fighting gravity with their vertically extended arm. You can solve both issues by creating a *talking queue*. All you have to do is acknowledge the people with their hands up and say their names in the order that you will call on them. Then you, as the teacher, must keep track of the talking queue and the order that you established. After you finish stating your question and you see hands go up, say something like "Andrew, Brandon, then Ebun, and then Rachel," and have them put their hands down. You will have to memorize the queue and stick to it, even as you manage all the other aspects of the discussion. When the queue is finished, you can encourage more hands to be raised, but it is probable that people will continue to raise hands as interesting new points are brought up in the discussion and you can continually add them to the talking queue as you go.

○ Summarizing each person's main point

- Once you have the initial talking queue set up and the first person is responding to your discussion question, you will need to listen carefully to what is being said. It is a mistake to think that you can just call on people lined up in the queue without moderating and summarizing each person's main point. This is not as easy as it sounds, and you will have to focus and practice over time to do it most effectively. What makes this challenging is the need to take thirty to sixty seconds of talking and restate it in ten seconds or less back to the class. As you listen, there will most certainly be distractions in the classroom with new people wanting to join the queue or side conversations starting that need to be redirected back to the main conversation. When you feel a person has made a solid point in the discussion, you can say something like, "You make an excellent point here. What I think you are saying is that…" as you try to encompass the main intent of their point. You can check to see if you were accurate by adding, "Did I get that right?" If the person affirms that you got the gist of the point, then you can move on in the queue to the next person. If they say you didn't quite get it right, then you can ask for clarification from them or you can try to summarize it slightly differently. The summary need not be comprehensive or complete, but it does need to demonstrate that you were listening and processing what was said. Besides affirming the speaker, your summary will also serve to help the class focus on what was said in order to advance the discussion.

- ## Using proximity and eye contact to keep everyone involved and focused

  - Keeping everyone in the class involved, on task, and focused during a discussion is one of the most challenging aspects of this teaching technique. How you move around the classroom (your use of proximity) will greatly affect your students' success in these behavioral areas. One general rule for you as the discussion leader is to move to a place in the room where everyone feels that they are part of the discussion. In most cases this means keeping a majority of the class between you and the person speaking. This is not a natural inclination for many people because in most social situations people move *closer* when they start a conversation with another person. But in a classroom setting you will need to move *away* from the person talking to invite the rest of the class into the discussion and to allow yourself to maintain eye contact with everyone in the room. The person talking will almost always direct their energy and eye contact toward where the teacher is standing, so the teacher must frequently move around the room to encourage the speaker to include as much of the class as possible. In the graphic (below) you will notice that the teacher (T) moves to keep most of the class between them and the speaker (SP). This is also true when the speaker is on the right side of the room. You will also see that when the speaker is in the center of the class, the teacher will need to *move back and away* from the front row in order to maintain eye contact with as many people as possible and to keep everyone feeling connected to the discussion activity.

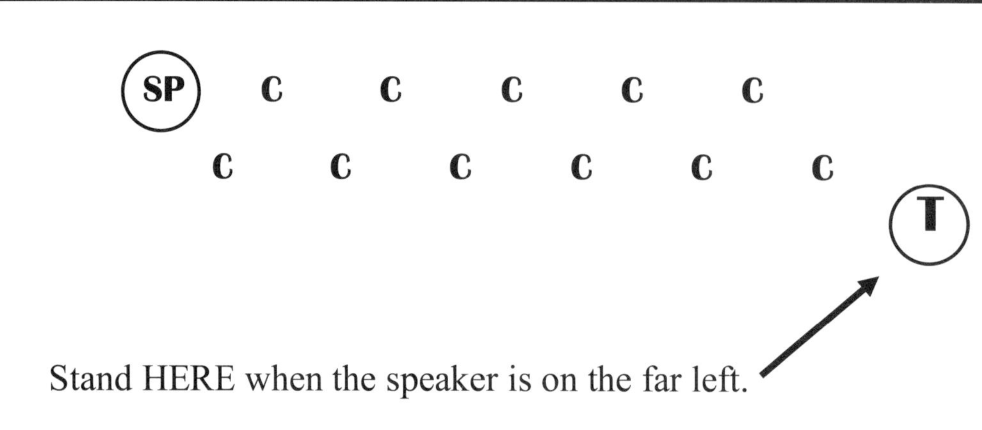
SP
C C C C C
C C C C C C
T
Stand HERE when the speaker is on the far left.

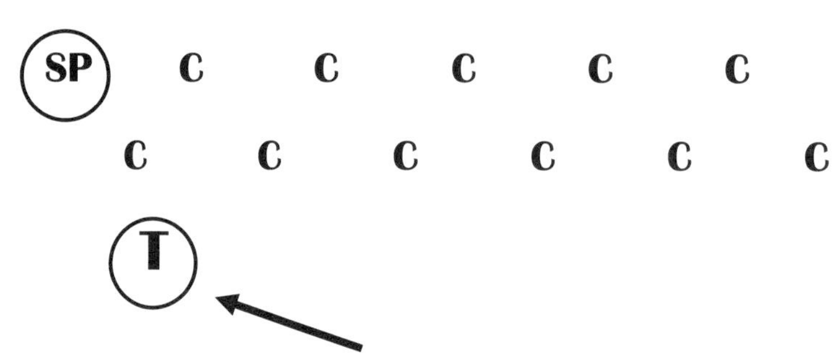
SP
C C C C C
C C C C C C
T
DO NOT stand here when the speaker is on the far left.

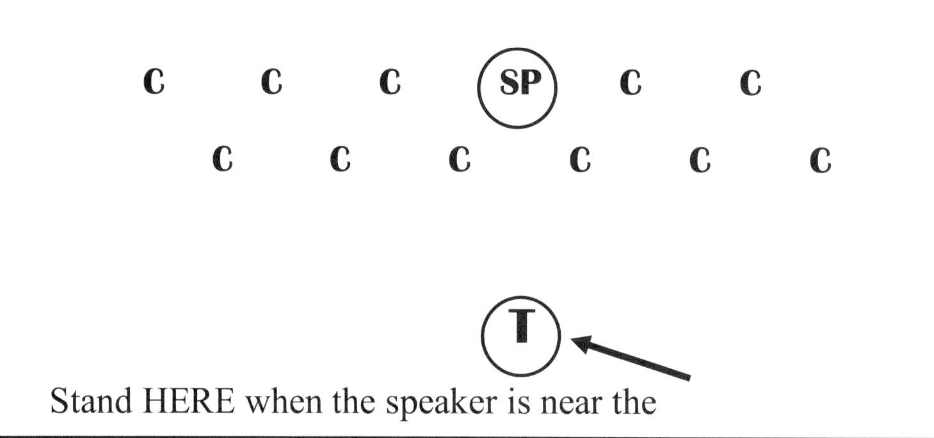
C C C SP C C
C C C C C C
T
Stand HERE when the speaker is near the

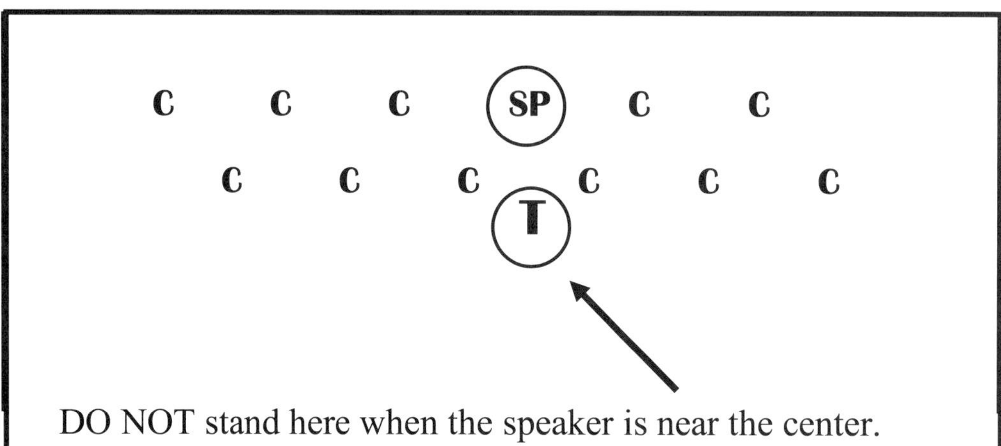
C C C SP C C
C C C C C C
T
DO NOT stand here when the speaker is near the center.

○ Encouraging everyone to contribute and participate equally

- Part of the art of leading an effective discussion is keeping everyone in the class engaged in the activity. It is easy to assume that all students will willingly participate, but that is rarely the case even when participation is tied to some sort of grade. Every class has a mix of introverts and extroverts, talkers and listeners, and participators and observers by nature. Your extroverted talkers will participate immediately and often if you have phrased your question well and set the stage for high-level thinking. But your introverted observers will probably not raise their hands and participate at first, and you will need to encourage them with your words, body language, and positive reactions to what other people have said. One thing that will keep people from participating is when your extroverted talkers have trouble wrapping up their point and when they start to ramble or make several points. This is when the class will stop paying attention and may even get off task by talking quietly or completely checking out. As the facilitator, you will need to listen for when a single point is made, and then you will need to intervene and summarize the main point and then move to the next person in the queue. This ability to help people wrap up and complete their point is not always as easy as it sounds. You will need to be sure that each person feels heard and that the class can understand each point as it relates to the discussion question. It's also all right to say, "I'd like to hear from people who haven't talked yet," as you ignore others who have already participated several times. Encouraging everyone to participate as equally as possible increases the chances that the class will stay on task and engage meaningfully.

○ Reframing the question when necessary

- There will be times when you think that your question has been well stated, but when the discussion doesn't seem to gather any momentum. Clues that this is happening are when people make points that are unrelated to the gist of your question or when people make points that seem to be randomly related to the topic. When this happens, you should consider reframing the question and asking it again using different words or by providing examples to clarify the theme of the question better. This problem is most likely to occur when you haven't set the stage for your question clearly enough or when the class wasn't focused and thinking when the question was posed. Sometimes the question, regardless of your intention, won't function to create critical thinking within a particular class of students; don't be afraid to reframe the question or even change the question if you don't think it is generating an interesting and engaging dialogue.

○ Keeping personal bias out of your own comments

- One of the most important aspects of using discussion as a teaching tool is affirming each speaker's contributions and thoughts with some sort of approval. This functions best when you keep your own personal biases about the question out of your reactions and approval segments. In other words, if you nod and smile and get excited about one student's point, but then have a neutral response and seem to disagree with another student's point, the class will "figure out" what they think the "correct" argument should be. But a great, high-level discussion question will not have a single correct answer or perspective; if you show a bias (either verbally or nonverbally) for one person's perspective over another one, your students will stop thinking creatively and will begin parroting what they suspect is a response that you prefer. Do your best to become a discussion moderator who reinforces everyone equally and positively. At the close of the discussion, if your students can't unanimously figure out what *you* think about the question, you have done well in this area.

○ Creating and maintaining a safe environment for discussion

- Leading a discussion is complicated, not just because of all the aspects described so far, but also because it requires a safe classroom environment to thrive and expand. This technique may not work when a teacher has not established a fully functioning contingent relationship with the students or when there is not sufficient trust among all the participants. Students must know that it's all right to offer an opinion that hasn't been stated or to say something that is contrary to what has already been heard in the room. The teacher has the responsibility to control the classroom environment so that everyone is respected and treated with kindness…even when points of disagreement come up. How you do *anything* affects how you do *everything*, and trust is created and maintained over time, in all your classes and with all your students. Discussion as a technique may be especially challenging to use with your students until you have built a solid foundation of trust and kindness within the culture of all your classes.

○ Wrapping up the discussion skillfully

- The final aspect to consider as you prepare to lead a discussion is how to end it. Ideally, the class will have found some cognitive momentum and will want to keep the discussion going for a while. You, as the moderator, will have to close the discussion when you find a good balance between a discussion that feels too short and one that has gone on for too long. Your class time might dictate the ending (such as the bell ringing) or you might need to move on to another activity in the curriculum. When you feel that it's time to wrap up, you can begin to let the class know with words such as, "We have time for a few more perspectives on this" or "Just a few more minutes, everyone." Giving a warning that the discussion is ending soon helps those who want to talk, but who have been reluctant, to muster up the courage to say something in the last few seconds. As you bring everything to a close, you can also make a few general summarizing statements about what was said, and you can encourage the students to continue talking about the topic when class is over. A good discussion, run and structured well, can leave participants feeling satisfied because of the rich exchange of ideas that can happen in a creative and safe classroom environment.

RECAPITULATION

1. Have you had teachers in your lifetime who have used discussion as a teaching technique? Describe what you remember about some of those experiences. Did you feel the classroom was a safe place for the exchange of ideas, and did you feel that the discussion was well managed based on the aspects described above?
2. Good discussions start with good questions. Do your best to write three rich discussion questions that could be used to initiate an interesting class dialogue. Include some extra sentences that you would actually say in the classroom to frame your question or to give examples or context. Read your complete questions to someone you know to see if they fully understand what your question is addressing and if they think it could generate a rich discussion.
3. It has been stated that leading a discussion is possibly the most difficult teaching tool to do well. Like any skill, the more experience you get, the better you will become, and beginning teachers can and should explore this technique in their emerging pedagogy. Reflect on your own experience and abilities in light of the "most important aspects" outlined above. Which ones do you think you could already do well, and which ones do you think you would have to work on to be completely effective? How difficult do you think it would be for you personally to keep all these aspects working effectively at the same time in front of a real class? Why do you think this is the case?
4. If you think about it, many of the elements of leading an effective discussion would also function well in general human social interactions. Make a list of which elements could be applied (and why) to general human social interactions and which ones are less applicable. In other words, how many of these techniques would help you in a small group of friends or even strangers when you are not leading a discussion or even in charge?

III. Coda

Chapter Twelve

Formulating Your Philosophy of Music Education

12. Formulating Your Philosophy of Music Education

"Your beliefs become your thoughts, your thoughts become your words, your words become your actions, your actions become your habits, your habits become your values, your values become your destiny."
~Mahatma Gandhi

Why Do You Want to Teach Music?

When you first start preparing to be a professional music educator, you will invariably spend a large amount of your time studying the pedagogy of the craft. Among the many things you study, you will learn about scope and sequence, classroom management, and how to create practical, detailed, and usable task analyses to create dynamic lessons for students of various ability levels in your classroom. You will spend a great deal of your time improving your musicianship and determining *what* to teach by writing detailed, step-by-step lesson plans. But at some point you will need to focus not only on what you teach, but also *why* you teach. The question of "why" you teach is very different than the question of "what" you teach, and unless you have a solid and grounded understanding of why you teach, you will probably not be as inspiring a teacher as you could be. Your ability to inspire others must be fueled by your impassioned drive to accomplish great and important things and to make a difference in the world. Every professional music educator should be able to articulate, in plain language, why they teach, what they teach, and why the study of music is essential to a comprehensive education.

If you think back to the moment you decided to become a music teacher, there was probably something significant that happened to you, something you thought about, or an experience that focused your attention toward the profession. You may have experienced a significant and transcending musical moment, or you may have been inspired by the teachers that you had. Perhaps you are someone who has always known that you are a teacher, but found your way to music later in life. It is also possible that you don't know or remember why you made the choice to pursue choral music education as a career, and you could still be searching for a basic explanation for why you want to teach. No matter how you describe the path that led you to where you are today, it is of great benefit for you to explore the reasons that you choose to study music and to clarify and describe why you want to become a great teacher.

How Have You Changed The World Lately?

The world is constantly changing. Catastrophic events and global unrest are routinely reported to all ends of the Earth on media streams, and it can seem at times like the world is out of control. Sometimes it feels like no single person can make a difference in the world, and it is not uncommon for people who are not important CEOs or powerful politicians to feel like their efforts and influence don't matter very much. This view does not take into consideration the immense effect that everything has on everything else. How you do anything affects how you do everything, and every positive thing you do does make a significant difference.

It has been calculated that a single butterfly flapping its wings in South America can change the weather patterns thousands of miles away.[1] This phenomenon, called the *Butterfly Effect*, can help us remember that every gesture of kindness, every face-to-face interaction, and every small action you embark upon in your day has a real and lasting effect on the world. It is not necessary to be a powerful executive to make a significant and positive difference in the lives of many people, and as a teacher, you will strive to change the lives of your students for the better every day. As you help change the world, one student interaction and one class period at a time, the effect of your influence will ripple out and continue to change the world in a positive way. Music teachers change lives, and your work with your students will indeed change the world for the better in powerful and meaningful ways.

What Is a Philosophy of Music Education?

The word *philosophy* is a noun that can be defined as "the study of the fundamental nature of knowledge, reality, and existence, especially when considered as an academic discipline."[2] A philosophy of music education could be described as your personal set of principles as to why you teach, what you regard as music, what music you consider worthy of study, who you think should study music, and who you believe should teach music. Your philosophy should reflect your personal values, but it should also make a strong case for music as an academic subject that is essential to the success of student learning across the curriculum. Your advocacy for the profession must be linked to your personal beliefs and aspirations for teaching, so that anyone you talk to will sense the personal enthusiasm tied to your thoughtful understanding of the benefits of a comprehensive music education.

---

1 http://www.stsci.edu/~lbradley/seminar/butterfly.html

2 http://www.oxforddictionaries.com/us/definition/american_english/philosophy

A good place to start a personal inquiry into your beliefs about a philosophy of music education is to think of a single word that best describes *why* you want to teach. A common reaction to this task is to think, "I can't sum it up in a single word. There are too many things to consider." Yet you can do it if you simply ponder what you want your students to be able to do because of your teaching, or the values you hope they will come to hold through the study of music in your program. Once you choose a word or two that describes why you want to teach, compose one or two sentences that elaborate on the word or words. Let these sentences represent a kind of personal "mission statement" about how you intend to change the lives of your students through music. If you take the time to refine these sentences so that they describe your intentions concisely, you are well on your way to writing a paragraph, and then a page, and finally a full statement of your music education philosophy.

RECAPITULATION

1. Because the motions of the wings of a butterfly can change the world in significant ways, you likewise change the world in even more significant ways every day when you are interacting with people, your environment, and even your own thoughts. Write a short narrative about some of these interactions by describing some specific things you have done or experienced in the recent past that may have affected a change in another person, the environment, or your own mind in a positive way.
2. Think about why you want to teach music. Then think about your potential to be a positive influence on your students through the experience of music. Consider what is in it for you and also what you expect your students to receive through the experience. Next, brainstorm as many single words as you can that embody your intentions as a teacher of music. Once you have this list of words, decide on which ones come the closest to representing your broadest and most positive intentions for the profession. From your continued thinking about these words and ideas, compose four sentences that start with each of the following:
    a. "I teach music because…"
    b. "As a professional music educator I intend to …"
    c. "Music has the power to…"
    d. (Compose the fourth sentence using any words you choose)

Starting to Write Your Philosophy of Music Education

Many educational institutions that train preservice music teachers will include within the curriculum a section on music education philosophy. Undergraduate students, who may not have much, if any, experience in authentic classroom environments are asked to articulate their beliefs regarding a profession that they are only just beginning to explore. In a sense this seems premature, or at least difficult, in the same way that creating a mission statement about fine art painting would be daunting if you only had experience finger painting. There is a reasonable argument that can be made that a philosophy of music education is best composed during post-graduate study by students who are experienced educators with knowledge of real-world classroom dynamics and outcomes. Indeed, life is the greatest teacher, so experienced educators are usually best able to reflect and articulate detailed explanations of why they do what they do, and why they believe music is important, in more powerful ways than beginning teachers can.

But preservice teachers can and should explore their own beliefs about the profession before they get their first job, even if those beliefs are not grounded in authentic teaching experiences. It is not unusual, therefore, for your first attempt at writing your philosophy of music education to feel like a rote exercise or a task of the mind rather than the heart. Hopefully you gained valuable insights and learned something about yourself when you brainstormed words earlier in this chapter and then completed the four sentences that might form the theme of your personal philosophy.

As you begin to write, it is perfectly normal for you to struggle to find your unique voice while you search to find the appropriate words, and it is perfectly appropriate for you to read other students' philosophies online and to talk to your fellow students and the community about the common philosophical beliefs of the profession. As you digest what other people have written, you should begin to think about what you agree with, what you do not agree with, and to begin writing about the beliefs that you hold strongly *in your own words*. If you simply copy someone else's words verbatim, you will not be able to own them later or talk to parents, colleagues, administrators, students, school boards, or hiring committees about your philosophy when it matters the most. As you read other's work, and as you think about your philosophy of music education, look for *themes of agreement*, and then strive to find your own voice through your own writing.

Themes of Philosophical Agreement

Even though you may be striving to find your own voice in your writing, know that there are some common themes that many successful educators articulate and several philosophical beliefs that music educators commonly share. As a public school music education professional, you may consider including the following themes in your personal philosophy of music education. Public school music educators generally agree that…

A. …music education is for everyone, not just the talented.
B. …music should be taught comprehensively as a core subject in the K-12 school curriculum.
C. …music should be taught by well-trained, credentialed music educators.
D. …all styles and genres of choral music should be represented in the curriculum.
E. …the study of music provides a unique way of knowing and understanding the world and provides insights into the realm of human artistic expression and perception.
F. …music education should be available in every school, and for all students, from pre-K to 12th grade, and beyond.

As you read these Themes of Philosophical Agreement, you may find yourself agreeing with some more than others. These ideas are specifically tailored to the common beliefs shared by professional choral music educators in the public schools of the United States. Let's look at the first statement, for example:

> *"Public school music educators generally agree that music education is for everyone, not just the talented."*

In the United States, music educators generally agree that the public schools exist to educate every student in the school and to provide opportunities for every student to learn, explore, experience, and grow through varied activities in singing, playing, composing, arranging, improvising, listening to, and moving to music. There are many countries in the world where music is not offered in the schools at all and where music is considered an after-school hobby that is paid for by parents who can afford to provide it for their children. Music education is not valued as a core subject, but rather as a special activity that would be wasted on students without innate talent or interest for music.

Professional public school music educators in the United States most often share the values that contend that every student can benefit from the study of music and that it is essential to provide music instruction as a core subject in the schools, regardless of the levels of musical aptitude of the students. They do not believe that the benefits of music study are limited to creating professional musicians, famous composers, conductors, or performers. Every student, with proper structure, experience, practice, and guidance, can improve their musical skills and abilities; every student can become a more well-rounded and better-educated human being through the study of music.

RECAPITULATION

1. As a starting point for writing your philosophy of music education, conduct a web search for other undergraduate (and possibly graduate) music education students around the country who have already completed this task and who have posted their work online. Some will be extensive and some will be quite brief. Find and read as many examples as you can, and then save and/or print two that you think align well with your personal beliefs at this point. From these two philosophy examples, excerpt three sentences or paragraphs that you think read well, or that express something that you believe strongly. Paste these sentences into a blank document and write, in your own words, why you chose these sentences and why you consider them to be significant statements that align to your beliefs.
2. The section on "Themes of Agreement" highlights the common beliefs of many professional music educators in the public schools of America. Briefly discuss your thoughts about this list in a short written paragraph. If you are strongly opposed to any of these belief statements, justify your opinions in a second short paragraph. Additionally, brainstorm, type, and print several "belief statements" that you think, in your opinion, could be added, or maybe should be added to this list. In other words, are there some belief statements that are not on the "Themes of Agreement" list that trained, credentialed music educators and conductors should believe about the profession, in your opinion? Come up with at least two, and be ready to discuss and share these ideas with the class or community.

Creating the First Draft of Your Philosophy of Music Education

Now that you have begun to explore the ideas that form the foundation of every philosophy of music education, it is time for you to create your first working draft. Even at this point, some preservice teachers mistakenly think that they are supposed to create an essay about how they decided to be a music teacher, and they proceed to write a historical accounting of their musical life. While this can be an interesting and insightful exercise that helps you understand how you got where you are, your philosophy of music education is not a story about what happened to you. It is, rather, a several-page narrative expressing your beliefs about the profession. It is a series of declarative paragraphs that take a philosophical stand on the core issues of the music education profession. Your philosophy is your personal creed that you can explain to other people when it is appropriate, but it is also the document that will help you make tough decisions throughout your career. When you know what you believe, and have articulated these ideas clearly, and when you know what you stand for, you can always guide your actions and choices based on those foundational assumptions of professional behavior. When you are discouraged (and we all get discouraged), you can remember what you wrote, why what you do is important to you and your students, and the ways that you make the world a better place through teaching music.

If you are just starting out in the profession as an undergraduate preservice music education major, it is recommended that you use the following template to write your first draft. The template will help guide your thoughts about what to write and will make it easier for you to put ideas to paper. You should feel free to copy ideas and beliefs that you agree with, but you should strive to use your own words and voice to elaborate on the themes of your philosophy. So in a paragraph that might start with, "I believe that all students should have access to a quality music education in the schools, regardless of age and ability," and if this was a verbatim statement that you found from another philosophy, you would then continue to finish the paragraph in your own original words to substantiate and defend the statement. Don't worry if what you write sounds similar to what others in your class or the online community have written, but rather focus on using words that you would recall and be able to communicate verbally to someone interviewing you for a job or a colleague who is interested in knowing why you love to teach. It should reflect your words, your voice, and your vocabulary. Write in the first person and take a strong stand through your words and ideas.

Music Education Philosophy Template

Paragraph 1: Discuss what you think music is. Is it any organized sound, or do you have a different definition of what music is? What would you consider to be "good" music and "bad" music? Add anything else that you think is important, including music's role in society and culture.

Paragraph 2: Discuss why music study should be part of the core educational curriculum. What does the study of music do for the student that benefits their educational development? Add anything else that you think is important, including the direct and collateral benefits of a comprehensive music education.

Paragraph 3: Discuss what kinds of music should be taught in the schools. Should all genre styles, time periods, and cultures be represented or just some specific ones? Include statements about the use, study, and inclusion of pop music, jazz, and multicultural literature in your discussion. Add anything else that you think is important, including a statement about your approach to concert programming.

Paragraph 4: Discuss who should be able to study music in the public schools. Is music for all students or just for students with musical aptitude who can already sing and perform well? Add anything else that you think is important, including how you would approach teaching students who are mainstreamed as exceptional students with disabilities.

Paragraph 5: Discuss how music should be taught in schools. How would you structure the curriculum? What classes should be included in a comprehensive choral program, and what classes could be included in the schedule if there were time, administrative support, and student interest? Add anything else that you think is important, including how you might structure the choirs in your program to address beginning, intermediate, and advanced student ability levels.

Paragraph 6: Discuss who should teach in public schools. Is it acceptable for people who like music, but who do not have training as professional musicians and music educators, to be teaching music in the public schools? Add anything else that you think is important, including some of the skills that you have gained through study in your music education program to this point with a focus on the knowledge, attitudes, and behaviors of well-trained, professional music educators.

Paragraph 7: Conclude with something personal that provides some insight into your personal passion for being a music educator. Consider your earlier answers to the following prompts:

a. "I teach music because…"
b. "As a professional music educator, I intend to …"
c. "Music has the power to…"
d. (Compose the fourth sentence using any words you choose)

Add anything else that you think is important in this paragraph that was not addressed by you in the first six paragraphs.

Creating The Final Draft of Your Philosophy of Music Education

Once you have created a first draft of your music education philosophy, it is a good idea to share it with someone who is willing to listen as you read it to them. This can be another student from your methods class or a good friend who may or may not be a musician, or perhaps a family member. By reading your first draft out loud to someone, you will discover that some of your ideas are clearly explained, while other ideas are less clear to the listener. This is valuable feedback for you as a writer. It is common for any author to make some mental assumptions that the reader may not be making and to leave out clarifying sentences or ideas that would make the text more easily understood on a first hearing. Before you start reading, ask the person to provide clarifying questions, when and if they get confused, while you are reading. Have a pen and a piece of paper available to keep track of their questions. Let these requests for clarification inform the final draft of your philosophy so that anyone hearing your words would understand your intent as clearly as possible. If you have the time and resources, and after making adjustments to your text based on your initial feedback, repeat this exercise with a different person listening. Ideally, every new version of your philosophy will be clearer and more concise and more easily understood by any listener.

Once you have a version that has been refined based on the feedback you received, your last step is to have your philosophy edited for grammar, spelling, sentence structure, and punctuation. While it seems like this should be a preliminary step in the process, your text will retain more of your personal, individual voice if you compose primarily for content and ideas initially, and then clean up the technical aspects of your writing in this final step. Your editor will probably be one of your professors, but it could also be anyone that you know and trust with the technical skills to edit written text. If you don't have someone who can edit your text with you, consider using one of the online grammar-checking programs, some of which are completely free as a download. It is important to fix the technical aspects of your writing in this final version so that you can feel comfortable submitting your music education philosophy to anyone who might request it as a writing sample for a job, a class, or as part of an application to graduate schools. Your ability to communicate well through the written word will send a positive first impression to anyone considering you for these opportunities, and as a professional educator, it is worth your time to improve your writing ability as much as possible.

RECAPITULATION

1. Discuss your personal process for creating your philosophy of music education by explaining what was easy for you, as well as the ways you struggled or were challenged as you explored these topics. Did you enjoy the process, or did you find it to be a tedious exercise that was not very interesting? Be honest and explain why you feel the way you do, and feel free to use different descriptors than "enjoy" or "tedious" if they come closer to describing your experience writing your philosophy of music education.
2. What insights do you think you have gained by writing your philosophy of music education? Do you feel that these ideas could be helpful to you as you begin your career? If so, brainstorm some specific professional scenarios where you might be able to use your philosophical ideas in a positive way. If you don't feel that this exercise has been helpful to you, explain why, and provide feedback regarding alternate ways that you think it could have been more meaningful or educational for you personally.

Creating An "Elevator Pitch" of Your Philosophy of Music Education

Once you have successfully created your personal, unique, and grammatically correct philosophy of music education, it can be a practical exercise to create an "elevator pitch" of your philosophy. The concept of the elevator pitch comes from a fictitious scenario where a young employee of a large business suddenly finds herself in an elevator with the Chief Executive Officer of the company, and she has only a short elevator ride of maybe sixty seconds to "sell" the executive on an innovative idea for the company. She "pitches" the idea while she has the brief attention of the CEO before the door opens again, and the opportunity ends.

The elevator pitch of your philosophy should be a brief synopsis of the main points of your text in a style that fits your normal speech patterns. It is best to employ words that you would use in your actual daily speech and to avoid sounding too "academic." You should strive to memorize your elevator pitch so that if you were asked by a hiring committee in a live job interview to address your philosophy of music education, you could do so without needing to pause and think. Ideally, you should work to be able to deliver the main points of your elevator pitch philosophy in sixty to ninety seconds. It is not necessary to address every paragraph of your philosophy in a single spoken sentence, but rather to pick and choose the parts that you are most passionate about…the parts that you feel resonate strongly with your personal beliefs about the profession.

Music Education Philosophy "Elevator Pitch" Template

[Refer to your written philosophy, and then complete the following steps.]

Paragraph 1: Re-read your words about what music is and what you consider to be good and bad music. Note what you wrote about music's role in society and culture and anything else you included on these topics. Is there anything in this paragraph that you are really passionate about or that you feel is central to your music education philosophy? If so, summarize these points in a sentence or two. You can use your words verbatim, or you can write new sentences if you want to. Be sure to use words that you would use in your actual speech, and avoid sounding too "academic."

Paragraph 2: Re-read your words about why music study should be part of the core educational curriculum. Review what you wrote about the study of music and how it benefits students' educational development. Is there anything in this paragraph that you are really passionate about or that you feel is central to your music education philosophy? If so, summarize these points in a sentence or two as you did in paragraph one.

Paragraph 3: Re-read your words about the kinds of music that should be taught in schools. Revisit what you wrote about the inclusion of varied musical genres, styles, time periods, and cultures, as well as concert programming. Is there anything in this paragraph that you are really passionate about or that you feel is central to your music education philosophy? If so, summarize these points in a sentence or two.

Paragraph 4: Re-read your words about who should be able to study music in public schools. Consider what you wrote about talent vs. skill building, as well as your views on teaching students who are mainstreamed as exceptional students with disabilities. Is there anything in this paragraph that you are especially passionate about or that you feel is central to your music education philosophy? If so, summarize these points in a sentence or two.

Paragraph 5: Review your words about how music should be taught in schools. Are you particularly passionate about issues of curriculum structure or teaching effectively to beginning, intermediate, and advanced students? If so, summarize these points in a sentence or two.

Paragraph 6: Review your words regarding who should teach in public schools, and if it is acceptable in your view for people who like music, but who do not have training as professional musicians and music educators, to be teaching music in public schools. Is there anything in this paragraph that you are really passionate about or that you feel is central to your music education philosophy? If so, summarize these points in a sentence or two.

Paragraph 7: Conclude this "elevator pitch" with words from your final paragraph that convey insights into your personal passions for being a music educator. Summarize these points in several short sentences.

RECAPITULATION

1. Once you have completed the first draft of your "elevator pitch," practice reading it while timing yourself with a timer. Ideally, you should be able to read the whole thing in the span of sixty to ninety seconds without sounding too hurried in your speech, but while also maintaining a rapid speaking pace. If you can't complete a recitation in this amount of time, go back and remove a few sentences based on the degree of passion you have for each concept. Remember that it is not necessary to hit every point that you included in your extended philosophy of music education, but rather to highlight your most

central beliefs. If you want, you can also rewrite longer sentences into shorter sentences while maintaining the inclusion of the baseline concepts. Time yourself again and see if you can speak your pitch in ninety seconds or less.

2. Read your elevator pitch to someone who has not heard it before. Ask them if it makes sense to them and if your language sounds clear and colloquial. Ask them if you sound like a normal person speaking or if you sound like someone reading words that are not really yours. Take their feedback and revise your pitch to make it even more natural and conversational.
3. Video yourself sharing your elevator pitch and then watch yourself on the video. Be aware that hardly anyone likes the sound of their own voice or the way they look on video. Be careful not to be too critical of yourself. At the same time, make notes to yourself about your tone, pace, word inflection, lighting, camera angle, and quality of the audio, and then give yourself feedback for improvement. Consider shooting the video again based on your feedback. Allow yourself to acknowledge the improvements. Consider showing your video to someone else and getting their feedback as well. If you feel your elevator pitch is in really great shape, consider posting it to social media.
4. Memorize your elevator pitch, and then recite it from memory to a person or to a group of people. This group of people could be from a college class or perhaps a panel of people in a mock job interview. Have the people listening give you feedback about what went well, as well as what you can improve to be even more effective communicating your music education philosophy in ninety seconds or less.

The Evolution of Your Philosophy of Music Education

Now that you have explored and articulated some of your beliefs about music and music education, you are much better prepared to communicate to friends, colleagues, school boards, and hiring committees why you teach, what you regard as music, what music you consider worthy of study, who you think should be allowed to study music, and who you believe should teach music. It is important to know that these ideas will change and evolve throughout your career as you gain experience and as you apply what you know in authentic settings. If you choose to pursue graduate studies in choral music education, you may find yourself revisiting and rewriting your philosophy, and you might be surprised to find that you have gained a fresh perspective on your original ideas. This is a good thing, and you should expect your years of professional experience to affect, clarify, and expand the details of your beliefs. As stated earlier, your advocacy for the profession must always be linked to your personal beliefs and aspirations for teaching, and these beliefs will most certainly be reshaped throughout your professional career.

It is natural for you to feel like you expended a lot of time, brainpower, and energy writing your philosophy of music education...you did! This exercise is not easy for many beginning teachers, and the focus required will certainly feel different than writing lesson plans or practicing your musicianship skills. Pause at this point and reflect upon the importance of knowing *why you teach*; you will be aided and guided by these ideas for years to come. Some people will put their philosophy away for a while and not think about it, while others will continue to refine the ideas in their mind or even on paper. The best time to re-read your philosophy is when you are a practicing teacher who is faced with tough decisions such as trimming a music budget or realigning or cutting classes within your curriculum. You will need to remember what you believe, what you are willing to stand up for, and why music is important to every student. Knowing who you are and what you believe is essential to making good decisions. Congratulations to you for taking this important step in your professional development.

Chapter Thirteen

Gender Identity in Choral Music Education

13. Gender Identity in Choral Music Education

by William Sauerland [he/they]

"Good teachers possess a capacity for connectedness. They are able to weave a complex web of connections among themselves, their subjects, and their students so that students can learn to weave a world for themselves."
~Parker Palmer

Introduction

A Wide-Angle Lens

As music teachers, we are asked to deal with a lot of different issues, from underfunded programs to overcrowded classrooms, from legal issues of copyrighted music to sorting out forms for competitions and field trips. Among our teaching duties, we are responsible for choosing repertoire, facilitating auditions, balancing a music budget, fundraising for concert attire, recruiting new members, interacting with supportive (and unsupportive) families, and many other important and menial tasks. We must not forget that vocal technique, piano skills, score study, and conducting are part of our job! If we were to formulate a list of the scenarios and situations we, as music educators, face, it might be overwhelming, especially as we consider the complex and diverse range of students and colleagues among us. It is a wonder how we do it all.

If we broaden our periphery to view the "complex web of connections" that Palmer mentions, we gain a greater awareness of the complexities that reach beyond pitches, rhythms, and musical nuance. The lens through which we view the world is only our perspective, yet we are called to understand and embrace each student as an individual, with unique life experiences, self-perceptions, identities, and diverse learning styles. The art of developing rapport and weaving connections among our students to engage them in and through our discipline is fundamental to teaching.

Critical thinking and reflection should be at the core of our profession. A deeper evaluation of teaching can unearth a "hidden curriculum" (Basow, 2004; Jackson, 1968), where our work implicitly teaches our students what is important and what is not — forms of empowerment and oppression. We might discover that our curriculum and pedagogies unintentionally reinforce stereotypes, racism, sexism, bigotry, Androcentrism, heteronormativity, and various kinds of discrimination. The way we address our students, or the way we select and teach repertoire, can reify belief systems and ideologies. Songs in the traditional choral canon, even some we have sung over and over, may fortify an oppressive or old-fashioned belief of a culture or way of life. "Music educators are so involved in the practice of music," Lamb (2010) suggests, "that reflection on what we are doing is difficult and often contradicts our practice" (p. 33). It can be complicated to see how our teaching empowers some students or ideas while oppressing others.

Investment in high-quality music-making is essential to our job, but if it deters you from the opportunity for reflection (as it frequently does in my own life), I invite you to consider these questions:

1. How does my pedagogy imitate the way I was taught and/or the learning styles of my students?
2. How does my choral repertoire mirror my musical interests and/or my students' interests?
3. What music is deemed worthy for my students, school, and community? (Why and by whom?)
4. How do I maintain or abate stereotypes and cultural expectations through repertoire, curriculum, and pedagogy?
5. How do I seek student input for curricular design and repertoire selection?
6. How does my teaching evolve with modern views and emerging technologies?
7. What do I prioritize: student experience or musical output?
8. How do I judge the success of my choir(s) and who gets to judge its outcomes?
9. How do I consider the individual identities and life experiences of my students?
10. How does my teaching foster access and belonging for a diverse range of students?

These questions endeavor to align Lamb's call for reflection with Palmer's web of connections. They also seek to be an entry for uncovering the "hidden curriculum" within our music programs. A choral teacher's role is a taxing balance between music teaching and administration, but I welcome you to widen your lens and reflect on your teaching (or the kind of teacher you want to be). Consider the complex web of connections among your students. Contemplate the wide range of students who do (and do not) enter our learning spaces and how we might foster connectedness (or instigate disconnectedness) through our actions and words.

In starting this chapter so broadly, my goal is to elicit critical thinking and reflection — to lead with questions, not answers. The purpose of this chapter is to offer a discussion on welcoming and affirming trans(gender) and non-binary singers in choir. When I embarked on research in this field several years ago, I did so from a desire to understand my students better and to explore my own gender identity. I came to realize that the teaching of trans and non-binary singers could not live in a vacuum, nor could it be essentialized and discussed in isolation separate from a bigger examination on how we move about in our classes and rehearsals. If we, as teachers, are going to create welcoming environments for gender-diverse students, we first ought to reflect on our ways of teaching, before implementing changes. In forging stronger connections with our students and our discipline, teaching trans and non-binary students is not merely a practice of doing specific affirming acts or adopting a welcoming posture (though, this is a part of it!); it is also in the undoing of other practices and conventions that marginalize students. Reflection seems a needed exercise in the pursuit of greater access and equity for all students, regardless of gender, sex, race, ethnicity, creed, socio-economic status, or identity.

This chapter is going to examine how choral music education conventionally expects singers to fit within culturally understood definitions of female and male voices and identities. I aim to share some of the important literature in this area of choral and vocal pedagogy, and provide a basic overview of trans and non-binary vocality. Strategies for increasing access and affirmation for singers in our classes, rehearsals, and concerts will be included. Throughout this chapter, I will refer to the wider population of transgender choristers as trans and non-binary singers. It is not my intent to subdivide trans from non-binary, but to bring attention to a population of the trans community who live outside the female/male gender binary.

From Wide to Narrow: Personal Motivation

I was born on a small dairy farm in Southwest Ohio. It was apparent to me from an early age that I did not quite fit the norm of other young boys. Football, tractors, cowboy boots, and other objects and activities considered masculine did not appeal to me. I was more interested in my older sister's dolls and activities. I recall once in elementary school being referred to as a "big boy," which caused me to guffaw. As the woman apologized to me, she amended her language by referring to me as a "young man." I did not have the rhetoric at that time to explain why that made me uncomfortable. I was not offended by the descriptive words "big" or "young," but rather by the assumption I was a boy. I knew from a young age that my gender identity did not conform with the expectations of my family and community. While I faced significant bullying and intolerance throughout my schooling, I was grateful to have supportive parents, friends, and teachers. My choir teacher provided me a space to be myself. Musical experiences in choir and band enabled to me to grow and explore my identity, helping me realize a richer understanding of myself. Not all gender-diverse students have it as easy as I did.

Today, I use he/him/his and they/them/their pronouns, and I am outspoken in my attempt to redefine masculinity and in encouraging others to construct their identity based on their inner sense of self and not on expectations as determined by their communities or culture. My professional work as a singer, voice teacher, choral conductor, and researcher in trans and non-binary vocality supports my understanding in this discussion. While this chapter aims to impart specific strategies and information for welcoming and affirming trans and non-binary singers, each choral director is responsible for making decisions appropriate for their program based on their school and community. While historical and environmental contexts are important for determining curricular and practical changes, marginalizing choristers to maintain time-honored conventions because "we've always done it that way" is inexcusable. I hope that ongoing reflection in this chapter prompts further questions as we, a collective body of choral teachers, seek to better understand the nature of our teaching.

A Trans "Tipping Point"

A 2014 cover article of *Time* magazine referred to the next American civil rights movement as the "Transgender Tipping Point" (Steinmetz, 2014). In the years that have passed since that article, discussions on the rights of trans and non-binary individuals have been consistently present in the national media, from Gavin Grimm's court case around bathroom use (Steinmetz, 2015) to the ability of trans folks to serve in the military (Klimas & Bender, 2018). While an exact number of trans and non-binary people cannot be given, it is estimated that 0.5-0.6% of the United States population identifies as "transgender" (Hoffman, 2016; Steinmetz, 2014). This may not account for trans and non-binary youth or non-binary folks who do not self-identify as transgender. If you are thinking, "A half of a percent doesn't sound like a lot," it accounts for around 1.5 million people in the United States alone. You may teach a trans or non-binary student every 200 students or less. For teachers with large choral ensembles, it does not take too many years to teach well over 200 students. Let's be clear. I am not discussing the whole of the LGBTQ+ (lesbian, gay, bisexual, trans, queer) community, but rather just the "T" of that population. You will most certainly teach many more students who identify as LGBTQ+.

As trans and non-binary students "come out" earlier and earlier in middle and high school (e.g., Beemyn & Rankin, 2011; Grossman & D'Augelli, 2006), it is important for teachers to understand the role they have in accepting and embracing these students. Research indicates that high school LGBTQ+ choral students perceive their choral classroom as a safe space (Palkki & Caldwell, 2018). Palkki and Caldwell suggest that music classes, which can be taken year after year with the same teacher, cultivate a space where students feel free to exhibit traits that define them against the norm. The authors uncovered that trans and non-binary students feel less safe in high school choral programs than their gay, lesbian, and bisexual peers. A study by Silveira and Goff (2016) examined the self-reported attitudes of music teachers towards trans and non-binary students. Their findings suggest music teachers perceive themselves as being supportive of trans and non-binary students. While these findings are heartening for the acceptance and affirmation of trans and non-binary students, other studies indicate LGBTQ+ students endure considerable bullying and discrimination in school.

Though Silveira and Goff (2016) found a perceived readiness of music educators to teach trans and non-binary students, other recent research indicates teachers feel ill-equipped to work with trans and non-binary students (Luecke, 2011; Nichols, 2013; Payne & Smith, 2014). Furthermore, the Gay, Lesbian and Straight Education Network (GLSEN) conducted a study with 10,000 LGBTQ+ students, ages thirteen to twenty-one and found that schools can be a hostile environment for LGBTQ+ students (Kosciw et al, 2016). Indeed, 43.3% of the trans and non-binary participants indicated they have felt unsafe at school. This sense of insecurity or harm can lead to lower self-esteem, class attendance, and test scores. It can also cause higher levels of depression and dropout rates. Kosciw and colleagues (2016) suggest that inclusive curriculums and supportive teachers can make an important difference in changing the climate for LGBTQ+ students in school. Faculty members with best intentions for creating inclusive classrooms should understand how gender impacts educational spaces, and how cultural expectations of gender can cause trans and non-binary students to feel marginalized or discriminated.

Returning to the notion of a hidden curriculum, Basow (2004) argues that gender is a player in the implicit teaching of privilege and oppression. Basow supports O'Toole's (1998) position, which asserts, "Teachers are not immune from society's notions of gender…their pedagogy is laden with subtle messages about who is important in the classroom" (p. 13). Rands (2009) "gender complex" education beseeches teachers to give trans and non-binary learners greater consideration in curricular design and pedagogy. In music teacher education, Palkki and Sauerland (2018) employ the concept of gender complexity by suggesting teachers modify classroom language, reassess music literature selection, and thoughtfully consider student teaching placements for gender-diverse student teachers.

Gender and Identity

When you think about your identity, what comes to mind? I am a husband, son, brother, uncle, nephew, cousin, and a friend. I am a teacher, singer, conductor, and scholar. I have or will be many other identities in my life. Gender is often a central part of one's identity. It is an indication of how you dress, fix your hair, and what kind of bag or purse you carry. Gender (how we experience and perceive it) influences our teaching and interactions with one another.

Gender is a cultural construct, often based on sex categorization, which is assigned intrauterine or at birth (Hausman, 2001). Sex categorization, is primarily based on body parts (genitalia), though chromosomes and hormones are a component of a body's sex. Children born intersex do not fit within the binary male/female paradigm as their sex categorization does not match the standard profile of male or female bodies. We see expectations of gender placed on a child even before birth based on the sex of the fetus. Gender reveal parties with blue or pink decorations suggest children assigned female at birth are supposed to like pink and dolls, while their counterparts are expected to like blue and toy trucks. As a socially constructed concept, gender imposes hegemonic influences on roles, expectations, and behaviors (Halberstam, 1994; West & Zimmerman, 1987). These expectations carry on much beyond childhood and they permeate all aspects of culture and education (Bornstein, 1998).

Gender is the inner identity of a person (Wilchins, 2002), which is expressed through visible cues of one's body or behaviors, such as attire, hairstyle, mannerisms, and voice. *Gender identity* is a term related to the inner compass of one's sense of self, whereas *gender expression* is how an individual articulates and displays their gender. For an individual assigned female at birth who feels comfortable within a feminine identity, the gender terminology is *cisgender,* meaning her sex categorization and gender identity are the same. Individuals who do not have congruent gender and sex categorization may identify as trans or non-binary.

Defining Trans and Non-Binary

If an individual feels the gender they were assigned at birth is incongruent with their authentic gender identity, they might identify as *trans* or *transgender* (Nagoshi & Brzuzy, 2010). Trans is an umbrella term for all folks who identify as non-cisgender. The term transgender stems from the concept of a person transitioning from the assigned gender to the one that feels authentic to their sense of self. In general, a trans woman is a woman who was assigned male at birth. In older articles, you might see a trans woman referred to as *MtF*, or male-to-female, which problematically emphasizes the assigned sex at birth. More recently, the acronym *AMAB* is being employed, to signify the individual was "assigned male at birth." Likewise, a trans man is a man who was assigned female at birth (*FtM*, female-to-male, or *AFAB*, assigned female at birth, is seen in some literature). Some people who identify as trans want to be publicly acknowledged as trans, while others may not wish their trans status to be a marker of their identity.

Not all folks who identify as trans wish to be known as female or male. Some individuals do not fit within the gender binary at all. People who identify as *non-binary* or *gender nonconforming* may see gender as fluid, living neither as male nor female, as both, or as a third gender, depending how they see themselves (Roen, 2001). There seems to be an intentional *in-betweeness* for some non-binary individuals. They may express their identity in ways seen as gender neutral or androgynous. Some individuals who identify as non-binary may use *ze/hir* for pronouns or *they/them/their* in a singular form (Andrews, 2017). Other individuals might craft pronouns that best fit their identity.

If you are unfamiliar with trans and non-binary identity, or are new to the uncoupling of sex categorization and gender, the above information can take time to process. I find it challenging to write a definition for trans and non-binary in the same way I find it unfeasible to define maleness or femaleness. Concepts of gender and identity are personal. Attempting to define a diverse population of trans and non-binary people is probably imprudent. I encourage everyone to maintain an open and adaptable notion when working to define gender and identity.

While information on sexuality is not the purpose of this chapter, it should be noted that gender, sex categorization, and sexuality are intertwined (Nagoshi, Brzuzy, & Terrell, 2012). Sexuality, or sexual orientation, concerns the physical and/or romantic attractions (or lack thereof) one individual feels for another. A man who is primarily physically and/or romantically attracted to another man is gay; likewise, a woman who is primarily attracted to other women is a lesbian. Individuals who are physically and/or romantically attracted to people independent of their gender or sex category might be bisexual or pansexual. Sexuality, like gender, is fluid and ever-expanding. Labels related to gender or sexuality should not be imposed upon by other people; each person is empowered to define their identity as it feels appropriate for them.

The Gender Unicorn (Figure 1) is an image created by Trans Student Education Resources (transstudents.com) to illustrate five concepts: 1. gender identity, 2. gender expression, 3. sex assigned at birth, 4. physical attraction, and 5. romantic attraction. An interactive version is available on their website (transstudents.com/ gender), which enables a person to include their name and pronouns, in addition to sliding a marker along the scales below each category.

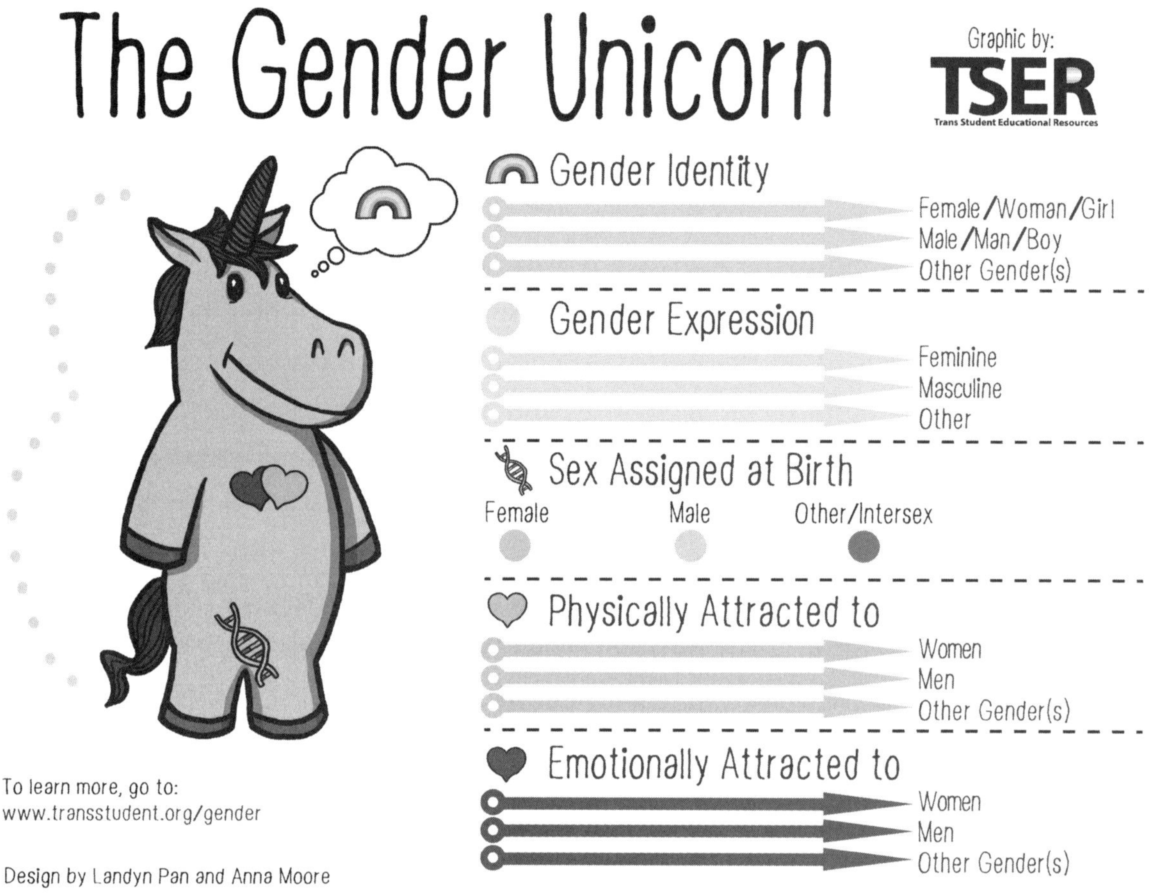

Figure 1: The Gender Unicorn illustrates the connections between gender identity, expression, sex categorization, and sexuality.

Making assumptions of gender or sex categorization based on someone's outward appearance can cause *gender dysphoria*, a feeling of discomfort or distress due to being misgendered or referred to by the wrong gender. Employing a tool like The Gender Unicorn cultivates an environment where we allow people to name their gender and sexuality without judgment or assumptions.

Though I do not want to disseminate non-inclusive language, I think it is pertinent to be clear on language deemed offensive. Never is a person *transgendered*, which connotes that a trans identity has been forced upon them. *Transsexual* is historically more for a person who modifies their body through surgery to align their sex categorization with their gender. Though the term transsexual is not seen as offensive by all, a person's physical body should be of little concern unless you interact with the individual on a more intimate level. It is a good rule of thumb to avoid referring to someone as transsexual, unless they have specifically requested it. The word *transvestite* is generally an outdated word (used frequently in the movie *The Rocky Horror Picture Show*) to intimate a person dresses as the opposite gender to fulfill sexual desires. Other words such as tranny, crossdresser, fag, or dyke are generally considered less appropriate, though you might still hear them used vernacularly. As I offered before, all words corresponding to gender or sexuality are for an individual to use for or about themselves. Some people use or reclaim a word or idiom because it is important to their lived experience. It is prudent to use words with good intentions and to stay up to date on evolving language.

Transphobia is the dislike, fear, or prejudice of trans people and can appear in obvious and covert ways. Outward harassment and denial of basic human rights for trans and non-binary folks is an obvious manifestation of transphobia. In educational or community spaces, transphobia appears less conspicuously when trans and non-binary individuals are not welcomed and affirmed. Finally, the oppression of women, trans or otherwise, is commonly known as *sexism.* Rands (2009) suggests *gender oppression* is a more appropriate term, as the oppression is based on gender, not sex categorization.

Vocal Identity

An aspect of identity sometimes overlooked is one's relationship with their voice. Andrews (1986) advocates, "Voice is a very important part of the self-concept, and our identity is projected through our voices" (p. 3). In singing and speaking, our voice reveals information about us to the outside world, beyond the content we mean to impart. For many adults, it informs others of our *sex categorization* based on pitch range. When I speak on the phone, an individual on the other end can usually discern I was assigned male at birth. The voice is a product of our biology. Titze (1994) reported that the average length of the vocal folds for an adult assigned male at birth is between 17.5 and 25 millimeters. For adult humans assigned female at birth, the average vocal fold length is 12.5 to 17 millimeters. Based on vocal fold length and thickness, speaking voices phonate at faster or slower frequencies, which we discern as being higher or lower. The pitch range of each person is individualistic and also dependent on habitual use and other vocal patterns. Research on trans and non-binary singers indicates the pitch range of the voice is an important part of gender expression for some individuals, but not important for others (Palkki, 2016; Sauerland, 2018a).

An examination of voice identity reveals that trans and non-binary singers are not all the same in how they perceive their voice or how it signifies (or doesn't signify) their gender identity. Palkki (2017) shares:

> Some trans singers may revel in the fact that their voice does not match society's notions of how their voice should sound. Some trans people, however, consider the voice a vital way that they "do" their gender in society. Choral music educators can determine through conversation the level of connection, if any, between a trans student's voice and gender identity (p. 25).

I am also mindful that words we use to describe voices such as high/low and masculine/feminine are problematic as they are based on personal perception in comparison to other voices. In spite of Titze's reporting of vocal fold length, there are countless examples of high-sounding "male" voices and low-sounding "female" voices. The vocal ranges of Nina Simone or Bea Arthur provide good examples of low-sounding women's voices. Likewise, the vocal stylings of Phillipe Jaroussky or Freddie Mercury show that not all male singers phonate in the tenor or bass range exclusively. If a trans women has a bass-baritone range, we should describe her voice as feminine, because she is feminine. Likewise, we should not describe a male countertenor's voice as feminine, nor a cisgender female tenor's voice as masculine simply because she sings tenor. Sims (2017a) argues, "A voice cannot be designated as male or female if we hope to change our binary way of thinking" (p. 280). Many texts on vocal pedagogy refer to "female" voices for bodies assigned female at birth and "male" voices for bodies assigned male at birth (McKinney, 1994; Miller, 1996). When we begin to consider trans and non-binary singers in music education, these gendered descriptors seem inadequate.

Vocal Considerations for Trans and Non-Binary Singers

The examination of vocal pedagogy for trans and non-binary singers is an emerging field. A few studies have begun to look at teaching gender-diverse singers (Constansis, 2008; Manternach, 2017; Manternach, Chipman, Rainero, & Stave, 2017; Sauerland, 2018a; Sims, 2017a; Sims, 2017b). This scholarship is just the start to a burgeoning area of study. This next section will provide an outline of the vocal changes some trans and non-binary people undergo as part of their transition. Vocal pedagogy for teaching trans women, trans men, non-binary singers, and adolescent students will be discussed.

Concerning Physical Changes

As part of a person's transition, some people modify their gender expression by changing their clothes, hair, or other outward traits. Some trans or non-binary people seek physical modifications through surgery and hormone therapies; others do not. Physically changing one's body might include surgical procedures to modify the chest, genitalia, or facial features. Alterations of the organs associated with sex categorization is known as *sex reassignment surgery*. As a choral teacher, it is unlikely you will need detailed information on sex reassignment surgery. Asking a person about their physical bodies is wildly inappropriate and vulgar. We should, however, be attentive to arranging appropriate private spaces backstage for costume/concert attire changing.

Another component to physical change is called *hormone replacement therapy* (HRT). Physical changes in a person's body hair and muscle mass are common due to HRT. Hormone replacement therapy typically involves trans women taking estrogen. An adolescent trans female might take a hormone blocker to stop the onset of puberty. If engaging in HRT, trans men take testosterone, otherwise known as androgen therapy. The administration of testosterone causes the vocal folds to increase in size, resulting in a lowering of the pitch range. The effects of HRT on singing will be discussed in further detail.

In respect to each person's body, we should be conscientious when making comments. A trans man (assigned female at birth) might be standing in a manner that minimizes his chest size. Though this physical alignment might not be optimal for breath support, forcing him to stand in a way that brings his chest forward is a probable cause of gender dysphoria. I think it is prudent to think about how our words and expectations impact others, especially when it comes to other people's bodies.

Trans Women Voices

Due to puberty during adolescence, the vocal folds of an adult trans woman have grown in length and thickness as consistent with a body assigned male at birth. The naturally produced testosterone at puberty causes an increase in the size of the larynx, causing the thyroid notch (also known as the Adam's apple) to protrude outward. While a trans woman may take estrogen to decrease overall body hair or other associated physical attributes, the vocal folds and larynx will experience little change from the estrogen. Lessley (2017) reports that some trans women experience change in vocal timbre from estrogen by a thickening of the mucous membrane. The author asserts:

> Depending on the balance and doses of the hormones involved in the student's hormone replacement therapy, she may be experiencing any number of symptoms that may feel like her voice is changing. However, these are not permanent changes, and they will only affect the quality of the voice, not the pitch (p. 69).

Since pitch-raising of the vocal range through hormone therapy is not viable, if a trans woman wishes to be an alto or soprano, exercises might be given to help foster development of the head register.

Kozan (2012) and Lessley (2017) provide insight on the vocal development of trans women. Vocal exercises using a semi-occluded vocal tract, such as [ð] as in "they," [v] as in "victory," or [z] as in "zoo" have been found useful. Lip buzz and rolled [r] similarly foster a released phonation. Three- to five-tone descending scales beginning in the lower-middle range are an effective starting place. If you are working with a singer one on one or working with a group of singers in preparation for solo repertoire, I advocate for the following suggestions:

1. Each voice is different, and so it is necessary to listen carefully, not just to the singer's instrument, but to their goals in singing.
2. Avoid gendered words such as "falsetto" when working in the upper range. While falsetto may seem like standard jargon, it tends to be connoted with masculine voices, and thus, could cause the singer uneasiness. Phrases such as "upper range," "head voice," or "upper register" will likely suffice.
3. When sharing models of singers, look for other trans women singers such as:
    a. Breanna Sinclairé, mezzo-soprano
    b. Lucia Lucas, baritone
    c. Veronica Klaus, chanteuse

    Showing trans women a video of a countertenor might be beneficial to illustrate what is vocally possible in the upper register, but I would be highly sensitive to showing them a male singer as an example of their potential sound.
4. When selecting repertoire, offer a wide range of pieces or allow her to choose something for herself with your approval. Songs that seem innocuous might be laden with gender. Jointly choosing repertoire engages the student and assures she is singing something that aligns with her identity and vocal goals.

While it is beyond the scope of this chapter to offer greater insight to studio voice teaching, additional resources listed at the end of the chapter will provide further reading.

Some trans women might seek what is called voice "feminization" from a speech-language pathologist. Many studies discuss voice feminization, which may include 1. making the speaking voice breathier (à la Marilyn Monroe), 2. making the intonation of the voice sound higher at the end of sentences (known as "uptalk" or "upspeak"), and 3. increasing the baseline pitch of the speaking voice (aka, the fundamental frequency) to be perceived higher. It is important to note that these studies are not designed for singers. These vocal goals or practices do not cover the full extent of voice therapy for trans women.

In some cases, a trans woman might undergo vocal surgery to raise her pitch frequency, but data indicates the results are inconclusive (Gross, 1999). Personally, I do not recommend vocal surgery for a singer until more research verifies the benefits. Trans women seeking voice modification from a speech-language pathologist or vocal coach would benefit from working with a professional who has specific training in working with trans and non-binary individuals.

It is important that we create choral environments where singing in the tenor-bass range is not a place just for men. Palkki's study (2016) on the experiences of trans singers in the high school choral setting suggests some trans women are proud to sing tenor or bass, feeling no need to adjust their voices to match the cultural expectations of a "feminine" timbre. A participant in Palkki's study disclosed, "I'm a girl and I'm a bass and I own that" (p. 138). The more we de-gender our language and perceptions around voices, the easier it might be for trans women to sing in whatever range is most comfortable for them – from low bass to high soprano.

Trans Men Voices

Not all trans men engage in voice modification, but when an adult trans man seeks to lower his voice, he is given testosterone. Over time, the vocal folds thicken, but do not typically lengthen. A lower range is commonly produced, enabling him to sing tenor, baritone, or bass. It is valuable to understand that every person's body will experience physical changes from the testosterone differently. The physical modification will be dependent on the dosage of the testosterone, age of the individual, and the organic composition of their body. Constansis (2008) found in studying his own vocal change that a smaller dosage of testosterone might allow for the voice to modify more gradually. Though a smaller dosage might be appropriate for some people, Sauerland (2018a) observed that a lower dosage of testosterone could increase dysphoria for a person wanting to see changes more rapidly. There is a need for scientifically driven research in this area.

While it is not wholly analogous to compare the vocal change of an adult trans man to the *cambiata* voice of a child, there are similarities; the voice of a pre-pubescent boy is difficult to predict in terms of when and how it will change, and this can also prove to be true with a trans man at the onset of hormone therapy. Some trans men experience a gradual and easy lowering of their vocal range, while others have difficult vocal transitions. Some singers seem to lose access of the head voice indefinitely, while others consistently maintain the upper range or regain it in time. In general, the first six to twelve months is vocally the most difficult. The vocal folds are in the initial stage of thickening, which can cause hoarseness, breathiness, and fatigue. For a singer, this can be challenging because he might one day be singing comfortably above middle C, and within a few weeks, have little treble range at all.

Research also indicates that age plays a factor in voice modification. An older singer whose larynx, made of cartilage, has become less pliable over time might find the vocal change to be more challenging. Beginning testosterone at a younger age seems to facilitate an easier transition, however, a word of caution: there is limited research on the long-term effects of androgen therapy on the body. Pragmatically speaking, once the voice change has taken place, the modification cannot be undone. A person should be certain of their desire for a lower range before embarking on androgen therapy.

You May Like This

Trans Men Singers - Adrian

The vocal pedagogy of a trans man is not severely different from teaching any singer in the tenor-bass range. Constansis (2008), Sims (2017a; 2017b), and Sauerland (2018a) provide more substantial information with regards to vocal development and repertoire. The four recommendations above for teaching trans women pertain to trans men too. There are many trans masculine singers to show students as models.

1. Adrian Angelico, mezzo-soprano
2. Holden Madagame, tenor
3. Lucas Silveira, singer-songwriter

As stated above, every person's voice is different, and thus, a voice teacher must enter each voice lesson as a learner in the process of teaching.

When one of your students starts androgen therapy, be prepared for their voice to become unsteady and initially decrease in range. It is important to keep the singer singing. Extra care and support from a teacher to boost confidence and self-esteem is valuable. Providing exercises that promote breath support and a vibrant tone is crucial. A choral director or voice teacher can help safeguard the singer from pushing into their lower range as it develops. If the student was a singer before the onset of testosterone, it is possible that old habits from singing soprano or alto will creep into their emerging lower voice. Vocal exercises on [u] can nurture a lower laryngeal position. Employing smaller intervals in exercises will also help keep the voice smooth and connected. Figure 2 shows an exercise built on minor thirds.

Figure 2: Stacked minor thirds for range development

Unlike a standard arpeggio, the exercise above does not ask the singer to vocalize over a series of different intervals. Indeed, for range development, an additional minor 3rd could be added to the bottom and/or top of each musical figure to increase the overall range of the exercise. Exercises constructed from whole tone or pentatonic scales are similarly beneficial in being able to increase the range by smaller intervals.

In working with trans male singers, a teacher should also be mindful that some trans men may bind their chests to reduce chest size. Some binders cover only the top half of the torso, while others cover the chest and belly. If possible, a top-only binder is preferable, as this will enable more dynamic breathing. Medical bandages or tape are not recommended for binding, as they can be harmful to the body when worn consistently. It is usually not appropriate to ask a student if they bind their chest, so be thoughtful with your language about posture and intercostal breathing. If you have a strong rapport with the student, they might offer personal information, but asking is intrusive.

Non-Binary Singers

The joy in working with a non-binary singer comes in allowing the individual to be the guide of their vocal development. A non-binary person might be assigned male, female, or intersex at birth, but intentionally living outside or in-between the female/male binary. Other non-binary people may see gender as fluid, living as both male and female or as a third gender. Regarding vocal concerns, non-binary singers might desire a bass or treble range, or a gender-neutral or androgynous voice. As a voice teacher or choral director, it is our obligation to see that the individual sings in a manner that enables their authentic voice to flourish, while simultaneously providing information on breath support, resonance, and articulation so their voice stays healthy and supple.

While knowledge of vocal pedagogy is paramount for teaching any kind of singer, there are a few paradigms to consider when teaching a non-binary singer:

1. If a singer is assigned female at birth but wishes to sing in the tenor or bass range without taking testosterone, the teacher needs to thoughtfully

offer range-lowering exercises, while simultaneously abating the singer from "pushing" into a bass clef range unsuitable for their instrument. Semi-occluded exercises, as mentioned above, might help a singer to find a comfortable lower range. Sliding on descending scales or intervals fosters movement into the lower range. Having a sensitive and honest conversation about range is pertinent to help set appropriate expectations.

2. Since the singer might not identify as male or female, choosing traditional repertoire might be problematic. While I have heard the argument that art songs transcend gender, this opinion might not be the perspective of a non-binary singer. Allowing them to select their repertoire or locating pieces that permit minor lyric changes are excellent options.
3. When teaching a trans or non-binary singer, changing the key of a song is advantageous to best fit their voice. Should an alto-range singer wish to sing a tenor solo, transposing the piece up a little bit might make the repertoire possible. Though this might not fit the expectations of an opera or musical theatre audition, for solo recitals, enabling a singer to present repertoire that makes them feel confident is the overriding intention.
4. A non-binary singer might not wish to be categorized as a traditional voice part (soprano, alto, tenor, bass), as these words are encumbered with gender stereotypes. Thinking of them as a "vocalist" or "singer" might be sufficient, and allowing them to sing a variety of repertoire focusing on different ranges could be a way for them to explore and build confidence in their voice.

A participant in my research shared that throughout their life, they had frequently been made to feel inadequate in voice lessons and choir. Even though they outwardly presented feminine at times, they were not interested in singing the repertoire they were assigned. They told me, "I was made to feel like I wasn't good enough, especially when it came to the types of music they wanted me to sing because it was always very hyper-feminine and just stuff that I couldn't really relate to" (Sauerland, 2018a, p. 124). As music educators, we should acknowledge that gender expression, or the way someone dresses or carries themselves, does not necessarily reflect their feelings or experiences of their inner self. Allowing all students, whether they present as trans or non-binary or cisgender, to guide their vocal practice and repertoire selection is advisable.

Trans Youth

Unfortunately, there is very little research on trans and non-binary youth singers. A young trans woman might take a hormone blocker to stop the onset of testosterone at puberty, which will enable her body to develop in a manner like an individual assigned female at birth. In speech-language pathology, Hancock and Helenius (2012) investigated adolescent trans female voices. For a trans man, if testosterone is administered as a teenager, the voice might develop exactly as it would in a natal male body. Following the tenets of vocal pedagogy outlined above provides a starting place for working with trans youth singers.

Teachers should be aware that trans youth are a vulnerable population. Supportive parents can make a tremendous difference, but sometimes a trans or non-binary teen is not supported by their families. Recognize that a young person might want to explore their vocal potential while not being fully "out" to you or their community. Having the capacity to enable the student to sing as their heart tells them to might be more beneficial than developing *bel canto* technique. I am not expecting a voice teacher or choral director to be a therapist, but creating a space where young people can be themselves is imperative.

As a choral conductor, you are not expected to be an expert in vocal technique, but having an awareness of the connection between vocal identity and gender can help guide the practices and pedagogies imparted in the classroom. Assisting a trans man to find comfort in his new lowering voice, or allowing a trans woman to access her upper range (or ensuring she is welcome to sing tenor or bass), is an emotional and rewarding experience. Empowering a person to sing in a section that makes them feel like their voice matters is key in creating access and belonging. Listening to the student's perspective and acknowledging their gender identity alongside their vocal abilities is useful when working with all singers, not only trans and non-binary musicians.

Creating Access and Belonging

Rands (2009) affirms that "students learn a great deal about gender in the educational system" (p. 242). As discussed before, gender expectations are apparent in music and music education. As an example of how gender norms are reified in music education, two recently published songbooks for young singers uphold stereotypes. One book for "young women" includes songs of flowers and lullabies, while a similar collection for "young men" contain songs about ships and young ladies (Boytim, 2008a; Boytim, 2008b). Not only do these books reinforce heteronormativity, they emphasize gender expectations of these young singers. In my experience, repertoire for "men's" and "women's" choruses often follow a similar trajectory.

Sometimes discourse on trans and non-binary people gets named as "the issues of transgender students," when instead it should be framed as, "the issues caused by transphobia and gender oppression." We should be asking: how do our historic (and sometimes beloved) traditions in choral music cause the marginalization and discrimination of trans and non-binary singers? It is useful to acknowledge that the issues experienced by trans and non-binary students do not belong to them. The issues belong to us, as educators, who create and uphold practices and policies that marginalize and discriminate. Several articles within the last two years have addressed the needs of trans and non-binary singers in the choral classroom (Agha, 2017; Miller, 2016; Palkki, 2017; Rastin, 2016; Sauerland, 2018b.) A version of the next section of this chapter originally appeared in an article I wrote for VOICE*Prints* in May-June 2018 called "Trans Singers Matter: Gender Inclusive Considerations for Choirs." These six considerations towards inclusion draw specific attention on language, names and pronouns, voice assignment, repertoire selection, concert concerns, and advocacy.

Six Considerations Towards Inclusion

Language Matters

It is imperative that we examine our language and ensure it is welcoming for all. I encourage everyone to avoid saying "ladies and gentlemen" or "boys and girls" or intentionally gendering any section of the chorus. If you want the tenors and basses to sing, say "tenors and basses," don't say "men." I acknowledge that traditional voice part names (soprano, alto, tenor, bass) are not wholly unfettered from gender implications, but using them is an improvement from more highly gendered words, such as calling all sopranos and alto "ladies." One chorus in the Pacific Northwest has done away with the custom monikers, referring to each part as Voice I, Voice II, Voice III, and Voice IV. I know it is asking a lot to dismantle traditions in our own field, but even if we cannot entirely change the entrenched language, at least we can be aware of the gender implications.

Though the phrase "guys" has become a colloquial word meaning "everyone," using it as such is a ripe example of Androcentrism inherent in our language. If calling a mixed group of people "girls" or "gals" is not widely practiced or considered appropriate, nor should "guys." Using

Androcentric language is oppressive, even if intentions are harmless. Instead, say, "everybody," "folks," "friends," "colleagues," "students," or "singers." Anything non-gendered is usually welcoming for all individuals. Stopping the use of "guys" is a hard habit to break, and I am not suggesting we all become language police, but if we model inclusive language, we provide an example to those around us.

I encourage every choir to adopt an open and affirming policy statement. All members of your ensemble should read, understand, and abide by a declaration that all individuals are welcomed and affirmed in your ensemble. Guest performers and clinicians should be sent this statement, providing them the appropriate framework for working with your ensemble. Being proactive and transparent with a statement of affirmation helps assuage issues from developing. Last, but not least, posting a safe space sign shows LGBTQ+ students they are accepted and welcomed. These signs are free and available online.

Names and Pronouns Matter

If a person has selected a name for themselves different from what appears on their birth certificate (or other legal documentation), it is important we use the name they have chosen, instead of the name chosen for them. Names and pronouns are often entrenched with gender implications. An official class roster might show the birth names of students, but if the student goes by Sarah and uses she/her pronouns, use her chosen name and pronouns. Keep the other name on the roster private; do not share it with other students. On the first day of class, allow each student to introduce themselves to avoid calling names from the roster; doing so would unintentionally expose Sarah as trans or non-binary. When introducing yourself, give your name and pronouns to signify your gender (and your approval for others to give their own, if they desire). You might also start each semester with an information sheet filled out by each student, where names and pronouns can be included. I avoid asking all students to publicly give their pronouns, as this might cause a student to "out" or "closet" themselves before they are prepared. Should you discover an incongruence on your roster from how a student identifies, privately speak to the student to ensure you have the correct student in class. The student will likely know the name on the roster is different, and they may appreciate your sensitive handling of the concern. If they are unaware of the incongruence, you might offer to serve as an advocate and get the official course roster updated. Partner with your administration to have school documents reflect the chosen name and pronouns of the student.

In contacting parents, legal guardians, and family members, you will need to know if the student is "out" at home. This can be highly sensitive information. If the student uses their birth name at home, you must be aware of this before e-mailing or speaking with family members. It is important to establish rapport with each singer so that they are comfortable talking to you.

Concert programs are also a matter of attention. Ask all students how they would like their name to appear in the program or if they want it to appear. Listing singers alphabetically, instead of by section, will avoid gender implications, in case a student is uncomfortable with a public acknowledgment of their voice part. This might seem overly considerate, but if a trans woman is listed as a bass in the program, it could cause her discomfort or embarrassment if she is not publicly out as trans with acquaintances and the general audience.

We should also consider the implication of language in an ensemble's name. If an ensemble is called "Generic High School Women's Chorus," this chorus should allow all women to sing in the ensemble, including those who sing tenor or bass. Otherwise, it should be called a treble choir, and thus, open to all treble voices. A men's chorus should be available to all men, including male sopranos and altos, or it would be more appropriate to call it a bass clef choir or tenor-bass ensemble. The phrase "treble choir" is a fine alternative for "women's choir," but our language does not have a good word alternative for choruses that sing in the tenor and bass range. It is increasingly popular for choruses to create ensemble names based on their location or school mascot. I think this is a great way to bring distinction to your ensemble, while avoiding the gendered-name issue.

From personal experience, the changing of an ensemble name is difficult if it is a historic demarcation. For community choruses, this can be particularly challenging as the chorus name might have been determined by distinguished founders or a part of local history. In the United States, "women's chorus" has been a safe space for women to connect and unify their voices in song. Similarly, many LGBTQ+ choruses use descriptors in their name as a form of awareness and advocacy work. For these ensembles, changing the names is akin to changing the very purpose of its existence. Nevertheless, I encourage ensembles to move beyond a "how it's always been" mindset to a vision with greater inclusivity for trans and non-binary singers. An outside organizer or mediator can be an enormous support in the facilitation of a name change process. A name-change facilitator will lessen the strain on the conductor or music director.

Voice Assignment Matters

The above discussion on trans voice modifications gives some context to how teaching a trans or non-binary singer might be distinctive. Nevertheless, research overall indicates there are many more similarities than differences (Lessley, 2017; Sauerland, 2018a). I believe one of the more difficult aspects of choral teaching is assigning voice parts to each singer. Not only does it take time at the beginning of a rehearsal period, it can be nerve-wracking for some members to sing a solo for you, if it is a non-auditioned ensemble. Moreover, as has been discussed earlier in the chapter, some singers hold a sense of identity in the voice part they have customarily sung. Switching a soprano to the alto part might be problematic if they have always seen themselves as a soprano. As part of my voice-assignment process, I always ask singers where they feel their voice is best suited. Hopefully, the perception of their voice and their physiological range is similar. If not, a personal conversation takes place explaining how their voice would be more comfortable singing in another section. It is also useful to have a chart showing the standard vocal ranges of each section of a choir and where their voice corresponds on the musical staff. This might help a singer understand that your decision to have them sing alto or tenor is not based on their gender, but on a musical construct.

If a trans man is beginning testosterone, remember that his voice might be developing at a rate determined by the hormone dosage and his biology. Check in with him during the transition to ensure he is singing in the range that best suits his current abilities. If range is an issue, Palkki (2017) suggests allowing the singer to switch parts during a song as necessary. This could be an excellent option for a trans woman who wishes to sing alto, but is unable to maintain the tessitura or comfortably phonate the higher pitches.

For many singers, the choral conductor is the only voice teacher they will ever have, so craft exercises that enable singers to build efficient habitual use. Do not skip over or go through the motions when warming up your ensemble. Doscher (1994) recommends no less than a ten-minute warm up at the beginning of each rehearsal. Consider it a group voice lesson, and supplement the experience with a cool-down exercise at the end of rehearsal to alleviate tension that may have built up.

Repertoire Matters

The repertoire we give our singers is not only the sustenance for building great choral artistry, it is also a reflection of the community and culture of our chorus. For an ensemble not specifically designed for a single style of music (i.e., madrigals or jazz music), it is vital to choose repertoire that reflects a wide variety of genres. Music selected for an entertaining and balanced concert that pedagogically benefits the ensemble is an important element in building or maintaining a strong choral program. As it is our responsibility as choral conductors to preclude repertoire that propagandizes racism and xenophobia, it is also our job to select music that avoids misogyny, sexism, gender oppression, and transphobia. There are too many great choral pieces in existence for us to select songs that uphold gender roles.

Though there is nothing wrong in programming traditional choral music, diversifying concert repertoire by selecting pieces of underrepresented composers can add greater meaning to a student's experience. Allsup (2010) argues, "We needn't fear a movement *away* from traditions we love; rather freedom creates the possibility of new unions, new inductees, and new encounters" (p. 229). As this pertains to choral literature selection, consider the purpose of each piece and the value it brings to your ensemble in learning not merely the rhythms and pitches, but the context and history of its authors. Discussing the significance of each piece can help students connect to the music as well as to each other. The texts we ask singers to perform deserve as much consideration as the style of the composition. Though it takes rehearsal time to facilitate these important discussions, students feel empowered and motivated by having the opportunity to discuss the repertoire apart from dynamic marks and other musical nuances.

One practice I have found constructive is encouraging my students to suggest repertoire. Though not every piece can be included in an upcoming concert, and others are unsuitable for various reasons, the opportunity to submit pieces for consideration can foster student motivation and connection to the concert programs. You might also affix a drop box somewhere near the rehearsal space where students can offer names of pieces.

Concert Matters

Whether you direct a church or show choir, think about how the attire you ask singers to wear becomes a signifier of their identity. If you choose to have all singers appear in a uniform choral dress or tuxedo, let each singer decide for themselves which to wear. Alternatively, you might allow each singer to select their own outfit entirely. When I did away with the choral dresses and tuxedos as a high school teacher, I provided time in class for the students to discuss and agree on their performance apparel. The students chose to wear formal "concert black" with a "splash" of a single color. This decision not only made my trans and non-binary students more comfortable, everybody felt more at ease in performance. The concert dresses and tuxedos were still available for use, but I did not force anyone to wear them. I also purchased additional black shirts and trousers for students needing to borrow clothing items.

If your school administration, board of directors, or booster club has spent a lot of money on concert uniforms in recent history, explain the importance of changing the performance etiquette and why it supports the long-term sustainability of the ensemble. The money raised to buy concert uniforms can be repurposed or used to build a wardrobe of gender-neutral clothes.

In addition to concert attire, we should also think about riser or stage formations. If you have students arranged by section, it would be prudent to allow female tenors or basses, or male sopranos or altos, to stand on the end of a section to be less conspicuous on stage. Though some students will be comfortable no matter the arrangement, other students might appreciate your sensitivity to the matter.

Advocacy Matters

Not only should we serve as advocates for trans and non-binary singers within our own ensembles and institutions, we should take note of the practices and policies of arts organizations in our communities. If you observe that the local theatre company produces transphobic shows or only honors traditional casting that reinforces gender roles, sensitively approach the organization with your concerns or stop sending singers to audition for their shows. If the local church that hosts your annual choral festival condones transphobia, find another venue. It will benefit you and your singers to know of open and affirming organizations in your area. Also, be aware of the behaviors and policies of state- and county-wide music honor ensembles and competitions that prohibit the participation of trans and non-binary singers in their musical events.

Part of being an advocate is staying informed on global and local issues. While we might look to our trans and non-binary students for guidance in crafting affirming policies and practices for our choirs, we must not use them as the authority on concerns or issues pertaining to the trans and non-binary population. As any woman or man is not the fount of information pertaining to male or female concerns, nor should we expect our gender-diverse students to be our primary source of information for learning about the trans and non-binary community. It is our role as teachers to practice cultural competency.

RECAPITULATION

Fostering Dialogue and Reflection

Reading about teaching trans and non-binary singers provides a foundation for the implementation of affirmative practices and pedagogies. An important step in moving forward is dialoguing and reflecting on the tenets of this chapter. Practicing the language and becoming comfortable in talking about gender in a non-binary way is a component to creating access and belonging for gender diverse students. Here are four activities to help facilitate additional consideration:

1. In a small group or on your own, select repertoire for a fictitious choral concert, consisting of ten to twelve songs. Analyze the text of the pieces. Is there an overarching theme? How will the texts help the students connect to the music? Do any of the pieces reinforce gender stereotypes? What explicit and implicit messages are found in the selected repertoire? Who is represented in the music? How does your repertoire signify that all students, regardless of gender, race, or creed, belong in your ensemble?
2. Write an affirmation policy for your school or choir. What should be included? How explicit must it be? What language best suits your community or the dominant culture of the area you live or wish to teach?
3. Consider the following scenarios. What should you do in each case below? How might you best address it in your community?
   a. A trans man in your choir asks to have his chosen name in an upcoming concert program (instead of his name assigned at birth), even though his parents do not recognize or use his chosen name.
   b. A trans woman wants to sing alto, even though the easiest and most beautiful part of her vocal range is E4 (above middle C) to B3.
   c. A cisgender female student asks to sing tenor.
   d. A non-binary student is uncomfortable singing any songs from a male or female perspective.
   e. You are interested in starting a choral festival for tenor and bass voices. What do you call it?
   f. An upcoming choral overnight trip means you need to organize

room assignments for your students. A trans woman wants to be housed with other women in the ensemble, but you worry parent chaperones will find it inappropriate.

g. Your school does not have an institution-wide affirmation policy, but you believe it is important to include one in your classes.
h. One student is continually bullied for being non-binary, but does not want the transphobic students to be disciplined for fear it will incite more mistreatment outside of school.

4. Return to the reflective questions at the beginning of the chapter. Reconsider them. How have your responses changed, if at all? How does creating access and belonging for trans and non-binary students change the way we, as choral music educators, should respond to those prompts?

Conclusion

During my undergraduate studies, I was the first countertenor at my university to major in music. I encountered misunderstandings about my gender frequently. I will never forget the occasion when I was a soloist in a local music series, and without my permission, the concert organizer added to my bio that I retain all my male body parts even though I sound like a "girl." In high school, I endured physical threats and homophobic and transphobic slurs daily. Had it not been for music and my choir teacher, I am not sure how I would have survived. In this small, rural town, this teacher accepted me and my voice without question, without pause. And thanks to her and my supportive parents, my life has meaning and is richly filled with music. I am inspired to make my music-teaching life about empowering and affirming all who want to sing. This does not mean we cannot have high standards or make exceptionally fine music, but we can do so in a manner that honors all students and their life experiences.

In May 2016, the United States Departments of Justice and Education put forth a document called the "Dear Colleague Letter on Transgender Students" (Lhamon & Gupta, 2016). In this letter, recommendations were put forth to protect trans and non-binary students in schools, including:

1. Schools should provide "safe and nondiscriminatory environments" for all students, including trans and non-binary students;
2. Schools should protect trans students by keeping their trans status, birth name, and assigned birth sex confidential;

3. Schools should permit trans students access to restrooms and overnight accommodations that align with their gender identity; and,
4. Schools should allow students to use their chosen name and pronouns in all classes and activities.

Although these recommendations were rescinded in February 2017 by the federal government under new administration, teachers can use these tenets as guidelines in teaching trans and non-binary students. While many of us do not have to worry about finding a bathroom to use, trans and non-binary students might. As leaders in our community, this must become our concern too.

Recently, I was presenting at a conference when I was informally asked by a teacher what they should do about a trans male student (assigned female at birth) in their choir who wanted to sing in the tenor section. According to the teacher, the student has a higher alto voice, and so he would not be able to sing the lowest tenor pitches. The student's parents have not allowed the teenager to start androgen therapy. I gently encouraged the teacher to let the student sing in the section where they feel most comfortable, suggesting that the student could switch to the alto part when not able to sing the lowest pitches of the tenor line. The teacher had serious concern for the student's vocal health, indicating that vocal health must be a teacher's chief concern. While I am aware of the potential issues in attempting to condition one's voice in a way that it is not best suited, I am more concerned with forcing a person to sing in a way that does not align with their identity. I asked the teacher to consider whether their greatest worry should be for the student's vocal health or for the student's emotional and mental well-being. I know where I stand in that concern: emotional health is paramount. Singing at the bottom of one's range a few hours a week in a choral ensemble might cause vocal fatigue, but so does shouting at an intense sports game or speaking loudly in a crowded room.

Concerns like the one above come up all the time in person and on social media. Many of us (voice teachers, choral directors, music educators) spend so much time learning music theory, history, and the traditional canon, that we sometimes miss the larger picture of how to treat our students like emotional beings. As the collective and historic tribe of choral conductors, let's stop honoring traditions that marginalize students. It is our duty as twenty-first century educators to reflect on our practices, even if this means dismantling beloved traditions. It is our role to create connections and make spaces where all students – cisgender, trans, and non-binary – can "weave a world for themselves" (Palmer, 2007, p.11).

Suggested Readings & Resources

1. Agha, A. (2017). Making your chorus welcoming for transgender singers. *The Voice, 41*(2), 18-23.
2. Beemyn, G., & Rankin, S. R. (2011). *The lives of transgender people*. New York, NY: Columbia University Press.
3. Palkki, J. (2017). Inclusivity in action: Transgender students in the choral classroom. *Choral Journal, 57*(11), 20-34.
4. Rands, K. E. (2009). Considering transgender people in education: A gender-complex approach. *Journal of Teacher Education, 60*(4), 419-431.

Citations

Agha, A. (2017). Making your chorus welcoming for transgender singers. *The Voice, 41*(2), 18-23.

Allsup, R. E. (2010). Choosing Music Literature. In H. F. Abeles and L. A. Custodero (Eds.) *Critical issues in music education: Contemporary theory and practice* (pp. 215-235) New York, NY: Oxford University Press.

Andrews, M. (1986). *Voice therapy for children: The elementary school years.* New York, NY: Longman.

Andrews, T. M. (2017). The singular, gender-neutral 'they' added to the Associated Press Stylebook. *The Washington Post.* Retrieved from http://wapo.st/2nuXMMf?tid=ss_mail&utm_term=.f9d27ba8097f

Basow, S. (2004). The hidden curriculum: Gender in the classroom. In M. A. Paludi (Ed.), *Praeger Guide to the Psychology of Gender* (pp. 117–131). Westport, CT: Greenwood.

Beemyn, G., & Rankin, S. R. (2011). *The lives of transgender people*. New York, NY: Columbia University Press.

Bornstein, K. (1998). *My gender workbook: How to become a real man, a real woman, the real you, or something else entirely.* New York, NY: Routledge.

Boytim, J. F. (Compiler). (2008a). *Young Ladies, shipmates & journeys: 21 classical songs for young men ages mid-teens and up.* [Songbook] Milwaukee, WI: Hal Leonard Corporation.

Boytim, J. F. (Compiler). (2008b). *Roses, laughter and lullabies: 18 classical songs for mezzo-soprano ages mid-teens and up.* [Songbook] Milwaukee, WI: Hal Leonard Corporation.

Constansis, A. (2008). The changing female-to-male (FTM) voice. *Radical Musicology, 3*. Retrieved from http://www.radical-musicology.org.uk/2008/Constansis.htm

Doscher, B. (1994). *The functional unity of the singing voice.* Metuchen, NJ: Scarecrow Press. "GLSEN Safe Space Kit: Be an ALLY to LGBTQ Youth," https://www.glsen.org/safespace (accessed February 11, 2018).

Gross, M. (1999). Pitch-raising surgery in male-to-female transsexuals. *Journal of Voice, 13*(2), 246-250.

Grossman, A. H., & D'Augelli, A. R. (2006). Transgender youth. *Journal of Homosexuality, 51*(1), 111–128. doi:10.1300/J082v51n01_06

Halberstam, J. (1994). F2M: the making of female masculinity. In L. Doan (Ed.), *The Lesbian Postmodern* (210-228). New York, NY: Columbia University Press.

Hancock, A., & Helenius, L. (2012). Adolescent Male-to-Female Transgender Voice and Communication Therapy. *Journal of Communication Disorders*

45(5), 313-324.
Hausman, B. L. (2001). Recent transgender theory. *Feminist Studies, 27*(2), 465-490.
Hoffman, J. (2016, June 30.) Estimate of U.S. transgender population doubles to 1.4 million adults. *The New York Times.* Retrieved from: https://www.nytimes.com/2016/07/01/health/transgender-population.html
Jackson, P. W. (1968). *Life in classrooms.* New York, NY: Hold, Rinehart and Winston.
Klimas, J., & Bender, B. (2018, March 3). *Trump moves to ban most transgender troops.* Retrieved from: https://www/politico.com/
Kosciw, J. G., Greytak, E. A., Giga, N. M., Villenas, C., & Danischewski, D. J. (2016). *The 2015 national school climate survey: Executive summary*. New York, NY: GLSEN.
Kozan, A. (2012). The singing voice. In R. K. Adler, S. Hirsch, & M. Mordaunt (Eds.), *Voice and communication therapy for the transgender/transsexual client: A comprehensive clinical guide* (2nd ed.). San Diego, CA: Plural Publishing.
Lamb, R. (2010). Music as sociocultural phenomenon: Interactions with music education. In H. F. Abeles and L. A. Custodero (Eds.) *Critical issues in music education: Contemporary theory and practice* (pp. 23-38). New York, NY: Oxford University Press.
Lessley, E. (2017). *Teaching transgender singers* (Doctoral dissertation). Retrieved from ProQuest Dissertations & Theses Global. (1943885845).
Lhamon, C. E., & Gupta, V. (2016). Dear colleague letter on transgender students. *U.S. Department of Education and U.S. Department of Justice.* Retrieved from http://www2.ed.gov/
Luecke, J. C. (2011). Working with transgender children and their classmates in pre-adolescence: Just be supportive. *Journal of LGBT Youth, 8*(2), 116-156.
Manternach, B. (2017). Teaching transgender singers. Part 2: The singer's perspectives. *Journal of Singing, 74*(2), 209-214.
Manternach, B., Chipman, M., Rainero, R., & Stave, C. (2017). Teaching transgender singers. Part 1: The voice teacher's perspectives. *Journal of Singing, 74*(1), 83-88.
McKinney, J. (1994). *The diagnosis & correction of vocal faults: A manual for teachers of signing and for choir directors.* Nashville, TN: Genevox Music Group.
Miller, J. R. (2016). Creating choirs that welcome transgender singers. *Choral Journal, 57*(4), 61-63.
Miller, R. (1996). *The structure of singing: System and art in vocal technique.* Belmont, CA: Wadsworth Group.
Nagoshi, J., & Brzuzy, S. (2010). Transgender theory: Embodying research and practice. *Affilia: Journal of Women and Social Work, 25*(4), 431-443.
Nagoshi, J., Brzuzy, S., & Terrell, H. (2012). Deconstructing the complex perceptions of gender roles, gender identity, and sexual orientation among transgender individuals. *Feminism & Psychology, 22*(4), 405-422.
Nichols, J. (2013). Rie's story, Ryan's journey: Music in the life of a transgender student. *Journal of Research in Music Education, 61*(3), 262–279. doi:10.1177/0022429413498259
O'Toole, P. (1998). A missing chapter from choral methods books: How choirs

neglect girls. *Choral Journal, 39*(5), 9–32.

Palkki, J. (2016). *"My voice speaks for itself": The experiences of three transgender students in secondary school choral programs.* (Doctoral dissertation). Retrieved from ProQuest Dissertations. (10141543)

Palkki, J. (2017). Inclusivity in action: Transgender students in the choral classroom. *Choral Journal, 57*(11), 20-34.

Palkki, J., & Caldwell, P. (2018). "We are often invisible": A survey on safe space for LGBTQ students in secondary school choral programs. *Research Studies in Music Education, 40*(1), 28–49. doi:10.1177/1321103X17734973

Palkki, J. & Sauerland, W. (2018). Considering 'gender complexity' in music teacher education. *Journal of Music Teacher Education*, 1-13.

Palmer, P. J. (1998). *The courage to teach: Exploring the inner landscape of a teacher's life.* San Francisco, CA: Jossey-Bass.

Payne, E., & Smith, M. (2014). The big freak out: Educator fear in response to the presence of transgender elementary school students. *Journal of Homosexuality, 61*(3), 399-418.

Rands, K. E. (2009). Considering transgender people in education: A gender-complex approach. *Journal of Teacher Education, 60*(4), 419-431.

Roen, K. (2001). "Either/or" and "both/neither": Discourse tensions in transgender politics. *Signs, 27*(2), 501-522.

Rastin, M. (2016). The silenced voice: Exploring transgender issues within western choirs. *The Canadian Music Educator, 57*(4), 28-32.

Sauerland, W. (2018a). *Legitimate voices: A multi-case study of trans and non-binary singers in the applied voice studio* (Doctoral dissertation). Retrieved from ProQuest Dissertations. (10825714)

Sauerland, W. (2018b). Trans Singers Matter: Gender Inclusive Considerations for Choirs. *VOICEPrints: Journal of New York Singing Teacher Association, 15*(5), 95-105.

Silveira, J. M., & Goff, S. C. (2016). Music teachers' attitudes toward transgender students and supportive school practices. *Journal of Research in Music Education, 64*(2), 138-158.

Sims, L. (2017a). Teaching transgender students. *Journal of Singing, 73*(3), 279-282.

Sims, L. (2017b). Teaching Lucas: A transgender student's vocal journey from soprano to tenor. *Journal of Singing, 73*(4), 367-375.

Steinmetz, K. (2014, May 29). The transgender tipping point: America's next civil rights frontier. *TIME, 183*(22), 38-46.

Steinmetz, K. (2015, July 28). Everything you need to know about the "bathroom bill" debate. *Time.* Retrieved from http://time.com/3974186/transgender-bathroom-debate/

Titze, I. R. (1994). *Principles of voice production.* Englewood Cliffs, NJ: Prentice Hall.

West, C., & Zimmerman, D. H. (1987). Doing gender. *Gender & Society, 1*(2), 125-151.

Wilchins, R. (2002). Queer bodies. In J. Nestle, C. Howell, & R. Wilchins (Eds.), *GenderQueer: Voices from beyond the sexual binary.* Los Angeles, CA: Alyson Books.

Chapter Fourteen

Other Considerations for Emerging Choral Music Professionals

14. Other Considerations for Emerging Choral Music Professionals

"Luck is what happens when preparation meets opportunity."
~Lucins Annaeus Seneca

The Student-Teaching Experience

There are several topics that will be addressed briefly in this last section as a sort of "tag" on the coda. These are important topics to consider conceptually, yet they may be site specific or dependent on your actual job and circumstances or dependent on how your particular state or university rules dictate the manner in which your experience will be structured. The first topic is the student-teaching experience.

Most emerging teachers look forward to the student-teaching experience as a time when they will be able to "show what they know" and finally get to be a "real teacher" in front of actual classes. Sometimes the thought of being in charge of actual classes is less exciting and more stressful for some people, but usually there is a mix of excitement and mild uneasiness associated with the start of student teaching. The circumstances of your student teaching may vary widely from the next person's experience, and rather than get too specific about what you might encounter, here is some general conceptual guidance to consider:

- **You may not get to do as much as you thought you would:** Sometimes student teachers do get excited to "show what they know" when they get into their placement, and they can sometimes get disappointed when they either have *too much* or *too little* to do. While this all depends on how the program is structured, music teachers who run choral programs rarely let student teachers lead all the choirs; but in a math classroom, it would be common for the student teacher to teach everything at some point. If your expectation is that you will get to do some things, but not everything, you will probably have those expectations met. If you do find that you are feeling really under-utilized or grossly over-utilized, you should alert your university supervisor to determine if your perception is valid and if adjustments can be made to your responsibility load in conjunction with your cooperating teacher.[1]

1 The term "cooperating teacher" is used to identify the person who is teaching in the public schools and with whom the student teacher works on a daily basis. In some situations, this person is called the "master teacher" or perhaps the "site teacher." The term "university supervisor" is used to identify the local teacher or professor who acts as the observing party for the university or college.

- **You are not there to teach your cooperating teacher:** When you are student teaching, you will be excited to try some of the activities and methods that you learned in your preservice classes. It is very possible that your cooperating teacher will not use every one of those specific methods in their own classroom, and they might want you to try the methods that they use instead of the ones that you learned in your university classes. Ideally, the cooperating teacher will let you try the techniques that you have learned with an open mind, but this is not always the case. It is a mistake, however, to try to change the mind of your cooperating teacher by trying to convince them that your chosen technique is better than theirs or to imply that you can teach them how to improve. Do your best to learn what you can from them, but do not expect them to be curious about the methods that you are excited to try out.

- **You are there to learn, but also to assist:** Student teachers can feel like they are not used by the cooperating teacher in a way that matches their skill and expertise. For example, when asked if they will run off 100 copies of the concert program instead of warming up the choir, the student teacher might feel like "office help" as opposed to a professional educator. This is normal, and this is probably going to happen on some level at some point. And while it's true that you might prefer to warm up the choir and learn something about your subject matter, your willingness to assist your cooperating teacher will go a long way toward building you up in their eyes as a colleague. You should be ready to jump in and teach when asked, but you should also be prepared to assist as needed in whatever capacity they need you to.

- **You are there to get a good recommendation:** One of the goals of student teaching is to get some good experience teaching real kids in an authentic setting. But your ability to teach, while supremely important to your future success, will be evaluated in conjunction with many other indicators of your future success, including being on time, being prepared, being a nice person, being good with kids, assisting as needed, being willing to attend meetings and concerts, and demonstrating a willingness to work on the extra things that the music program is involved in, as well as many other possible things. Your recommendation from your cooperating teacher will be important to your future job prospects, and you want to be perceived as a good teacher, a good colleague, and a committed professional. If that means that you don't get to lead as many songs in concerts, that's OK.

- **Student teaching is temporary:** Whether you are placed for a semester or for a year in your student-teaching assignment, you will eventually have your own job and your own students. All of the joys and concerns of the student-teaching time should be considered as temporary experiences. Use the time to refine your approach and to plan for how you will run things when you are in charge of your own room and program. Be positive and remember that no matter how much you love it or are challenged by it, student teaching is only temporary.

- **Be a reflective practitioner, even if your cooperating teacher is not:** Some cooperating teachers are "teachers of teachers" and some simply are not. Not every good teacher will have the skills or desire to be a great mentor, so, you may have to look at your own teaching style with the intention to improve, if you want to progress. You can video your teaching and review it on your own, journal about what you remember, or discuss it with a friend or a colleague. If your cooperating teacher has the time and desire to work with you on your pedagogy, that's great. Just be ready to grow on your own if need be.

Teaching Outside of Your Content Area

There are places in the country where a full-time music teacher is the exception and not the rule. Many states allow a single-subject certified teacher (such as a music teacher) to receive an "emergency certification" to teach other subjects such as math, English, technical theater, drama, or other subjects as needed. There is no way to prepare you for this possibility, though you will probably be able to decide what you feel comfortable teaching if it is not your specialty. You might also be asked to teach something within your content area as well, such as a band class, an orchestra class, or an elementary general music class. Here are a few things to consider:

- **Good teaching is good teaching:** If you have developed a good approach to sequencing academic material, balanced with an ability to manage a classroom in a positive, kind, and consistent manner, you can *learn* to teach anything. Take what you know about teaching a great choral class and transfer what you know to the new subject matter.

- **Decide if you like the subject matter:** If you don't like drama and have never done it before, you might not want to take an assignment teaching drama. But if you have an open mind and are willing to learn more about it to teach it, you might be able to learn enough about it to be successful. This concept applies to anything you might be asked to teach.

- **Seek expertise from people in your environment who can help:** If you are suddenly assigned to teach a band class (presuming that you don't have experience playing in concert band or conducting a band), you can contact people you know who are accomplished band directors and ask them to give you some advice. You can observe them teaching, if possible, or you can consult online resources. If you are not a member of NAfME (which you should already be), then you can join and scour their website for "how to" tips on teaching band as a choral director or whatever subject area you need to learn more about.

- **Classes that are not music-related often have set curricula:** If you are willing to teach math, for example, there will probably be a text book and a set curriculum to follow. This will help you determine your scope and sequence, which is half the battle. Then you just have to get familiar with the academic subject matter and write your lesson plans.

All the Things That Are Not Teaching Music

Many emerging teachers are surprised to discover that music teachers do a lot more than teach music. You learned in Chapter 2 "Career Paths in Music Education," that depending on your specialty area, you will need to spend more or less time after school and more or less time doing administration to run your program. Teachers have to correct homework, take attendance, write lesson plans, attend meetings, organize events, pick music, and manage so many things apart from the actual time that they get to teach music. This topic alone could probably fill a textbook with "how to" tips for each thing. In reality, you will have to be curious about the things that you are required to do in your actual job, and you will need to find out how your school handles the "extras" so that you can do them professionally and efficiently. Here are some considerations:

- **Fundraising**: If you are required to fundraise for your program, then you are in good company. Many music educators find themselves in an underfunded position, and they need to find systems and activities to raise extra money for music, equipment, trips, and performance attire. Some schools have mandatory "pay to play" systems where parents have to pay a certain amount for their student to participate in music, even when it is offered during the school day. In many states, this practice is being replaced with a voluntary system where parents are encouraged, but not required, to donate to the program. When you do have to fundraise, you can contact one of many companies that specialize in helping schools in this area, or you can create your own fundraisers. One big concept to remember about raising money is that when you can, use music as part of the fundraiser. If students can create, learn, perform, and showcase their music during the fundraiser, you are using the subject matter to enhance the music program. It is a win-win. Programs like "Singing Valentines," caroling during the holidays, or preparing a benefit concert with proceeds going to offset student costs for a choir trip, all use music to raise funds for the things that are needed to keep the program fully funded.

- **Managing money**: When you are in charge of taking students on trips, and raising money and collecting money, you need to have a transparent system for keeping the money safe and accounted for. You can end your career if you don't have accurate accounting, or if money and equipment that is the property of the school ends up permanently under your control off campus. In other words, if you are handling money for any reason, check with your administration to find out how they want you to handle it, where it needs to be deposited and when, and how you can keep a public accounting record that can be seen and checked by the office staff.

- **Building a booster program:** This one topic could easily get a full chapter in any choral methods book, but again, what your school wants and what it has done in the past is the most important information that you first need to know. Conceptually, you need to know if there is already a music booster group that is active, and then you need to know how the former teacher managed it. Some booster groups, which are run by parents in most cases to support the music program, sometimes manage the choral educator in subtle or overt ways, and they may try to influence decisions they should not be influencing. In other cases, the booster group might be collaborative and ready to assist in any creative ideas that the choral educator has in mind. If you need to start a booster group, your first job should be to find out what other choral music programs in your area have for booster organizations. Look at what they have, how they function, and see if you could emulate their system. Again, your professional organizations have large amounts of information regarding this and other topics (ACDA, NAfME, and your state music associations) and you will get the most out of their resources if you are a paid member.

- **The teacher's room:** You will need to make a conscious choice as to whether you want to eat your lunch in the teacher's room. It is not unusual for a choral music teacher to have students in the choir room at lunch who are practicing or hanging around, and on those days you will need to be supervising your learning space while you eat. But if you have the opportunity to eat with other faculty members in the teacher's room, remember that it is a public space where people will say all kinds of negative and unprofessional things. How do we know this? It seems to be universal that teachers (not necessarily music teachers) love to congregate and complain, and maybe this is just a human expression in any setting like this. The main concept here is not to get drawn into being negative yourself, especially if you're talking about your students. If you can, just chew, listen, and add a positive comment every now and then. If you never show up in the lunchroom, your colleagues will wonder why, so you should make an appearance when you can. Of course, there will be some very fun and positive people there as well, so be sure that you are one of them.

- **Organizing trips:** If you are a secondary choral music educator in charge of a growing program, yearly trips with your choirs may help your program grow in numbers and quality. There are many tour companies that can help you organize a trip with as many students as you want to bring to almost any destination that you are interested in. Most choir trips will include a concert performance and perhaps a choral clinic along with time to sight see and travel in your chosen destination as a group. A concept to lock in here is the idea that some schools travel with everyone who is a member of the choir program (all students), some travel with only one or two choirs (perhaps the advanced choirs), and some offer trip options for any student in the program who wants to go on (and pay for) the trip. This last scenario can be considered a "choir of the willing" and you will have to schedule rehearsals outside of the school day if you want this choir to learn a common repertoire, since you will have a few members from every choir, but not all members from any one choir. If you choose to organize a trip yourself and will not be using an outside, professional tour company, be sure you check with your administration to be sure that you are covered by school insurance and that you have liability insurance in case anything goes wrong. That is one big advantage to using a tour company (using the company's insurance coverage). But you will pay for it through the fees they charge you, so you will have to decide if what they provide is a value for you and your students. Finally, always opt for "trip insurance" if it is offered, and look for an independent provider if it is not an option from the tour company. Imagine, for example, all the choirs that paid to travel in spring of 2020, just before the Covid-19 pandemic ended all travel and music performances. With "trip insurance" you would be able, in most cases, to get all of your money refunded.

- **Purchasing music:** In Chapter 8, "Materials for the Choral Music Educator," we examined how to choose music and build choral concert programs that will be both educational and engaging for the choir and audience alike. It is important to reemphasize here that you should insist to your administration that the program needs money to buy new music every year. Your music is your textbook, and you need to have a wide variety of high-quality music available for your students to study and perform. If you steal and photocopy music to run your program, you are teaching your administration that you don't need the funding and that you are willing to break the law and put your school at great financial risk to run your program. Everyone is going to make a photocopy now and then, but if you run your program on photocopied music without buying any music legally, you are helping to put music publishers and composers out of business. Be sure that part of your administrative work includes getting funding for music purchases, and then do your best to buy music that you believe in, music that you will use and reuse over the years.

- **Budgeting:** Music purchasing is not the only thing you will have to manage through your budget. If you are lucky enough to have a line-item budget, then you will have to decide each year what you want to prioritize for your program's needs. You will have to learn the process that your school district goes through to request budget items, what the approval process entails, and strategies for creating budget requests. For example, if you can determine that your school cuts all budget requests by 10% every year, you would do well to ask for a 10% increase every year if you want your funding to remain steady from year to year. Budgeting is a process that is kind of like a game, so do what you can to learn the rules of your school district and play the budgeting game as well as you can. Every school district will have set budgeting procedures that you will need to learn and follow, so be ready to figure out how to complete this important task.

- **Auditioning students for advanced choirs:** This topic is important depending on the school you teach in and the traditions that you inherit. In some schools, students work really hard to audition up into the advanced choirs, and students that don't make it can sometimes feel discouraged and quit the program. In some cases, there can be political issues when parents get involved and want to meet with the choir director to find out exactly why their student didn't make a certain choir. There are two concepts to think about here. First, you will need a concrete and public grading system for your audition rubric so that everyone knows how to prepare and how they are being evaluated. Like you learned in Chapter 10, "Assessment Strategies for the Music Classroom," your audition rubric needs to be based upon observable behaviors that you can count and score. There are music educators who simply pick who they want in the advanced choirs without an audition, and there are some who do an audition but pick who they want anyway, making up scores in some cases. This is not recommended, even if this has been done in the past at your school. Secondly, it would be smart to make a video of all choir auditions so that you can go back and reevaluate a score when two auditions come out to be the same score (and one has to be cut) or to review an audition with a student and their parents if needed. People will believe what they see and hear much more easily than they will believe what they are told. This way you have a system to help your students understand your audition criteria, and also a tool to help them improve their auditioning skills in the future.

- **Teacher burnout:** Even though we get to teach music and change lives every day, there are going to be days where you don't feel like doing your job. The great basketball star Julius Erving (Dr. J as he was called) once said, "Being a professional is doing the things you love to do on the days you don't feel like doing them." We do indeed have to do our job no matter how excited we feel about doing it, and that is true for any profession. But if you feel that you have lost your passion for choral music and teaching, stop and take a look at the following things:

  - Have you balanced your professional and personal life carefully? Do you need to spend more time at home and less time at school?
  - Do you have a creative outlet for your own music making? You might be missing making music yourself.
  - Have you been doing the same thing over and over again? When we grow both personally and professionally, life is more interesting. Do you need to learn something new? Have you been teaching for ten years, or for one year ten times?
  - Are you supported by your school and administration? Sometimes, when you have been putting in overtime hours for too many years to keep a program running because of a lack of support, you need to pull back and do less. This can mean many things, including looking for another position at another school, or just reducing the hours that you are willing to put in for free.
  - Do you have a support system of friends and colleagues to connect with when you need to? Your professional conferences and organizations are a great place to reconnect and re-energize professionally and personally. You can also join groups that meet in your area even if they have nothing to do with music. You might be inspired with some new ideas and new friendships too.
  - If you are really feeling sad or depressed for a while, seek professional help. We all need help once in a while, and it's OK to ask for and seek help from trained people who know how to listen and who can help you get back to your very best, centered self.

- **Interviewing for your first job**: Interviewing for employment is an essential skill that must be examined and practiced before your first interview. These simple tips and sample questions will help you to prepare for the interview process and will allow you to be you best during that inevitably stressful first interview experience.

1. Don't apply for a job you don't really want to take, or that you are not qualified to accept. It's unprofessional and wastes the time and money of the school district.
2. Dress professionally. It's never casual Fridays when you are interviewing.
3. Arrive a little early. Wait quietly. Be polite and smile at people.
4. Do some research to find out about the school, the mission statement, and the history of the arts program before you arrive. Have something nice to say about the school and program.
5. Review your philosophy of music education (and your elevator pitch) so that it is in the forefront of your mind when you are asked questions. It should positively inform virtually every answer you give.
6. Answer each question briefly and concisely, but don't talk too much. Show that you understand the question and have an informed answer, but don't use the opportunity to pivot and talk about another topic. Make your point directly and then wrap it up.
7. Picture yourself as a colleague, not as a student teacher. Be positive and professional, but don't make any excuses or tell stories about times that you were not successful.
8. If the question could be considered controversial in some way, speak to both sides of the issue to show that you are open minded, and that you can see more than one point of view.
9. Have fun and enjoy the time as much as you can. Make eye contact and smile. Think to yourself "I am going to get a wonderful job somewhere, and maybe it is here."
10. If you do not understand a question, feel free to ask a clarifying question to the panel if this helps you focus your response. Be sure you know and understand what they are asking so that your answer is clear and to the point.
11. Have a question or two for the interview panel (if they ask) and have these memorized. Do NOT ask about salary in the interview because you have not been hired yet, and there will either be time to negotiate this if you are hired, or the salary schedule will already be set by union and school district contracts. You might ask about the music program budget, or parental support for the arts in the school or district, or maybe how they envision the program growing over time. Ask questions that you are fairly confident will function well in this setting. Consider running your questions by a colleague or professor before your actual interview.
12. Always be gracious and say "thank you" when you are done interviewing. Let them know you enjoyed meeting them, and shake

hands with everyone using a friendly, firm handshake and solid eye contact. (Unless social distancing is being observed, of course.)

To help in your preparation for interviewing, practice answering the following questions. While there are hundreds of possible questions that might be asked, here are some of the big ones that are more likely to be included in some form or another. Practice your answers both in your own mind and also out loud with someone listening and giving you honest feedback about your responses and body language.

- Tell us a little bit about yourself.
- How much, on average, do you teach by rote and how much do you teach the students to read music on their own? Describe to us your strategy for teaching musicianship in the rehearsal, and what you expect students to be able to do, as musicians, after one year of choir, and also after FOUR years of your musicianship instruction.
- What is your personal philosophy of music education? Do you think everyone can and should study music? Why or why not?
- What kinds of music would you include in the repertoire across the choirs in a single year? Comment on your approach to concerts and programming.
- Would you consider yourself to be more of a teacher-centered instructor, or more of a student-centered instructor? What do these terms mean to you?
- Do you strive to create student leadership in the choirs? If so, explain how you structure and build this leadership.
- Describe your approach to auditioning students for your choirs. What would a typical audition look like? Would you have ALL choirs be auditioned, or just some choirs? Which ones, and why?
- Discuss your abilities both as a conductor and as a pianist. How will you balance and hone those abilities to be most effective for your students?
- What does the title "professional music educator" mean to you, and what qualities and behaviors do you personally possess that would earn you that title?
- Are you interested, willing, and able to be part of an all-

school musical production? What skills could you bring to the team, and what kinds of musicals do you think fit well in a diverse high school population?

- Talk about your plan to recruit for the choir program. What would you do first, second, third, and on an ongoing basis?
- Discuss your ideas for fundraising for the choral program. How would you supervise and organize your music booster group?
- Discuss your training in working with diverse populations such as ESL students and students with physical and mental challenges. How would you help them be successful in your choral program?
- What is your greatest personal or professional strength and also what do you consider to be your greatest personal or professional weakness?
- Do you have any questions for us?

RECAPITULATION

1. This section is a sort of "potpourri" of topics that could easily fill a large chapter in any choral methods textbook. List the top three topics that you found to be most interesting to you, and then go online and find out as much as you can about them. Prepare a half-page summary of what you found for each of the three topics, including websites, resources, articles, and blog summaries. Present these to your class or to a colleague.
2. This textbook has a lot of information for the emerging choral music teacher. No book could possibly address every topic that you will need to know in your career. Make a list of any topics not mentioned in this text that you would want to know more about at some point in your career. Share this list with a friend, a colleague, or with the class. Keep that list with you (or in your mind) whenever you attend professional music conferences in the future to help guide your learning and curiosity. Be curious…always.

IV. Cadenza

Chapter Fifteen

Cadenza and Resources

15. Cadenza and Resources

"The best teacher in life is experience."
~ LeBron James

Living in the Real-World Classroom

If you have read and studied the concepts in this text and have made it to this final section, congratulations! I hope you have enjoyed the presentation of ideas in this book, and I hope you feel more prepared and ready to change the world through your teaching. You have gained many insights into some of the important aspects of becoming a professional choral music educator. You have been exposed to a lot of ideas, and you have had the opportunity to explore these concepts with open-ended prompts that did not have one specific "right" answer. For some people, the absence of one "correct" answer is stressful and for others, it is freeing. Some people thrive when they can think creatively while others need to "get it right" and move on. Which kind of person are you, and how does it affect your approach to teaching and learning?

One semester a few years ago, one of my students asked a very telling question during class. The question made me think hard about how people learn, and how I sequence my own training of future teachers. It was about three weeks into the semester, and she raised her hand and asked, "Are you ever going to tell us what to do…like *exactly* what to do in our classrooms?" I smiled and answered, "Yes, *sometimes* I will. But most of this class and this year you will hear me teaching you about how to *figure out* what to do, as opposed to *telling* you what to do." She didn't seem to be particularly satisfied with that answer in the moment, though she came to appreciate the methodology behind the pedagogy over the year. She also came to realize that even the prescribed sequences I provided like "movable do with a la-based minor" and "Menu Programs" and "Teaching Units" and "Whole-Part-Whole" rehearsing were only placeholder techniques for addressing larger values. My students know that I will make them learn specific sequences in methods class, but I will never judge them if they use different techniques in their classrooms, as long as they function to implement the values we share. I really do want them to "figure it out" when the real world appears in their reality, and I want them to feel confident that they have tools to do this effectively.

As I thought about her excellent question after class, I thought back to all the teachers who trained me. How much did they prescribe what I should do, and did they balance that information with conceptual problems for me to consider and solve in the real world? I came to the conclusion that, as far as I could remember, they mostly taught me specifically what to do. They gave me tools and sequences and games and ideas and lessons and literature lists. During my student teaching and my early teaching years, I was excited to try all the things they taught me, and for the most part I did what they taught, and I emulated my mentors to the best of my ability. For the most part, what they told me to do worked. The struggles came for me, however, when I encountered situations that were not part of their "how to" lectures; there were a lot of times when I felt completely unprepared to face things that I encountered in my schools and classrooms. It wasn't a fault of my professors; it just isn't possible in the time allotted in methods classes to cover everything that could possibly happen in the real world. I came to the conclusion that I wanted my methods classes and teaching pedagogy to reflect a balance of "giving my students some fish," but also "teaching my students how to fish" as much as it was practically possible.

Knowing *about* something is much different than *knowing it*. I always tell my students that what they learn in my classes to become student teachers is nothing compared to what they will learn during student teaching and in the real world, in authentic classroom and rehearsal situations with real students. Words do not teach…it's life that teaches. It's real life that wakes us up and makes us take notice so that we ask the critical questions that then bring the answers that we are ready to hear. Life is your classroom, and you must be ready to face the unpredictable challenges and problems in your professional world. You have to be ready to figure out the concepts that are interacting with any specific challenge, try to predict how various possible courses of action might function, and then make the best choices you can. When your choices function well, great! When they don't, you have to reassess and try again and acknowledge that you learned something new about that specific problem. Be humble, be open, and be ready to learn through your successes as well as your failures. You are not supposed to know everything. All you can do is keep learning in Life's Classroom and demonstrate for your students that learning never ends.

Keeping Your Questions Alive

Remember that your curiosity drives your questions, and your questions summon the answers that you need so that you can grow. The questions that are important to you now are not the same questions that you will be asking after one, three, five, or twenty years of teaching. Even if you go on to earn graduate degrees and you "know about" so much more, keep your curiosity stoked and your questions alive. Nurture the *Learning Cycle* in your life so that you always move through comfortable times when you feel like you know everything and into uncomfortable times where you suddenly realize that you don't know *anything*. If you go too long without that uncomfortable feeling, it might be a sign that you need to ask tougher questions. Life, of course, usually does a good job of motivating us to that uncomfortable space where we can learn. I urge you to consciously keep track of your journey through the Learning Cycle throughout your career to be sure you don't stall out and stop asking your questions. Ideally, learning never ends for anyone. We are never done learning...unless we decide to stop learning. This fact is a great motivator for me as a teacher, and as a student in life.

Finding Resources To Answer Your Questions

As we have established, when you ask a question that is important to you, you immediately summon answers into your experience. In other words, as soon as you ask a question, the answers come to you in many forms such as conversations, TV commercials, and in emails that you might normally delete without reading. While the answers will start to flow automatically to you, it's also a good idea to have "go to" resources and places you can look to find quick and specific answers. The richest and most-related sources are on the websites of your professional organizations. As a member of NAfME (The National Association for Music Education) and ACDA (The American Choral Directors Association) along with the aligned state organizations that are included in your membership, you have access to incredible information provided by music educators all over the country, and with decades of real teaching experience. There are forums and articles and "how to" lessons for virtually anything you are curious about. There are many other organizations and websites available for you if you look for them, such as Chorus America, the National Association of Teachers of Singing (NATS), and the National Collegiate Choral Organization (NCCO) just to name a few. If you find the information on a website particularly relevant to your questions and interests, consider donating to the organization or becoming a member.

Another resource for you is attending your professional conferences, both state and national. We all know that COVID-19 halted in-person conferences starting around March of 2020, resulting in the creation of many virtual conferences that could be attended without leaving one's home. As the world returned to some sort of new "normal" with travel and live in-person conferences, new opportunities have arisen that allow us to take advantage of the virtual aspects of these events. I think this could be considered one of the "Covid benefits" that has been created through the pandemic that has allowed us to be even closer as a choral community. Take advantage of these

opportunities to network with other choral educators, to meet people who share your interests, and to ask your questions in rich professional settings. Consider becoming a volunteer or an active board member in one of your state professional organizations; you will learn about managing groups of people, communicating clearly across multiple platforms of information, and you will be able to affect positive change for music education in your state.

Final Cadence

I want to thank you for interacting with this text. Creating this book has been a labor of love and without *you,* it has no purpose. Consider this information as a foundation…a starting point…on your journey to a rich and purposeful life in the choral music education profession. I love choral music, and I love teaching, and I appreciate every one of my students, including you. Your gifts will change the lives of your students, and their students, and their students. I am so grateful that we get to be in a profession that is more *Art* than science. I am so glad that what we do as choral educators can *Resonate* out far beyond the individual, affecting positive changes in others who are far away or that we may never meet in person. I tell my students that their ultimate goal is to be better than their own teachers. I want them to strive to integrate the best aspects of all their teachers while identifying and minimizing the things their teachers didn't do as effectively. We are who we are because of the many people who have loved, taught, and supported us along the way, and we have an obligation to *pay it forward,* lifting others up with our sound pedagogy and positive teaching approach. Make music, but always make a difference.

Finally, I would like to share an image created by one of my former students, Jonny Dolan, now a choral music educator in Southern California. Like many of my students through the years, Jonny kept a running list of "Dr. P-isms" that came up in my classes, and many of these you have already encountered in the body of this book. He took the time to create this graphic, and I think it is a fitting testament to how the little concepts add up to the bigger ones, so that from a distance it is just a single treble clef. Thanks, Jonny, and thanks to all of you who have started your journey into this amazing profession. We are never done, and we are always learning.

"The Gestalt nature of learning: many steps become fewer and fewer steps."

"Choose a job you love and you'll never work a day in your life." ~Confucius

"The first line of reinforcement is to ignore behavior unless it is dangerous, or if it interferes with learning."

"Teach proper associations: When you do nice things, nice things happen to you, and when you do bad things, bad things happen to you."

"People would rather be praised than punished, but they would rather be punished than ignored."

"Intention vs. function"

"4-step teaching process"

"Behavior is situational."

"Every Rule will be broken."

"Everyone is trying their best."

"Everything we do, we do together."

"Teach to disengage the Autopilot."

"Perception is reality." [intention/function]

"Meet them where they are, and make them better."

"You can do anything, but you can't do everything."

"The use of Sarcasm is not a good teaching tool."

"Use high-level questions with more than one right answer."

"You control the environment that, in turn, controls you."

"What other people think about me is none of my business."

"Don't stop a behavior, replace it with something you want."

"Call them custodians, not janitors." [office staff/counselors]

"Give directions from big to small: page, system, measure, beat."

"Behavior that goes unrewarded will be extinguished."

"Contingent relationship" and success in curriculum.

Taking a group from "really suck" to "kinda suck."

"Beginning teachers must be self-focused at first."

"Use proximity to keep the whole class involved."

"Behavior is relative to the situation."

"Social behavior vs. academic behavior."

"Ignoring cannot be observed."

"Learning IS the modification of behavior."

"Decide who talks, and who is in the queue to talk."

"Facial expressions, touching, tokens."

"The Doomsday Contingency"

"Choose your battles."

"The token economy"

"Emotional Vampires"

"Rote before Note"

"Take control of your life."

"Prioritize musicianship."

"Posture: Feet on the floor, elbows off the lap, back away from the chair."

"There is no rule until someone breaks it and they are publicly punished."

"Whatever you focus on, you get more of."

"Be encouraging and validate when students contribute by occasionally repeating or rephrasing what was said."

"It's my first mistake of the year."

"The Learning Cycle"

"If you can't say something nice, try harder."

"Movable 'Do' with a La-based minor"

"Every rehearsal is a coup in progress."

"Do No Harm accompanying"

"You teach the way you were taught."

"Feed forward."

"The ZAP"

"Burn no bridges."

"Flow"

"Magnitude"

Approval, disapproval, approval error, disapproval error, ignoring.

"4-1 Ratio"

"The Payoff"

"Be the most interesting thing in the room"

"Catch people being good."

"Impulse of Will"

"The Fatal Flaw"

"Bus Song"

"Teacher vs. Coach"

"Attention grabber"

"Compared to WHAT?"

"It's not about you."

"Work Hard, Play Hard."

"Hierarchy of teaching."

"It's easier to be average."

"Students want structure."

"You don't get to have bad days."

"Behavior is always being modified."

"Don't be fair, be kind and consistent."

"Balance who talks so that everyone participates."

"How you do anything affects how you do everything."

"If you want anything done, give it to a busy person."

"Insanity is doing the same thing, but expecting a different result."

"Be a student-centered teacher, not a teacher-centered teacher."

"The contingent relationship: If you do this…then THIS will happen."

"Once a discussion gets going, know when to move onto another person"

"Leading a discussion with the class is the most difficult teaching strategy."

"Redefine the questions or start the conversation yourself if need be."

"Ignore behavior that is not dangerous and doesn't interfere with learning."

"Preparing to teach means planning to control the environment." "

"There is no such thing as an academic emergency."

"What can kids do? Whatever you teach them to do."

Addressing posture: "Sit up, sit down, stand up."

"You teach best what you struggled to learn"

"Words don't teach, real life teaches"

"Who decides…the teacher decides!"

"Approval, disapproval, threat of disapproval, ignoring."

"Don't take the short-term gain for the long-term loss."

"Good says nothing. Give specific feedback on Step 4."

"Motivation vs. Inspiration"

"Rhetorical questions are not real questions."

"Teach manners, then teach music."

"Sound before symbol"

"Values vs. Techniques"

"May I have All Eyes please?"

"Empathy vs. sympathy"

"Maintain eye contact."

"Do what fits you."

"Burn no bridges."

"Task analysis"

"Start on time, end on time"

"Watch body language to see who is open and who is shutting down."

"Don't use Guess What I'm Thinking teaching."

"The best predictor of future behavior is past behavior"

"Focus on the behavior, not the person."

CSUF

"You only know what you know."

"What you know is easy, but what you don't know may be difficult."

"No one wants to hear the answer to a question that they are not asking."

"Have you been teaching for 30 years, or for one year 30 times?"

"IP-AP=TO" (The Ideal Performance minus the Actual Performance equals your Teaching

"Art is never finished, only abandoned." ~Leonardo di Vinci

Photo: Hugo Alberto Mata, Jr.

William Sauerland is an Assistant Professor of Music and Director of Choral Studies for the School of Music at Purdue University – Fort Wayne. He conducts the university ensembles, teaches classes in conducting and music education, and supervises student teachers. He was previously a Lecturer in Voice at San Francisco State University, and the Director of Choral and Vocal Studies at Chabot College in Hayward, California. Dr. Sauerland taught choral music at Lick-Wilmerding High School for six years, and served as Associate Music Director for the Grammy Award-winning Pacific Boychoir Academy.

Praise by the San Francisco Chronicle for his "limpid tone and astonishing eloquence," Dr. Sauerland remains active as a professional countertenor. His recent solo appearances include the American Bach Soloists, Echoing Air, Festival Opera Company, Folger Consort, Handel Opera Project, Musica Angelica Baroque Orchestra, Oakland Symphony Orchestra, and Pacific Chorale. A former member of the Grammy Award-winning vocal ensemble Chanticleer, Dr. Sauerland has sung throughout the world, and recorded multiple albums for Warner Classics.

Dr. Sauerland received the Doctorate of Education in Music and Music Education from Teachers College, Columbia University. His research interests include social justice pedagogy in vocal music education, trans and gender expansive vocality, and student-centered teaching. His publications appear in the Journal of Singing, Journal of Music Teacher Education, VOICEPrints (Journal of the New York Singing Teacher's Association), and in *The Choral Conductor's Companion* (GIA Publication, 2020). As a Marshall Scholarship recipient, he earned a Master of Music and Post-graduate Diploma in Advanced Vocal Performance from the Royal College of Music in London. Raised on a small dairy farm in Ohio, he received a Bachelor of Music in Music Education and Vocal Performance from Miami University in Oxford, Ohio.

CHRISTOPHER PETERSON is a teacher, conductor, choral clinician, author, editor, composer, and choral arranger of music and books published in the United States and around the world. In his over thirty years as a music educator Dr. Peterson has taught in elementary, middle school, high school, church, community, festival, and collegiate settings. He earned the Bachelor of Science in Music Education from the University of Southern Maine in choral and instrumental music education and taught music for nine years in the public schools of Maine. He earned the Master of Music in Choral Conducting degree at the University of Maine, and the Doctor of Philosophy in Music Education and Choral Conducting at Florida State University.

He had the honor of teaching at the University of Wisconsin-Milwaukee for seven years before moving to Southern California to teach at California State University, Fullerton in 2007. At CSUF he has trained and mentored undergraduate and graduate choral music educators and conductors and has directed the Concert Choir and the Singing Titans Chorus. In May of 2019 he was honored as the University-wide recipient of the CSUF Carol Barnes Award for Excellence in Teaching. He has served as State Choral Representative and Southern Section President for the California Music Educators Association (CMEA), as well as the Western Division Representative for the National Association for Music Education's (NAfME) Council for Choral Education. He has also served the California Choral Directors Association in various offices, including CCDA President from 2021–2023.

He has been invited to teach, judge, and conduct choirs in more than thirty US states, five Canadian Provinces, and nine countries including China, England, Sweden, Japan, Germany, New Zealand, and Holland, and has conducted All-State Choirs across the nation including Maine, North Carolina, Oregon, and California. Dr. Peterson also holds the position of Director of Music at Irvine United Congregational Church in Irvine, CA. His "hobby" for many decades has been enjoying singing barbershop harmony, and he is a BHS District Quartet Champion baritone, a top-5 medalist chorus director, and a four-time gold medalist with the Masters of Harmony, nine-time International Men's Chorus Champions of the Barbershop Harmony Society.

Index

Symbols

A

B

C

D

E

F

G

N

O

P

Q

R

S

T

U

V

W

X

Y

Z